Effective Multicultural Team

Advances in Group Decision and Negotiation

Volume 3

The book series, Advances in Group Decision and Negotiation — as an extension of the journal, *Group Decision and Negotiation* — is motivated by unifying approaches to group decision and negotiation processes. These processes are purposeful, adaptive and complex – cybernetic and self-organizing – and involve relation and coordination in multiplayer, multicriteria, ill-structured, evolving dynamic problems in which players (agents) both cooperate and conflict. These processes are purposeful complex adaptive systems.

Group decision and negotiation involves the whole process or flow of activities relevant to group decision and negotiation – such as, communication and information sharing, problem definition (representation) and evolution, alternative generation, social-emotional interaction, coordination, leadership, and the resulting action choice.

Areas of application include intraorganizational coordination (as in local/global strategy, operations management and integrated design, production, finance, marketing and distribution – e.g., as for new products), computer supported collaborative work, labor-management negotiation, interorganizational negotiation (business, government and nonprofits), electronic negotiation and commerce, mobile technology, culture and negotiation, intercultural and international relations and negotiation, globalization, terrorism, environmental negotiation, etc.

Claire B. Halverson • S. Aqeel Tirmizi
Editors

Effective Multicultural Teams: Theory and Practice

Editors
Claire B. Halverson
School for International Training
Brattleboro, VT
USA

S. Aqeel Tirmizi
School for International Training
Brattleboro, VT
USA

ISBN: 978-1-4020-8697-7 e-ISBN: 978-1-4020-6957-4

Library of Congress Control Number: 2007941590

Printed on acid-free paper

9 8 7 6 5 4 3 2 1

springer.com

I dedicate this book to my daughter Renya Halverson Larson who encouraged me to write this book and helped me with her outstanding writing skills

- Claire

My mother Nighat Sultana taught me to embrace kindness and patience which continue to enrich my life and my father Ahmad Raza has always encouraged me to pursue my dreams

- I dedicate this book to them - Aqeel

Preface

Multicultural and multinational teams have become an important strategic and structural element of organizational work in our globalized world today. These teams are demonstrating their importance from the factory floors to the boardrooms of contemporary organizations. The emergence of multicultural teams is evident across a variety of organizations in the private, public, and civil society sectors. These developments have led to an increasing interest in the theory and practice of multicultural teams. Management educational and training programs are giving increasing attention to these developments. At the same time, there is emerging interest in research about and study of multicultural teams.

This book emerged from our teaching, research, and consulting with multicultural and diverse teams in multiple sectors over the last several years. In particular, we have developed and refined our ideas about the concepts in this book from teaching an advanced course called Effective Multicultural Teams in the Graduate Program at the School for International Training (SIT) in Vermont. We have learned from the rich background of students who are from, and have worked in, six continents, and who are, or plan to be, working in the public, educational, not-for-profit, and for-profit sectors. Additionally, we have engaged with a variety of teams through our consulting and training, providing consultation to teams in a variety of sectors and continents as they struggled to become more effective.

During our work we have developed a great appreciation for the roles that teams play in our lives and organizations, the complexity surrounding the individual and organizational factors that make them effective, and how the larger contextual and cultural dynamics impact them. We have been excited to see the potential of teams, particularly ones that are committed to shared leadership, participation, and/or self-management. We truly believe in the potential of diversity—international and multicultural—which for us includes age, race/ethnicity, gender, religion, class, and ability. In addition, diversity of viewpoint, personality, and professional role can improve effectiveness. There is also the potential that teams with this diversity will be less effective than more homogeneous teams. We see the study and practice of multicultural and international teams and how to manage them as an important discipline.

We believe that this discipline is a complex and continuously emerging area of knowledge and practice. We have not found any textbook that is relevant to our students and participants who are working, or will work, globally in a variety of sectors. For years we kept hearing, "Why don't you publish your own book?" So we took on this project and asked our colleagues to contribute some of the chapters. It has been a rich learning process. We bring our own diversity in age, race/ethnicity, nationality, ability, religion, and gender to the process, but we bring a common commitment to the potential of effective multicultural teams. We have both said that we could never have edited this book alone.

The book is written for graduate students, advanced undergraduate students, or those pursuing a certificate in management or leadership. Cultural background, social identity, and individual characteristics provide an overlapping tri-lens through which to view the complexity of team member diversity. The chapters use a variety of examples, exercises, questions, specific ideas, and practical suggestions that we hope will engage you. Case studies and an assessment inventory are at the end of each chapter.

Chapter 1 opens with a broad overview of the emergence and importance of multicultural teams, the different forms these teams may take, and the numerous factors that impact team effectiveness.

Chapter 2 defines culture, and presents an integrated cultural framework that can be used to explain and understand behavior in multicultural teams.

Chapter 3 discusses foundations of individual behavior, including social identity, personality, and multiple intelligences.

Chapter 4 provides the reader with an understanding of typical stages a team experiences as it develops to a level of high performance, and describes team-building processes that may enhance this development.

Chapter 5 discusses team process, both overt and covert, functional and dysfunctional roles team members may take, and how to conduct successful meetings.

Chapters 6–9 discuss specific team processes: leadership, communication, conflict, and problem solving and decision making.

Claire B. Halverson
S. Aqeel Tirmizi

Acknowledgments

Our multicultural team of contributors included individuals who are engaged scholars and reflective practitioners in the field of multicultural teams. They included Linda Gobbo, John Ungerleider, Ken Williams, and Teressa Moore Griffin. We greatly appreciate their commitment and dedication to this project.

Anitra Ingram, Susan Peters, Chulin Jiang and Mariana Syrotiak provided valuable support in terms of background research, formatting, editing and indexing. We are thankful to all of them for their contributions and attention to detail throughout the project.

Veronica Johnson helped us edit all of the chapters in this version of the book. She provided a series of valuable comments and suggestions, which brought clarity and coherence to a number of our discussions appearing in different chapters.

We are thankful to Adam Weinberg, Provost of the School for International Training, and Marla Solomon, Dean, for providing a grant to support the research and editorial work for this project.

We would like to express our appreciation to Melvin Shakun, Myriam Poort and Esther Otten at Springer. Their encouragement and support greatly helped with the timely completion of this project.

We recognize all those individuals who, over the years, have taught us the value and importance of culture in making work authentic and meaningful in multicultural settings.

Contents

About the Authors

Co-editors

Claire B. Halverson, Ph.D., is a Professor of Intercultural Service, Leadership, and Management, and designed the course Organization Behavior I: Effective Multicultural Teams at SIT. She has taught the course for 20 years, and has been the lead faculty for five simultaneous sections. Halverson compiled the text that is currently used, *Effective Multicultural Teams*, which includes overviews and additional articles for eight chapters. She has also published several articles on Edward Hall's Cultural Context including "Cultural Context Inventory: The Effects of Culture on Behavior and Work Style" in the 1993 Annual: Developing Human Resources. She has taught at the University of the Northwest in South Africa, and the Global Partnership Program in NGO Management in Lima, Peru she is a professional member of the National Training Laboratories Institute for Applied Behavioral Science and the recipient of World Learning's first annual Diversity Award. Halverson is currently doing research and planning writing on the applications of racial/ethnic social identity development theory internationally.

S. Aqeel Tirmizi, Ph.D., is an Associate Professor of Intercultural Service, Leadership and Management at the School for International Training. During his tenure at SIT, he has chaired the Management Degree and Co-directed the Ford Foundation IFP Leadership for Social Justice Institutes Initiative. Dr Tirmizi's professional portfolio includes more than 13 years of international experience in teaching, capacity building, research and management. He has a Masters degree in International Administration and a Ph.D. in Management. He teaches in the areas of organizational behavior, multicultural teams, performance management, human resources management and leadership and change. He has taught at the State University of New York, Binghamton, The Lahore University of Management Sciences, and The Global Partnership Program in NGO Leadership and Management, BRAC, Bangladesh. Dr. Tirmizi conducts research on impact of culture on human processes including teams and interpersonal interactions, leadership, decision-making and human resource management. He has presented his work at several leading international conferences in Asia, Europe and the U.S., including the Academy of Management Conference, the European Academy of Management Conference, and the Global HRM Conference. He has undertaken training and consulting assignments for clients such as the Ford Foundation's International Fellowship Program–New York, Heifer International–Arkansas, Eisenhower Fellows Program–Philadelphia, The World Bank-Pakistan, Canadian International Development Agency - Pakistan, DESCON Engineering Group-UAE, The Aga Khan Rural Support Program - Pakistan. Dr Tirmizi is a member of The Academy of Management, International Leadership Association and Leadership Learning Community.

Contributors

Linda Drake Gobbo is an Associate Professor, and the Chair of the International Education degree at the School for International Training. Linda teaches courses in International Education, Strategic Planning, and in the management core of the Program in Intercultural Service, Leadership, and Management. With over 20 years of service to SIT, Linda has served in several administrative capacities and received the Sustained Excellence Award. She is currently the Chair for the Teaching, Learning, and Scholarship knowledge community of NAFSA: The Association of International Educators, and was the lead curriculum designer for NAFSA's Academy for International Education program. She has published in the International Educator journal on various occasions.

Teressa Moore Griffin is the President of Freeman Associates, LLC. Her experience spans the pharmaceutical, financial, and consumer products industries. Since 1977, she has managed organization-wide culture change efforts, and has designed and implemented numerous training and management development processes and programs. Currently, Ms. Griffin specializes in individual development, the effective creation and utilization of a diverse workforce, executive coaching and leadership development. Providing services to public and private sector organizations, her work focuses on maximizing productivity through the development of people. While this is the first contribution to a text, Ms. Griffin is in the process of writing a book. The working title is *Unmask the Lies*. The book challenges readers to examine the limiting beliefs they hold which disempower and diminish their opportunities for success and satisfaction. Mrs. Griffin is a professional member of National Training Laboratories Institute for Applied Behavioral Science (NTL Institute).

John Ungerleider, Ed.D., is a Professor at SIT where he teaches graduate courses in Conflict Transformation, Intercultural Communication and Organizational Behavior.

Ungerleider also teaches Conflict Resolution at Hampshire College and recently taught in Spain at the master's program at the Bancaja Institute for Peace and Development. In 1997–98, he was a Fulbright Senior Scholar in Cyprus, coordinating bi-communal conflict resolution activities. Since 1990 he has designed and directed summer programs for youth at SIT. These include Youth Peacebuilding Camps for teenaged Greek and Turkish Cypriots, Catholics and Protestants from Northern Ireland, Arab and Jewish Israelis, and Muslims and whites from England, as well as Confidence Building Workshops for university students from Cyprus. He also directs the Governor's Institute on Current Issues and Youth Activism for Vermont teens. With a start up grant from the United States Institute of Peace, Ungerleider co-founded the CONTACT (Conflict Transformation Across Cultures) graduate certificate program for international peacebuilders. With grants from the US Departments of Labor and Education, Ungerleider created and directs the Child Labor Education and Action project to teach US youth about the global issue of oppressive child labor.

Kenneth Williams, who has a certificate of Education and a B.A. from the University of the West Indies, and Master's degrees from London School of Economics and Columbia University, is completing his doctorate in Organization and Leadership at Columbia University. He is degree chair of Social Justice in Intercultural Relations and an assistant professor at the School for International Training, where he teaches courses in Social Identity, Research Methods, Organizational Behavior and Multicultural Team Effectiveness, Organizational Behavior and Leadership, and Multicultural Organizational Development. His doctoral dissertation focuses on Transformational Leadership and Organizational Learning in education.

Chapter 1
Towards Understanding Multicultural Teams

S. Aqeel Tirmizi

We write to taste life twice, in the moment and in retrospection.
–Anais Nin

Introduction

Consider the following two anecdotes:

A French-Senegalese manufacturing organization in Senegal was struggling with ways to increase production. The company's leadership was mostly comprised of French and Italian expatriates. Following some initial efforts and calculations, the French production manager concluded that it was impossible to increase the production levels by 25%. Coincidentally, he fell ill during this time and his assistant, a Senegalese national, took over the negotiation and decision making temporarily. A Senegalese worker approached the assistant with a proposal that workers were willing to increase the daily production by 30% or more in return for two hours' additional pay. The Senegalese assistant did some calculations and consulted some influential people and accepted the proposal. The daily production increased between 30 to 40%. Upon his return, the French production manager did not fully support the agreement since he thought that his authority had been undermined, which led to worker dissatisfaction and low morale. It was clear that both the Senegalese staff and expatriate managers were equally interested in increasing performance. However, they did not manage their cultural differences well and thus were not able to work effectively as a team.

The tragic earthquake in Northern Pakistan and India, in the autumn of 2005, killed around 75,000 people, and left thousands injured and sick and about three million people homeless and at the mercy of harsh mountain winter weather. The urgent relief work included acquiring and supplying tents and food for the homeless and medical aid to the sick. Among several organizations, a major U.S.-based international relief organization mobilized its human and organizational resources to respond to this tragedy. Successful planning and delivery of relief service, in a large part, depended

C.B. Halverson and S.A. Tirmizi (eds.), *Effective Multicultural Teams: Theory and Practice*,

on the effective working of individuals from the international, national, and local offices of the agency and its partner organizations. While the organization was able to act quickly, the highly dedicated individuals from different nationalities found it difficult to understand and work with each other.

The individuals represented in the two anecdotes represent different backgrounds and were working in formal and informal teams to achieve the organizational objectives within multicultural settings. They exemplify the trends, possibilities, and challenges that surround teamwork in the various sectors of our society, including the for-profit, not-for-profit, and relief and development contexts.

According to Young (1998), some of the key challenges of managing multicultural teams are related to how people relate to each other, how they communicate with each other, and differences in their cultural orientations. Iles (1995) observes that misunderstanding, stereotyping, lack of competence and contribution, and mutual blaming create conflict and tension in teams. He goes on to add that such issues are likely to be multiplied when working with people who are culturally different and when working with gender, racial, ethnic, and ability diversity (Iles 1995). The work of Shenker and Zeira (1992) highlights the fact that cultural differences can contribute to increased conflict and misperceptions, which results in poor performance. Brett et al. (2006) sum up the major challenge in multicultural teams as follows:

> The challenge in managing multicultural teams effectively is to recognize the underlying cultural causes of conflict, and to intervene in ways that both get the team back on track and empower its members to deal with future challenges themselves (p. 1).

Management and leadership of multicultural teams involves effectively and creatively dealing with a variety of challenges that emerge as people from different cultural backgrounds interact with each other to accomplish the team task.

The purpose of this chapter is to introduce what is known about multicultural teams and the factors that play a role in understanding and making these teams effective, using research and practice-based knowledge. The chapter begins with a broad overview of the emergence and importance of multicultural teams, the different forms these teams may take, and the role of diversity in multicultural team dynamics and effectiveness. Additionally, the chapter systematically identifies numerous factors embedded in the individual, team, organizational, and societal levels that impact multicultural team effectiveness.

Learning Objectives

After reading this chapter you should be able to:

- Discuss the discipline of teams as an emerging area of study and practice
- Define the concept of teams and discuss some differences between teams and groups
- Discuss different types and categories of teams
- Discuss the importance and relevance of multicultural teams

- Discuss some key effects of multicultural teams on organizational performance
- Describe an overall model for articulating and highlighting the different factors that contribute to effective teamwork

The Emergence and Study of Multicultural Teams as a Discipline

Why do teams emerge, or why do we create teams? Human beings have been working together and learning to cooperate since the dawn of time. Cooperation and working together are considered valuable in and of themselves. However, there is more here. Cooperation and working together result in efficiency and satisfaction that may not be possible otherwise. In addition to efficiency there is a bigger consideration that leads to the emergence and creation of teams. This consideration has to do with the sense of individual and collective satisfaction, achievement, and learning that occurs as individuals combine their efforts to achieve team and organizational goals. These variables directly and indirectly strengthen team processes and outcomes.

The successful completion of tasks, projects, and missions in community, organizational, and larger arenas of human interactions requires a certain degree of interdependence and relationship building among a group of individuals. In that sense one can argue that when a number of people in some kind of an informal or formal organization regularly interact and depend upon each other to accomplish desired outcomes, they are working as a team. An example of this is a core group of half a dozen individuals comprised of indigenous farmers from Mexico and a young couple from the US working under the Fair Trade umbrella to sell their products in the USA In order to work effectively, the members of the group interact with each other formally and informally on a regular basis; they depend upon each other for completion of significant tasks (e.g., timely preparation of shipments).

Recent developments around the world have affected all sectors in which society is tightly and loosely organized (private, public, civil society, etc.). Accordingly, the nature of work in each of these sectors has been affected by globalization and technology. Changes in the workforce composition resulting from globalization, combined with the rising popularity of team-based management techniques, have led to a practical concern with the management of multicultural teams (Thomas 1999). Technological advances have changed the way work is done and the way people communicate. Globalization and technology have added layers of complexity to the organization of work, which makes it necessary for people to depend upon one other to develop their goals and missions successfully and effectively. In that sense, teams and teamwork are integral to the way work in different organizations, sectors, and cultural settings gets done. From the above discussion we can infer that the notion of interdependence is central to defining and understanding teams in a complex and diverse world. The section of this chapter explaining different types of teams highlights how the degree of interdependence determines the nature of a team.

The academic and popular literature of the 1990s fully embraced the notion that multicultural teams were becoming a way of organizational life in the USA and other parts of the world, and therefore, it was important to understand how such teams could be managed and led effectively (e.g., Iles 1995). Equally important has been the concern with preparing individuals so that they can be effective in their roles as team members. This trend continues in the new millennium (e.g., Laroche 2001; Matveev and Milter 2004). As a result of this recognition, the theory and practice of effective multicultural teams started emerging. While this was a much needed and important start, our knowledge of different factors that contribute to building effective, especially high-performance multicultural teams, remains somewhat scattered and not fully integrated.

Harnessing the synergy or potential for high performance that is present in a multicultural team can lead to more creative approaches to problem solving and decision making (Marquardt and Horvath 2001), and this in turn means that we need to refine our understanding of the factors and processes that contribute to creating synergy and making the team effective. The remaining sections of this chapter introduce the basic ideas and a conceptual framework to define and contextualize the theory and practice of multicultural teams. The additional chapters offer comprehensive explanations, ideas, and suggestions for both understanding and working effectively with multicultural teams.

Teams Defined

The academic and popular literature offers many ways of defining teams. In their extensive review, Bailey and Cohen (1997) examined a large set of team definitions. Following this comprehensive review, they proposed the following definition of teams:

> A team is a collection of individuals who are interdependent in their tasks, who share responsibility for outcomes, who see themselves and are seen by others as an intact social entity, embedded in one or more larger social systems and who manage their relationships across organizational boundaries (p. 241).

Offermann and Spiros (2001) observe that an important issue in linking theory and practice of teams is the proper use of the term *team*. From a theoretical perspective, the interdependent nature of teams differentiates them from other collectives. On the other hand, groups are broadly constituted, their members consider themselves as social entities and are perceived by others this way, and they may have shared goals but are loosely connected (Offermann and Spiros 2001).

Katzenbach and Smith (1993) differentiate between teams and groups.
Looking at their list in the table below we see possible differences in the areas of leadership, accountability, meeting processes, and output. However, looking closely at some of these differences—for example, the focus on purpose and goals—one

Teams	Groups
• Shared leadership roles • Individual and mutual accountability • A specific purpose that the team itself delivers • Collective work products • Open-ended discussion and active problem solving in meetings	• Strong, clearly focused leader • Individual accountability • Purpose is the same as the larger organizational mission • Individual work products • Focus on efficiency in meetings

can easily argue that any collective is concerned with the overall purpose that may be rooted in the larger organization or community. In that sense, teams and groups share a purpose that cannot be separated from the mission of the larger organization, since members are part of, and identify with, the organization or community.

While some writers have attempted to differentiate between *teams* and *groups* by attaching different conceptual meanings to them, others, such as Bailey and Cohen (1997), do not agree with this differentiation and approach these two concepts interchangeably. Bailey and Cohen (1997) observe that the popular management literature has tended to use the word *teams* more often, and the academic writing has used the word *groups* more regularly. While we lean towards defining team as entities characterized by a high degree of task interdependency, we do not see this as a major issue one way or the other.

Since we are concerned here with understanding and defining not just teams but teams that are diverse and multicultural, we need to take that into consideration in our definition. Marquardt and Horvath (2001) define multicultural teams as task-oriented groups comprising people of different cultural backgrounds. Following Marquardt and Horvath (2001) and Bailey and Cohen (1997), we define multicultural teams as a collection of individuals with different cultural backgrounds, who are interdependent in their tasks, who share responsibility for outcomes, who see themselves and are seen by others as an intact social entity embedded in one or more larger social systems, and who manage their relationships across organizational boundaries and beyond.

Types of Teams

Several typologies have been offered to categorize teams (e.g., Katzenbach and Smith 1993; Mohrman et al. 1995; Bailey and Cohen 1997). These typologies include formal and informal teams, task forces, committees, self-managed team and virtual teams. While the conceptual characteristics that differentiate these typologies are useful and important, in many cases the features attributed to a certain type of team may overlap with another team type. For example, a task force may be self-managed, and an on-going work group may be formal or informal. Each of these categories is briefly discussed below.

Based on the works cited above and similar sources, the following categorization of teams may be useful in understanding the different forms that teams take and some of their important features.

Formal teams are the building blocks of organizations. The formal team has a high level of boundary spanning in that it may operate across departments within organizations. The formal team has a more rigid organizational structure, as team members tend to have distinct roles and the workload is distributed accordingly. Formal teams may be set up to address particular tasks that the organization seeks to accomplish within a specific time period. The members have a high degree of interdependence and both the process and performance are integral to the success of the formal team. A product development team consisting of members from the engineering, marketing, and production departments of an air conditioning manufacturing plant would be considered a formal team.

Informal teams meet to solve specific problems, and their membership may change with the task that the team seeks to accomplish. Informal teams thus have a high level of boundary spanning, similar to that of formal teams. However, members of informal teams have a lower level of interdependence than formal teams, consistent with a less-rigid organizational structure. An informal group might be formed in a micro-credit organization, for example, to understand and offer some suggestions about motivational and turnover issues among its loan officers. Members of the group might primarily be loan officers.

Task forces are teams organized for a specific project, and they are generally managed by the organization that initiated them. The task force has a great deal of interdependence between members and a strong emphasis on performance and timetables.

A *committee* is similar to a task force in that it is focused on a specific project for a discrete period of time. A committee can be a group of people who are formally delegated to perform a task, such as a search process or a decision-making process. Committees can also be formed to take action on a matter without the explicit involvement of the organization the committee members belong to. In other words, a committee can have different levels of member interdependence and varying degrees of autonomy from the members' organizations. Along the spectrum of team autonomy, committees can have more autonomy than task forces.

Self-managed teams have the greatest degree of autonomy from the organization, and have a strong emphasis on performance. Self-managed teams combine aspects of formal and informal teams, since they are inaugurated by the organization's management but take on the responsibility for their own management. In self-managed teams, most decision-making authority is turned over to a group that works interdependently in order to accomplish an assigned task (Katzenbach and Smith 1993).

Virtual teams are formed and joined electronically, with negligible face-to-face contact. Although virtual teams are not necessarily as autonomous as self-managed teams, team members have a high degree of autonomy. In contrast to formal and self-managed teams, virtual teams are less interdependent due to the nature of virtual communications and the multiplicity of organizations that can be involved.

Virtual teams are characterized by a permeable boundary between organizations, facilitated by networking. Globalization and widespread access to communication and collaboration technologies has caused virtual teams and networked organizations to proliferate (Mohrman et al. 1995). Virtual teams have the advantage of spreading the workload among long-distance players. However, the challenges present for non-virtual teams can be enhanced for virtual teams (Mohrman et al. 1995). These challenges are likely to be overcome with increased experience and the use of continually improved technologies. Both self-managed and virtual teams are increasingly common team types for organizations, and ongoing research that examines the complexities of these team types can help us learn how to make them more effective.

Multicultural Teams and Team Performance

To assess the impact of multiculturalism on team performance, it is important to consider the organizational context of the team, the nature of the team's diversity, and the relationship between these factors and the team's task. Organizational cultures derive from the history and experience shared by members of an organization and individual behaviors formed by the national culture. Because of this, many organizational cultures with a wide range of differences co-exist in a national culture (Brannen 1994). Team members might be more homogeneous than the national cultures they are part of, because they belong to similar educational, occupational, and socioeconomic subgroups. On the other hand, team members might differ in age, religion, race, locality, or other subgroup affiliations within a national culture. Membership in diverse subgroups and social identity help explain why individuals from the same national culture bring different behavioral expectations to a team (Brannen 1994). In other words, members of a team represent both the national cultures that they come from and quite possibly many other subcultures and identities. Thus, multicultural teams must be seen as having many facets that are not limited to diversity in national cultures.

Brannen and Salk's (2000) research reveals the effects of multifaceted diversity and suggests that cultural differences do not necessarily have a negative impact on team performance. Differences do not cause team conflicts; rather, the organizational context and individual team members' responses to cultural norms mediate differences. Team members of an increasingly diverse workforce must actively cope with cultural differences in order to bridge cultural boundaries. One such mechanism may be the formation of a hybrid culture within the multicultural team (Kopp 2005). In line with past work on power and influence, Brannen and Salk's (2000) work indicates that uncertainties experienced by teams determine which individual attributes will influence team behavior. Since team members, having many potential identities, do not necessarily exemplify the values of their culture or organization, the organizational context is an important variable in determining which attributes will affect team performance. The work of Brannen and Salk's (2000) highlights the multiplicity of cultural identities, and shows that organizational context plays a central role in deciding the relative importance of those identities.

Empirical research on the output of multicultural teams has yielded divergent results. Many studies have shown that heterogeneous groups outperform homogenous groups. In contrast, some studies have shown that homogenous teams avoid the "process loss" caused by unpracticed communication and the subsequent conflict of more diverse teams. Recently, Williams and O'Reilly (1998) reviewed 40 years of diversity research and came to the conclusion that diversity does not have any predictable effects on team performance. Their review called for further research incorporating a more complex conceptualization of diversity and inclusion of context (e.g., organizational aspects, task type), types of diversity (informational and demographic), and process variables such as conflict and communication. A study by Jehn et al. (1999) attempts to synthesize these concepts with a model that illustrates how various types of diversity affect performance. The model includes three types of diversity discussed in past team research (informational diversity, social category diversity, value diversity). Informational diversity originates in differences between team members' educational background, work experience, and specialties. Social category diversity, or visible diversity, refers to the differences that people perceive first, such as gender, race, and ethnicity. Value diversity is essentially differences in what team members perceive the team's task and purpose to be.

The Jehn et al. study found that low value diversity and low social category diversity allow a multicultural team to take advantage of its informational diversity. Nonaka and Takeuchi (1995) affirm that informational diversity is not an advantage unless team members can capitalize on it. Tsui and O'Reilly (1989) have also found that even when teams possess advantageous aspects of diversity, performance will only improve to the degree that team members can overcome conflictual aspects of diversity. The Jehn et al. (1999) study also implies that some similarity in perspective among team members is necessary to facilitate successful group interaction. Their research correlated specific types of diversity with advantageous outcomes. For instance, high information diversity and low value diversity creates a high-performing team and maximizes effectiveness, while low value diversity alone leads to more efficient teamwork. Jehn et al. (1999) also found that value diversity becomes more important for team performance over time while social category diversity becomes less significant over time. This conclusion is supported by a study of R&D teams (Owens and Neale 1999) and by Salk's (1996) research on the relative prominence of national cultural differences in multicultural teams.

In addition to understanding how diversity affects team performance, the relationship between team process and diversity has been the subject of some research. The Jehn et al. (1999) study found that social category diversity led to higher team morale when task interdependence was high. In a study by Trefry and Vaillant (2002) multicultural team members reported enhanced capability to deal with unexpected events and increased self-confidence. Team members also stated that they had re-examined their perspectives when confronted with different perspectives. These individual benefits, including flexibility in response to unanticipated events, give multicultural teams a distinct competitive advantage. The competitive advantage of multicultural teams can be observed in the team's output, especially when members are able to mediate conflicts caused by value diversity.

Thus, research on multicultural teams has led to three conclusions about team performance. First, certain types of diversity affect team process and performance more than other differences. Second, team members' responses to diversity and conflict are a major factor in determining how teams will be affected, in both process and performance. Third, the type of task the team is responsible for and the level of task interdependence are also important variables in the success of a multicultural team. Accordingly, the nature of a team's diversity can be an advantage or a disadvantage depending on the task involved and how the teamwork is managed.

A Model for Multicultural Team Effectiveness

A number of theorists have put forward models conceptualizing what makes teams effective. It is a difficult task to build a model that captures complex behavioral and psychological phenomena, such as teamwork and team effectiveness, in a comprehensive and meaningful manner. In addition to adequately representing behavioral and psychological dynamics at the team level, such models need to include higher-level variables connected to organizational and societal dynamics. However, despite these difficulties it is important to develop such models to inform theory building and practice. Following a valuable observation by Offermann and Spiros (2001), I see this model as an attempt to integrate the comprehensive existing knowledge about teamwork and processes through a usable framework facilitating transfer to practice. In Fig. 1.1, I propose a model representing the factors that affect team effectiveness. The components of the model are societal/institutional factors, organizational factors, team factors (structure, membership, and processes), team climate, and team effectiveness criteria. Many of the components and relationships presented here have been included in previous models and conceptualizations of team effectiveness (e.g., Ancona 1990; Guzzo 1986; Hackman 1987; Salas et al. 2003). However, I believe that the previous models have not examined all the variables and the relationships among these variables in the manner presented here. Some of the factors, important for our purposes, that have lacked integrated attention are culture and social identity and their impact on the effectiveness of multicultural teams. In addition, previous models have not categorized the team-level factors according to the structure, membership and process dimensions. Offermannand Spiros (2001) list a number of these factors as important to researchers and practitioners alike but do not pinpoint factors at the team level or differentiate between team- and organizational-level factors. These distinctions are important for both conceptual and practical purposes. Additionally, the model includes and builds on the works of Williams and O'Reilly (1998) and Jehn et al. (1999) by including a number of factors at the contextual and team levels.

Overall, the model proposes that team structure, membership, and processes determine team effectiveness. The model further asserts that the relationship

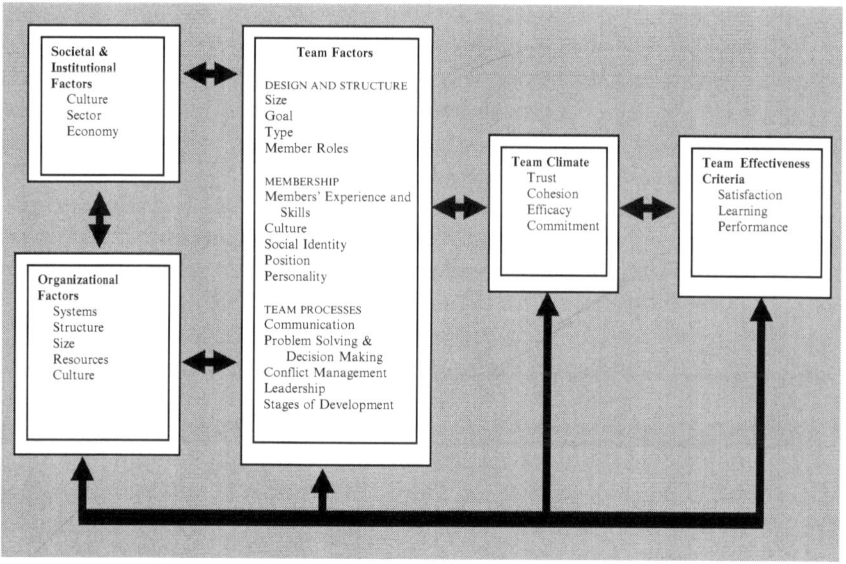

Fig. 1.1 Multicultural team effectiveness model

between team effectiveness and team-level factors is mediated by the level of trust, cohesion, efficacy, and commitment that are present in a team, labeled as team climate in the model. In addition, team effectiveness and its team-level determinants are impacted by variables in the organizational and societal contexts.

Many of the relationships presented in the model have been studied and accepted by some of the existing conceptualizations and models of team effectiveness. For example, Hackman (1987) was one of the major initial works on this subject, which included a number of variables such as team size, norms, satisfaction and task accomplishment. However, neither Hackman nor many of the subsequent works on the subject fully dealt with some of the other relevant factors that impact the working and effectiveness of multicultural teams. Therefore, in the model presented below, I attempt to link several of these factors and provide an integrated approach to understanding and working with multicultural teams effectively. Some of the linkages and dynamics presented in the model have already been discussed in previous sections. For example, the sections on Types of Teams and Multicultural Teams and Performance relate team effectiveness to team design.

Societal and Institutional Factors

The above definition of multicultural teams stated that teams are embedded in one or more larger social systems. One such system is culture or national culture.

For our immediate purposes I use Schein's (1985) definition of culture as the assumptions, values, and artifacts that are shared by the members of a group (society). Since the major focus of our work is to understand multicultural teams, it is important to examine culture and how it impacts teams and individual team members. Some of the cultural dynamics and their impact on multicultural teams have been discussed above. Chapter 2 includes an overview of the major cultural frameworks and their implications for team processes and dynamics.

In addition to culture, other macro-level variables such as the sector of work (development, education), industry (high technology, manufacturing), etc., may play some role in impacting the nature and effectiveness of teams in a certain context.

Organizational Factors

Team achievement, to a large extent, depends upon the resources and authority required to complete the assignment successfully. A number of organizational arrangements play a key role in this area. These arrangements include systems such as compensation, performance management, and training and development; structural arrangements that help create and maintain teams; and organizational culture that promotes and encourages teamwork.

Tata and Prasad (2004) studied the impact of organizational formalization and centralization on self-managed teams and their effectiveness. They concluded that self-managed teams may be more effective in organizational settings with limited explicit rules, procedures, and polices. In addition, they found that these teams were effective in organizational environments that were characterized by distributed authority and decision making. Thomas et al. (2000) reported that the organization in their study that had comprehensively transferred power successfully created a feeling among its workforce that it valued employee involvement. In the same study, the authors report that most effective teams obtained a substantial part of their rewards based on team efforts. Such organizational systems support and encourage teamwork.

The fact that organizational culture is a key determinant of organizational behavior and performance is now well recognized. It is important to emphasize here that within the same national culture, organizational and group cultures may take many different forms (Brannen 1994). When understanding team effectiveness, organizational culture becomes an important variable to consider.

Team-Level Factors

The team-level factors have been divided into three subcategories: team design and structure, membership, and team processes. I briefly discuss each of these below.

Team design and structure elements include team size, goal, type, and member composition. Team size is an important variable as it plays a role in management of team dynamics and if not managed properly could negatively affect the team's performance. The size is defined by the nature and complexity of the task to be performed. It also depends upon the resources available. In some teams the size may not be constant, but depend upon the progress of the task and the available resources.

The quality of a team's output and the efficiency with which it is achieved, in some ways, are sensitively linked to a team's size. While it is obvious that the higher the size, the more resources a team will have, it is important to consider that with increased size comes a more complex web of intra-team dynamics. Specifically, a five-person team has ten two-person relationships, but when the size is doubled a ten-person team will have about 44 dyadic relationships, an almost exponential increase in the number of relationships to be managed (Jones and Bearley 2001). Jones and Bearley (2001) argue that it is difficult to sustain high levels of performance in teams of people with more than about 15 members (p. 57).

According to Gardenswartz and Rowe (2003), team goals are the means to articulate and translate the overall mission. Collective understanding and clarity around team goals is crucial for a team's success. In our experience with both monocultural and multicultural teams, we recall many instances when there was no discussion of the team's overall goal. In such cases, the individual members assume that the goal is understood and clear to everyone, which is not always the case. In such cases, there is potential for frustration, lack of timely progress, and unmet or incomplete goals. This potential is even greater in multicultural teams due to the variety in expectations, individual goals, and backgrounds that members bring to the team. Therefore, it is very important for multicultural teams to develop collective understanding of their goals and link them to the members' individual expectations and aspirations to the extent possible.

The type or form of a multicultural team is another important element of team design. These forms may include a task force, self-managed team, committee, or virtual team, which were explained in the section on team types.

Team membership variables include team members' experiences and skills, cultural background, social identity (issues such as class, race, gender, ethnicity) and individual aspects of personality and intelligence. At the team level the variable of social identity, personality, and culture intersect in complex ways. These intersections may be seen as a tri-lens, which may exist as overlapping personal, social, and collective identities that members bring to a multicultural team. The role of culture will be discussed in Chapter 2, and the role of social identity and personality will be explored in detail in Chapter 3.

Team processes include a number of important areas such as communication, problem solving and decision making, conflict management, stages of development, and leadership. All of these processes play an extremely important role in the working and effectiveness of multicultural teams. For example, norm setting and clarification is an important team development process. A norm in the context of multicultural teams is a behavior, a way of doing, which the team practices on an ongoing basis, and it serves as a ground rule. Kopp (2005) talks about the notion of *hybrid culture* as a set of communication norms that are designed by the group. She goes on to observe that such norms may be explicitly agreed upon or emerge over a period of time. This notion and team roles that contribute to effective group process are explored further in Chapter 5. Chapters 6 and 7 provide comprehensive discussions on leadership and intercultural communication. Conflict processes are discussed in Chapter 8 and problem-solving and decision-making processes in Chapter 9.

In many ways the major focus of our examination in the book will be the team-level factors. While we consider other larger variables at organizational and societal levels as important and integral to understanding teams and their effectiveness, what happens within a team and how team processes and dynamics are managed play a central role in a team's success.

Team Climate

The areas of trust, commitment, cohesion, and efficacy have received some much-deserved attention in the organizational and behavioral literature. I consider them as mediating variables linking the team-level factors and the effectiveness criteria. Druskat and Wolff (2001), while examining the emotional intelligence of teams, argued that team trust, identity, and efficacy play a key role in determining a team's effectiveness as they form a foundation for collaboration and cooperation. They further asserted that team processes of appropriate norm building contribute to the team trust and efficacy building. The model indicates that the team and higher-level factors determine the team climate. The resulting climate not only plays a role in team effectiveness, but could also impact team processes and higher-level variables. In other words, a synergistic relationship between team climate and team process exists. For example, increased trust among team members may strengthen the communication and decision-making processes.

Team Effectiveness Criteria

Over the years, the theory of multicultural teams has recognized the importance of multiple effectiveness criteria when considering team success. In addition to productivity and performance, team members' satisfaction and learning are now considered integral to understanding the team's effectiveness. The team effectiveness model explicitly recognizes that in addition to performance and productivity, individual and collective sense of satisfaction and learning is integral to judging a team's success. The model further asserts that factors of learning and satisfaction may contribute to strengthening teamwork. For example, on-going learning may strengthen a shared sense of efficacy or unlock new means of communicating and decision making. Further, team member satisfaction creates positive feedback that boosts the effectiveness of multicultural teams.

As we attempt to understand what makes for appropriate effectiveness criteria for multicultural teams, it is again important to consider how these criteria may be influenced by culture as well. Cultural norms influence team members' perceptions of team process and performance. In other words, as observed by Thomas et al. (2000), what is considered "going nowhere" in some cultures may be seen as "getting there" in other cultures. In their two-year study of multicultural teams in the Australasian region, Thomas and Ravlin (1995) found that members' effectiveness criteria related to both task and interpersonal factors. Their findings revealed that a majority of team members from different cultural backgrounds felt that both task achievement and how well members worked together were important. The study also reiterates the importance of organizational context. Thomas and Ravlin (1995) found that team performance was positively correlated with management support for teams, diversity support and training, team status, and team rewards. Team rewards were not material, but again related to members' satisfaction with task accomplishment and feelings of positive self-esteem. Thus, team members' effectiveness criteria relate to their satisfaction with team process, or the "getting there," as well as task accomplishment.

Application of the Model

Now that we have examined the components of the model, it would be useful to look at how it can be applied, highlighting the factors that play an important role in determining team effectiveness, and the complex ways in which these factors can be linked. Let's take the example of a team responsible for organizing and implementing executive development programs for the Executive Development Unit (EDU) in a university setting in Thailand. The core team has three Thai, one Indian, and one British national on it. Two Thai support and administrative staff assist the team. The team has two female members. The overall mandate of the team is to plan, market, and implement highly reputable portfolios of open-enrollment short training programs on leadership and management for professionals across the South East Asia region. The team works closely with the management school faculty from the university, which provides the conceptual leadership and human resources for the actual program design and delivery.

The societal factors in this case include the opportunities and constraints that come with the emerging market economy and the educational and training sectors in Thailand and the neighboring countries. These factors will partly determine the nature of marketing and success of these programs. The organizational factors in this case will include the university faculty resources whose availability and competence will impact the timely planning and delivery quality. Financial resources, information technology, and support from the organization will play a role in the success of the marketing efforts.

At the team level, clarity of goals and member roles in terms of structural factors are clearly important. In terms of membership factors, the member's relevant experience and skills, social identity and personality will have a critical impact on the team's working, its overall climate and subsequent performance. The British female has been hired as the Program Director a few months ago. Though she is coming to this job with four years relevant managerial experience from a university in Singapore, there are important questions about how she is perceived by the Thai team members as a foreigner.

The team processes of communication, decision making, management of developmental stages, and leadership are key determinants of how this multicultural team will manage its dynamics and meet its goals and mandate. There may be a leadership challenge here as the Indian team member, who grew up in a hierarchal and male-dominated society, may have to adjust to a female leader. This team's climate and effectiveness will be determined by how the team-level factors will be managed and the impact of the organizational and societal factors.

Relevant Competencies

- Articulate the contextual factors that impact the work of multicultural teams
- Understand the team-level factors and the overall role they play in determining the effectiveness of multicultural teams
- Identify the variables that determine the team climate
- Understand the nature and relevance of multiple criteria for team effectiveness
- Observe connections among various factors that determine the effectiveness of multicultural teams

Summary

The purpose of the chapter was to introduce what is known about multicultural teams and the factors that play a role in understanding and making these teams effective, using research and practice-based knowledge.

The model proposed in this chapter provides a conceptual framework for the discussions to follow in subsequent chapters. It lists the most relevant factors that play an important role at different levels in determining the effectiveness of multicultural teams. In addition, the model articulates some of the key causal linkages among the different factors and variables.

While all the factors listed in the framework are important and relevant for understanding how multicultural teams work, our major focus in this book is on exploring and discussing the team-level factors. However, several of the other factors, particularly culture and effectiveness criteria, will be examined and linked to various team processes and dynamics.

The discussions in the next chapters will explore cultural frameworks and operationalization of culture most relevant to teams, individual factors with particular attention to personality and identity, team development, group process, leadership dynamics, communication dynamics, conflict management, and problem solving and decision making.

Case Study: Evaluation Mission[1]

As you read the case study below, consider the following questions:

- *What is the evaluation team's goal?*
- *What are key contextual variables at the societal and organizational levels that may impact the team's work?*
- *What aspects of the team members' social identity are important in this context, if any?*
- *What are your thoughts on the experience and skills of the team for conducting this mission?*
- *What would be your recommendations to the team to facilitate their work?*

Rada International Development Agency (RIDA) sponsors development initiatives around the world. As part of its learning and monitoring activities, it regularly organizes evaluation missions. Let's assume that RIDA is forming an evaluation mission to assess the five-year impact of a major regional development program in Indonesia. This particular mission is aimed at evaluating a project focusing on strengthening local governance. The team will pay close attention to gender equity, policy reforms, and participation and strengthening of civil society organizations.

The evaluation team will consist of four members representing different nationalities, which will initiate and complete the assessment in a three-month period. The work will include a detailed review of program documentation, extensive meetings with stakeholders, analysis, and report writing. Two of the team members are from Canada and the remaining two members are from Indonesia. The team leader is a Canadian male of European descent. The other Canadian team member is a male of Ugandan origin. Both Canadians work for a small consulting firm in Ottawa that specializes in the monitoring and evaluation of international development programs. One of the Indonesians is a female who has just returned to Indonesia with a degree in public administration. Her previous work in Indonesia and her recent degree research focused on issues of local governance. The other Indonesian is a professor at a national university who regularly consults with international organizations.

RIDA considers Indonesia as an important partner in its development efforts and is assisting the country in a number of areas. Until the late 1990's, Indonesia had limited experience with democracy. The country is still recovering from the financial and political crises of 1997–98 and the tsunami disaster of 2004. Indonesia is predominantly a Muslim country. During the mission's work, Indonesia will celebrate the month of Ramadan (the Muslim month of fasting).

---

[1] This case study is based on a hypothetical scenario. However, the context, complexities, and dynamics summarized here are representative of situations experienced during evaluation of international development projects.

During the mission, the team will work closely with the Development Section of the relevant Embassy and the staff of local government and leading civil society organizations. The team will have about three months to complete the project. The project deliverables include a major presentation to the stakeholders to discuss findings and receive feedback, report writing, and debriefing at the RIDA headquarters.

Multicultural Team Effectiveness Inventory

The Multicultural Team Effectiveness Inventory (MTEI) allows a team to perform an overall assessment of its working and performance with attention to larger organizational and societal factors. Think of a formal or informal team that you have been a part of and assess your experience along the following dimensions.

How clear was the goal or purpose of teamwork? (Consider most members' shared understanding of the goal and purpose)	Not clear			Very clear
	1	2	3	4
How appropriate was the team size? (Consider the task complexity and member interdependence)	Not appropriate			Very appropriate
	1	2	3	4
Was the team type appropriate for the task? (Formal, informal, self-managed)	Not appropriate			Very appropriate
	1	2	3	4
How clear were the member roles and responsibilities? (Roles, deadlines, reporting)	Not clear			Very clear
	1	2	3	4
How do you characterize the team's understanding and managing of the following team processes?	Not effective (inappropriate, weak)			Highly effective (appropriate, strong)
	1	2	3	4
Communication				
Decision making and problem solving				
Conflict management				
Leadership				
Stages of development				

(continued)

(continued)

Did the following aspects of team membership get appropriate attention?	Did not receive appropriate attention			Received appropriate attention
	1	2	3	4
Experience				
Skills				
Social identity				
Personality				
What kind of role did the following societal and institutional factors play in influencing the team's work?	Not significant			Very significant
	1	2	3	4
Economy (consider the overall economic conditions at a national or regional level)	Not significant			Very significant
Culture (think about the norms, traditions, and values at the national and/or regional levels)				
Sector (not-for-profit, private, health, etc.)				
What kind of role did the following organizational factors play in influencing the team's work?				
	1	2	3	4
Systems (performance management, information technology, monitoring and evaluation, etc.)				
Structure (simple, matrix, flat, hierarchical, etc.)				
Size				
Resources (human, financial, technological)				
Culture				
Assess the overall level of team climate along the following dimensions	Low			High
	1	2	3	4
Trust				
Cohesion				
Efficacy				
Commitment				
Assess the overall level of team effectiveness on the following dimensions	Not effective			Highly effective
	1	2	3	4
Satisfaction				
Learning				
Performance				

Scores of 3 or more on the individual dimensions of this instrument indicate these areas of team dynamics are satisfactory to strong.

Scores of 2 or less on the individual dimensions of this instrument suggest these areas of team dynamics are weak and need appropriate attention.

References

Ancona, D. (1990). Outward bound: Strategies for team survival in an organization. *Administrative Science Quarterly*, 24, 382–404.

Bailey, S., Cohen, D. (1997). What makes teams work: Group effectiveness research from the shop floor to the executive suite. *Journal of Management*, 23(3), 239–290.

Brannen, M.Y., Salk, J. (2000). National culture, networks, and individual influence in a multinational management team. *Academy of Management Journal*, 43(2).

Brannen, M.Y. (1994). Your next boss is Japanese: Negotiating cultural change at a Western Massachusetts paper plant. Unpublished doctoral dissertation, University of Massachusetts, Amherst, MA.

Brett, J. Behfar, K. and Kern, C. (2006). Managing multicultural teams. *Harvard Business Review*. November, 1–8.

Druskat, V., Wolff, S. (2001). Building the emotional intelligence of groups. *Harvard Business Review*, 79(3), 80–90.

Gardenswartz, L. and Rowe, A. (2003). *Diverse teams at work: Capitalizing on the power of diversity*. Alexandria, VA: Society for Human Resources Management.

Guzzo, R. (1986). Group decision making and group effectiveness in organizations. In P. Goodman (Ed.), *Designing Effective Work Groups* (pp. 34–71). San Francisco, CA: Jossey-Bass.

Hackman, J. (1987). The design of work teams. In J.W. Lorsch (Ed.), *Handbook of Organizational Behavior* (pp. 315–342). Engelwood Cliffs, NJ: Prentice-Hall.

Iles, P. (1995). Learning to work with difference. *Personnel Review*, 24(6), 44–60.

Jehn, K.A., Northcraft, G.B., Neale, M.A. (1999). Why differences make a difference: A field study of diversity, conflict, and performance in workgroups. *Administrative Science Quarterly*, 44, 741–763.

Jones, J., Bearley, W. (2001). Facilitating team development: A view from the field. *Group Facilitation: A Research and Applications Journal*, 3, 56–65.

Katzenbach, J.R., Smith, D.K. (1993). *The wisdom of teams: Creating the high performance organization*. Boston, MA: Harvard Business School Press.

Kopp, R. (2005). Communication challenges between Americans and Japanese in the workplace. *Transcultural Management Review*, 2 (November), 70–77.

Laroche, L. (2001). Teaming up: Multicultural teams are becoming more common in Canadian organizations. *CMA Management*, 75(2).

Marquardt, M. and Horvath, L. (2001). *Global teams: How top multinationals span boundaries and cultures with high-speed teamwork*. Palo Alto, CA: Davies-Black Publishing.

Matveev, A., Milter, R. (2004). The value of intercultural competence for performance of multicultural teams. *Team Performance Management*, 10(5/6), 104–111.

Mohrman, S.A., Cohen, S.G. & Mohrman, A.M. (1995). *Designing team-based organizations: new forms for knowledge work*. San Francisco: Jossey-Bass Publishers.

Nonaka, I., Takeuchi, H. (1995). *The knowledge-creating company*. New York: Oxford University Press.

Offermann, L., Spiros, R. (2001). The science and practice of team development: Improving the link. *Academy of Management Journal*, 44(2), 376–392.

Owens, D.A., Neale, M.A. (1999). *The dubious benefit of group heterogeneity in highly uncertain situations: Too much of a good thing*? Working paper, School of Business, Vanderbilt University, Nashville, TN.

Salas, E., Stagl, K.C., Burke, C.S. (2003). 25 years of team effectiveness in organizations: Research themes and emerging needs. In C.L. Cooper and I.T. Robertson (Eds.), *International Review of Industrial and Organizational Psychology*. New York: Wiley.

Salk, J.E. (1996). Partners and other strangers: Cultural boundaries and cross-cultural encounters in international joint venture teams. *International Studies of Management and Organization*, 26(4), 48–72.

Schein, E.H. (1985). *Organizational culture and leadership: A dynamic view*. San Francisco, CA: Jossey-Bass.

Shenker, O., Zeira, Y. (1992). Role conflict and role ambiguity of chief manager officers in international joint ventures. *Journal of International Business Studies*, 23, 55–75.

Tata, J., Prasad, S. (2004). Team self-management, organizational structure, and judgements of team effectiveness. *Journal of Managerial Issues*, 16(2), 248–266.

Thomas, D.C. (1999). Cultural diversity and work group effectiveness: An experimental study. *Journal of Cross-Cultural Psychology*, 30(2), 242–263.

Thomas, D.C., Ravlin, E.C. (1995). Responses of employees to cultural adaptation by a foreign manager. *Journal of Applied Psychology*, 80, 133–146.

Thomas, D.C., Ravlin, E., Barry, D. (2000). Creating effective multicultural teams. *University of Auckland Business Review*, 2(1), 10–25.

Trefry, M., Vaillant, G. (2002). Harnessing cultural diversity to stimulate learning. In M.A. Rahim, R. Golembiewski and K. Mackenzie (Eds.), *Current Topics in Management* (Vol. 7, pp. 47–60). Somerset, NJ: Transaction Publishers.

Tsui, A.S., O'Reilly, C.A., III. (1989). Beyond simple demographic effects: The importance of relational demography in superior-subordinate dyads. *Academy of Management Journal*, 32(2), 402–423.

Williams, K.Y., O'Reilly, C.A. (1998). Demography and diversity in organizations. In B.M. Staw and R.M. Sutton (Eds.), *Research in Organizational Behavior* (Vol. 20, pp. 77–140). Stamford, CT: JAI.

Young, D. (1998). Global efficiency: Team heat. *CIO Magazine* [Online] September. Available at: http://www.cio.com/archive/090198_team-content.html

Chapter 2
The Impact of Culture in Multicultural Teams

S. Aqeel Tirmizi

One has to recognize that countries and people differ in their approach and their ways of living and thinking. In order to understand them we have to understand their way of life and approach. If we wish to convince them, we have to use their language as far as we can, not language in the narrow sense of the word, but the language of the mind.

–Jawaharlal Nehru

Introduction

Japan is widely recognized for its success as an economic power. Despite some of the challenges in the last few years, it remains one of the world's largest economies. The chances are that most of us have used, seen, and heard of Japanese brands ranging from automobiles to consumer electronics. Lesser known to the outside world but equally impressive is Japan's highly service-oriented society domestically. This national and global success has been intriguing the rest of the world. The last 20 years have seen the adapting of Japanese management and organizational practices in small manufacturing plants in Asia to the assembly lines of American automobile giants such as General Motors. Many observers directly attribute Japan's success to Japanese cultural values and the emphasis on teamwork. At the same time, Japanese organizations have been open to adapting and embracing some Western-style managerial practices. A major consequence of these developments is that in many of these international settings multicultural teams are attempting to work effectively where Japanese and other cultures may be significantly impacting the teamwork.

Cultural values can deeply affect organizational and team structure, rewards and motivation, interpersonal interactions, decision making, and effectiveness. Chapter 1 highlighted some of the broad ways in which culture impacts and manifests the working of teams at organizational, team, and individual levels. When an organization consists of individuals with the same value orientations, policies and procedures follow naturally and smoothly, and expectations are mutually understood. When an organization consists of individuals with different value orientations, three

C.B. Halverson and S.A. Tirmizi (eds.), *Effective Multicultural Teams: Theory and Practice,*

possibilities exist: the organization can lack awareness of the differing value orientations or their significance and proceed with the orientations of the dominant group; the differences can be acknowledged and made explicit but those in the minority forced to assimilate; or the differences can be acknowledged and pluralistic norms developed that meet the needs of all. These and related approaches will be discussed in subsequent chapters. In this chapter we will look at the notion of culture and cultural influences on multicultural team dynamics.

Learning Objectives

After reading this chapter, you should be able to:

- Define culture and recognize the challenges involved in defining it
- Describe selected cultural values frameworks used to conceptualize and compare cultures
- Describe an integrated framework for explaining and understanding behavior in multicultural teams

Defining Culture: The Challenges Involved

Culture is a complex and fuzzy phenomenon, and it is difficult to encompass its richness and intricacies in a single definition. Early attempts at defining it were too broad to be operationalized easily. Capturing the breadth of the concept while at the same time narrowing it so that it is useful—in the words of Clifford Geertz (1973), making it a "more powerful concept"—has been a major focus of anthropological theorizing for decades. The various narrower definitions have taken different directions, and theorists have not reached agreement on any one definition.

The question then is, how do we tackle the concept of culture for our purposes in this book? We need both a working definition of culture relevant to the context of multicultural teams, and a practical framework for conceptualizing it in order to examine its impact on multicultural teams. It seems to me it is unnecessary to reinvent the wheel here when we can offer a workable definition drawing upon earlier work. Let us now explore some ways of defining and understanding the notion of culture and its related complexities.

Redfield (1948), as quoted in Triandis (2004), defined culture as "shared understandings made manifest in act and artifact" (p. vii). According to Triandis (2004), "This (definition) is consistent with the definition used by the GLOBE[1] research project, which examines culture as practices and values." Practices are acts or "the

---

[1] GLOBE refers to the Global Leadership & Organizational Behavior project.

way things are done in this culture," and values are artifacts because they are human-made and, in this specific case, are judgments about "the way things should be done." The issue of defining culture is further complicated by the fact that culture is dynamic and constantly changing. Certainly technology, such as the introduction of automobiles, home computers, email, and electricity, has had profound effects. The move from agricultural societies to industrialized societies and rural to urban has resulted in changed conceptions about gender roles, time, and space. The change from industrialized to information societies has resulted in changes in communications patterns and approaches, and in concepts of time. Additionally, cultural intermingling due to such factors as colonization, diasporas (which have scattered groups such as Africans and Jews), and immigration has impacted culture.

Connaughton and Shuffer (2007) observe that most existing classifications of culture according to national origin may not fully represent the "mobile nature of contemporary populations who relocate for professional, economic and social reasons" (p. 397). Smith (2002) states "...they [national cultures] seem to me to be increasingly characterized by numerous and mutually contradictory trends and sources of influence, to the point where one no longer needs to treat culture as a hold-all concept." Smith's observations emphasize that it is hard to describe the culture of a society in the midst of change; norms, rules, rituals, and practices are not set, and there is a lot of confusion and disorientation.

Chao and Moon (2005) offer a meta-framework to highlight these complexities and also provide a way to conceptualize culture in a meaningful and practical fashion. Their approach includes a three-component taxonomy labeled the Cultural Mosaic. According to this framework, an individual's cultural identity results from interactions among demographic (age, gender, race, ethnicity), geographic (country/regional, urban/rural, climate) and associational (family, religion, profession, politics) dimensions.

This meta-framework overlaps with the notion of a tri-lens that we are using in this book. The cultural lens overlaps with a geographic component; the social identity lens overlaps with demographic and associational components. This framework addresses some of the complexities related to understanding the impact of culture on human behavior and interactions noted above. The Cultural Mosaic framework emphasizes that culture includes societal differences at the national level and in addition also incorporates differences rooted in ethnicity, gender, religion, and profession.

Two definitions reported by Connaughton and Shuffer (2007) are particularly relevant in forming a useful working definition. Maznevski and Chudoba (in Connaughton and Shuffer 2007) define culture as "...the set of deep-level values associated with societal effectiveness, shared by an identifiable group pf people." Gibson and Gibbs (in Connaughton and Shuffer 2007) define it as "characteristic ways of thinking, feeling, and behaving shared among members of an identifiable group."

Building on all these ideas, I offer the following definition:

> Culture consists of shared ways of thinking, feeling, and behaving rooted in deep-level values and symbols associated with societal effectiveness, and attributable to an identifiable group of people. Culture may manifest at different levels including national and organizational, may take several forms, and may evolve over time.

This definition recognizes the complex and dynamic nature of the concept and at the same time offers some concrete ways to understand it by focusing on shared patterns of thinking, feeling, and behaving.

A useful way to build upon this definition and operationalize it can be found in the cultural values approach, in which cultures are conceptualized and compared in terms of their orientation to certain basic social values such as time, uncertainty, and individualism/collectivism. The remainder of this chapter will focus on the impact of culture on multicultural teams as seen through various cultural values frameworks.

Cultural Values Frameworks

There have been numerous attempts in the last few decades to conceptualize culture. It will not be possible to review all the major contributions. In deciding which frameworks to discuss here, I used three criteria. Firstly, I examined those ideas and frameworks that have consistently influenced the thinking about how to conceptualize culture and its impact on studying organizational behavior. Secondly, I considered their conceptual and practical relevance to multicultural teams. Thirdly, I paid attention to the frameworks that represented a wide variety of cultural settings and their present realities.

Kluckhohn and Strodtbeck's Value Framework

An early study on cultural values was carried out by anthropologists Florence Kluckhohn and Fred Strodtbeck, through their field research with Navajos, Spanish Americans, and Anglo-Americans in the southwestern United States. They drew on the earlier work of Clifford Geertz, which emphasized the importance of cultural values. In *Variations in Value Orientation* (1961), Kluckhohn and Strodtbeck describe a value orientation as

> complex but definitely patterned (rank-ordered) principles, resulting from the transactional interplay of three analytically distinguishable elements of the evaluative process—the cognitive, the affective, and the directive elements—which give order and direction to the ever-flowing stream of human acts and thoughts as these relate to the solution of "common human" problems (p. 4).

Previous work with values by others did not include the directive element, which guides or directs behavior. The Five Value Orientations as conceptualized by Kluckholn and Strodtbeck are described below.

Human Nature

This value orientation has to do with how humans are perceived: basically Good, basically Evil, Neutral, or a Mixture of Good and Evil. If one has a perception that humans are basically Evil, there is a lack of trust. At work, people would need to be heavily monitored and disciplined. If one believes that people are basically Good, trust in team members would be high, even in the early stages of team formation. Probably the most common response for most cultures is that humans are basically a Mixture of Good and Evil.

Relationship of Humans to Nature

According to this dimension, there are three ways humans can relate to nature: Subjugation to it, Harmony with it, or Mastery over it. The West has traditionally believed that nature can be mastered by alterations such as dams, building tunnels through mountains, building new lakes, extending life, etc. However, natural disasters such as the 2005 earthquake in Pakistan, the 2004 tsunami in Sri Lanka, and the 2005 hurricane in New Orleans repeatedly remind the world that this approach is unrealistic. There are subgroups in the West, such as environmentalists, who advocate an approach of Harmony with nature. Kluckhohn and Strodtbeck note that this was the dominant orientation in many periods of Chinese history, in Japan, and among the Navajos in the US Southwest. These groups see no distinction between humans and nature. Some indigenous societies believe there is no other course but to subjugate oneself to nature and accept the fate of situations such as floods, pests, and illness. The expression Ayorama (It cannot be helped) of the Inuit in Canada reflects this orientation.

Time

According to this value dimension, the possible orientations toward time are Past, Present, and Future. All societies must encompass each of these, but they are rank-ordered differently. Cultures that have an orientation of Subjugation to nature also are likely to be oriented toward the Present. They pay little attention to the Past and believe little can be done about the Future, so it is best to focus on the Present. Other cultures rank-order the Past as the most important. Ancestor worship was important. There was the belief that nothing ever happened in the Present or the Future; it all happened in the Past. In Past-oriented cultures, planning and decision-making reflect tradition and what has worked in the Past. Europeans value the Past and tradition more than US Americans, who value the Present and near Future.

Activity

The range of variation in human activity is Being, Being-in-Becoming, and Doing. The Doing orientation values accomplishment. This is prevalent in the USA, where a person's value is measured by what he/she does. Standards are objective and external to the person. The Being orientation values a spontaneous expression of impulses and desires, and living in the moment, although Kluckhohn and Strodtbeck point out that this does not mean pure license. It exists within societal morals, rules, and policies. A person focused on Being wants to experience life as it is. The type of work and relationships with others, not external rewards, motivates employees in these cultures. Being-in-Becoming is also concerned with what the human being is rather than what he or she can accomplish. It is the kind of activity "which has as its goal the development of all aspects of the self as an integrated whole" (p. 17). In Europe, employees generally have at least a 4-week vacation a year, which reflects this orientation.

Relational

This value orientation pertains to human relations and has three subdivisions: Individualistic, Lineal, and Collateral. All societies and subgroups must pay attention to all of these, but they rank-order them differently. Individualistic societies value individual autonomy over the welfare of the group. Families are more nuclear, and mobility is often high. Lineal refers to the relationship through age and generational differences that gives cultural continuity. There is a definite position in a hierarchy of ordered positions based on hereditary factors. Collateral refers to social status. Relationships are extended to larger household groups and communities in group-oriented societies.

Hofstede's Value Dimensions

An extremely important cultural framework was advanced by Geert Hofstede in 1980, in his book *Culture's Consequences*, based on extensive multinational survey data comprising 1,660,000 respondents from 40 nations. This work has profoundly impacted the fields of cross-cultural psychology, organizational behavior, and management. In his initial work, Hofstede conceptualized a four-dimension framework for understanding culture across nations. These dimensions were: Individualism-Collectivism (I/C), Power Distance (PD), Masculinity-Femininity (M/F), and Uncertainty Avoidance (UA). Subsequently, Hofstede (1991) added a fifth dimension, Long-Term Orientation (LTO), to his framework.

Individualism–Collectivism

This dimension is the extent to which needs and aspirations of individuals get priority and importance compared to needs of others and of collectivities. In individualistic cultures, personal autonomy, freedom, individual achievement, and right to privacy are valued. Collectivist cultures emphasize "we" awareness, loyalty to groups and clans, security and order from organizations, and group decisions. Australia and Great Britain are examples of Individualistic societies and Pakistan, Greece, and Peru are perceived to be Collectivist cultures.

Power Distance

This is the extent to which differences in status, hierarchy, class, etc., are accepted and preserved. In low-PD cultures, attempts are made to minimize inequality, people in subordinate positions find it easy to access people in superior positions, and equal rights are emphasized. In high-PD societies, power holders are entitled to privileges and power is considered a basic fact of society. Austria and Norway are considered low-PD societies, and Spain and Indonesia are examples of high-PD societies.

Masculinity–Femininity

This is the extent to which assertiveness, performance, independence, and role differentiation (by gender, or sex) are valued by societies. In Masculine societies, sex roles are clearly differentiated, individual performance and independence are valued, and visible manliness is acceptable. In Feminine cultures, interdependence and relationships are important, roles are not clearly defined according to sex differences, and quality of life is important. Norway and Finland are considered Feminine cultures and Japan and the USA are examples of Masculine societies.

Uncertainty Avoidance

This is the extent to which uncertainty and ambiguity are perceived as a threat in a society. In low-UA societies, there is less emphasis on rules, the younger generation is considered more trusting, emotions are expressed rarely, and deviation is easily tolerated. In high-UA cultures, experts are valued, hard work is considered important, and a strong need for consensus is felt. Canada, the USA, and Hong Kong are considered low-UA cultures, and Argentina and France are considered high-UA cultures.

Long-Term Orientation

Following some additional research in collaboration with researchers in East Asia, Hofstede (1991) added the dimension of Long-Term Orientation to his cultural framework. This dimension is concerned with the extent to which societies include a Long-Term Orientation towards tradition and change. Considering these finding in light of the teachings of Confucius, it is argued that Long-Term Orientation cultures emphasize persistence, thrift, and sense of shame, whereas cultures with Short-Term Orientation give more value to personal steadiness and stability.

Hofstede's work has come under scrutiny and has been criticized for a number of reasons. Since its publication, Hofstede's work has been revised twice, in 1991 and 2001. In these revised editions, Hofstede offered clarifications of his earlier work and also responded to some major critiques. In one critique, Roberts and Boyacigillar (1984) raised concerns about the measurement validity. A number of individuals, including McSweeney (2002), suspect levels of analysis problems with Hofstede's work. Basically, this critique is concerned with the appropriateness of the levels at which data was collected and generalized respectively.

Trompenaars' Value Framework

Another important cultural framework relevant for understanding the impact of culture on organizational practices was developed by Trompenaars and colleagues (e.g., Trompenaars et al. 1996; Trompenaars and Hampden-Turner 1998). This framework is based on seven dimensions:

Individualism Versus Communitarism

In Individualistic cultures, there is an emphasis on individual freedom, aspirations, and personal needs. Communitarism emphasizes the needs of the collective. This dimension is similar to the Individualism/Collectivism dimension conceptualized by Hofstede and others.

Universalism Versus Particularism

Universalist societies are formal in their emphasis on rules and procedures that guide agreements and actions, considering them "sacred." Particularist cultures are less attached to formal rules and procedures and consider relationship and situational contingencies as important determinants of decisions and actions.

Specific Versus Diffuse

This dimension deals with communications and interactions within societies. Specific cultures approach communication directly, with attention to clarity of words, frankness, and facts. Diffuse cultures approach communication indirectly, considering contextual variables carefully.

Neutral Versus Affective

In Neutral cultures, emotions are not shown in visible ways, as this is considered to show a lack of self-control. A certain physical distance is maintained by avoiding touching. In Affective cultures, individuals express emotions freely, and interactions are characterized by passion, frequent use of gestures, and physical contact in the form of touching.

Achievement Versus Ascription

In Achievement-oriented cultures, status and recognition are based on one's competencies and performance. Titles and position in hierarchy are limited in meaning in themselves. In cultures that value Ascription, the titles and hierarchy are important in themselves. People in higher positions in hierarchy deserve respect and find it easy to access resources and exert influence.

Attitudes Toward Time

Past, Present, or Future. Cultures valuing the Past pay a great deal of attention to history, traditions, and established ways of doing things. Present-oriented societies place importance on current circumstances in determining what is appropriate and in making decisions. Future-oriented cultures consider a long-term view in making judgments on what is appropriate, and focus on achievement of future goals.

Internal Versus External Control

Societies valuing Internal Control view individual action and effort to have a large ability to influence and control outcomes, and External Control-oriented cultures consider external circumstances and factors to play an important role in determining outcomes.

Schwartz's Value Framework

Another important framework that has made useful contributions to conceptualizing culture is a value survey developed by Shalom Schwartz. Schwartz studied the value orientations from several cultures using multiple perspectives (Schwartz 1992, 1994). According to Hanges and Dickson (2004), Schwartz's work has two major strengths: (1) It is theory-driven and based on understanding the philosophical, religious, and empirical literatures from different cultures and societies (Smith and Schwartz 1997); and (2) it carefully considers prior works on culture and builds on them—for example, works by Kluckhohn (1951) and Rockeach(1973).

Schwartz identified seven cultural value dimensions for examining differences across societies: Embeddedness, Affective Autonomy, Intellectual Autonomy, Hierarchy, Egalitarianism, Mastery, and Harmony (Schwartz 1994; Schwartz and Melech 2000). See Table 2.1.

House and Colleagues' GLOBE Cultural Framework

Robert House, at the University of Pennsylvania, initiated a major research project called Global Leadership and Organizational Behavior Effectiveness (GLOBE, House et al. 2004) to study the impact of culture on leadership and organizational behavior

Table 2.1 Schwartz's cultural value dimensions

Value dimensions	Definitions
Embeddedness	The extent to which societies value traditional ways and status quo, such as respect for tradition and social order
Affective autonomy	The extent to which individuals within a society feel free to express emotions and feelings
Intellectual autonomy	The extent to which societies encourage and safeguard freedom and choice in intellectual pursuits
Hierarchy	The extent to which societies tolerate (and protect) differences in power, hierarchy, and allocation of resources
Egalitarianism	The extent to which societies value and demonstrate concern for the welfare of others
Mastery	The extent to which societies encourage active participation to change (improve) the prevailing environment
Harmony	The extent to which societies emphasize the need for and importance of harmony with the natural and social world

practices. The project team comprised 172 researchers who gathered data from 17,300 respondents in 951 organizations across 62 societies. Following works of Hofstede (1980, 1991), Kluckhohn and Strodtbeck (1961), and McClelland (1985), among others, this project conceptualized nine dimensions of culture, shown in Table 2.2. The table uses definitions of these dimensions presented by Javidan et al. (2004).

This work is quite comprehensive and thorough at two levels. Firstly, it offers linkages between three well-established frameworks to understand the cultural implications on human behavior. Secondly, the research approach and methodology focused on careful linkages between theory and practice. For example, during the data collection phase, respondents were asked to report on leadership practices in their societal contexts.

Table 2.2 The GLOBE project cultural dimensions

GLOBE cultural dimensions	Definitions
Power distance	The extent to which members of a society expect power to be distributed equally
Gender egalitarianism	The degree to which societies discourage differences in gender roles and inequality
Uncertainty avoidance	The extent to which societies rely on rules, policies, and procedures to minimize ambiguity and unpredictability of future events
Collectivism I (institutional collectivism)	The degree to which societies encourage and reward collective action and distribution of resources
Collectivism II (in-group collectivism)	The extent to which members of a society express pride, loyalty, and cohesiveness in their relationship with others
Future orientation	The degree to which members of a society engage in future-oriented behaviors such as planning, preparing for, and investing in the future

(continued)

Table 2.2 (continued)

GLOBE cultural dimensions	Definitions
Assertiveness	The extent to which members of a society are aggressive, demanding, and confrontational toward each other in their interactions
Performance orientation	The extent to which societies reward and encourage individuals for innovation and performance excellence
Humane orientation	The extent to which a society encourages its members to be generous, altruistic, and caring, and to show concern for the welfare of others

Edward Hall's High/Low Context Framework[2]

Another important work in this regard is the conceptualization of culture by Edward Hall. His original fieldwork was with the Navajo, Hopi, and Spanish Americans in the Southwestern United States. Hall's first two books, *The Silent Language* (1959) and *The Hidden Dimension* (1966), discuss the importance of orientation toward time and space in human interactions. In *Beyond Culture (*1976), Hall developed a theoretical model related to context. Culture, he notes, "designates what we pay attention to and what we ignore" (Hall 1976, p. 85). Hall describes context as the connection of social and cultural conditions that surround and influence the life of an individual, an organization, or a community.

Cultures range on a continuum from Low to High context. In Low-Context communications, for example, people pay attention to the explicit words. Other factors such as tone of voice, gesture, social status, history, and social setting are not considered, or, if they are, they are made explicit. Low-Context cultures are more individualized, somewhat fragmented, and there is little involvement with people. In High-Context interactions, people pay attention to the surrounding circumstances or context of an event. It is not necessary to provide explicit information since people already know it through continuous interaction. A High-Context communication requires more time, since trust, friendships and family relationships, personal needs and difficulties, weather, holidays, and other factors must be considered.

In *The Silent Language* (1959), Hall identified ten separate dimensions of human activity, which he has labeled Primary Message Systems: association (relationships), interaction (verbal and nonverbal communication), subsistence (work), bisexuality (gender roles), territoriality (use of space), temporality (time, orientation), learning (what and how knowledge and skills are developed and transmitted), play (importance of and approach to diversion), defense (what, when, and how protection occurs), and exploitation (relationship to others and to environment)

Halverson (1993) argues that the dimensions of association, interaction, territoriality, temporality, and learning are most relevant to interactions in multicultural environments. Based on Hall's work, she points out some concrete ways in which High- and Low- Context cultures vary across these dimensions in Table 2.3.

Halverson has developed a Cultural-Context Inventory to measure and assess one's High-/Low-Context preferences based on these dimensions. The inventory is provided at the end of this chapter.

[2] I am thankful to Clarie B. Halverson for her contributions to this section.

Table 2.3 High/low cultural context characteristics (Halverson 1993)

High context (HC)	Low context (LC)
Association	
Relationships depend on trust, build up slowly, and are stable. One distinguishes between people inside and people outside one's circle.	Relationships begin and end quickly. Many people can be inside one's circle; circle's boundary is not clear.
How things get done depends on relationships with people and attention to group process.	Things get done by following procedures and paying attention to goal.
One's identity is rooted in groups (family, culture, and work).	One's identity is rooted in oneself and one's accomplishments.
Social structure and authority are centralized; responsibility is at the top. Person at the top works for good of the group.	Social structure is decentralized; responsibility goes further down (is not concentrated at the top).
Interaction	
High use of nonverbal elements; voice tone, facial expression, gestures, eye movement carry significant parts of the conversation.	Low use of nonverbal elements. Message is carried more by words than by nonverbal means.
Verbal message is implicit; context (situation, people, nonverbal elements) is more important than words.	Verbal message is explicit. Context is less important than words.
Verbal message is indirect; one talks around the point and embellishes it.	Verbal message is direct; one spells things out exactly.
Communication is seen as art form—a way of engaging someone.	Communication is seen as a way of exchanging information, ideas, and opinions.
Disagreement is personalized. One is sensitive to conflict expressed in another's nonverbal communication. Conflict either must be solved before work can progress or must be avoided because it is personally threatening.	Disagreement is depersonalized. One withdraws from conflict with another and gets on with the task. Focus is on rational solutions, not personal ones. One can be explicit about another's bothersome behavior.
Territoriality	
Space is communal, people stand close to each other, share the same space.	Space is compartmentalized and privately owned, privacy is important, so people are farther apart.
Temporality	
Everything has its own time. Time is not easily scheduled; needs of people interfere with keeping to a set time. What is important is that activity gets done.	Things are scheduled to be done at particular times, one thing at a time. What is important is that activity is done efficiently.
Change is slow. Things are rooted in the past, slow to change, and stable.	Change is fast. One can make change and see immediate results.
Time is a process; it belongs to others and to nature.	Time is a commodity to be spent or saved. One's time is one's own.

(continued)

Table 2.3 (continued)

High context (HC)	Low context (LC)
Learning	
Knowledge is embedded in the situation; things are connected, synthesized, and global. Multiple sources of information are used. Thinking is deductive, proceeds from general to specific.	Reality is fragmented and compartmentalized. One source of information is used to develop knowledge. Thinking is inductive, proceeds from specific to general. Focus is on detail.
Learning occurs by first observing others as they model or demonstrate and then practicing.	Learning occurs by following explicit directions and explanations of others.
Groups are preferred for learning and problem solving.	An individual orientation is preferred for learning and problem solving.
Accuracy is valued. How well something is learned is important.	Speed is valued. How efficiently something is learned is important.

Exercise: Personal Application

Reflect upon the cultural values described in the various frameworks and which of these values you relate to conceptually and practically. You may focus on a number of values from the different frameworks or choose a particular framework to guide your reflection.

Now think about a multicultural team setting from your past experience. Alternatively, think about an intercultural interaction from your personal experience. Consider the key players involved in this interaction and try remembering their expressed feelings, behaviors, and approaches during that experience.

Now carefully and objectively consider your own thinking, feeling, and behaviors during that experience. How do some of the cultural values you reflected upon above explain your and others' behaviors and approaches during these interactions?

An Integration of Cultural Frameworks for Multicultural Teams

The frameworks reviewed above offer important approaches to the understanding of culture. Table 2.4 summarizes these frameworks. Taken together, these frameworks, while overlapping in certain dimensions, also diverge in some significant ways. For example, the dimension of Individualism/Collectivism appears quite consistently across the various frameworks, whereas Gender Egalitarianism is fully or partially present in just a few. This naturally presents some difficulties in determining which dimensions should be employed to understand human behavior within the context of teamwork, the focus of this book.

Additionally, there is not an established body of research that might provide clear and meaningful guidance about which of the cultural frameworks and the dimensions

Table 2.4 Summary of cultural values frameworks

Kluckhon and Strodtbeck (1961)	Hofstede (1980, 1991, 2001)	Trompenaars and Hampden-Turner (1998)	Schwartz (1994)	House et al. (1999, 2004)	Hall (1990)
Relationships: individualistic versus groups	Individualism/ collectivism	Individualism versus communitarism	Embeddedness	Collectivism I and II	Association
Relationships: hierarchy	Power distance	Achievement versus ascription	Hierarchy	Power distance	
Activity orientation	Uncertainty avoidance	Universalism versus particularism		Uncertainty avoidance	Defense
	Masculinity/femininity			Gender egalitarianism	Bisexuality
Time orientation	Long-term orientation	Attitudes towards time		Future orientation	Temporality
Relation to nature: subjugation and domination		Internal versus external control	Mastery harmony		Exploitation
			Egalitarianism	Humane orientation	Play
Human nature: good, evil, or mixed		Neutral versus affective	Affective autonomy	Performance orientation	Learning
			Intellectual autonomy	Assertiveness	Subsistence
		Specific versus diffuse			Interaction and territoriality

they offer are most relevant for understanding and working effectively in multicultural teams. Therefore, I have developed a summary framework, integrating what seem to me to be the most relevant cultural dimensions, according to three criteria: face validity, robustness and stability based on research evidence, and practical relevance of the cultural dimensions to understanding and working in multicultural teams. This integrated framework contains eight dimensions: Individualism/Collectivism, Universalism/Particularism, Specific/Diffuse, Neutral/Affective, Achievement/ Ascription, Temporality, Gender Egalitarianism, and Intellectual Autonomy.

Individualism–Collectivism

As noted above, in Individualistic cultures, individual needs, preferences, and desires receive more attention than collective needs, whereas, Collectivism focuses on the needs of the collective. This dimension has been conceptualized by most of the frameworks reviewed above and has been demonstrated as one of the most robust dimensions of culture.

Universalism–Particularism

Interactions, exchanges, and agreements are guided by formal rules and procedures in Universalist societies. There is a lot of emphasis on contracts and laws. In Particularist cultures, emphasis on formal rules and procedures is limited and contextual factors and relationships play an important role in how situations and decisions are approached. In terms of its face validity and practical relevance, this dimension seems quite appropriate for understanding various aspects of team dynamics, especially conflict resolution, problem solving, and decision making.

Specific–Diffuse

Following Trompenaars and Hampden-Turner (1998) and Hall (1990), this dimension deals with how individuals communicate and interact within societies. As noted above, Specific cultures approach communication directly with attention to clarity of words, frankness, and facts. In Diffuse cultures, indirect communication is acceptable and understood and even preferred in some cases along with attention to contextual factors. This dimension deserves special consideration for our purposes in this book, especially relating to communication, conflict, and leadership dynamics in multicultural teams.

Neutral–Affective

Building on Trompenaars and Hampden-Turner (1998), Schwartz (1994), and Schwartz and Melech (2000), Neutral cultures emphasize self-control by discouraging visible display of emotions and feelings. On the other hand, emotions are expressed somewhat openly and comfortably in Affective cultures. Interpersonal exchanges are characterized by passion, use of gestures, and physical contact in the form of touching. This dimension has clear implications for organizational behavior and teamwork, especially in the areas of communication and conflict resolution.

Achievement–Ascription

To some extent, several of the frameworks reviewed above—including Hofstede (1980, 2001) and House et al. (2004)—deal with the Achievement orientation of societies. As mentioned previously, recognition and position are determined by considering one's competencies and performance in Ascription-oriented cultures. In cultures that value Ascription, people in higher levels of traditional and organizational hierarchy find it easier to access resources; they are able to influence others based on their position and may get respect by virtue of their higher position. This dimension has implications for how multicultural teams may define effectiveness criteria and dynamics around leadership.

Temporality (Time Orientation)

Orientation toward time has been an important dimension of culture across various frameworks. However, I feel Hall's (1990) work on temporality to be most relevant for our purposes. Working with deadlines and schedules and pace of work are issues central to team task achievement and process, and different culture-based perceptions of time could complicate a team's dynamics.

Gender Egalitarianism

As discussed above, Gender Egalitarianism is the extent to which societies differentiate between people on the basis of gender when assigning roles, power, status, etc. This is an important dimension of cultural differences that has not been widely employed. Hofstede's work should be credited with generating interest in it. Houseet al. (2004) also employed it in their cultural framework. Gender has increasingly become part of organizational life and the dynamics of multicultural teams, and therefore needs to be taken into consideration in order to manage the internal and external dynamics of teams.

Intellectual Autonomy

Intellectual Autonomy is the extent to which societies promote and protect freedom and choice in intellectual pursuits. Most teams are formed to deal with complex issues and problems. Innovation, creativity, and intellectual expression contribute to high-quality problem solving and decision making. The challenge for teams is how to manage differing expectations around intellectual autonomy.

The purpose of the above discussion is to highlight the importance and relevance of some of the key cultural dimensions presented in different cultural frameworks discussed above. It is not my intention to suggest that the cultural dimensions not included in this synthesis are not important. In that sense, this discussion provides an initial platform to link learning and knowledge based on the cultural frameworks to understanding and working with behavioral dynamics in multicultural teams and organizations.

Relevant Competencies

- Discuss the complexity of defining and conceptualizing the idea of culture
- Apply cultural frameworks to explanations of human behavior in organizational settings
- Use the cultural frameworks and integrated framework to link culture and behavioral dynamics in the context of multicultural teams
- Critically approach the discussions related to culture's impact on teams in subsequent chapters

Summary

An important objective of this chapter was to familiarize the readers with the notion of culture and highlight some of its complexities. The initial sections of this chapter discussed some key definitions of culture offered over the last five decades and at the same time highlighted a number of challenges and issues in conceptualizing culture. Additionally, the chapter offered a working definition of culture which is sensitive to some of the challenges in understanding and defining cultural complexity and at the same time provides a concrete way of thinking about its key components of shared thinking, feeling, and behaving.

The cultural frameworks discussed in this chapter offer important and practical ways of approaching cultural issues and questions related to understanding behavioral dynamics in multicultural teams and organizational settings. However, it is important to consider the following when working with these frameworks:

- While general patterns and tendencies included in the various frameworks may be attributable to different societies, most cultures include sub-cultures, which may be different in some significant ways from the society within which they exist.
- When working with generalizations about societies and cultural groups, it must be recognized that cultural attributes may not apply to all the individuals for a variety of reasons, including differences in background, experiences, and preferences.

Case Study: ANZ Foundation

As you read the case study below, consider the following questions:

- *Choose one of the cultural frameworks above and apply it to develop some overall understanding of Moroccan, South Korean, and South African cultures. You may find it useful to conduct a basic Internet search to understand the cultural orientation of these countries.*
- *Identify at least three cultural dimensions from the integrated framework above that explain the impact of culture on this team's dynamics.*
- *What challenges and opportunities related to culture are presented in this case?*

ANZ Foundation was established in South Africa to promote and strengthen the social entrepreneurship field in the African region. An initial endowment established by a group of South African business groups provided the necessary organizational and program-related funding. The main organizational strategy has been to identify and support emerging social entrepreneurs by providing funding and networking opportunities. The organization has selected about 50 fellows so far and plans to select another 200 fellows in the next four years.

ANZ recently formulated a team to refine and lead its communication strategy. The team has been charged with developing a stronger communications strategy for the foundation. The aim is to support the ANZ mission impact by making its achievements more visible globally, develop a virtual platform to strongly connect the existing and new fellows, and continuously strengthen engagement with different stakeholders.

The core communication team consists of three members. Saba Hassan is a 35-year-old Moroccan female who worked for a UN family organization program based out of South Africa for four years prior to joining ANZ. Saba grew up in Morocco as a Muslim in a well-educated, middle-class environment. She received her advanced training in communications at a French university. Following the completion of her graduate degree she started working in the communications field at a private, for-profit organization within the service sector before she joined the UN project. She joined ANZ as the Director of Communications and will lead the communications strategy development.

Lee Yong has a technology background. He became interested in the development sector during a six-month study-abroad assignment in East Africa. Before joining ANZ, he was with a Singapore-based technology consulting firm working on web marketing projects for NGOs and foundations in Asia and Africa. Yong is 32 years old and has been with ANZ for about six months coordinating the development of its new website.

Nkosana Sipho, a specialist in communications and marketing, is the third team member. He comes from the Xhosa tribe of South Africa. He attended University of Pretoria, studying economics and management. He has been with ANZ since its inception about three years ago. He is 36 years old and has been working with international development organizations promoting social enterprise development in Sub-Saharan Africa prior to joining ANZ.

Over the past four weeks, the team has met about four times and is in the initial stages of articulating the overall strategy direction. Meetings usually start within thirty minutes of the scheduled time. Meetings appear friendly, and team members are respectful of each other. Nkosana enthusiastically participates in the team discussions and is comfortable expressing opinions when important points are to be made. Saba comes to the meetings well-prepared with the agenda and detailed relevant information. She feels that pertinent facts and detailed analysis are crucial to this strategy-development process. Yong is usually quiet during these meetings. He speaks when he is invited to share his thoughts. Most of his contributions are confined to the technical matters. The team is expected to complete most of its work in the next five weeks and make a presentation to the top management team.

Cultural-Context Inventory

Instructions: For each of the following 20 items, circle 1, 2, 3, 4, or 5 to indicate your tendencies and preferences *in a work situation*. Then use the scoring sheet on p. 53 to see how you rank.

	Hardly ever		Sometimes		Almost always
1. When communicating, I tend to use a lot of facial expressions, hand gestures, and body movements rather than relying mostly on words.	1	2	3	4	5
2. I pay more attention to the context of a conversation—who said what and under what circumstances—than I do to the words.	1	2	3	4	5
3. When communicating, I tend to spell things out quickly and directly, rather than talk around and add to the point.	1	2	3	4	5
4. In an interpersonal disagreement, I tend to be more emotional than logical and rational.	1	2	3	4	5
5. I tend to have a small, close circle of friends rather than a large, but less close circle of friends.	1	2	3	4	5
6. When working with others, I prefer to get the job done first and socialize afterward, rather than socialize first and then tackle the job.	1	2	3	4	5

(continued)

	Hardly ever	Sometimes			Almost always
7. I would rather work in a group than by myself.	1	2	3	4	5
8. I believe rewards should be given for individual accomplishments rather than for group accomplishments.	1	2	3	4	5
9. I describe myself in terms of my accomplishments rather than in terms of my family and relationships.	1	2	3	4	5
10. I prefer sharing space with others to having my own private space.	1	2	3	4	5
11. I would rather work for someone who maintains authority and functions for the good of the group than work for someone who allows a lot of autonomy and individual decision-making.	1	2	3	4	5
12. I believe it is more important to be on time than to let other concerns take priority.	1	2	3	4	5
13. I prefer working on one thing at a time to working on a variety of things at once.	1	2	3	4	5
14. I generally set a time schedule and keep to it rather than leaving things unscheduled and go with the flow.	1	2	3	4	5
15. I find it easier to work with someone who is fast and wants to see immediate results than to work with someone who is slow and wants to consider all the facts.	1	2	3	4	5
16. In order to learn about something, I tend to consult many sources of information rather than go to the one best authority.	1	2	3	4	5
17. In figuring out problems, I prefer focusing on the whole situation to focusing on specific parts or taking one step at a time.	1	2	3	4	5
18. When tackling a new task, I would rather figure it out on my own by experimentation than follow someone else's example or demonstrations.	1	2	3	4	5

(continued)

	Hardly ever	Sometimes			Almost always
19. When making decisions, I consider my likes and dislikes, not just the facts.	1	2	3	4	5
20. I prefer having tasks and procedures explicitly defined to having a general idea of what has to be done.	1	2	3	4	5

Scoring Instructions: Transfer the circled numbers to the appropriate blanks provided below. Then add the numbers in each column to obtain your totals for High Context and Low Context.

High Context (HC)	Low Context (LC)
1. 4	3. 2
2. 5	6. 5
4. 2	8. 5
5. 5	9. 4
7. 1	12. 4
10. 1	13. 4
11. 5	14. 5
16. 5	15. 4
17. 2	18. 5
19. 4	20. 5
Total: 34	Total: 43

Subtract your smaller total from your larger total using one of the equations below. This will give you either a high context or a low context score. If your two totals are equal, your score is zero.

_____High Context Score	_____Low Context Score
_____Low Context Score	_____High Context Score
_____High Context Score	_____Low Context Score

Interpretation:

* Scores between 0-3 indicate a relative bi-cultural orientation along the high/low context dimension
* Scores close to 20 indicate a strong preference towards very high or low context.

References

Chao, G.T. and Moon, H. (2005). The cultural mosaic: A Meta-theory to understanding the complexity of culture. *Journal of Applied Psychology 90*, 1128–1140.

Connaughton, S.L. and Shuffer, M. (2007). *Multinational and multicultural distributed teams: A review and future agenda. Small Group Research 38/3*, 387–412.

Geertz, C. (1973). *The Interpretation of Cultures*. New York: Basic Books.

Hall, E. (1959). *The Silent Language*. Garden City, NY: Doubleday.
Hall, E. (1966). *The Hidden Dimension*. Garden City, NY: Doubleday.
Hall, E. (1990). *Understanding Cultural Differences*. Yarmouth, ME: Intercultural Press.
Halverson, C. B. (1993). Cultural context inventory: The effects of culture on behavior and work style. In W. Pfeiffer (Ed.), *The Annual (1993) Developing Human Resources*. San Diego, CA: Pfeiffer.
Hanges, P. J. and Dickson, M.W. (2004). The development and validation of the GLOBE culture and leadership scales. In R.J. House, P.J. Hanges, M. Javidan and P.W. Dorfman (Eds.), *Leadership, Culture, and Organizations: The GLOBE Study of 62 Societies* (Vol. 1, pp. 122–151). Thousand Oaks, CA: Sage.
Hofstede, G. (1980). *Culture's Consequences: International Differences in Work-Related Values*. Thousand Oaks, CA: Sage.
Hofstede, G. (1991). *Cultures and Organizations: Software of the Mind*. London: McGraw-Hill.
Hofstede, G. (2001). *Culture's Consequences: Comparing values, behaviors, institutions, and organizations across nations*. Thousand Oaks, CA: Sage.
House, R.J., Hanges, P.J., Ruiz-Quintanilla, S.A., Dorfman, P.W., Javidan, M., Dickson, M. and Gupta, V. (1999). Cultural influences on leadership and organizations: Project GLOBE. In W.H. Mobley, M.J. Gessner and V. Arnold (Eds.), *Advances in Global Leadership*. Stamford, CT: JAI.
House, R.J., Hanges, P.J., Javidan, M., Dorfman, P.W. & Gupta, V. (Ed.). (2004). *Culture, leadership, and organizations: the GLOBE study of 62 societies*. Thousand Oaks: SAGE
Javidan, M., House, R.J. and Dorfman, P.W. (2004). In R.J. House, P.J. Hanges, M. Javidan, P.W. Dorfman (Eds.), *Leadership, Culture, and Organizations: The GLOBE Study of 62 Societies* (Vol. 1, pp. 29–48). Thousand Oaks, CA: Sage.
Kluckhohn, C. (1951). Culture and Behavior. *Handbook of Social Psychology*, 921–976.
Kluckhohn, F. and Strodtbeck, F. (1961). *Variations in Value Orientation*. Evanston, IL: Row, Peterson.
McClelland, D.C. (1985). *Human Motivation*. Glenview, IL: Scott, Foresman.
McSweeney, B. (2002). Hofstede's model of national cultural differences and their consequences: A triumph of faith—a failure of analysis. *Human Relations*, *55*(1): 89–118.
Roberts, K.H. and Boyacigiller, N. (1984). Cross-national organizational research: The grasp of the blind men. In B.L. Staw and L.L. Cummings (Eds.), *Research on Organizational Behavior* (pp. 423–75). Stamford, CT: JAI.
Rokeach, M. (1973). *The nature of human values*. New York: Free Press
Schwartz, S.H. and Melech, G. (2000). National differences in micro and macro worry: social, economic, and cultural explanations. In E. Diener and E. Such (Eds.), *Culture and Subjective Wellbeing* (pp. 219–256). Boston, MA/London: MIT/Cambridge University Press.
Schwartz, S.H. (1999). A theory of cultural values and some implications for work. *Applied Psychology: An International Review*, *48*, 23–47.
Schwartz, S.H. (1994). Beyond individualism and collectivism: New cultural dimensions of values. In U. Kim, H.C. Triandis, S.C. Choi, G. Yoon and C. Kagitcibasi (Eds.), *Individualism and collectivism: Theory, method, and applications* (pp. 85–122). Thousand Oaks, CA: Sage.
Schwartz, S.H. (1992). Universals in the content and structure of values: Theoretical advances and empirical tests in 20 countries. In M. Zanna (Ed.), *Advances in Experimental Social Psychology* (pp. 1–65). Orlando, FL: Academic.
Smith, P. (2002). Culture's consequences: Something old and something new. *Human Relations* *55*(1), 119–135.
Smith, P.B. and Schwartz, S.H. (1997). Values. In J.W. Berry, M.H. Segall and C. Kagitcibasi (Eds.), *Handbook of Cross-Cultural Psychology: Social Behavior and Applications* (Vol. 3, pp. 77–118). Boston, MA: Allyn & Bacon.
Triandis, H.C. (2004). The many dimensions of culture. *Academy of Management Executive*, *18*(1).
Trompenaars, F., Smith, P.B. and Dugan, S. (1996). National Culture and the Values of Organizational Employees. *Journal of Cross-Cultural Psychology*, *27*(2), 231–264.
Trompenaars, F. and Hampden-Turner, C.M. (1998). *Riding the Waves of Culture: Understanding Cultural Diversity in Global Business* (2nd ed.). Chicago, IL: Irwin.

Chapter 3
Social Identity Group and Individual Behavior

Claire B. Halverson*

Every individual nature has its own beauty.
–Ralph Waldo Emerson

Introduction

Emerson recognized and celebrated the unique beauty of each individual. Diversity consultants Frederick Miller and Judith Katz (2002) note that while on some level we are all alike as humans, we are like some others who share similar culture and experience, and finally, we are unique and like no other. Understanding individuals—ourselves and others—is crucial for members of a high-performing team since problematic interpersonal issues are destructive. Without that understanding, we are apt to think that others feel and respond as we do and if they do not something is wrong with them. Even if we have a clear handle on ourselves—our values, attitudes, and emotions—we may not understand how we impact others. Once we understand how we impact others, we might want to modify our behavior.

The importance of the tri-lens of overlapping personal, social, and cultural identities that members bring to a team was discussed in Chapter 1. The previous chapter looked at how that unique beauty is shaped by an individual's culture; in this chapter we will look at the impact of membership in social identity groups, and unique aspects which influence individual behavior: personality and multiple intelligences. Models for personal change are presented. It is beyond the scope of this chapter to discuss other aspects that influence individual behavior such as motivation, skills and experience, and learning style.

C.B. Halverson and S.A. Tirmizi (eds.), *Effective Multicultural Teams: Theory and Practice*,

Learning Objectives

After reading this chapter you should be able to:

- Define personality and the factors that determine personality
- Describe the impact of social identity groups
- Describe the Myers-Briggs personality-type framework and its cross-cultural relevance
- Identify the factors in the Five Factor/Big Five personality models and their cross-cultural relevance
- Identify multiple forms of intelligence and their importance for teams
- Discuss a model of personal change and adaptation

The Impact of Social Identity

What It Is

Social identity speaks to common experiences based on group identity. Social group identities include such dimensions as family, community, nationality, "race," ethnicity, age, religion, gender, physical and mental ability, sexual orientation, marital and family status, socio-economic class, educational level, language and accent, geographic location, military status, job function, and job level.

We are members of social identity groups whether we think so or not. Both how others perceive us and how we perceive ourselves frame our social identity. In Western psychology, with its individualistic orientation, individuals often see themselves as autonomous and able to seek their own goals and beliefs.

Erik Erikson, in his classic *Childhood and Society* (1950), introduced the idea that in Individualistic societies, the individual develops his or her unique identity. In Collectivist societies, the individual defines his or her identity by social group—he or she is a part of family, community, and culture. Anthropologist Clifford Geertz (1975) noted this difference:

> The Western conception of the person as a bounded, unique, more or less integrated motivational and cognitive universe, a dynamic center of awareness, emotion, judgment and action organized into a distinctive whole and against a social and natural background is, however, incorrigible. It may seem to us a rather peculiar idea within the context of the other world cultures (p. 48).

Privilege and Marginalization: One-Up and One-Down

Every society values and privileges some groups (the *one-ups*), while targeting others for discrimination and marginalization (the *one-downs*). A process is created that impacts individuals in both the one-up and the one-down groups in society, in organizations, and in teams. This process can be described as follows:

- The group in power creates societal beliefs and *stereotypes* about the capabilities, characteristics, and personalities of members of their own group and the group seen as the "other." A stereotype is a description of characteristics or behavior perceived to be true for all members of a group. It is usually based on limited or inaccurate information, often evaluative, and usually rigidly held even when confronted with dissonant information.
- Individuals, both one-up and one-down, internalize the beliefs and stereotypes as *prejudices* and come to see them as normal and natural. Prejudice is a negative attitude toward a socially defined group and toward any person perceived to be a member of that group (Ashmore in Collins 1970, p. 253).
- Discriminatory institutional practices are put into place in institutions: housing, health care, justice, and the workplace which, intentionally or unintentionally, create barriers for the one-down group and privileges for the one-ups. Discrimination is the act of making or recognizing differences, giving privileges to some and creating barriers for others.
- Individual beliefs and institutional practices create a reality so that, in fact, the one-down's potential and performance are not fully realized and the one-up continues to easily access the privileges and benefits of society.
- This process is often apparent to one-downs while one-ups are apt to be oblivious to it and see themselves as individuals.

Group identities that have the greatest impact are those that are determined early in life, have high social significance, and are relatively difficult to change. Although there are variations in each country, these core identities often include: "race"/ethnicity, gender and gender identity, social-economic class, religion, physical and mental ability, age, and sexual orientation. Clarification for a few of these is given below.

"*Race*" is "an imprecise and unscientific concept" (Wright 1998). It is a sociological not a biological construct (Johnson 2006; Bamshad and Olson 2003), which was developed in the 19th century in the United States in order to justify the presence of slavery. The Race Literacy Quiz developed by California Newsreel (www.Newsreel.org) states that none of the 30,000 human genes separate all members of one "race" from all members of another.

Gender refers to the roles and behaviors defined by society: male, female, and transgender. Transgender is an umbrella term, which includes cross dressers/transvestites, third gender people, transsexuals, and intersexuals. *Gender identity* refers to how we identity ourselves.

Sexual Orientation refers to one's orientation towards the same or other gender: sexually, affectionally, or romantically.

Most of these social identities will be classified as either "one-up" or "one-down" in any given culture. However, cultures may classify a social identity differently. For example, older people are one-down in the United States but one-up in many Asian cultures.

Cultures also vary in the extent to which they acknowledge individual social identities at all. For example, "race" is a very significant identity group in the United States, as is evident from the fact that racial data is collected on the census in this country. However, some countries do not classify their populations by "race" at all but rather by religion. This is the case in Bangladesh. When a culture uses a social identity to classify its population, this is usually in order to determine who will be one-up and who will be one-down. In Bangladesh, the Muslim majority uses religion to restrict Hindus from positions of power. Similarly, Europeans use ethnicity to classify the Roma (gypsies) as a one-down group that can be marginalized from the mainstream.

Each of us has multiple social identities, and we may experience being one-up in some situations and one-down in others; we may also experience being both one-up and one-down at the same time. For example, as a heterosexual European American woman, I am two-up as a European American and a heterosexual, and one-down as a woman. A white, gay man is one-up as a European American man, and one-down as a gay. We usually are more aware of how we are marginalized or discriminated against as one-downs, while as one-ups we are often not aware of our unearned privileges and advantages.

In Table 3.1, consider the following questions: *How do you identify which of your social identity groups are one-up and which are one-down in the country(ies) in which you grew up, and in the country(ies) in which you have lived as an adult? How many of your identities are one-up and how many are one-down?*

Table 3.1 One-up/one-down social identity group

Social identity groups	One-up	One-down
Gender/gender identity		
"Race"/ethnicity		
Socio-economic class		
Religion		
Sexual orientation		
Age		
Physical/cognitive ability		
Other		

Social Identity in Organizations and on Teams

Work teams frequently reflect the organizational culture. The organizational culture usually reflects the values, patterns, and behaviors of the social group that was dominant in numbers and leadership in the organization at its founding. For most organizations in the United States, that social group is European American men. Miller and Katz (2002) point out that according to Census 2000, "while women comprise 51% of the adult population of the United States and people of color comprise 49%, 95% percent of the senior leaders of business are white men"

(p. 10). Their cultural patterns include linear thinking processes, focus on a single task, direct expression of thoughts, and individualism. Work hours may start early with perhaps a long lunch or after-work social patterns. Socialization at the golf club may limit information flow to those who are not in there. Leaders in these organizations seek out people most like themselves. Taylor Cox, a professor of organizational behavior and a diversity consultant, describes the "similar to me" phenomenon—one-ups are simply more comfortable with those like them (Cox 1994, pp. 216–218).

Affirmative action and changing demographics due to immigration have brought those who were previously excluded into the workplace. These newcomers, often one-downs, have frequently been expected to assimilate into the organizational culture and behave like the founders. Thus, the founding culture continues unless an intervention changes it.

The following are examples of how one-downs have been discriminated against or marginalized in organizations and on teams. Some are examples of overt, intentional discrimination, and others are examples of unintentional, subtle discrimination. *Have any of these happened on a team on which you have worked? Can you think of similar examples?*

Someone who has a circular thinking process and indirect expression of thoughts cannot maximize his potential on a team where linear thinking is valued.

A woman who has child or elder care is unable to make arrangements for spontaneous meetings after work hours.

An older worker is assumed to be incapable of learning new skills and is not provided with training in technology.

An African American manager finds that one of the members on his team has bypassed him and gone to his supervisor to receive input on a project he is developing.

An Asian technician is not recognized for his leadership potential.

A gay man does not as feel free to display a photo of his partner, or talk about his weekend, as those who have partners of the other sex do.

A man from Brazil working with first-language English speakers finds they are impatient with his accent.

A Muslim woman is unable to attend an important meeting that is scheduled during an important religious observance.

A colleague in a wheelchair cannot get to an important meeting that is not accessible.

A woman is ignored at a meeting while a man with the same input is given accolades.

A woman receives unwanted sexual verbal or physical attention from her boss but does not feel she can say anything.

A Jewish man is taunted when he wears a yarmulke.

A young colleague is not recognized for her talents and skills, and is dismissed because of her age.

Some of these situations may indicate overt, intentional discrimination toward one-downs—for example, the Jewish man being taunted. In many countries and organizations, this type of blatant discrimination is not officially tolerated. However, unintentional discrimination and marginalization are frequent due to the practice of following norms established by and favoring one-ups. Let us take the case of a team that ignored a woman's input at a meeting. Perhaps she presented her ideas with a more equivocal style. Perhaps she spoke more softly. Perhaps she was more hesitant to jump into the fast-paced conversation, or she was interrupted before she finished her point. In any case, her input was ignored while that of her male colleague was appreciated. If this was pointed out during the meeting, the response is likely to have been, "But I didn't *intend* to ignore you." While it may have been unintentional, it still could have an *impact*. The woman could feel less sure of presenting her view next time, thinking she had not articulated it correctly. Or she could believe she had presented her idea sufficiently, but that the man was unjustly given the praise. This could cause some emotional pain or anger for her. Either way, the cost to the team could be that significant ideas are not heard.

Was the woman being overly sensitive to feel upset by this? Well, perhaps, if this was the only time it happened. But if it has happened frequently or she has observed it happening to other women, this incident becomes part of a pattern that hurts. It's like getting a paper cut. If you got one, you wouldn't complain, but if you had many, it could feel like a knife cut.

If this woman is the only woman on the team or at her level in the organization, men observe her carefully. Since they cannot observe differences between her and other women, her behavior may be interpreted as "women's behavior." Rosabeth Moss Kanter (1980) describes this in her landmark video and book, The *Tale of O*, where Os are the *onlys* and there are lots of Xs. *What do you notice most below?*

Numbers count. Most people notice the O, and not the differences in size and font style among the Xs. When Os are both onlys and one-downs, the identity group differences between them and the one-ups often get highlighted, and the differences between the one-ups are not recognized. For example, when there is one woman in a group of men, attention is focused on the woman being different and not the differences in style, personality, or age among the men. One-ups are apt to notice when one-downs make a mistake, but not when they are performing well. One-ups expect one-downs to represent their group rather than themselves, and to speak for it. And, if one-downs mention this problem, one-ups may discount them. When

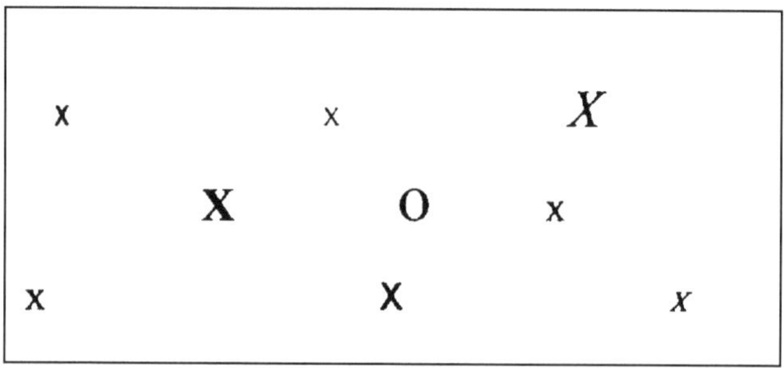

one-downs are onlys, they often expend a great deal of energy dealing with the experience of being one-down, while one-ups generally are unaware of their status as one-up (Andrews 1999). Although onlys have often been referred to as tokens, Miller and Katz (2002) refer to them as modern pioneers since they are breaking ground for others who will come later.

When one-downs feel discounted or stereotyped and believe that they have to check some of their identity at the door in order to fit in, they are not able to utilize their creativity and skills. Their contributions are not maximized. Assimilation and uniformity may have worked in organizations in the past where individuals worked alone, but it is not effective today where people work interdependently in teams. Creativity and differing views are needed. Organizations and teams need the broadest talent pool possible for complex tasks. Teams need to create a climate where the contributions of all are valued, and different styles and thoughts are the norm.

Taking Responsibility

As both one-ups and one-downs, we all have some responsibility to interrupt the one-up/one-down process in organizations and teams. Here are some starting points.

As one-ups, we can:

- Be Self-aware. Acknowledge that we have privileges due to our social identity that one-downs do not have, and that these may give us an advantage in our ability to accomplish our work.
- Educate Ourselves. Read, attend training and presentations, work with other one-ups in this identity to learn more about our own one-up experience, and the experience of one-downs. Remember, we are frequently blind in our one-up identity.
- Listen. Listen as those in one-down identities relate their experiences. Take it in, as their experiences and feelings are real, even though they may seem unfamiliar to us. Ask for their individual experience, but do not expect them to be a spokesperson for their group.
- Speak Up. If we see discrimination or marginalization, name it. As one-ups we are frequently in situations where discriminatory comments are made when one-downs are not present.
- Review Team Norms. Advocate review of team norms so that they are based on a principle of inclusion and pluralism, not on a principle of assimilation.

As one-downs we can:

- Be Self-aware. Believe our own experiences and that they are real. Acknowledge feelings of anger, frustration, discomfort which we may have.
- Seek Out Support. Seek support from those in our one-down group and those in one-up groups who are supportive.
- Assume Positive Intent. Remember that one-ups have blind spots, and that they may be reasonably well-intentioned, at least until proven otherwise.

- Speak Up. Name those practices and behaviors that marginalize or discount us. Explain their impact.
- Review Team Norms. Advocate review of team norms so that they are based on a principle of inclusion and pluralism, not on a principle of assimilation.

Personality

What It Is and What Determines It

While we think we all understand what personality is, social scientists have many definitions of it. Gordon Allport (1937), a prominent social scientist, looked at over 50 different definitions of personality, and consolidated them into one definition: "the dynamic organization within the individual of those psychophysical systems that determine his unique adjustment to his environment" (p. 48).

More recently, David Funder (1997) stated that personality is "an individual's characteristic pattern of thought, emotion, and behavior, together with the psychological mechanisms—hidden or not—behind those patterns" (pp. 1–2). This second definition is more specific than the first, but this chapter will draw on both.

Having defined personality, we will now look at factors that shape it. These factors fall into two categories: *nature* (the genetic characteristics a person is born with) and *nurture* (factors of socialization). Over the decades, there has been a controversy about the question of nature-nurture in determining personality. The question has been phrased as "nature versus nurture," and social scientists have sought to determine the relative weight of *heredity* (nature) versus *environment* (nurture).

Studies of twins separated at birth have produced evidence that heredity influences personality. Wright (1998) reports that The Minnesota Twin Study anticipated finding similarities in I.Q. and temperament dimensions such as timidity or gregariousness. The study found similarities that had not been anticipated in such areas as speech patterns, body carriage, sense of humor, matrimonial histories, professional careers, tastes in clothes, and choice of hobbies. Since the researchers had not even designed their questionnaires to find these similarities, Wright believes the results are most likely conservative.

Unfortunately, heredity has been used to categorize and oppress groups of people (women, working class people, racial/ethnic minorities, etc.). Assuming genetic group differences in intelligence or personality sometimes misguides social policy and organizational practices as well as individual beliefs. Arthur Jensen, a psychologist at the University of California, argued in 1969 that African Americans scored as a group consistently lower on intelligence tests than European Americans and that this was due to lower intelligence. He further concluded that this group difference was hereditary, but as has been previously discussed, no human genes separate all members of one "race" from all members of another. Environmental factors, such as access to quality education is more helpful when looking at group differences.

Environment can make a huge impact on personality. Some factors are: physical and psychological factors of the mother before birth; environmental factors such as air pollution and noise after birth; nutrition; family socialization including birth order, bonding, and family values; and cultural values as discussed in Chapter 2.

Most social scientists posit that personality is a product of both heredity and environment (Goldberg 1993; Myers and McCaulley 1985; McCrae and Costa 1989, 1997). Culture is an aspect of the environment; some research has investigated the influence of culture on personality. For example, R.R. McCrae has extensively researched personality across cultures. In 2002, McCrae and co-researcher, Allik, wrote, "acculturation studies and other natural situations offer the only feasible way to disentangle genetic from cultural effects" (p. 24). In a study of Hong Kong Chinese who immigrated to Canada, for example, McCrae and others (2004) found that the Chinese progressively adopted Canadian personality traits of openness and agreeableness. However, they also note that a previous study found that even Chinese born and raised in Canada were more introverted than Canadians of European ancestry.

In a seminal paper in *Psychological Review* in 1958, Anne Anastasi posited that the nature-nurture debate is asking the wrong question (Lerner 1986). It is not a question of which is more salient, but of how they interact:

> [T]here would be no one in an environment without heredity, and there would be no place to see the effects of heredity without environment. Genes do not exist in a vacuum. They exert their influence on behavior in an environment. At the same time, however, if there were no genes (and consequently no heredity), the environment would not have an organism in it to influence. Accordingly, nature and nurture are inextricably tied together. In life they never exist independent of the other (Lerner, p. 84).

Rather than attempting to determine what percent of personality is hereditary and what percent is environmental, one should assume that 100% of heredity and 100% of environment always contribute. Heredity and environment always interact. Therefore, the same hereditary influence will lead to different outcomes in different environments, and vice versa.

Although many people assume that personality is stable and consistent once adulthood has been reached, some argue that one's personality changes according to the setting. Different aspects of our personality appear in different settings: work, religious, social, and home. However, some theorists question whether personality changes in different settings, or just behavior. Is our personality more than our external behavior?

This question is even harder to answer when a person's setting significantly changes. For example, living in a different culture over a long period of time arguably may change one's personality in a way that persists even when one returns to one's native culture. In the following case study, Patrick experienced living in different cultures for extended periods of time. *Do you think he changed his personality or just his behavior?*

Case Study:

Patrick is a man from the Sudan who has lived in Minneapolis, Minnesota, for six years. While there, he saw that many immigrants from Africa were working below their capacity and skill level, and organized an initiative to link them to local employers. He is currently in a master's program and is seen as a leader there also. He is a risk taker—he entered the graduate program without finances, but was able to secure some funding. He is an initiator, is outgoing, open, trustful, and friendly. He is adaptable, but also challenging—even stubborn—when he disagrees.

Was he always like this?

Patrick lived with his family as a refugee in Uganda until he was 19. Many of the characteristics described above were already apparent in high school—he was on the debating team and in positions of leadership. He was outgoing, open, trustful, and friendly. At age 19 he moved back to the Sudan, took a responsible job, and became active politically. After about five years, in 1982, the political situation changed, and another war broke out. His life was threatened and he changed his behavior, and seemingly his personality. He became secretive, closed, mistrustful, and even dishonest. He felt defeated. He even did not trust telling his wife as he made plans to leave the country.

In 1996, at age 38, Patrick moved to Syria, an Arab country where the Sudanese military often went to recruit. Although he did not feel his life was threatened, he was without a job and without a passport. There were times he had to lie to get what he wanted. As Patrick describes this change in his attitude and behavior, he becomes most passionate when he describes how he hated being dishonest. He says he was not himself during these years in the Sudan and Syria. In 1996, he left for the United States. He misses his wife and children and is sad when he talks about not being able to be in contact with them. He has thrown himself into new projects and initiatives and has a network of friends.

Research on Personality Types

Many 20th-century Western psychologists, such as Freud, Adler, Maslow, and Fromm, worked from the premise that people are basically alike and are driven by the same needs. Others have pursued the theory that there are different personality types. The Greek Hippocrates identified four temperaments: Sanguine, Choleric, Phlegmatic, and Melancholic (Keirsey and Bates 1978). Keirsey and Bates note, "Many since [Hippocrates] have proposed other basic differences in personality, temperament or character, each in turn ignored" (p. 3).

This chapter will discuss two theories of personality type that have received a lot of attention in the applied behavioral sciences in the 20th century: The Myers-Briggs Type Indicator and the Big Five/Five Factor Model. Using these theories can be useful in understanding and working with individual differences on teams.

The Myers-Briggs Type Indicator

Over 50 years ago, two US American women, Katherine Myers and her daughter Isabel Myers, developed the Myers-Briggs Type Indicator (MBTI), which is based on the concepts of Swiss psychiatrist Carl Jung's Function Type. They derived their distribution standards from a white, middle class, US population. In 1975, the MBTI was published commercially in the USA. The MBTI helps people identify their own psychological type and their interpersonal needs. It has been widely used in US organizations for the last three decades and internationally since the 1990s.

What It Measures

The MBTI measures four sets of preferences on a scale that, in turn, creates 16 personality types. We can behave outside of our type, but it may be awkward and take more energy and practice. The developers of MBTI, Myers and Briggs, believed the preferences are inborn but that culture and environment are influential.

When you complete the MBTI, you have a score on each of the four preferences anywhere from slight to very clear. The preferences are as follows:

- Extraversion (E) – Introversion (I)

  Extraverts get their energy from being with people and are lonely when they are alone—the larger the group the better! They enjoy being the center of attention. Introverts need some private time to become reenergized—time to reflect, read, or work by themselves or with only a few other people. They can feel lonely in a crowd because of their preference for deep connection. The US seems to value the outgoing personality, and introverts can believe they ought not to want private time. This has implications for roles on teams, and in the context in which work gets done.

- Sensing (S) – Intuition (N)

  Sensors are practical; they want and trust facts. They seek the details of a situation. Intuitors, on the other hand, grasp the whole situation, the probable. They seek metaphors and imagery. Sensors see the trees and Intuitors see the forest. Extreme differences between teammates in this function can cause conflict in gathering data for decisions, although both Intuitors and Sensors are needed.

- Thinking (T) – Feeling (F)

  This dimension has to do with what type of information is considered relevant when making decisions. The Thinker chooses impersonal, objective, and logical information. Laws, policies, and criteria are important to thinkers. Feelers use their values and consider the impact on others. Both are equal in emotionality, but the Feeler shows this more outwardly. Both can think logically, but the Feeler may not verbalize it. These differences need to be clarified on teams as they relate to problem solving and decision making.

- Judging (J) – Perceiving (P)

  The Judger is anxious to get something settled and feels relief once the decision has been made. The Judger would rather not have a lot of options, but would like a deadline. The US population is equally distributed on these dimensions. Perceivers prefer to keep options open and fluid, since making a decision can make them uneasy. The Perceiver may reopen the decision. This is the list maker; each day has a multitude of opportunities.

By combining the four preferences, 16 personality types emerge. An additional 16 types describe people with even scores in any of the types. Practitioners who use MBTI have extrapolated on each type. Many practitioners, for example, believe that ENFJs (Extraversion/Intuition/Feeling/Judging) are outstanding leaders of task groups. They are charming, have charisma, and place a high value on cooperation from others. People are their highest priority, and they feel responsible for others. They communicate caring and concern. They have high expectations of relationships, which seldom can be sustained in a work environment. They believe they are understood and understand others, which may not always be true. On the other hand, practitioners find that ISTJs (Introversion/Sensation/Thinking/Judging) are decisive and dependable. They are often managers. They are quiet, serious, and concerned with details and thoroughness. They like materials and people to be in the right place at the right time, and may be impatient when this does not happen. They do not have much interest in socializing at work.

Validity and Reliability

Academic psychologists have criticized the MBTI in research, claiming that it lacks convincing validity data. In particular, the dichotomous scoring of the preferences is questioned (McCrae and Costa 1989; Stricker and Ross 1964; Pittenger 1993). The scores on the preferences are distributed in a centrally peaked manner similar to a normal distribution. Scores are divided at the center so that a score on one side is classified as one preference, and a score on the other side is classified as the other preference. This raises questions about type since the norm is for people to be near the middle.

The reliability of the MBTI is questionable. A wide range of 36–76% of those tested are assigned a different type upon retesting weeks or years later, and many people's types were also found to vary according to the time of the day (Pittenger 1993; Matthews 2004). The instrument has been criticized for its terminology being so vague that it allows any kind of behavior to fit any personality type. An individual can give a high rating to a positive description that supposedly applies to them so that when they are asked to compare their preferred type to that assigned by the MBTI, only half of them pick the same profile (Pittenger 1993; Carskadon and Cook 1982).

Cross-Cultural Research

Linda Kirby and Nancy Barger (1998) have studied the reliability and validity of the MBTI cross-culturally. Although the research was originally standardized and validated among white middle class populations, the more recent forms include a much more representative sampling of US co-cultural groups. Kirby and Barger contend that "the great majority of multicultural and international MBTI studies report results comparable to those found in similar studies in the United States, and support the validity of the MBTI instrument when it is used appropriately in those cultures" (p. 369). Almost every culture for which there are type data reports a predominance of Sensing Judging types, and the great majority report STJ as the modal type. Kirby and Barger report research by others that found distributions comparable to those in the USA using similar populations in the United Kingdom, Canada, and Australia.

Dozens of studies of the MBTI in more diverse cultures also replicate the results found in the English-speaking countries. These studies include students from Spanish-speaking countries (Call and Sotillo 1993 in Kirby and Barger 1998), female school administrators from the People's Republic of China (Yao 1993 in Kirby and Barger 1998), Singaporean high school students (Lim 1994 in Kirby and Barger 1998), and South African female managers (Van Rooyen 1994 in Kirby and Barger 1998).

However, Kirby and Barger (1998) note that the use of the MBTI may be inappropriate in cultures that combine high Collectivism with the experience of oppression. This was pointed out by practitioners working with Black South Africans and New Zealand Maori. One researcher, Colin Hopkirk (1997 in Kirby and Barger 1998), gave the following explanation as to why the MBTI may be inappropriate for the Maori:

> They perceive and experience themselves first as part of the whole creation, second as part of the hapu (tribe) of which they are the product, third as part of the whanau (extended family) from which they descend, and only last as a distinct individual personality (p. 369).

Practitioners working with Hopi and Navajo Native Americans in the USA suggest that indigenous cultures:

> [I]nclude traditional ways for members to discover the meaning of their lives and to understand how their individual existence fits within the history and tradition of the family and tribe. It may be that the culturally identified ways for developing self-understanding for individuals in these cultures will work better and be more appropriate than the MBTI and psychological type theory (Salazar and Sanchez 1997 in Kirby and Barger 1998, p. 370).

Eduardo Casas, Professor of Psychology at the bilingual University of Ottawa, Canada, has a data bank of over 5,000 profiles. He states that all the data coming from outside the USA indicate a preference for Introversion (in Barger 1992). Research has not yet determined why this is true; possibilities include differences in language or preferences in temperament. Another possible reason might be a self-reporting bias for Extraversion in the United States or Introversion in other countries. For example, Barger (1992) found that one Korean who is an Extravert on the MBTI felt that he received a message while growing up that he should refrain from being outspoken or from calling attention to himself. He views his culture as being majority Introverted, where Extraverts are not favored, whereas in the USA, Introverts often feel their style is not favored.

Battle (in Gaskins Jones 1992) researched the MBTI among African Americans and found them more heavily clustered in two of the 16 types, Sensing and Thinking, than the MBTI type distribution of the general population. Twillman (in Gaskins Jones 1992) found the same to be true in a study of African American university students. Research has not yet determined for sure why this clustering occurs, but Twillman and Gaskins Jones both suggest that African Americans may tailor their MBTI responses to either match or challenge preferences of the dominant, white culture. This example demonstrates how difficult it is to confirm the validity of the MBTI cross-culturally.

Establishing both the existence of types and the distribution cross-culturally is complex. Translations for the Myers-Briggs Type Indicator instrument have been available since the early 1990s, and it is now currently published in 21 countries. Kirby and Barger (1998), Allik and McCrae (2004) and Williams et al. (1998) name the following difficulties:

- Translations may be semantically accurate, but some meaning might be lost in the way the sentence reads, the idioms and word usage
- Individuals in different cultures have different response styles, self-presentational motives, and/or standards of comparison
- Managers and students may be more Westernized than the general population
- Personality test taking and self-reports on behavior may not be considered appropriate in some cultures

Barger and Kirby (2005) point out that there is wide variation in how these types are expressed in other cultures:

> The surface behaviors of people with similar type preferences will look somewhat different, much as a rose that grows in the rich soil and moist climate of Portland, Oregon, looks quite different from the same plant trying to survive in the clay soil and climate of Denver, Colorado. They are both still identifiable as a rose, but outward appearance varies tremendously (p. 1).

How It Can Be Applied

The MBTI has enjoyed immense popularity in organizations in the last three decades in the USA and, more recently, globally. It is one of the most widely used personality frameworks (Quenk 2000 in Robbins 2003). Licensed practitioners often use the MBTI in team building to facilitate the development of a trusting and committed environment. Potential outcomes include:

- Enabling team members to realize their unique contributions and gifts
- Creating the potential to understand different contributions as assets that can benefit the team
- Assisting team members to understand potential conflicts in style and negotiate around these differences to work more productively
- Enabling a team to realize their team profile and identify important styles that may be lacking or underrepresented

Personality differences can be aggravating and produce tension, or they can be helpful. Let us take the example of a team composed of some individuals who are extreme on Intuition and others who are extreme on Sensing. The Intuitors will dream broadly and envision limitless possibilities, whereas the Sensor will look at the details—for example, how resources will constrain possibilities. When the Intuitor is cut off from dreaming, important possibilities may be lost, but if the details and resources are not considered, the dream will crash. Both are needed and can be helpful if the team understands the value of each. *Do you find some types are more valued than others in your team or organization*?

It should be remembered that we all have access to the other preferences if we try. To experience this, try writing your signature as you normally do. Now try it with the other hand. Most people find that doing it with the non-dominant hand is harder and they feel more awkward doing it, but they are able to do it. Our MBTI type is like our dominant hand—it is what we prefer to use but it is not the only "hand" available to us.

The Big Five/Five Factor Model (Big 5/FFM)

Another attempt to identify personality types came in the 1930s with the development of the so-called lexical approach. In 1936, Gordon Allport and Harold Odbert posited that socially relevant personality characteristics are encoded in language. They listed all the words found in a dictionary related to personality and came up with 18,000. Their approach led to numerous attempts to develop a taxonomy of personality that could be used to predict human behavior. The lexical approach had no single theory or model—just different ideas based on descriptive definitions. Perhaps for this reason, this approach never gained recognition.

In the 1960s, R.R. McCrae and P. Costa developed a model, the Five Factor Model, based on the lexical approach as well as a number of theoretical perspectives and cross-observer data. In the 1970s, a similar model was developed by L.R. Goldberg called The Big 5 (Cattell et al. 1970).

In the last 10 years, the Big 5 and FFM models have influenced psychological researchers and organizational psychology literature. There is currently a considerable amount of research being done to determine if these models can be replicated cross-culturally.

What It Measures

The Big 5 (developed by Goldberg in the 1970s) and the FFM (developed by Costa and McCrae in the 1960s) are the most popular of many similar models that measure broad personality traits. Since there is similarity in the two models and in the method of research to determine them, they are often spoken of together. The dimensions are as follows:

- Big 5—surgency, agreeableness, conscientiousness, emotional stability, intellect. The International Personality Item Pool (IPIP) is the instrument that measures this.
- FFM—agreeableness, extraversion, conscientiousness, neuroticism, openness to experience. This is known as the OCEAN model. The Neuroticism, Extraversion, Openness Personality Inventory (NEO) or the Revised Neuroticism, Extraversion, Openness, Personality, Inventory (NEO-PI-R) are the instruments that measure this.

While the MBTI identifies 16 personality types, the Big5/FFM model could produce trillions of combinations of traits. It describes differences, but does not provide an underlying theory to explain those differences. These traits are seen as dimensions, not types, so people vary on a continuum, with most people being in a middle range. The traits are seen as stable over a 45-year period beginning in young adulthood (Soldz and Vallaint 1999). The source of these differences is seen as both genetic and environmental (Allik and McCrae 2004).

Many other psychologists have developed very similar models with five dimensions; a few have developed models with three dimensions (generally combining Agreeableness, Conscientiousness, and Emotional Stability/Neuroticism). A few additional models identify six dimensions: the Big 5 plus the additional dimension of Interpersonal Relatedness (Digman 1997; Griffin and Bartholomew 1994; John 1990; McCrae and Costa 1997). A fuller explanation of the five dimensions, combining other frameworks, follows.

- Extraversion/Surgency

  Extraversion/Surgency means liking a lot of action. Other words associated with it are gregariousness, assertiveness, energy, enthusiasm, seeking excitement, demonstrating a lot of positive feelings, trusting others, sociability, outgoingness, independence, and warmth. Those who score high on this enjoy the responsibility of leading others. On the low end of this dimension would be desiring privacy and being reserved. This dimension is often seen as the most salient, and therefore it is listed first in the Big 5/FFM.

  This dimension is listed in all models, although it is variably described as Ambition and Sociability, Low Ego Control, or Dominant Initiative. It is highly correlated to Extraversion-Introversion on the MBTI. Extraversion can be helpful in facilitating a positive climate between team members; however, too much can lead to dominance of conversations and insufficient time accomplishing tasks.

- Agreeableness

  Agreeableness means the tendency to accommodate the wishes and needs of others, being interested in others' needs, and being uncomfortable with acknowledgment. Other words associated with it are affection, harmony seeking, and adapter. On the low end of this dimension would be challenger, and attending to one's own personal priorities.

  Other models describe it as Love, or Consensuality. This dimension does not show up on all models, or is combined with Conscientiousness and Neuroticism/Emotional Stability. It is somewhat correlated to Thinking-Feeling on the MBTI. Agreeableness can be helpful in harmonizing and establishing group cohesion, but too many team members high in Agreeableness can lead to lack of challenging of ideas and procedures.

- Conscientiousness

  Conscientiousness describes the tendency to consolidate energy and resources on one or more goals, to plan for everything and keep organized, and to refine and polish. Other words associated with it include dependable, self-disciplined. The extreme can be a workaholic. On the low end of this dimension would be someone who is spontaneous in their work style, flexible, less focused, has weak control over impulses, and likes being involved in many projects at the same time.

  Other models describe this as Conformity, Prudence, or Impulsivity. It is somewhat correlated to Judging-Perceiving on the MBTI. Conscientiousness is generally helpful on a team, but the extreme can be wearing. Some spontaneity and flexibility can be a relief.

- Neuroticism/Emotional Stability

  Neuroticism describes the need for stability. One scoring high on this does not work well under stress, and takes longer to rebound. Other words associated with this are alert, attentive, concerned, quick to feel anger, and worrying. Someone on the low end of this dimension would be described as calm, non-reactionary, never missing a beat, stable, and sometimes cool and aloof.

  Other models describe this as Emotional Stability, Adjustment, Emotionality, and Affect. There is nothing similar to this in the MBTI. Neuroticism is not generally positively associated with teamwork, particularly in situations which are stressful and/or changing, although individuals high in this dimension can provide a strong sense of concern about problems, which might balance someone who is very low in this dimension and minimizes problems.

- Openness/Intellect

  This dimension is perhaps the most controversial because its meaning is the least clear. In the FFM it means openness to new experiences and ideas, open-mindedness, presenting the broad view and resisting details, accepting changes and innovation, and seeking complexity. Those scoring low in this dimension are described as practical and traditional. The Big 5 model and others describe it as Intellect.

It is highly correlated to Intuiting-Sensing on the MBTI. Members with high levels of openness are useful to the team in generating ideas, whereas those at the low end might question their practicality.

Validity and Reliability

Researchers generally agree that nearly all clusters of personality-relevant adjectives can be subsumed under the Big 5/FFM (Saucier and Goldberg 1998; Digman 1990). For example, Digman notes that the dimensions can be measured with high reliability and impressive validity. He further states that the five variables that compose the FFM provide a good answer to the question of personality structure. However, Paunonen and Jackson (2000) found that up to 20% of clusters of traits fell outside of the Big 5. The Big 5/FFM Model is seen as the best available to date, although there is some disagreement as to the number of dimensions and their exact description. Practitioners also disagree about whether there is correlation between dimensions or if they are mutually independent. For example, whereas McCrae and Costa (1997) conceived of their dimensions as independent, Yoon et al. (2002) report that Conscientiousness, Neuroticism/Emotional Stability, and Agreeableness are interrelated.

Cross-Cultural Research

McCrae et al. (2004) point out that fixed personality traits could be a phenomenon of Individualistic cultures, whereas Collectivist cultures view personality characteristics as fluid and determined more by the situation. As noted previously in the discussion of the MBTI, there are several challenges to validating personality instruments across cultures.

Despite these challenges, several studies have found that the FFM can be replicated cross-culturally. For example, one project used a lexical approach in Dutch and German whereby researchers studied dictionaries in these languages for words related to personality and categorized them into personality factors. These factors replicated the factors of the FFM (Yoon et al. 2002). In another study, using one of the FFM instruments translated into Czech and Russian, McCrae et al. (2004) found that responses still fell into the same five factors as in the original FFM. Observer correlation showed moderate to high agreement, especially for Extraversion.

Yoon et al. (2002) report on a number of studies in China, Korea, Hong Kong, and Japan using the lexical approach, which found five factors of personality that generally correlated with the Big 5. For example, in a study of Korean employees using a translated version of the NEO, researchers examined the construct validity of the FFM and found it fit the normative data for the USA. The pattern of intercorrelation was similar to that in the USA, with the only noteworthy difference being the stronger relation between Agreeableness and Conscientiousness in the Korean sample. They hypothesized that this was due to the Confucian values of loyalty, filial piety, social responsibility, ethics, and integrity.

Using an FFM instrument and the Chinese Personality Assessment Inventory (CPAI) with Chinese students, Cheung et al. (2001) found four factors similar to the FFM. However, they found an Interpersonal Relatedness factor in their scales (which the FFM does not find) and they did not find an Openness factor (which the FFM does find). The Interpersonal Relatedness factor also appeared in a study with Hawaiian students of differing ethnic backgrounds. Rolland (in McCrae and Allik 2002), using the FFM, found Extraversion, Agreeableness, and Conscientiousness universally replicated, but Neuroticism/Emotional Stability, and especially, Openness, to be more culturally contingent.

The largest cross-cultural study to date was conducted by McCrae in 2001 and 2002 (Allik and McCrae 2004). It compared the FFM in 36 cultures in Europe, North America, South America, Africa, and Asia. Language translation often determined who was represented. For example, in India it was given in Marathi and Telugu, in Zimbabwe in Shona, in the United States in English and Spanish, and in Yugoslavia in Serbian. Separate results were given for Black South Africans and White South Africans. The tests measured self-reports by college-age and adult men and women. College students predominated, which may have moderated differences. The study yielded some surprising results. For example, Black Africans and Asians had less standard deviation than respondents did in all other cultures. McCrae hypothesizes that this could be due either to a stigma against extremes in collectivist cultures, or to more homogeneity among members of these groups.

By examining the total scores from each country and grouping together countries with the most similar cultures, McCrae (Allik and McCrae 2004) found that similar cultures often show similar personality profiles. For example, Hispanics in the USA and Peruvians scored similarly, as did Hungarians and Serbians, Canadians and US Americans, Danes and Norwegians, Black South Africans and Zimbabweans, and Chinese from Hong Kong and Taiwan. However, some dissimilar cultures yielded similar personality profiles. For example, people from Japan and the Peoples Republic of China scored similarly to a mixed group of Europeans and Latin Americans, people from Turkey scored similarly to people from the USA and Canada, people from Belgium similarly to people from Spain, and people from Portugal similarly to people from Russia.

McCrae (Allik and McCrae 2004) also analyzed the data in another way by mapping Neuroticism (correlated with Conscientiousness) and Extraversion (correlated with Openness and Agreeableness). In doing so, McCrae found that Europeans and Americans (with the exception of those of Dutch, Croatian, Spanish, or Portuguese descent) scored high in Openness and Extraversion and low in Agreeableness, and Asians and Africans scored high in Agreeableness and low in Openness and Extraversion. This tendency of Asians and African cultures towards introversion, traditionalism, and compliance (low Extraversion, high Agreeableness), Allik and McCrae believe, is related to their tendency towards High Power Distance (see Hofstede, Chapter 2). European and American cultures put self-interest before the group and ascribe to self-actualization (high Openness and high Extraversion), which they believe is related to high Individualism. McCrae did not find any correlation between the scores of people from similar cultures in the Neuroticism/ Conscientiousness factor.

As Allik and McCrae (2004) note, the FFM attributes differences in personality to an interplay of shared cultures and shared genes. Openness does not appear in a variety of cultures, while another dimension, Interpersonal Relatedness, does appear. It is important to remember that there are many difficulties in researching differences in personality and one must not overinterpret results. Generally, research shows that variations across cultures tend to be small compared to variations between individuals within cultures.

How It Can Be Applied

The Big 5/FFM has received a lot of attention from researchers in the past 10 years, including cross-culturally. Important relationships between the Big 5/FFM and job performance have been found. Conscientiousness predicted high job performance for all occupations in studies in the USA and European Community (Salgado in Robbins 2003). Agreeableness and Openness were more related to specific job categories (Barrick and Mount 1991 in Robbins 2003; Mount et al. 1994 in Robbins 2003). The Models are not used as much as the MBTI in organizations. This may be because there are questions about which five dimensions to use, whether there are five or six dimensions in total, and whether the dimensions are interrelated. Additionally, the terminology may not be sufficiently neutral—who would like to be identified as being low on Agreeableness or high on Neuroticism?

As was discussed previously with the application of the MBTI, these models can be useful in developing awareness of oneself and others, and of the team profile. Recognizing and discussing how to manage these differences is crucial, both intrapersonally and interpersonally. Personality is rather fixed, so dramatic changes are not to be expected, but it is possible to modify one's behavior. This will be discussed later in the chapter.

Limitations on the Effects of Personality

Both MBTI and Big5/FFM have been useful in predicting individual employee performance. Their usefulness in the team performance context, however, is questioned; some of the personality variables behaved as expected, some behaved unexpectedly, and most had no effect on team performance (Yeatts and Hyten 1998 in Kline 1999). The organizational context is important here. When the organizational culture and norms are strong, individual personalities are subjugated; when they are weaker, the personalities are more differentiated. The self-selection factor is also important here; individuals seek out and stay in situations in which they are comfortable. *Have you ever wanted to leave a work situation because you felt your personality was not valued?*

Multiple Intelligences

Are some people more skilled at working with others, and in particular, with others who are different from them? Recent research suggests this to be true. What enables this, and how does knowing about it help us understand the effectiveness of individuals on teams?

In the West, "intelligence" has traditionally meant abstract reasoning. This idea dates back to Ancient Greece, where the cognitive sphere was split from other ideas of intelligence such as the aesthetics. Half a dozen or more definitions of intelligence were offered in a symposium in the *Journal of Educational Psychology* in 1921 (Peterson and Seligman 2004). The predominant view was that intelligence was narrowly defined as abstract reasoning. However, this definition of intelligence does not speak to diverse abilities such as those needed by mediators of interpersonal conflict, Aborigines navigating a boat in the South Seas without instruments, strategists working to overthrow Apartheid, midwifes, hunters and food gatherers, composers of music, acupuncturists, or athletic coaches.

More recently, Howard Gardner (1993) posited that there are multiple intelligences that are independent of each other. He defines intelligence as "the ability to solve problems, or to fashion products that are valued in one or more cultural communities" (p. 7). Gardner studied a wide set of circumstances in which one can look at intelligence, such as the development of children, breaking down of abilities under conditions of brain damage, learning disabilities, and different cultures. He identified seven intelligences as a preliminary organizing system. Intelligence from this point of view is found in different people in different ways. We have different combinations of intelligence. Gardner's seven intelligences are:

- Linguistic Intelligence

  Ability to use words and language. These learners have highly developed auditory skills and are often eloquent speakers and excellent writers. They think in words.

- Logical/Mathematical Intelligence

  Ability to use reason, logic, and numbers. These learners think conceptually, in logical and numerical patterns, making connections between pieces of information. They are curious about the world around them, and ask a lot of questions.

- Spatial Intelligence

  Ability to think in pictures. These learners need to create a mental picture to retain information. They like maps, charts, pictures, videos, and movies.

- Bodily/Kinesthetic Intelligence

  Ability to control body movements and handle objects skillfully. These learners are able to remember and process information through the use of space. They like physical coordination, acting, using their hands to create, and sports.

sical Intelligence

Ability to produce and appreciate music. These learners think in sounds, rhythms, and patterns. They enjoy singing, playing musical instruments, and the rhythm of music.

- Intrapersonal Intelligence

Ability to access one's internal emotions and moods, to know one's strengths and weaknesses, and to understand one's mental processes. These learners are good at understanding their role in relationship to others.

- Interpersonal Intelligence

Ability to relate to and understand others. These learners are effective in seeing things from other people's points of view. They can sense feelings, intentions, and motivations. They are excellent in building trust and establishing positive relations with other people.

Gardner's work is helpful in broadening the understanding of intelligence beyond abstract reasoning. It is very similar to the ancient Chinese "Six Arts" educational program (Chongde and Tsingan 2003 in Connerley and Pedersen 2005).

Peterson and Seligman (2004) put forth another framework for intelligence. They posited that intelligence can be categorized in two groups: *cognitive intelligences* (verbal, perceptual-organizational, spatial, etc.) and *"hot" intelligences*, so called because they possess "hot" information: signals concerning motives, and feeling about oneself and others. They name three "hot" intelligences that are crucial for teamwork: Personal Intelligence, Social Intelligence, and Emotional Intelligence. There is virtually no research related to the possible genetic basis of these intelligences.

Personal Intelligence is similar to Gardner's Intrapersonal Intelligence. Research shows that people who have a relatively realistic sense of their ability perform better in their occupations than those who do not (Peterson and Seligman 2004). Understanding one's own emotions and skills is also important when interacting with others, and is essential in establishing boundaries in interpersonal relationships. The tests for measuring the hot intelligences are weakest for Personal Intelligence.

Social Intelligence is related to Gardner's Interpersonal Intelligence. It has the longest history, having been introduced by Thorndike in the 1920s. People with Social Intelligence understand the dynamics in a team meeting—they know when to step in, how to influence and make an impact through people. They understand and appreciate working with others to accomplish a task.

Karl Albrecht (2004) claims that Social Intelligence can be developed. He gives an example of an employee whose behavior was quite toxic in almost all his interactions with others. One day his manager asked him to take a questionnaire related to Social Intelligence. After he completed it, he remarked, "This is me, isn't it? All the things on the toxic side are the things I've been doing. I never really thought about it this way." The manager reported that from one day to the next he went from being a complete grouch to being helpful, considerate, and even friendly. Albrecht claims that he has many times seen convincing evidence that a big cause of low

Social Intelligence is lack of insight, and these people simply need help in seeing themselves as others see them.

Emotional Intelligence concerns the ability to use emotional information in reasoning. It overlaps with Personal/Intrapersonal and Social/Interpersonal Intelligence. Emotional skills are divided into four types as follows:

- *Perceiving emotions*: the ability to perceive emotions in oneself and others accurately
- *Using emotions to facilitate thought*: the capacity to integrate emotions in thought and to use emotions in a way that facilitates cognitive processes
- *Understanding emotions*: the capacity to understand emotional concepts and meanings, the links between emotions and the relationships they signal, and how emotions blend and progress over time
- *Managing emotions*: the capacity to monitor and regulate emotions for personal and social growth and well-being

Emotional Intelligence was first defined and measured in the 1990s. Of the three "hot" intelligences, the most studies have been published on Emotional Intelligence; therefore we will discuss this in more detail. People high in Emotional Intelligence generally have a smoother social functioning. The concept has been popularized through a best-selling trade book, *Emotional Intelligence*, by Daniel Goleman (1995), and then *Working with Emotional Intelligence* also by Goleman (1998). Other books have followed: *The Handbook of Emotional Intelligence*, by Bar-On and Parker (2000), *Emotions in the Workplace*, by Lord et al. (2002), and *Emotions in Organization,* by Fineman (2000). The term has become a catch phrase and its clarity is sometimes lost.

Clearly, emotions and rationality are interrelated, and some ability to understand emotions can contribute to group dynamics, understanding sources of conflict, and positive team relations. Some traditional corporate workplaces strive to eliminate emotions from work life, but, in fact, emotion is an integral part of any organization. Ashforth and Humphrey (1995) argue that rather than view emotion as the dysfunctional antithesis of rationality, it is important to recognize the functional complementarities.

There is some variance in Emotional Intelligence between groups. Women perform above men (a moderate group difference) on scales of Emotional Intelligence. Some cultural differences in emotional expression have been researched. Mesquita (2001) conducted a study of Dutch (representing Individualist cultures) and Surinamese and Turkish (representing Collectivist cultures) participants. She first identified the most frequent emotion words in each language and found five classes: anger, sadness, shame, happiness, and pride. In a second study, participants reported events that led them to feel one of the emotions. She found that the Surinamese and Turkish were differentiated from the Dutch in the following ways: (a) more grounded in assessments of social worth and shifts in relative social worth, (b) reflected the external world rather than the inner world of the individual, and (c) belonged to the self-other relationship rather than being confined to the subjectivity of the self. This study seems to indicate that emotions in Collectivist cultures are characterized as relational and contextual, whereas in Individualist cultures they are intrapersonal and subjective.

A study by Scollon et al. (2004) of emotions across cultures (European American, Asian American, Japanese, Indian, and Hispanic) asked participants to identify emotions as being pleasant or unpleasant. The most significant difference was found in pride, which was seen as unpleasant in India, but not in the other groups. Indigenous emotions in India and Japan clustered with Western emotions, rather than forming separate clusters. While in the USA, employees in service situations are expected to smile, in Israel, this is seen as inexperience, and in Moslem cultures, it is often taken as a sign of sexual attraction, so women are socialized not to smile at men (Rafaeli 1989 in Robbins 2003).

Cultural Intelligence is the capacity to adapt to new cultural settings. Christopher Earley (2002) argues the other "hot" intelligences are not transferable across cultures. For example, one can understand and relate to how others think and feel very effectively in one's own culture, but norms and values shift across cultures and, therefore, one cannot transfer Social Intelligence across cultures. According to Earley, Cultural Intelligence is the capacity to adapt to new cultural settings by using the following intelligences:

- Cognitive

    Knowing oneself is a starting point to cross-cultural competence. The self is a representation of one's personality and identity formed through experience, feelings, and thoughts, and encoded in memory. This overlaps with Gardner's Intrapersonal Intelligence. But Earley's Cultural Intelligence adds a flexible concept of self so that one can reshape and adapt to new settings. Bicultural people have an advantage here. Earley also includes high inductive reasoning: the ability to sort out and make sense of a multitude of social and environmental clues. This higher-order learning is often referred to as "learning how to learn."

- Motivational

    Motivation is tied into a feeling of efficacy—capability to accomplish a level of performance. People who believe in their own capability to understand different cultures are likely to proactively engage with these cultures. Obstacles and setbacks will not cause them to give up. Furthermore, they will be willing to engage in problem-solving. This might be difficult for people with High Uncertainty Avoidance.

- Behavioral

    Behavior depends on a person's being able to persist over a period of time. Earley posits that people with this intelligence will not merely act the same as others to mimic their culture, but they will engage in actions that put others at ease and make them comfortable. They are able to use various behavioral clues provided by others to interpret their actions and underlying motives.

People with high Cultural Intelligence not only know themselves and how their culture has influenced their identity, but they are able to sort out culturally derived behavior from individual, idiosyncratic behavior of a given team member.

Case Study: Euro American Female Working in an Asian American Organization

In the following case study, how successful is the Euro American in using Cultural Intelligence? I am a Euro American female who was working in an Asian American cultural organization in the U.S. The executive director was born and raised in Panama and was of Chinese descent. Although she spoke no Chinese, had never been to Asia, and seemed to have only a very limited knowledge of Chinese customs or history, she appeared to identify strongly with both Asian and Latin cultures. She, for example, frequently prefaced statements with, "We Asians," or "We Latinos."

I gained the greatest amount of insight into my strengths and weaknesses as a manager in a multicultural setting from an unexpected event. After writing a document that was to be mailed to twenty Asian American and non-Asian community leaders, I gave a copy to the Executive Director for her review in accordance with procedures. I was expected to check all important documents with both the Executive Director and the Chairperson of the organization's steering committee.

At this time, she was running late for an appointment. Very quickly, she glanced over the papers, crossed out one of the sections and said she wanted it deleted. As it turned out, I had included that section for a very specific reason, which I then briefly explained. She responded by saying, "Then do whatever you think is best," and went on her way.

After carefully thinking about what had happened, I left the document in its original form, made copies, and posted them. I thought the Executive Director felt the reason I had given for including the section was sufficient. When she returned from her meeting, however, I learned that this was not the case. She was upset I had not changed the document. I was surprised by her response and, initially, felt her reason was rather "unprofessional." In her culture, she expected me to go along with her.

When caught in this type of misunderstanding, my first reaction was to judge the Executive Director from a very Western perspective and view her behavior in a negative light. Perhaps I would have been much less likely to respond this way if the whole scenario had happened abroad, where it is easier to keep my cultural biases in check.

The research on multiple intelligences, and the "hot" intelligences is important for team work. Individual cognitive intelligence is less significant than the potential of the group. Hill (1983) found that results from hundreds of groups showed that the group scores were almost always higher than those of the best individual. Adler (2002) points out, however, that it is only with effective teamwork that this potential can be realized.

nging Oneself to Improve Team Effectiveness

This chapter has outlined the many factors that shape us as individuals and form our unique composite of strengths and weaknesses. Reflecting on this usually generates the desire to become more effective. Feedback from others can increase this desire. Sometimes changing behavior can feel daunting. We've probably all heard the expression, "That's just who I am," indicating that the individual believes change is not possible. As we saw in the discussion on nature-nurture, it is probably true that there are some things about ourselves that we cannot change. Howard and Howard (2001) suggest three approaches to working with a person whose individual behavior does not fit what is needed for the job: *Developmental* (teach, learn, train, educate, practice, study); *Supportive* (mentor, coach, adapt the job to the person); *Compensatory* (offset, substitute, work around, redesign, rely on others).

Since much of our behavior is due to socialization, we can make some modifications. The following is a model for personal change, which is adapted from the work of Kurt Lewin (1951), a prominent social psychologist.

- Stage 1: Unfreezing

  In this stage, old behaviors are "unfrozen," become less habitual, and the individual questions them. A desire for change has been created and a climate of psychological safety has been reached. In order to reach this stage, three conditions are needed. The first condition is the awareness of aspects of one's own behavior that are dysfunctional in a given situation. This awareness may be reached through observation, or direct or indirect feedback from others. Many times a person's ability to actually hear this feedback and reach this awareness is blocked because he or she is not comfortable enough to accept the feedback, or because it is given in such a manner as to disaffirm the person rather than the specific behavior. After having reached an awareness, one must truly have a desire to change. People who have become aware of dominating the discussion, for example, may wish to continue doing this because they believe it is important to push their ideas; thus, there is no desire for change. Finally, a climate of psychological safety and trust is important in a group so that people are able to accept feedback on their behavior and use it productively.

- Stage 2: Changing

  In this stage, people practice new behavior. For example, the person who dominates may decide to pull back entirely and observe the group for a while. Or, she/he may decide to set a specific goal, such as only speaking one time, or writing down responses first. It is helpful at this stage for people to let others know what behavior they are working on. In this way they can get feedback on their progress. Role models are helpful.

- Stage 3: Refreezing

  In this stage, new behaviors are "frozen," become habitual, and the individual does not question them. New behavior has become at least temporarily integrated and normal. One is no longer practicing and has, for example, achieved some desirable balance between the old and new behavior. Those with whom we need to exhibit these new behaviors help to reinforce them. If affirmation does not take place, the change cannot be sustained.

An additional model, The Learning Stages (no date), describes the change process in individual behavior in four stages using two variables: awareness and behavior or skill. At first, in the Naïve Stage, we are unaware of the impact of our behavior and therefore have some areas of incompetence. As we become aware of our behavior through observation, feedback, and assessments, we enter the Learning Stage, where we are conscious of our incompetence (and competence). As we practice new behavior, we reach the Performing Stage, where we are conscious of our new competence. Finally, after considerable practice, we reach the Habit Stage, where we become unconscious of our acquired competence. Figure 3.1 outlines this process.

BEHAVIOR OR SKILL

AWARENESS		**Incompetent**	**Competent**
	CONSCIOUS	LEARNING STAGE **Conscious Incompetence** We are conscious of our lack of skills and unable to behave differently. We learn from mistakes. Acceptance of ignorance is critical in order to move forward. **We know that we do not know.**	PERFORMANCE STAGE **Conscious Competence** Awareness and skills come together in proficiency and high performance. **We know that we know.**
	UNCONSCIOUS	NAÏVE STAGE **Unconscious Incompetence** The beginning of the learning journey for all of us. **We know that we do not know.**	HABIT STAGE **Unconscious Competence** We act skillfully without awareness of either positive or negative implications. **We do not know that we know.**

*Author Unknown

Fig. 3.1 Learning process stages

Relevant Competencies

- Be aware of the impact of your behavior on others
  - Understand your personality and its impact
  - Understand how culture has impacted your values and behavior
  - Understand your emotions
  - Acknowledge your privileges and seek to learn about blind spots in one-up identities
  - Acknowledge your experiences in one-down identities and seek support
- Engage constructively with differences: individual, social, cultural
  - Clarify and communicate your needs.
  - Listen: Take in the experience of the other. Do not expect individuals to be spokespersons for their group. Do not deny their experience.
  - Learn: Be able to observe, sort out, and make sense of clues that enable your to see what the other person needs. Educate yourself.
- Clarify and communicate your needs
  - Speak up: Speak out against acts and name practices that marginalize, stereotype or discount yourself or others
  - Be persistent
  - Be flexible, and adjust

Summary

The concept of personality describes the way each individual within a culture is unique. Both environment and heredity determine personality. Although we are still not sure of the exact roles of these two determinants, we can say that both are significant and interact with each other.

We each belong to multiple social identity groups which have a one-up or one-down status in society. Power and privilege are ascribed to the one-up groups, whereas one-down groups are targets for discrimination and prejudice. This can impact team dynamics.

It is useful to understand one's own personality type and those of others on a team. Myers-Briggs Type Indicator (MBTI) and the Big Five/Five Factor Model are two models for identifying personality type. The MBTI, based on Jungian theory, describes 16 types. Cross-cultural research confirms the existence of these types except in Collectivist societies with the experience of oppression. More research is needed to establish the distribution. Cross-cultural research is complicated by factors of language, context, and meaning, and differences in whether one sees oneself as a member of a group or as an individual. The FFM/Big 5 Model, using a lexical approach, outlines five dimensions that could produce trillions of combinations, since each dimension is on a continuum. Cross-cultural research shows some consistency across cultures, but also some deviation. For example, the Big 5/FFM universally replicated Extraversion, Agreeableness, and Conscientiousness, but Openness was culturally contingent. Additionally, a new dimension, Interpersonal Relatedness, appeared in some cultures. Further research is needed to determine the cross-cultural relevance of these models. This should be done using culturally relevant instruments and by researchers from within the culture, not translations.

Intelligence is more than abstract cognitive ability; there are multiple intelligences. "Hot" intelligences (Personal Intelligence, Social Intelligence, and Emotional Intelligence) are important for group work. Additionally, Cultural Intelligence is crucial for multicultural teams.

Since both environment and heredity determine our individual behavior, we can modify our behavior. Awareness, the desire to change and practice, are necessary for this.

In interacting with others, we may make the error of assuming that they are impacted in the same ways as we are. Whereas the Golden Rule is "Do unto others as you would have them do unto you," the Platinum Rule, "Do unto others as they would like," can be more effective.

Case Study: The ITT Team

As you read the case study below, consider the following questions:

- *Which dimensions of the Big Five/FFM are represented on the ITT team?*
- *How might the personalities of the members help or hinder their functioning and change management?*
- *Which team members might be in conflict?*
- *What should Mary do to make the meetings most effective?*

Healthcare for Elders is a nonprofit organization headquartered in Chicago which employs field staff in four regions in the US. It provides direct support to nursing homes and assisted living centers, and also works with advocacy groups and research programs. The Information Technology Team (ITT) is support staff to administration, monitors the physical computer system, plans acquisitions, installs machines, and provides training and user support. ITT has a Director, Mary, and five Group Leaders. Masud and Sue are computer specialists, Sam is an electronic engineer, Speth is a management analyst and is responsible for the budget, and Tom is responsible for training and support. The Group Leaders' responsibilities represent both a wide diversity of assignments and a potential for conflict due to overlap.

Due to the nature of the information technology business, there is constantly a need for change. Mary believes they are ten years behind in technology. The team needs to work effectively together in the areas of decision making and task/role relationships. They need to understand what others do, what their pressures are, and what problems they face.

Two of the leaders, Masud and Sam, get engrossed in details and do not have sufficient technical information. They are resistant to doing things differently since they have been doing things the same way here for while, and they think Mary is too focused on change. They wonder why all of a sudden things have to be changed quickly. They feel she runs a crisis shop. Sam is quite open with Mary about his displeasure with her. This aggravates Sue, who is uncomfortable with conflict and seeks harmony.

Tom has recently come from a high-tech job on the West Coast, and is eager to introduce new technology and systems. He is very gregarious and enjoys working with others. He likes to bounce his ideas for training of others, which can be frustrating due to the time pressures they face. At meetings, he talks a lot, trying out new ideas which he is formulating as he speaks. This is in contrast to Speth, who rarely talks at meetings. He has a good sense of financial situations and numbers. If he has time to prepare something ahead of time, he will present it at a meeting.

A series of planning meetings has been scheduled to discuss the need for change and several alternatives. Sam has said the meetings might be counterproductive since they have so much to do. Sue has told Mary she dreads the meetings because of the potential for conflict.

Case Study: Out at Work

As you read the case study below, consider the following questions:

- *What are the barriers to inclusion Carol faces?*
- *What could Sue have done to help Carol be accepted on the team?*
- *What do you think Pat should do?*

Elizabeth is a new employee in the loan department at the Bank of England in Birmingham, England. Nigel is manager of the loan department, and there are three full-time employees from the community and two part-time employees from the nearby university. Elizabeth is an open lesbian who is new to the Bank and to the community. Nigel assured her when she interviewed that the environment would be supportive. There are other gays and lesbians who are out in the Bank; there is Hear Us Out, a support group; and Bank of England was the first bank in the city to offer domestic partners health benefits. Elizabeth has had a good experience previously at another bank, and has put her partner's picture on her desk. After a few weeks, she told a few co-workers that others never ask about her partner when they are discussing families, that none of the others in the unit went to the Coming Out Day or have pink triangles on their doors indicating support for GLBT issues.

One time, Mary, one of the full-time workers, overheard Fanin and Charles, two student co-workers, saying they just didn't want to hear about all these personal issues, such as people's sexual orientation, at work. Fanin remarked, "In my country people are accepting of homosexuality, but it is not appropriate to put it in your face." Charles agreed that that is the way it should be at the Bank. Mary told Elizabeth what she overheard. Elizabeth asked Mary what she had said to them, and Mary said she told them to talk to Elizabeth. Elizabeth got upset and asked Mary, "Why didn't you talk to them; why does everyone expect me to always educate these homophobics?"

Today both Elizabeth and Mary have come to Nigel. Elizabeth told Nigel that she feels that the others are just tolerating her. Mary has complained that Elizabeth is asking too much when she expects others to take on her issue.

Assessment Instruments

Prejudice

Psychologists at Harvard, the University of Virginia, and the University of Washington developed Implicit Association Tests, or IATS, to measure unconscious bias in the areas of race and ethnicity, religion, sexual orientation, age, and gender. There are translations in Chinese, German, Spanish, French, Italian, Hebrew, Japanese, Korean, Dutch, Polish, Portuguese, Romanian, and Turkish. See implicit.harvard.edu.

Emotional Intelligence

There is a plethora of instruments that claim to measure emotional intelligence, including non-scientific ones that appear in newspapers and on websites as well as some scientific examples. Since there are so many interpretations of what emotional intelligence is, content validity is hard to ascertain. Three scientific examples with different methodological approaches are listed below.

Ability Approach: Mayer, Salovey, and Caruso Emotional Intelligence Test (MSCEIT) (Mayer et al. 1999). MESCEIT measures an overall emotional intelligence score as well as subscores for four distinct abilities: ability to perceive emotion, ability to use emotion to facilitate thought, ability to understand emotion, and ability to promote emotional and intellectual growth.

Self-Report Approach: Bar-On EQ-I (Bar-On 1997). EQ-I measures intrapersonal and interpersonal aspects, stress management, adaptability, and general mood.

Informant/Self-Report Approach: Emotional Competence Inventory (ECI) (Boyatzis et al. 1999). The Inventory measures self-awareness, social awareness, self-management, and social skills.

Temperament

The Myers-Briggs Type Indicator (MBTI Form M) is published by Center for Applications of Psychological Type (www.capt.org). The MBTI is administered by qualified facilitators who are required to provide a consultative interpretation.

Keirsey Temperament Sorter (Keirsey 1998) is mapped to the existing Myers-Briggs system groupings SP, SJ, NF, and NT.

Big Five

The most commonly accepted measure of the Big Five/FFM, Costa and McCrae's Psychological Assessment Resources, Inc. NEO PI-R, is based on 500 men and 500 women pulled randomly from three different well-respected studies. NEO-FFI is a smaller version. Pierce J. Howard and Jane Mitchell Howard (2000) have created a model based on the NEO PI-R, WorkPlace Big Five ProFile, which is designed with only the workplace in mind (Howard and Howard 2001).

The instrument below, *Team Big Five Assessment*[1], was created with teams in mind.

Team Big 5 Assessment[1]

For each item, check one response. Your score will range from 4 to 12, with scores of 4–6 being low in this facet, 7–9 being medium, and 9–12 being high. It is helpful for your teammates also to complete this Assessment for you and compare results. You can also benefit from sharing your own results with other teammates.

- Neuroticism

When presented with a problematic situation,

1. I tend to go to a problem-solving mode
2. I tend to take a few minutes to release my anxiety before moving to a problem-solving mode
3. I take it personally and worry a lot

Under stressful situations such as making a major mistake,

1. I remain calm
2. I need to take a break before I can become calm
3. I tend to panic

[1] © Claire B. Halverson

When I feel I have been wronged,

1. I am slow to anger
2. I am seldom angry, but it can be provoked
3. I get angry quickly and need to vent

I see myself as

1. Insensitive or uncaring
2. Moderately stable
3. Concerned and oversensitive

- Extraversion

My preferred style of communication with teammates is

1. Email or writing
2. Both email or talking; it depends on the situation
3. Talking

As far as teamwork goes, I prefer

1. To do as much as possible by myself without interruptions
2. Both to work with others and to work alone
3. To do as much as possible with others

In discussions, I usually

1. Keep my opinion to myself
2. Express my opinion only when I feel it is not represented
3. Speak often and am assertive

I see myself as

1. Reserved and formal
2. Somewhat friendly
3. Very friendly and more of a talker than a listener

- Openness

When we are discussing changes in how we do things, I usually

1. Prefer to hold on to what we do now
2. Am open to new ideas, but want to maintain the value of what we do now
3. Am excited about the potential and variety of new ways

When different emotions arise with myself and others on the team, I usually

1. Ignore or discount them
2. Can accept them if necessary
3. Value them and would like them expressed

I work best when I need to

1. Tend to the details
2. Tend to a variety of details as well as the big picture
3. Focus on the big picture and problem solving

I see myself as

1. Focusing on what exists
2. Somewhat open to novelty
3. A visionary

• Agreeableness

When there are different points of view, I like to

1. Jump in and debate
2. Listen and express my point of view
3. Defer or seek harmony

When others need help, I usually

1. Consider what I have to do first
2. Try to balance their needs and my own
3. Drop my own needs

When I have done something well, I

1. Like public acknowledgment
2. Like private acknowledgment
3. Am embarrassed by acknowledgment

• Conscientiousness

In terms of my work habits, I am

1. Usually unorganized
2. Somewhat organized
3. Well-organized

When I have big task to do, I

1. Usually procrastinate
2. Am usually on-task
3. Am very focused on the task

My work usually reflects

1. A low level of refinement
2. A medium level of refinement
3. A high level of refinement

I see myself as

1. Uninterested in high achievement
2. Somewhat interested in high achievement
3. Driven to high achievement

References

Adler, N. (2002). *International Dimensions of Organizational Behavior*. Canada: South-Western Thomson Learning.

Albrecht, K. (2004). Social Intelligence: Beyond IQ. *Training*, *41*(12), 27–32.

Allik, J. & McCrae, R. (2004). Toward a Geography of Personality Traits: Patterns of Profiles Across 36 Cultures. *Journal of Cross-Cultural Psychology*, *35*(1), 13–28.

Allport, G. (1937). *Personality: A Psychological Interpretation*. New York: Holt.

Andrews, R. (1999). Being the Only. In *Reading Book for Human Relations Training* (pp. 83–86). Alexandria, VA: NTL Institute for Applied Behavioral Sciences.

Ashforth, B. E. & Humphrey, R.H. (1995). Emotion in the Workplace: A Reappraisal. *Human Relations*, *48*(2), 77–125.

Bamshad, M. & Olson, S. (2003). *Does Race Exist?* Scientific American.

Barger, N. (1992). The Myers Briggs—Crossing National Cultures. *Cultural Diversity at Work*, *4*(6), 19.

Bar-On, R. (1997). *Bar-On Emotional Quotient Inventory (EQ-i): Technical Manual*. Toronto, Canada: Multi-Health Systems.

Bar-On, R. & Parker, J.D.A. (Eds.) (2000). *The Handbook of Emotional Intelligence: Theory, Development, Assessment and Application at Home, School and in the Workplace*. San Francisco, CA: Jossey-Bass.

Barger, N. & Kirby, L.K. 2005. Working in a Multicultural World. Downloaded Feb. 10, 2005 from www.bargerkirby.com/services.

Boyatzis, R. E., Goleman, D. & Hay/McMer (1999). *Emotional Competence Inventory*. Boston, MA: HayGroup.

Cattell, R.B., Eber, H.W. & Tatsuoka, M.M. (1970). *The Handbook for the Sixteen Personality Factor Questionnaire*. Champaign, IL: Institute for Personality and Ability Testing.

Cheung, F.M., Leung, K., Zhang, J.X., Sun, H.F., Gan, Y.Q., Song, W.Z. & Dong, X. (2001). Indigenous Chinese Personality Constructs: Is the Five-Factor Model Complete? *Journal of Cross-Cultural Psychology*, *32*(4), 407–433.

Carskadon, T. & Cook, D. (1982). Validity of MBTI Descriptions as Perceived by Recipients Unfamiliar with Type. *Research in Psychological Type*, *5*, 89–94.

Collins, B.E. (1970). *Social Psychology*. Reading, MA: Addison-Wesley.

Connerley, M.L. & Pedersen, P.B. (2005). *Leadership in a Diverse and Multicultural Environment*. Thousand Oaks, CA: Sage.

Cox, T., Jr. (1994). *Cultural Diversity in Organizations: Theory, Research and Practice*. San Francisco, CA: Berrett-Koehler.

Digman, J.M. (1990). Personality Structure: Emergence of the Five-Factor Model. *Annual Review of Psychology*, *41*, 417–440.

Digman, J.M. (1997). Higher-order Factors of the Big Five. *Journal of Personality and Social Psychology*, *73*, 1246–1256.

Earley, P.C. (2002). Redefining Interactions Across Cultures and Organizations: Moving Forward with Cultural Intelligence. *Research in Organizational Behavior*, *24*, 271–299.

Erikson, E. (1950). *Childhood and Society*. New York: Norton.

Fineman, S. (Ed.) (2000). *Emotion in Organizations*. Thousand Oaks, CA: Sage.

Funder, D. (1997). *The Personality Puzzle*. New York: Norton.

Gaskins, J.K. (1992). Myers Briggs: Valid with Co-Cultures? *Cultural Diversity at Work*, *5*(1).

Gardner, H. (1993). *Multiple Intelligences: The Theory and Practice*. New York: Basic Books.

Geertz, C. (1975). On the Nature of Anthropological Understanding. *American Scientist*, *63*, 47–53.

Goldberg, L.R. (1993). The Structure of Phenotypic Personality Traits. *American Psychologist*, *48*(1), 36–34.

Goleman, D. (1995). *Emotional Intelligence*. New York: Bantam.

Goleman, D. (1998). *Working with Emotional Intelligence*. New York: Bantam.

Griffin, D.W. & Bartholomew, K. (1994). The Metaphysics of Measurement: The Case of Adult Attachment. In K. Bartholomew & D. Perlman (Eds.), *Advances in Personal Relationships* (vol. 5, pp. 17–52). London, England: Jessica Kingsley.

Hill, G.W. (1983). Group Versus Individual Performance: Are N + 1 Heads Better Than One? *Psychological Bulletin 91*.

Howard, P.J. & Howard, J.M. (2001). *The Owner's Manual for Personality at Work: How the Big Five Personality Traits Affect Performance, Communications, Teamwork, Leadership, and Sales*. Austin, TX: Bard.

John, O.P. (1990). The "Big Five" Factor Taxonomy: Dimensions of Personality in the Natural Language and in Questionnaires. In L.A. Pervin (Ed.), *Handbook of Personality Theory and Research* (pp. 66–100). New York: Guilford.

Johnson, A. (2006). *Privilege, Power and Difference*. Boston, MA: McGraw-Hill.

Keirsey, D. (1998). *Please Understand Me II: Temperament, Character, Intelligence*. Del Mar, CA: Prometheus Nemesis Books.

Keirsey, D. & Bates, M. (1978). *Please Understand Me: Character & Temperament Types*. Del Mar, CA: Prometheus Nemesis Books.

Kirby, L.K. & Barger, N. (1998). Uses of Type in Multicultural Settings. In L.K. Myers, M.H. McCaulley, N.L. Quenk & A.L. Hammer (Eds.), *MBTI Manual: A Guide to the Development and Use of the Myers-Briggs Type Indicator* (3rd ed. pp. 367–385). Palo Alto, CA: Consulting Psychologists.

Kline, T. (1999). *Remaking Teams*. San Francisco, CA: Jossey-Bass.

Lerner, R.M. (1986). *Concepts and Theories of Human Development*. New York: McGraw-Hill.

Lewin, K. (1951). Field Theory in Social Science, New York: Harper.

Lord, R.G., Klimoski, R. & Kanfer, R. (Eds.) (2002). *Emotions in the Workplace*. San Francisco, CA: Jossey-Bass.

Matthews, P. (2004). The MBTI is a Flawed Measure of Personality (http://bmj.bmjjournals.com/cgi/eletters/328/7450/1244). bmj.com Rapid Responses

Mayer, J.D. Caruso, D. & Solovey, P. (1999). Emotional Intelligence Meets Traditional Standards for an Intelligence. *Intelligence*, *27*, 267–298.

McCrae, R.R. & Costa, P.T., Jr. (1989). Reinterpreting the Myers-Briggs Type Indicator from the Perspective of the Five Factor Model of Personality. *Journal of Personality*, *57*, 17–40.

McCrae, R.R. & Costa, P.T., Jr. (1997). Toward a New Generation of Personality Theories: Theoretical Contexts for the Five-Factor Model. In. J.S. Wiggins (Ed.), *The Five-Factor Model of Personality: Theoretical Perspectives* (pp. 51–87). New York: Guilford.

McCrae, R.R. & Allik, J. (Eds.) (2002). *The Five-Factor Model of Personality Across Cultures*. New York: Kluwer.

McCrae, R.R., Costa, P.T., Jr., Martin, T., Oryol, V., Rukavishnikov, A., Senin, I., Hrebicková, M. & Tomáŝ; Urgbánek, T. (2004). Consensual Validation of Personality Traits Across Cultures. *Journal of Research in Personality*, *38*(2), 179–201.

Mesquita, B. (2001). Emotions in Collectivist and Individualist Contexts. *Journal of Personality and Social Psychology*, *80*(1), 68–74.

Miller, F.A. & Katz, J. (2002). *The Inclusion Breakthrough: Unleashing the Real Power of Diversity*. San Francisco, CA: Berrett Koehler.

Moss Kanter, R. (1980). *The Tale of O, On Being Different in an Organization*. New York: Harper & Row.

Myers, I.B. & McCaulley, M.H. (1985). *Manual: A Guide to the Development and Use of the Myers-Briggs Type Indicator*. Palo Alto, CA: Consulting Psychologists Press.

Paunonen, S.V. & Jackson, D.N. (2000). What is Beyond the Big Five? Plenty! *Journal of Personality*, *68*(5), 821–835.

Peterson, C. & Seligman, M. (2004). *Character Strengths and Virtues: A Handbook and Classification*. London, England: Oxford University Press.

Pittenger, D. (1993). Measuring the MBTI… And Coming Up Short (http://www.indiana.edu/~jobtalk/HRMWebsite/hrm/articles/develop/mbti.pdf) *Journal of Career Planning & Placement*.

Robbins, S. (2003). *Organizational Behavior*. Upper Saddle River, NJ: Prentice-Hall.

Rolland, J.P. (2002). Cross-Cultural Generalizability of the Five-Factor Model of Personality. In McCrae, R.R. & Allik, J. (Eds), *The Five-Factor Model of Personality Across Cultures*. New York: Kluwer.

Saucier, G. & Goldberg, L.R. (1998). What Is Beyond the Big Five? *Journal of Personality*, *66*(4), 495–524.

Scollon, C.N., Diener, E., Oishi, S. & Biswas-Diener, R. (2004). Emotions Across Cultures and Methods. *Journal of Cross-Cultural Psychology*, *35*(3), 304–326.

Soldz, S. & Vaillant, G.E. (1999). The Big Five Personality Traits and the Life Course: A 45-year Longitudinal Study. *Journal of Research in Personality*, *33*(2), 208–232.

Stricker, L. & Ross, J. (1964). An Assessment of Some Structural Properties of the Jungian Personality Typology. *Journal of Abnormal and Social Psychology*, *68*(1), 62–71

Williams, J.E., Satterwhite, R. & Saiz, J. (1998). *The Importance of Psychological Traits: A Cross-Cultural Study*. New York: Plenum.

Wright, W. (1998). *Born That Way: Genes, Personality and Behavior*. New York: Knopf.

Yoon, K., Schmidt, F. & Ilies, R. (2002). Cross-Cultural Construct Validity of the Five Factor Model of Personality among Korean Employees. *Journal of Cross-Cultural Psychology*, *33*(3), 217–235.

Chapter 4
Team Development

Claire B. Halverson

> *"Cheshire puss," Alice began, "can you tell me which way I aught to go from here?" "That depends on where you want to get to," said the Cat.*
>
> –Alice's Adventures in Wonderland

Introduction

If you want to "get to" a high-performing team, you need to understand the developmental process groups go through to reach that stage. You can have some comfort in knowing that issues the group is facing such as inclusion, authority, and conflict are normal. You also need to be able to diagnose the stage and issues the team is working with, and have the patience and skills to help move the group along toward becoming a team. Those who do not have these insights and skills may, like Alice, feel they have fallen down a rabbit hole into a strange land where they do not know the way. As mentioned in Chapter 1, Thomas et al. (2000) observed what is "going nowhere" in some cultures may be seen as "getting there" in others.

Team development is important for all teams, but especially for multicultural ones. As noted by researchers (Adler 2002; Ely and Thomas 2001), teams that are highly developed are able to use their diversity, whereas those that are undeveloped will experience their diversity as a hindrance.

There are many models to describe the process that groups go through to get to a level of high productivity and inclusion. This chapter will provide an overview of the models, and then use a five-stage model to describe the process as it relates to multicultural teams. Additionally, another that focuses on teams with a time-bounded task experience will be introduced. A discussion of processes for team building will follow. A case study provides an opportunity to increase skill in diagnosing task and relationship issues that need to be addressed in a team, and in suggesting an intervention.

C.B. Halverson and S.A. Tirmizi (eds.), *Effective Multicultural Teams: Theory and Practice*,

Learning Objectives

After reading this chapter you should be able to:

- Discuss predictable stages of team development
- Assess task, relationship, and leadership issues that need to be addressed
- Identify behaviors that members and leadership can use to help a team progress effectively through the stages to high performance
- Describe an alternative model that is appropriate for short-term teams
- Discuss approaches to team building

Overview of Team Development Models

Research describing stages that small groups go through started with group-therapy groups and human relations training groups (Bales and Strodtbeck 1951; Schutz 1971; Bion 1959). Tuckman (1965) summarized the results of over 50 studies of small-group development to create a four-stage model of group development consisting of: Forming, Storming, Norming, and Performing. He later expanded it to a fifth stage, Adjourning (Tuckman and Jensen 1977). The model describes typical stages based on studies of therapy groups, human relations training groups, and natural groups (professional). Each stage describes both task and relationship issues. Although the Tuckman model is decades old, it is still widely used for teams in the workplace and often cited in the literature (Robbins 2003). Mary Maples (1988) found that her graduate students in group work thought the Tuckman stages were too limited, so she conducted research by having students describe the stages they were in using a list of 200 descriptors. Maples' study extended the Tuckman model to create four substages to each of the five stages.

Other models developed by organizational theorists replicate the original Tuckman four-stage model. They apply to virtual teams as well as face-to-face teams (Lipnack and Stamps 1997). Table 4.1 identifies models relevant to work groups. You can see there is much similarity among them. One difference is that Adler (2002) does not include a conflict stage.

A model not shown in Table 4.1 is the Punctuated Equilibrium Model by Gersick (1988, 1989), which provides a model of group development for temporary work groups. This model, which is quite different, will be discussed later in this chapter.

There is some controversy over whether the models are descriptive of how teams usually develop or prescriptive for what they should do to become high performing. As Bushe and Coetzer (2007) note, "development is not something all groups achieve over time, but is instead a journey toward optimal functioning only some groups attain" (p. 185). Tuckman (1965) is careful to note that in reality a group may be in several stages at any give time, although more probably, one stage is predominant. Teams need to resolve the issues at each stage before they can

Table 4.1 Group development models (Adapted from Jones and Bearley 2001)

Author	Stages				
Schutz (1971, 1984)	Inclusion	Control	Openness		
Tuckman (1965, 1977)	Forming	Storming	Norming	Performing	Adjourning
Francis and Young (1979)	Testing	Infighting	Getting	Mature organized	closeness
Woodcock and Francis (1980)	Ritual sniffing	Infighting	Experimentation	Effectiveness and maturity	
Weber (1982, 2002)	Infancy	Adolescence	Adulthood		Transforming
Moosbrucker (1988)	Orientation to group and to task	Conflict over control	Group formation and solidarity	Differentiation and productivity	
Osburn et al. (1990)	State of confusion	Leader-centered	Tightly formed	Self-directed	
Varney (1991)	Formation	Building	Working	Maturity	
Lipnack and Stamps (1997)	Start-up	Launch		Perform/Test	Deliver
Adler (2002)	Entry	Work		Action	
Busche and Coetzer (2007)	Membership		Competence		

progress to the next stage, and teams rarely skip stages. They may, however, never resolve the surfacing or hidden issues of one stage and become unable to move on or may revert back to an earlier stage. If there is a change in the team, such as new leadership or membership, or a change in task/purpose, the team may cycle back to a previous stage, but will progress more quickly.

Harrison et al. (2000) researched cultural factors affecting adaptation to fluid work groups and teams in Taiwan and Australia. They found Taiwanese organizations had more difficulty adapting to fluid teams with changing membership and leadership than those in Australia. They ascribe this to the differences described in Hofstede's Individualism-Collectivism and High Power Distance dimensions.

The Five-Stage Model

An overview of Tuckman's Five-Stage Model (1965; Tuckman and Jensen 1977) is presented in Table 4.2, Team Stages: Characteristics and Questions Needing Resolution. This is followed by a discussion of each stage, including Climate, Characteristic Behavior, Relationship Issues, Task Issues, Leadership Issues, Issues Resolved, and Competencies Needed. Issues Resolved and Competencies Needed may provide some guidance, since, as was noted earlier, not all teams progress through all the stages. In some teams leadership is shared, either because the team is self-managed, or, as discussed in Chapter 6, because there is a model of shared leadership due to organizational or cultural preferences. As noted earlier, not all teams progress through all the stages. As you read, consider the following questions: *Which stages have you experienced in a team? What issues were resolved or not resolved? What competencies have you used to help the team?*

Forming

Climate

During the forming stage, individual team members seek to create a safe environment for their interactions, and establish their purpose. There are no agreed-upon norms for forming, especially if individuals come from different cultures or organizations. Norms start to emerge related to task and relationship, but these are not discussed; they are implicit norms. In monocultural teams the climate is polite; in multicultural ones, politeness can be exaggerated to awkwardness. There may be periods of extended silence. Individuals with previous positive group experiences often have a feeling of excitement and anticipation. Maples' (1988) research describes this stage as Courtesy, Confusion, Caution, and Commonality.

Table 4.2 Team stages: characteristics and questions needing resolution[a]

Stage	Characteristics	Questions needing resolution
Forming	• Task productivity is low and confused • Irrelevant visible socio-cultural differences are noticed • Assumptions and stereotypes are associated with differences • Invisible and significant socio-cultural differences are not addressed • Attention is paid to finding commonalties • Use of dominant communication patterns results in some members being excluded • Communication is awkward and hesitant	Relationship • Who are we in this group? • What do we want/need to know about each other? • Can we trust each other? • What is the price of membership? • How are we alike? • Can our differences be accepted? • How can we all fit in and be included? • How can we establish common communication methods? Task • What is our overriding purpose? • Who is on this team? • Do we have the needed competencies (knowledge, skill, awareness) to do the work? • Do we have the needed resources? Leadership • Who is in charge here? • What type of leadership style do we want?
Storming	• Task productivity is low • Disagreement over purpose and goals/objectives emerges • Leadership is challenged • Struggles surface around differences • I/me is used more than we/us • Norms previously developed are challenged • Competition and power struggles occur • Previous biases, lack of inclusion, and assumptions are confronted • Sub-grouping by social-cultural identity group can occur	Relationship • How can we differ and disagree in a way that maintains the respect and dignity of all? • How can we give and receive feedback? • How can we understand the difference between intent and impact of non-inclusive language and behavior? • How can we work with individual and cultural differences in conflict styles? • How is power and influence distributed? Task • How do we do our work (tasks, roles)? • What are our standards and expectations? • What are previous assumptions, bias? • How can we work with individual and cultural differences in problem-solving and decision-making styles, procedures and expectations for accomplishing task, and meetings Leadership • What style of leadership do we want? • Can we accept the leadership we have?

(continued)

Table 4.2 (continued)

Stage	Characteristics	Questions needing resolution
Norming	• Task productivity is medium high • Members work interdependently • Norms are followed most of the time • Norms are revisited and revised as appropriate • Differences are used to deepen relationships and enhance task productivity • Conflicts are addressed and feedback is given appropriately • We/us is used more than I/me • Leaders provide coaching and support	Relationship • How close and personal do we want to be? • How should we appreciate and support each other? • How can we balance attention to task and relationship? Task • What are our explicit norms around decision-making, communication, and meetings? • How can we find ways to support each other's work? • How flexible should we be? Leadership • How strong a leadership role do we need?
Performing	• Task productivity is high • Team members are committed to the team and the task • A high degree of interdependence is demonstrated • Conflicts are transformed to lessons learned • Humor is genuine • Norms are followed consistently • Norms are revisited and revised as appropriate • Members are appreciated • Flexibility and ability to cope with ambiguity are apparent	Relationship • How can we adjust to changes in membership? Task • How can we sustain high quality work? • How can we incorporate changes in purpose and the external environment? • How can we continue to provide excitement and learning? • How do we want to celebrate our accomplishments? Leadership • How can we incorporate a process for change and renewal? • How can we share leadership?
Adjourning	• Task productivity is lower • Focus on wrapping things up	Relationships • How can we continue the relationships we have built? Task • Do we have a purpose to continue? • How can we celebrate what we have done?

[a]Claire B. Halverson

The following behavior is characteristic:

- Task productivity is low and confused
- Irrelevant visible socio-cultural differences are noticed
- Assumptions and stereotypes are associated with differences
- Invisible and significant socio-cultural differences are not addressed
- Attention is paid to finding commonalties
- Use of dominant communication patterns results in some members being excluded
- Communication is awkward and hesitant

Relationship Issues

Individuals usually move in tentative and polite ways to be included on a team. They grapple with issues of Who am I in this group? And Who are the others? They look for solutions to ease the uncertainty of their interactions as they attempt to discover what behaviors are accepted and valued. They seek to understand how they are like others.

Those who are Extraverted (see Chapter 3: Big 5/FFM) are outgoing and exhibit a lot of positive feelings and gregariousness, while those low in this dimension are more private and reserved and less apt to personally share or reach out to others.

Multicultural teams must manage a more complex fabric of issues than monocultural teams as they form. The familiar patterns of compatibility are layered by an array of cultural differences and values. For example, simple things that individuals take for granted in a homogeneous group—such as common norms related to pacing of speech, use of silence, and type of emotional expression—may not be present.

Cultural differences related to Individualism-Collectivism (see Chapter 2) are crucial here. Erez and Earley (1993) note that self-enhancement for members of Individualistic cultures (North America, Great Britain, Australia, The Netherlands) motivates individuals toward personal and individual achievement. The self is differentiated from the group. Team members with these values often find the joining-up process hard and may prefer to work by themselves. They want to get right to the task, and consider time spent on developing relationships wasted.

People in Collectivist cultures (Asian, African, Latin American) stress similarities and connectedness; their concept of self is interdependent. Erez and Early (1993) note that they seek similarities in order to strengthen group identity. Self-enhancement for members of Collectivist cultures motivates individuals to contribute to the success of the group, to avoid social loafing (not doing one's share of the work), and to meet the expectations of significant others. Team members from these societies often assume that the group has a higher value than individual needs and preferences, and consider it important to spend time connecting both during and outside of team meetings.

Membership in one-up/one-down groups (see Chapter 3) can also impact the team. Team members of one-up status in the society and/or organization are easily included. They may be unaware of the complexities and assume that all should conform to their norms. This is particularly true if they predominate numerically. Familiar patterns may emerge. They may take charge, initiate procedures, and do much of the talking. They may be unaware that norms they take for granted such as pacing of speech, jokes, use of analogies and metaphors, and type of emotional expression may not be effective for all. They may make assumptions about hidden identities—for example, assuming that all are heterosexual and using language that excludes gays and lesbians. A participant who is a nonnative speaker of the dominant language may appear to have no difficulty, but may find it strenuous to keep up with the pace of communication.

Members of one-down groups may be angry at attempts to push conformity. They may be consciously or unconsciously excluded. They want to be included, but wonder what the price of membership is. If they are an "only" (the only one of their group on the team), this feeling is exaggerated. They may be struggling with the cost of relinquishing their cultural norms, language, and communication style in order to be accepted. One-down group members may need longer to develop trust since they may have been excluded in the past, or their ability may have been questioned, and they are wondering if the same thing will occur on this new team. For example, a lesbian may feel she needs to guard this identity until she is sure she can be safe and accepted.

If there is a group numerical majority, members who are minority often take a low participatory role either to observe the behavior and attitudes of dominant status members and ascertain their own safety, or, if they are new to the country, to understand the cultural norms. Members of majority and one-up groups may attempt to include others in their participation, but their actions may not be appreciated since they do not fully understand the perceptions, values, and cultural behavioral patterns of members of the minority or one-down groups. For example, North Americans may not understand the preference of many Asians to hold back on participation and speak only if something important needs to be said, and to allow intervals of silence. Also, nonnative speakers can be hesitant to participate.

Virtual teams are at a disadvantage because they do not have the regular face-to face social contacts they need to develop relationships that are so important for building trust (Lipnack and Stamps 1997; Noble 2004; Ratcheva and Vyakarnam 2001). It is desirable to have an initial face-to-face meeting with some informal time such as a dinner and evening activity to develop these relationships. If this cannot be arranged, Noble suggests that a virtual relationship-building activity should be arranged. This might include, for example, everyone creating a symbol that personally represents them in some way. These can be arranged on a screen, and in a virtual meeting, members can explain why they chose their images. Similarities and differences are then shared. Members can build one-on-one relationships through phone calls or emails with each other, since they do not have the opportunity for informal contacts such as breaks or hanging around the water cooler.

The team needs to resolve the following questions:

- Who are we in this group?
- What do we want/need to know about each other?
- Can we trust each other?
- What is the price of membership?
- How are we alike?
- Can differences be accepted?
- How can we all fit in and be included?
- How can we establish common communication methods?

Task Issues

At this stage it is important to agree on the team's purpose and establish clear goals. The work of the team needs to be compelling and challenging. All need to be committed to it. For a multicultural team, a compelling goal that transcends individual differences is even more crucial than it is for a monocultural group. With the recent popularity of teams, many times organizations, in their zeal to join the popular team movement, create teams that have no common purpose or real reason for being interdependent. A basketball team needs to work together more than a bowling team. A group of teachers in primary school, for example, could function independently, each one teaching the students in their own classroom. If they have a need to share resources and skills, integrate curriculum, and understand previous experiences of students, they would have a reason to become a team.

Although it is generally taken for granted who is a part of the team, this is not always true. There may be levels of inclusion and different stakeholders that need to be clarified. Noble (2004) notes this is particularly true for virtual teams where there may be core, extended, and ancillary members. It is important to clarify who will be fully accountable for the results and how others will contribute. Identifying skills of individual members is also important. Role clarity and clear expectations have been noted to be important for successful virtual teams (Lipnack and Stamps 1997). Assumptions and stereotypes may exist about roles members should take in accomplishing the work. For example, the team may assume that Asian Americans can be good technicians but not good leaders.

Little work gets done at this stage, and that which is accomplished is often not of good quality. If decisions are made, they are often rushed, and represent the thoughts of the dominant cultural group. At this stage it is important to experience some success with a short, doable task.

The team needs to resolve the following questions:

- What is our overriding purpose?
- Who is on this team?
- Do we have the needed competencies (knowledge, skill, awareness) to do the work?
- Do we need to negotiate for the needed resources?

Leadership Issues

Leadership is critical to creating an environment that is either inclusive or exclusive. When leadership fails to address inclusion needs, the team will not achieve the level of trust necessary to move successfully past infancy. It is also essential that the leader see that the team has a purpose and goals to which it is committed. Team members are uncomfortable if there is lack of clarity about leadership at this stage. Teams with established leaders face less difficulty than self-managed teams. In self-managed teams, leadership tasks need to be identified and distributed. Multicultural teams often follow a path of least resistance and form around the leadership of members of the dominant culture. With the dynamic of social conformity and politeness typical of this stage, members may overtly go along even if leadership is not providing effective task and relationship behavior.

Group members from High Power Distance cultures in Asia and Latin America can become more uncomfortable with unclear leadership than those in Low Power

Distance cultures (North America and Europe). Additionally, members from High Power Distance may be uncomfortable with leaders who are the same age or younger than they are. In a study of Taiwanese and Australian workers, researchers (Harrison et al. 2000) found that the Taiwanese were uncomfortable with leaders who were not their seniors, while Australians found expertise and knowledge to be more important.

The team needs to resolve the following questions:

- Who is in charge here?
- What type of leadership style do we want?

Issues Resolved and Competencies Needed

When the issues at this stage have been successfully resolved, the group has developed an overriding purpose with a clear goal to which members are committed. Task and member competencies are clear, and a short-term, doable task has been achieved. All feel included and valued in the group. The competencies listed below can help a group successfully face the challenges of this phase. If there is not a formal leader, members should assume both member and leadership behaviors.

- Member competencies needed
  - Asking open-ended questions
  - Listening without making assumptions and judgments
  - Disclosing one's needs appropriately
  - Using inclusive communication patterns
  - Observing group patterns of communication
- Leadership competencies needed
  - Helping the group to articulate its purpose and overriding goal
  - Maintaining equity and being fair
  - Facilitating discussions
  - Intervening to include all

Storming

Climate

During this stage, politeness wears off and members start to disagree. Conflict may bristle openly or it may be subtler and hide under the surface. Implicit norms related to roles, communication, and decision making that emerged during the forming stage get challenged. The morale may be low, and little work gets done. The more time that the team took in the initial forming stage to develop commitment to a common goal, include everyone, and develop relationships, the easier this stage can be. Sometimes the team experiences this stage more as a light shower than a full-blown storm. And sometimes, as in a thunderstorm, the air is clear and fresh after what has been brewing for a while is expelled. There can be rainbows. The important task in this stage is to find ways of working with differences in personality and task accomplishment. Maples' (1988) research describes this stage as Conflict, Concern, Confrontation, and Criticism.

The following behavior is characteristic:

- Task productivity is low
- Disagreement over purpose and goals/objectives emerges
- Leadership is challenged
- Struggles surface around differences
- *I/me* is used more than *we/us*
- Norms previously developed are challenged
- Competition and power struggles occur
- Previous biases, lack of inclusion, and assumptions are confronted
- Subgrouping by social-cultural identity group can occur

Relationship Issues

The team now faces issues of difference of personality, social identity, and culture that affect work styles, communication, and managing conflict. Members speak in terms of *I/me* more than *we/us*. Conflict may be overt or covert. A conflict about how to approach a task may really be about a relationship issue where one team member is working out his or her own covert concern about wanting more recognition on the team.

Much research has documented that people feel more comfortable, safe, and trusting in homogeneous groups (Schneider 1997; Tsui et al. 1992; Brief 1998 in Foldy 2004; Cox 1994). This dynamic can contribute to more conflict. Additionally, there are individual and cultural differences in styles of conflict. While someone high on Agreeableness (see Chapter 3: Big 5/FFM) may be working to harmonize, a member who is low in this personality characteristic may be concerned with his/her own personal priorities and challenge the group. Those from Neutral cultures (see Chapter 2), where indirect communication is valued, may not want to express differences directly, creating a win-lose situation, whereas others from Affective cultures, where direct communication is valued, are ready to deal more openly with conflict in either a competitive (win-lose) or collaborative (win-win) style. The team needs to understand different preferences for giving and receiving feedback and managing conflict. Then it needs to develop norms that are effective for all. Giving and receiving feedback and styles of conflict are discussed more thoroughly in Chapters 7 and 8.

Expression of emotions also differs. It may be hard to interpret emotions cross-culturally. In some cultures, facial expression rarely changes with changing emotions. Women may show frustration or anger by crying, and this may be difficult for a man to experience.

In multicultural teams, group members who are in the minority numerically or in one-down positions may have been ignored or excluded in the Forming stage. They may have been unintentionally excluded because they do not share the same jokes, language, style of communicating, social habits, or work style. In the Storming stage they may express the impact of previous exclusion. They may have felt pressure to conform in order to be a member of the team, but have experienced anxiety and stress.

If members of one-down groups form relationships among themselves, they could be accused of sub-grouping and not becoming a part of the team. Their participation may be ignored due to covert or unconscious feelings of superiority of members of one-up groups, or unwillingness to accept members who are breaking the traditional demographics of the team. This may trigger anger in members of one-down groups since it is apt to repeat a pattern of exclusion in daily life.

Those in one-up groups or who are in the majority numerically may have been unaware of tensions keenly felt by others. They may have been challenged to change behavior because of the new members on the team, but they often do not feel they need to change.

The team needs to resolve the following questions:

- How can we differ and disagree in a way that maintains the respect and dignity of all?
- How can we give and receive feedback?
- How can we understand the difference between intent and impact of non-inclusive language and behavior?
- How can we work with individual and cultural differences in conflict styles?
- How is power and influence distributed?

Task Issues

At this stage, a team needs to assess how realistic the goals are and develop a work plan to achieve them. Whereas the task in the previous stage focused on what the team is to do, now the team needs to focus on how to do it. Tasks need to be defined, standards set, and methods of benchmarking progress identified. A decision-making process needs to be established. Although multicultural teams may generate many and creative ideas, decisions are harder to reach than they are in monocultural teams due to the diversity of perspectives (Adler 2002).

Roles of members need to be specified, both drawing on competencies of team members, and allowing opportunity for learning and growth. This can cause some conflict as different personality styles emerge and members jockey for their preference on how the work should be done and what responsibilities they would or would not like to take on. Someone high in Conscientiousness (see Chapter 3: Big 5/FFM) may push to keep focused on one goal, to plan for everything, and keep organized, whereas someone low in this dimension may like things to be more flexible and prefer to be working on many projects at the same time. Openness/Intellect (see

Chapter 3: Big 5/FFM) also is significant—someone who is high in this factor may present the broad view, like changes and innovation, and resist details, whereas someone who is low would like to keep things practical and traditional.

Hofstede's Uncertainty Avoidance (see Chapter 2) can come into play here. Members from strong UA countries (Japan, Greece, Portugal, Belgium and Latin American countries) often want to have plans firm and concrete, while those from weak UA countries (Denmark, Sweden, Ireland, Singapore, Hong Kong) may be more willing to keep plans open and subject to change. Members of Individualistic cultures usually prefer to work independently on a task that can contribute to the team, while members of Collectivist cultures often prefer to work more interdependently on a particular task.

Stereotypes can creep into the process of delegation—someone who is using a second language could be seen as less capable, or someone from a different culture could be seen as not having valuable expertise. For example, an Asian may be seen as being only capable in technical matters, while a Hispanic may be seen as incapable in this.

The team needs to resolve the following questions:

- How do we do our work (tasks, roles)?
- What are our standards and expectations?
- What are our previous assumptions, biases?
- How can we work with individual and cultural differences in
  - Problem-solving and decision-making styles
  - Procedures and expectations for accomplishing task
  - Meetings

Leadership Issues

In the Storming stage, leadership is often confronted. If a member of a one-up group is the designated leader, there may be less of a challenge than if the person is in a one-down group. In a culture or organization where women have rarely been leaders, for example, a team member may bypass a female leader and go to the next level to get approval of ideas. Team members may ignore ideas of a female leader, or a man may attempt to subgroup and build a coalition to undermine the power and influence of the leader.

In self-managed teams, it may seem easy and natural to have leadership fall to, or be taken over by, a member of the one-up group. There can be a subtle, covert struggle for leadership. Women frequently assume traditional roles by supporting male leadership.

Those from High Power cultures may have a hard time with conflict over leadership in leader-led teams and may be uncomfortable with self-managed teams where leadership has not been established, is not hierarchical, and will be distributed. Leadership styles will be more thoroughly discussed in Chapter 6.

The team needs to resolve the following questions:

- What style of leadership do we want?
- Can we accept the leadership we have?

Issues Resolved and Competencies Needed

When the issues at this stage have been successfully resolved, the group has developed a way to face differences related to task accomplishment and interpersonal styles. Differences are seen as opportunities for learning and growth. Biases and assumptions are discussed and there is a way to provide feedback and manage conflict. A work plan has been developed, with standards and expectations set, and roles utilizing the skills of all established. There is agreed-upon leadership.

These are tricky waters and all members need to help identify issues and work through them. Members who are high in Emotional and Cultural Intelligence (see Chapter 3) have the ability to be aware of their own emotions and sense the emotions of others. They have the capacity to monitor and regulate their emotions. The competencies listed below can help a group successfully face the challenges of this phase. If there is not a formal leader, members should assume both member and leadership behaviors.

- Member competencies needed
  - Using inclusive language and behaviors
  - Intervening when stereotypes and noninclusive behavior surface
  - Using diverse methods of feedback and conflict transformation
  - Giving and receiving feedback appropriately
  - Managing emotional expression
- Leadership competencies needed
  - Establishing an agreed-upon work plan
  - Using mediation skills

Norming

Climate

The climate is now comfortable; issues of difference have been negotiated and members have an understanding of how they can disagree. There is apt to be a feeling of tentativeness, but energy for proceeding. Maples' (1988) research describes this stage as Cooperation, Collaboration, Cohesion, and Commitment.

The following behavior is characteristic:

- Task productivity is medium-high
- Members work interdependently
- Norms are followed most of the time
- Norms are revisited and revised as appropriate
- Differences are used to deepen relationships and enhance task productivity
- Conflicts are addressed and feedback is given appropriately
- *We/us* is used more than *I/me*
- Leaders provide coaching and support

Relationship Issues

Patching up previously conflicting relationships has reduced emotional conflict. There is a strong sense of group identity and expression of interpersonal support. *We/us* is used more than *I/me*. Differences are openly expressed, and there are agreed-upon methods for managing them effectively. Idiosyncrasies are accepted. Relationships are functional, and in many cases, very enjoyable.

The team needs to resolve the following questions:

- How close and personal do we want to be?
- How should we appreciate and support each other?
- How can we balance attention to task and relationship?

Task Issues

The team must recommit to its goals, and establish realistic norms that incorporate the needs of its diverse members. When this is accomplished, it can be highly productive, drawing on the diverse skills of all team members and no longer hindered by stereotypes and assumptions.

At the Forming stage, implicit norms are usually established. For example, some may get to the meeting late, and the group waits for 15 minutes or so. Or the norms might be more explicit such as *Start and end meeting on time*, but they might not be followed. It could be that the meetings start on time, but those who come late want to revisit decisions made. At the Norming stage, the team discusses issues that might affect time management differences such as childcare, transportation, or time orientation. The norm might be revised to indicate that the first 15 minutes are connecting time, and once the meeting starts, decisions will not be revisited.

Creating common explicit norms is more complicated in multicultural teams due to culturally different patterns of behavior regarding styles of decision making, conducting meetings, communications, and conflict management. A team will often find it easier to continue with business as usual and use norms that reflect the culture of the dominant group. This happens particularly when there is only token representation of non dominant status groups. Differences need to be addressed in a way that allows all to contribute and the team to benefit from the richness of diversity. For example, one team composed of all first-language English speakers except one finally recognized its need to slow down in order to paraphrase and summarize more frequently so this member could understand. When it adopted this norm, the team found that all benefited from increased understanding.

Norms also should address behavior and be specific, especially in multicultural groups. Words such as *polite*, for example, imply different meanings in different cultures. A Japanese group member may think it's impolite to interrupt, but a Brazilian might call this overlapping speech patterns and think of it as showing interest.

The team needs to resolve the following questions:

- What are our explicit norms around decision-making, communication, and meetings?
- How can we achieve quality?

- How can we find ways to support each other's work?
- How flexible should we be?

Leadership Issues

At this stage there is less attention to status and hierarchy. The leadership of various team members is utilized, particularly in Low Power Distance cultures. In High Power Distance cultures, the leader may use the ideas of others in decision making, while formally retaining the decision-making power. Lines of authority are followed and not circumvented as in the Storming stage. The team uses different styles of leadership, and they are all recognized and valued. For example, it recognizes and values women's experience in listening and supporting as important to team building and coaching. The leader increasingly moves to a supportive, coaching role.

The team needs to resolve the following question:

- How strong a leadership role do we need?

Issues Resolved and Competencies Needed

At the end of this stage, the task productivity is medium high, and members are working interdependently. They are committed to clear criteria for quality. Norms are explicit and followed most of the time. Differences are used to deepen relationships and enhance productivity. Members feel supported and appreciated. The following competencies are needed to maintain the new energy and move to a highly productive stage:

- Member competencies needed
  - Demonstrating support on task and in relationships
  - Recognizing individual and cultural differences in how appreciation is shown
- Leadership competencies needed
  - Reinforcing high standards for task
  - Coaching where needed

Performing

Climate

Interpersonal support and a high energy for accomplishing the task characterize this stage. Morale is high, and the work is fun and very productive. Synergy has been reached. A. G. Banet (in Casse 1982) describes synergy as "a creative combination of two elements to produce something new or greater than the sum of its parts. The conception of the human being from egg to sperm is the highest form of synergy" (p. 112). Maples' (1988) research describes this stage as Challenge, Creativity, Consciousness, and Consideration.

The following behavior is characteristic:

- Task productivity is high
- Team members are committed to the team and the task
- A high degree of interdependence is demonstrated
- Conflicts are transformed to lessons learned
- Humor is genuine
- Norms are followed consistently
- Norms are revisited and revised as appropriate
- Members are appreciated
- Flexibility and ability to cope with ambiguity are apparent

Relationship Issues

Relationship issues have been resolved. The team members genuinely enjoy each other. Banet (in Casse 1982) notes that synergy can be achieved through the use of three basic teamwork skills: active listening (truly listening, hearing all ideas, practicing empathy), supporting (building on all ideas, feeling free to take a risk and freely express oneself), and differing (avoiding oversupport; probing all ideas). These skills will be discussed more thoroughly in Chapter 7.

The multidimensionality of members is perceived, so that, for example, a gay man is not seen only as gay, a Latin American as just Latin American—the whole person is recognized. As the team has bonded personally, if a member leaves, a loss is experienced. Conversely, if a new member joins the team, members are challenged to find a way to include him or her.

The team needs to resolve the following question:

- How can we adjust to changes in membership?

Task Issues

The group has a good ability to focus on the task. The diversity that may have caused problems in decision making in the Storming stage is now beneficial. Adler (2002) finds multicultural teams that reach this stage have advantages over monocultural ones. They have increased creativity, special insights and observations, and an opportunity to rethink norms and processes that may be taken for granted in a team with less diversity. Increased creativity is particularly important on tasks that require new solutions and an expanded understanding of the problem.

The team needs to resolve the following questions:

- How can we sustain high-quality work?
- How can we incorporate changes in purpose and the external environment?
- How can we continue to provide excitement and learning?
- How do we want to celebrate our accomplishments?

Leadership Issues

At this point in a high-performing team, the role of the leader is more "back seat," particularly in cultures with Low Power Distance. A leader who has a need to become too involved in daily operations can be problematic. The leadership needs to watch for change due to change in the organization or the external environment, and to see that the team is rewarded for its accomplishments. Even leader-led teams may find it productive to move to a model of distributive leadership.

The team needs to resolve the following questions:

- How can we incorporate a process for change and renewal?
- How can we share leadership?

Issues Resolved and Competencies Needed

The team has now reached a high level of trust and is very productive. Accomplishments are regularly celebrated. The competencies listed below can help a group maintain this high performance:

- Member competencies needed
  - Adapting and changing
  - Including new members
- Leader competencies needed
  - Establishing a process for incorporating change and renewal
  - Sharing leadership

Adjourning

This stage is relevant for temporary groups such as committees, project teams, task forces, and learning/study groups. The group anticipates its end and if it has reached the performing stage, most members feel a sense of loss. Task productivity is lower than in Performing, and the focus is on wrapping things up. Robbins (2003) notes that some members are upbeat, feeling successful, while others are feeling sad over the loss of the strong interpersonal connections. Some members want to slip away without making formal closure, while others want to acknowledge and celebrate their accomplishments. Sometimes a task group will attempt to rebirth itself and form a support or friendship group. Often plans are made to continue to get together, but it seldom happens that the whole group is able to schedule this. If a reunion is attempted, it is important that the purpose is clear; the group no longer has its original purpose. Maples' (1988) research describes this stage as Compromise, Communication, Consensus, and Closure.

There are several points to consider in the application of the Five Stage Model. Although many teams find the model helpful in understanding their process, it is important to remember that the literature on team development is based on studies that have been over-represented in the therapy-group and human relations training group settings rather than teams at work. The studies have had many independent variables such as purpose, duration, and composition of the group.

Time is an important factor. Busche and Coetzer (2007) note, "Teams that exist for only a few months may well be able to complete the phase of competence and not have to grapple with interpersonal relationships to effectively complete their work and disband" (p. 192).

Moreover, the organizational context of teams is not considered. If a strong set of commonly understood task procedures and effective norms for running meetings, addressing conflict, and decision making exists within the organization, the process of team development may go more smoothly. One study of an airline cockpit crew found that three people could come together and within 10 minutes be a high-performing team (Ginnett 1990). Contrarily, in an organization where lines of authority and tasks are unclear, or there is a lack of resources, or lack of rewards for individual performance, the team may not progress through all the stages.

Finally, it is important to remember, as was stated earlier, that not all teams follow the model precisely. Teams may slip back, or may experience several stages at once. It is possible that the task and relationship issues do not progress simultaneously. Jones and Bearley (2001) have developed a model that discusses this. For example, a team may have established harmonious relationships at Stage 3, Forming, but not have resolved the task issues at Stage 2, Storming.

The Punctuated Equilibrium Model

An alternative model, the Punctuated Equilibrium Model (Gersick 1988, 1989), studied special project groups that had to complete creative products with a deadline, and found that they did not complete the traditional Tuckman stages. Instead, they experienced a punctuated equilibrium, or alternation of inertial movement and radical change. Gersick found that these groups had an initial approach to the task that she describes as *inertia* or Phase 1; this lasted until precisely halfway through the group's allotted duration. This approach was set immediately at the first meeting, and groups remained locked into it. Then the groups underwent what she calls *transition*. In a "concentrated burst of activity, groups dropped old patterns, re-engaged with their outside supervisors, adopted new perspectives on their work, and made dramatic progress" (1989, p. 276). They developed a new approach and process. The timing of the transition did not correlate to accomplishments of results; instead, it seemed to occur when members felt particularly strongly that it was time to move ahead.

The new approach carried the group through the second major phase, Phase 2, as they completed their plans created at the transition. In Phase 2, a new equilibrium or inertia was reached. Finally, there was a final burst of activity just before the deadline, which she calls *completion*. Figure 4.1 illustrates this development.

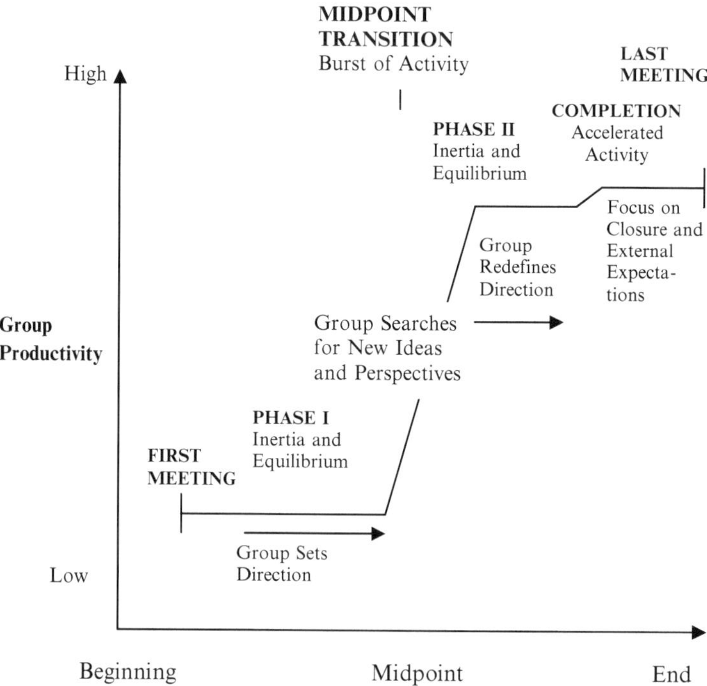

Fig. 4.1 Punctuated equilibrium model of group development adapted by C. Halverson

Team Building

Team building is an effort to increase the effectiveness of an intact team. Many effective work groups are involved in an ongoing process of renewal. A team may review its progress at the end of each meeting, discussing both what progress it made on the task, and how members felt about the interaction process. The team may assign a group member to observe group process norms. Chapter 5 presents an assessment tool which the team could use. The team may also have social events with each other occasionally, in order to increase the interpersonal fabric of their relationships.

A more formal team-building intervention involves identifying what the team does well, and issues that are hindering the team through a needs assessment. Based on the assessment, plans for improvement need to be developed. Team-building needs readiness and commitment from team members, an outside-trained consultant, and time to accomplish designated goals. It is usually more effective if it is conducted off-site for at least two days, and if follow-up is built in. It can be done on a regular basis, a few times a year, when the team is in the Forming stage, to help arrive at the Performing stage of development more quickly, and as needed when the team is in a Storming stage.

It is important for a team to have a vision of what their ideal team would look like, hopefully, early in the team's life. One technique I have often used in team building is to have each member describe their best experience with previous teams. Extrapolating from these examples, the team members can develop a visual collage of what their ideal team would look like. They may want to develop their own assessment, which they can use to check progress toward their ideal.

Both task and relationship issues are important. Team building is a good time to deepen relationships with both structured activities that allow participants to disclose more about themselves and informal time to socialize such as meals and activities. Structured activities can include values clarification, disclosing relevant information about oneself, and the use of instruments that indicate personality, work style, and conflict management preferences. Relationships may be strengthened by appreciating strengths in one another, and also by making requests that a person do more of/less of a specific behavior. These activities should lead to developing realistic norms.

Task issues that may need to be addressed include developing or clarifying a purpose statement, clarifying and negotiating roles, defining criteria for success, and developing processes for solving problems and making decisions. Follow-up sessions to check on progress are essential. Often individual conflicts may need to be addressed outside of the formal team-building session.

Beckhard (1972) advocates working on goals first and interpersonal issues last. He stated that beginning a team-building effort with work on interpersonal relationships may be a misuse of time and energy, as it is possible that problems in this area are a result of misunderstandings in other areas. Clarifying goals, roles, and responsibilities or team procedures and processes may eliminate certain interpersonal problems among team members; clarifying roles and responsibilities may in itself eliminate some of the problems with the team's working procedures and processes; and clarifying team goals and their priorities may in itself eliminate certain problems team members may have with their roles and responsibilities.

Beckhard's preference for focusing on goal clarity first may be different from other cultural preferences since it focuses on the task before relationships.

A team-building intervention in an organization located in Kenya with team members who were East Africans from several countries, Europeans, and US North Americans started out with several days of unstructured time away at a retreat center. After these days, which were used to develop relationships, the formal team-building process focusing on the task dimensions started. Imre Lövey (1996), a Hungarian management consultant, describes the use of *camp meetings* to bring Hungarians and North Americans closer together for self-managed teams in a US corporation with a site in Hungary. The idea for camp meetings, he explains, came from the Native Americans, who from time to time got together around the campfire to address major issues, make important decisions, and celebrate their accomplishments. These team camp meetings lasted two to three days and included experiential activities in which participants shared how differences and similarities between the two cultures impacted them.

Team building is usually built on the following values and beliefs:

- *Equality*: Reduced power distance between the manager and others on the team; joint responsibility for team functioning
- *Openness/explicitness*: Open discussion of problems; increased use of feedback between team members
- *Task/relationship*: Belief that a balance between task procedures and relationships is important
- *Change*: Belief that personal and organizational change can be planned and achieved

The values of openness, change, and equality of leadership, identified here, are the values of organization development (OD) consultants and are sometimes at odds with those of managers in US organizations. They are probably even more at odds with the values of managers in some other cultures. Malcolm Rigby (1989), a British OD practitioner who has worked extensively in Asia, has identified two dimensions of culture researched by Hofstede (1984) as being important to multinational team development—Uncertainty Avoidance and Power Distance. Rigby has the following suggestions to make about team building in many non-Western cultures which have a more hierarchical relationship to authority and a higher need for certainty than the USA:

- Keep data-gathering, such as interviews and questionnaires, confidential before and during team building
- Retain hierarchical relationships
- Consider holding sessions, or parts of sessions, separate from the manager to gain more openness from team members
- Provide a clear agenda, objectives, activities, and rationale to reduce ambiguity
- Provide expertise and leadership, especially at the beginning
- Use activities that promote success, not failure
- Use activities with a low level of confrontation and a wide margin of escape at first
- Subgroup with similar age, seniority, or culture for some issues

- Build in structures for equalizing communication among team members, such as the round robin method, so members who have less status have an opportunity to participate
- Ask people to describe what the session would be like if it were successful
- Monitor frequently for anxiety, confusion

Team-building sessions are designed considering data that the needs assessment shows. The data will indicate the stage the team is in. Cultural and organizational context are important. Resources for team-building activities are listed at the end of the Reference section.

Relevant Competencies

At each stage the team needs competencies related to task, relationships, and leadership. These have been identified throughout the chapter, at the end of the description of each stage.

Summary

Most teams go through several stages before they become high-performing teams. Many authors have described these stages in similar frameworks. The most common framework is Tuckman's (1965; Tuckman and Jensen 1977), which names the stages Forming, Storming, Norming, and finally, Performing—the stage at which the team is high performing. Although a team may exhibit behaviors in all stages at once, most teams are predominantly at one stage in a given period of time. Issues of task, relationship, and leadership need to be addressed at each stage so that the team can progress to the next one. In order to do this, specific member and leadership behaviors are needed. Tuckman later identified a fifth stage, Adjourning, which describes what needs to happen if the team is to disband.

If a team is functioning in a strong organizational culture that has clearly articulated and utilized process norms, the team formation process may be smooth and rapid. On the other hand, organizational challenges such as a lack of resources, unclear expectations, or lack of rewards for team efforts may make it difficult for the team to progress.

An alternative model, the Punctuated Equilibrium Model (Gersick 1988, 1989), is more appropriate for short-term special project groups that have to complete a product with a deadline. This model describes a punctuated equilibrium, or alternation of inertial movement and rapid change.

In addition to on-going attention to team processes, formal team-building sessions can enhance team effectiveness.

Case Study: The Affirmative Action/Human Development Team

As you read the case study below, consider the following questions:

- *In what stage of the Five Stage Model does the team appear to be?*
- *What are some of the relationship, task, and leadership issues the team faces?*
- *What do you think needs to be done to move this team to the next stage?*

The team, part of a US federal agency, consisted of two programs: the Affirmative Action Program and the Human Development Program (HDP). HDP referred to programs for older US. Americans, women, Native American Indians, and low-income youth. The government mandated these programs. The leader of the team, Sam, reported to Ed, the division director. The agency was currently experiencing layoffs.

The team consisted of the following persons:

- *Sam, team leader - an African American male in his early 40's. He was the only person among 40 people at his level that was not a Euro American male. Sam had recently had a heart attack due to work stress.*
- *Maria, program leader - a Latina woman in her late 30's who had been with the unit about six months.*
- *Ruth, program leader - a Euro American woman in her late 30's*
- *Ellen, program leader - a Euro American in her late 40's who had previously held a clerical position*
- *Jeff, program leader - a Euro American male in his early 40's*
- *Sarah, secretary - an African American woman in her late 20's*

A consultant had been contracted by Sam to conduct team building. Initial discussion with Sam indicated that he believed the team was not performing as well as it could, and that there were some interpersonal problems. He indicated that he wanted to know what he should be doing better. Sam had discussed the idea of a team retreat with team members in order to work on becoming more effective. The consultant conducted a needs assessment that included individual interviews with each member of the team, a written questionnaire completed by each member, and a review of team documents including purpose and job descriptions. The results of the needs assessment are described below.

Most team members thought that the rest of the agency did not value the purpose of the team. In fact, the purpose of the team was seen differently by those on the Affirmative Action Program and those on the Human Development Program. The government mandated the programs. In particular, Ed, the division director, was seen as having no commitment to issues of race or gender. He was also seen as an incompetent administrator with sporadic bursts of demands for work that must be produced in a certain way. The team thought he had impossible timelines *and that the procedures did not make sense.*

Generally, people in the unit had little faith in Sam. They thought he was not strong enough in dealing with Ed, the division director. They used words like "task master," "driven," and "authoritarian" to describe Sam's management style. People sometimes circumvented Sam and went to Ed, his boss, when they did not get the answer they wanted from him. Sam was in the field frequently, and during this time, his boss would often make demands of the team. When Sam returned, he would have a lot of demands waiting for him, and he would be unaware of what had happened between Ed and the team. Sam was feeling pressure because of the huge workload, and lack of support from Ed. Sam thought that because he was the only person of color at his level, people were watching him to see if he would be able to be successful. Some team members were concerned about his use of English, which they thought had too much "Black English."

Jeff, in particular, seemed to be quite angry with Sam. He thought Sam did not think he was doing his job well. He was annoyed when Sam would give him work to do and then take it away because he thought Jeff was not doing it right. People on the team thought there was much tension between Sam and Jeff. They believed this was partially due to the fact that Sam had previously had Jeff's job in the Human Development unit, and Sam interfered too much with Jeff's work. They also believed Sam lacked an understanding of and interest in their work, particularly those in the Affirmative Action Program.

Jeff was seen as creative. His job, however, involved much detail work. Sam said he frequently had to do Jeff's work for him because he would not get right to the point; he would take some work that was just matter-of-fact and blow it up into a big, involved project. Sam also thought that Jeff was undermining his position by going around him to Ed, Sam's boss, and even spreading rumors about Sam's competency to others. At one time, Sam discussed some of his concerns with Jeff, but thought he didn't get anywhere. Sam believed Jeff had some problems with authority with him. He thought Jeff had difficulty accepting an African American as his boss.

Jeff liked to talk a lot, and others were concerned they could not get their work done. They tried to avoid getting in a conversation with him, except for Ruth, with whom he spent a lot of time discussing work projects. Sam felt these discussions did not look good; people who passed by from other departments would think the unit was not working. Jeff thought his abilities were not being used and that Sam was out to get him. He was very concerned about getting laid off due to reductions in the workforce.

Maria, who was new, was concerned that there was so much tension in the team. Her previous work experience for the agency in other parts of the country had been satisfying—productive and harmonious. Others saw her as energetic and able to get along easily with everyone. She commented that she had enjoyed socializing with people she worked with before coming to the team, and that she missed that.

Sam saw Ellen as capable of moving up in the organization. She was in charge when he was away. She seemed to have no conflicts with others, and was very motivated and eager to perform. She had moved from a clerical position to program leader, and was very interested in her work.

Ruth and Jeff liked to work on projects together. Sarah saw Ruth as uncooperative and rude. One example was when Sarah kept knocking on the door to get into the office, and Ruth would not get up to open it. Ruth, for example, would not answer the phone when Sarah was away from her desk, even though Ruth's desk was next to Sarah's. Ruth was not very interested in putting out much effort in her work. She was looking for another job.

Sarah did not say much in her interview and seemed somewhat angry with the team. The workload seemed huge to Sarah, and she was annoyed that she would sometimes get work from team members instead of from Sam. She was supposed to be his secretary, and the others were supposed to use another secretary from the agency pool. The agency had gone to a new computer system, for which she had taken a short training. Sarah and others saw the system as problematic.

Sam was concerned about Sarah's ability to perform and to learn the computer system. Her position was a considerable upgrading from her previous one in the agency. He found out later that she had misrepresented herself on the application, and that she did not have the experience and skills she had claimed. Additionally, Sarah had difficulty interacting with the leader of the secretarial pool when she brought work from the unit to Sarah. Team members felt trapped between the boss's demands for work, and the tie-up in the secretarial pool. Work seemed to get delayed and lost. Team members felt that Sarah was away from her desk too much, and they did not know what she was doing during these periods.

Multicultural Team Assessment

Each member should complete the form individually, and then the scores should be tallied.

Goals

1. Members are committed to the purpose and the goals of the team.

Very much				Not at all
5	4	3	2	1

2. Members share common values, beliefs, and assumptions about their work.

Very much				Not at all
5	4	3	2	1

3. Members have clear and high expectations about standards of work.

Very much				Not at all
5	4	3	2	1

4. Members feel proud of their work output.

Very much				Not at all
5	4	3	2	1

Roles

5. The team has the essential skills and abilities to accomplish its work.
Very much Not at all
5 4 3 2 1

6. All team members do what it takes to get the work done.
Very much Not at all
5 4 3 2 1

7. Work is organized and implemented in a way that helps get it done efficiently.
Very much
5 4 3 2 1

8. Members are able to grow and develop skills by learning from each other.
Very much Not at all
5 4 3 2 1

9. Members are satisfied with the way leadership is handled.
Very much Not at all
5 4 3 2 1

Procedures

10. Clear norms are established which are based on an understanding of individual and cultural differences.
Very much Not at all
5 4 3 2 1

11. Information that is important for doing the work is shared so that all can understand.
Very much Not at all
5 4 3 2 1

12. Meetings are effectively managed.
Very much Not at all
5 4 3 2 1

13. Diverse perspectives are utilized to improve decisions; decisions are made when fully supported.
Very much Not at all
5 4 3 2 1

14. Conflicts among members are effectively managed utilizing appropriate styles of conflict management.
Very much Not at all
5 4 3 2 1

15. Members are able to give and receive feedback constructively.
Very much Not at all
5 4 3 2 1

Interpersonal Relations

16. All members feel included in and supported by the team.
Very much Not at all
5 4 3 2 1

17. Members understand and respect cultural and individual differences.
Very much Not at all
5 4 3 2 1

18. Members enjoy each other and have fun working on the team.
Very much Not at all
5 4 3 2 1

19. Members trust each other.
Very much Not at all
5 4 3 2 1

20. List 5 words that describe your team climate.

Scores of 4 and 5 indicate a high performing team. The team should discuss any items which show a range of 3 points or where there are scores of 2 or 1. Items are related by stage as follows:
Forming: 1, 2, 5, 16, 17
Storming: 14, 15
Norming: 3, 6, 7, 8, 9, 10, 11, 12, 13
Performing: 4, 18, 19

References

Adler, N. (2002). *International Dimensions of Organizational Behavior* (4th ed.). Cincinnati, OH: Southwestern.

Bales, R.F. and Strodtbeck, F.L. (1951). Phases in Group Problem-solving. *Journal of Abnormal and Social Psychology*, *46*, 485–495.

Beckhard, R. (1972). Optimizing Team-Building Efforts. *Journal of Contemporary Business*, *1*(3) 23–32.

Bion, W.R. (1959). Experiences in Groups. New York: Basic Books.

Bushe, G. and Coetzer, G. (2007). Group Development and Team Effectiveness. *Journal of Applied Behavioral Science 43*(2).

Casse, P. (1982). *Training for the Multicultural Manager*. Washington, DC: SIETAR.

Cox, T. (1994). *Cultural Diversity in Organizations*. San Francisco, CA: Berrett-Koehler.

Ely, R. and Thomas, D. (2001). Cultural Diversity at Work. *Administrative Science Quarterly*, *46*, 229–273.

Erez, M. and Earley, P.C. (1993). *Culture, Self-Identity and Work*. New York: Oxford University Press.

Foldy, E. (2004). Learning from Diversity: A Theoretical Exploration. *Public Administration Review 65*(5) 529–538.

Francis, D. and Young, D. (1979). *Improving Work Groups: A Practical Manual for Team Building*. San Diego, CA: University Associates.

Gersick, C.J.G. (1988). Time and Transition in Work Teams: Toward a New Model of Group Development. *Academy of Management Journal*, *31*, 9–41.

Gersick, C.J.G. (1989). Marking Time: Predictable Transitions in Task Groups. *Academy of Management Journal*, *32*(2), 274–309.
Ginnett, R.C. (1990). The Airline Cockpit Crew. In J.R. Hackman (Ed.), *Groups That Work (and Those That Don't)* (pp. 444–447). San Francisco, CA: Jossey-Bass.
Harrison G., McKinnon, J., Wu, A. and Chow, C. (2000). Cultural Influences on Adaptation to Fluid Workgroups and Teams. *Journal of International Business Studies*, *31*(3), 489–505.
Hofstede, G. (1984). Motivation, Leadership, and Organization: Do American Theories Apply Abroad? In D.A. Kolb, I.M. Rubin and J.M. McIntyre (Eds.), *Organizational Psychology*. Englewood Cliffs, NJ: Prentice-Hall.
Jones, J.E. and Bearley, W. (2001). Facilitating Team Development: A View from the Field. *Group Facilitation*, *3*, 56–64.
Lipnack, J. and Stamps, J. (1997). *Virtual Teams*. New York: Wiley.
Lövey, I. (1996). Culture Changes and Team Building in Hungary. In M. Berger (Ed.), *Cross-Cultural Team Building*. New York: McGraw-Hill.
Maples, M.F. (1988). Group Development: Extending Tuckman's Theory. *Journal for Specialists in Group Work*, *13*(1), 17–23.
Moosbrucker, J. (1988). Developing a Productivity Team: Making Groups at Work Work. In W. B. Reddy and K. Jamison (Eds.), *Team Building* (pp. 88–97), Alexandria, VA: NTL Institute for Applied Behavioral Science.
Noble, S. (2004). Starting up a Virtual Team. *Link & Learn E-Newsletter*. Retrieved January 31, 2005 from http://www.linkageinc.com/company/news_events/link_learn_enewsletter/archive/2004/02_04_oble_virtual_team.aspx
Osburn, S.D., Moran, L., Musselwhite, E. and Zenger, J. (1990). *Self-directed Work Teams: The New American Challenge*. Homewood, IL: Business One Irwin.
Ratcheva, V. and Vyakarnam, S. (2001). Exploring Team Formation Processes in Virtual Partnerships. *Integrated Manufacturing Systems*, 12/7/2001, 512–523.
Rigby, M. (1989). *The Challenge of Multi-National Team Development* (unpublished document).
Robbins, S. (2003). *Organizational Behavior*. Upper Saddle River, NJ: Prentice-Hall.
Schutz, W. (1984). *The Truth*. Berkeley, CA: Ten Speed.
Schutz, W.C. (1971). *Here Comes Everybody*. New York: Harper & Row.
Tuckman, B.W. (1965). Development Sequence in Small Groups. *Psychological Bulletin*, 384–399.
Tuckman, B.W. and Jensen, M. (1977). Stages of Small Group Development Revisited. *Group and Organizational Studies*, *2*, 410–427.
Varney, G.H. (1991). *Building Productive Teams: An Action Guide and Resource Book*. San Francisco, CA: Jossey-Bass.
Weber, R. (1982). The Group: A Cycle from Birth to Death. In *Reading Book for Human Relations Training* (pp. 68–71). Alexandria, VA: NTL Institute for Applied Behavioral Sciences.
Weber, R. (2002). The Group: Opportunity and Reality. In *Transforming Interpersonal Relationships* (pp. 107–112). Alexandria, VA: NTL Institute for Applied Behavioral Sciences.
Woodcock, M. and Francis, C. (1980). Team building: Yes or No. In W.W. Burke (Ed.), *Trends and Issues in OD: Current Theory and Practice*. San Francisco, CA: Jossey-Bass.

Resources

Casse, P. (1982). Training for the Multicultural Manager. *Training and Research* (Chapter 4). Washington, DC: Society for Intercultural Education.
Eitington, J. (1996). *The Winning Trainer*. Houston, TX: Gulf Publishing.
Gardenswartz, L. and Rowe, A. (1994). *Diverse Teams That Work*. Chicago, IL: Irwin.

Hackman, R. (1990). *Groups That Work (and Those That Don't)*. San Francisco, CA: Jossey-Bass.
Francis, D. and Young, D. (1979). *Improving Work Groups: A Practical Manual for Team Building*. San Diego, CA: University Associates.
Johnson, D.W. and Johnson, F.P. (1991). *Joining Together: Group Theory and Group Skills*. Boston, MA: Allyn & Bacon.
Myers, S. (1996). *Team Building for Diverse Work Groups*. San Francisco, CA: Jossey-Bass.

Chapter 5
Group Process and Meetings

Claire B. Halverson*

We all went to the same different meeting together.
–Marvin Weisbord quoting Jim Maselko, at ODN Conference

Introduction

In any culture or organization there may be effective or ineffective meetings. There often are individual perspectives on what happened during a meeting and how effective it was, as illustrated by the quote above. It is not unusual to find subgroups of people rehashing a meeting after it has ended, offering criticisms they did not voice during the meeting. Although at the meeting the discussion addressed the content of such issues as problems to be solved, work to be coordinated, or progress on projects, team members were most likely also noticing the process of how discussions were conducted.

Many teams do not overtly discuss the process that is used to accomplish a task. Particularly in multicultural teams, where there are differing beliefs, assumptions, and values that impact how people behave and how they think others should behave, it is important to be aware of group process. Those who are aware of the process may then be able to intervene to improve the group's effectiveness. This will help move covert processes to more overt and intentional ones. This chapter will discuss principal components of small-group process: leadership, communication, conflict, and problem solving. The four chapters that follow will each focus on one of these components.

The chapter will also discuss roles and behaviors of team members, and describe procedures for effective team meetings.

* The author wishes to acknowledge the research provided by Anitra Ingham for the sections on Power and Group Process, and Components of Team Process.

C.B. Halverson and S.A. Tirmizi (eds.), *Effective Multicultural Teams: Theory and Practice,*

Learning Objectives

After reading this chapter, you should be able to:

- Define group process
- Describe covert processes and the reasons for them
- Describe power dynamics in group process
- Identify individual functional and dysfunctional roles and behaviors
- Describe factors that are important for effective meetings

Overt and Covert Group Process

In any interpersonal or group interaction there are always two things happening simultaneously: content and process. Content is the *what*, or the task of a team. Process is *how* it is being discussed. For example, in a firefighting team, the content is about what equipment should be used, and where and how to rescue individuals. The process is who is giving directions, who is responding, the speakers' tones of voice, the pace and rhythm of the communication, and nonverbal communication. In a team of human resources managers from Japan and the United States in a multinational corporation, the content could be about methods of performance review and managerial development. The process would involve the same issues mentioned for the firefighters, with the added complication of differing cultural assumptions. These assumptions could lead to unexpressed emotional reactions related to both the communication process and the content of performance review and managerial development.

One can think of content/process as an iceberg with only one-eighth of what is happening, the content, above the water, and seven-eighths, the process, below. As with a steamship when it encounters an iceberg, it is the seven-eighths of group process below the water that is the most dangerous. What is not seen can cause damage. It is often not discussed, or brought above the surface, and therefore people can leave a meeting with different understandings and feelings about what went on. This underwater or covert process usually is not helpful, although, as explained below there are times when it might be strategic.

Covert processes derive from behaviors and beliefs that are not, or cannot be, openly discussed in team meetings. Marshak and Katz (1997) posit that something is likely to become covert when

> untested assumptions, beliefs, or constructs are limiting either reasoning or choice; the basis of the covert dynamic is in the unconscious or shadow of the individual, group or organization, or, behaviors, thoughts or feelings are defined by the prevailing rules, norms, and/or culture as inappropriate, unacceptable or out-of-place (p. 33).

They describe three dominant types of covert processes, which arise in the following circumstances:

- *Blind Spots and Blocks*. Members of the team are not able to think "outside of the box"; they are controlled by their beliefs, assumptions, values, and paradigms. They may be constrained because "this is the way we've always done it." An outside consultant or observer may wonder why they seem so constrained when the answer is clear. To the observer "it may appear as if everyone is trying to push open a door that is locked, while simultaneously ignoring a nearby window" (p. 34). For example, a team delivering a study abroad program may not discuss the implications of changes in passport requirements. If anyone suggests they revise procedures, he or she is challenged.
- *Unconscious or Shadow Dynamics*. The behavior of the team is influenced by collectively repressed or projected emotions, desires, or needs. Teams often operate as if everything is fine when there is physical, emotional, or psychological danger, behaving as if the danger does not exist. Higher values and creativity that could be sources of energy and high performance are untapped. For example, a team operating a soup kitchen in an area hit by a hurricane may minimize the dangers involved.
- *Conscious Disguises and Concealments*. Some or all members of the group keep things closed to discussion because of the prevailing culture of the group—certain beliefs, rules, or norms are considered unacceptable or out-of-place. There are two subcategories of this type:

  – *Protective Disguises and Concealments*. These are used when some or all members of a group are afraid of raising certain issues because of fear of harm. This is especially common in teams where there is a high degree of suspicion. For example, a team member could hide a "wild idea" or creative vision for fear of criticism. One way to manage this type of covert process in teams is to create a team climate that is supportive of "wild ideas" and respectful of a truly diverse array of viewpoints.
  – *Strategic Disguises and Concealment*. These are used to gain some advantage or goal. When cultures have different norms and values, they are sometimes used for strategic advantage. For example, North Americans want to work through conflict as rapidly as possible, whereas other cultures such as the Chinese engage in conflict regularly, enjoy it, and have procedures for managing it as part of normal business transactions (Nadler et al. 1985). The North American propensity to resolve conflict quickly could be used as an advantage by the Chinese team members.

Have you ever thought any of these covert processes were happening on a team? Have you, yourself, ever behaved covertly?

Sometimes subgroups will meet to covertly frame a discussion in order to have their idea approved. They may meet to anticipate types of resistance and plan how to respond. Members of an ongoing subgroup may support each other consistently, rather than considering the substance of their teammates' ideas. In multicultural teams, subgroups may form around demographics such as gender, nationality, or "race"/ethnicity.

Diagnosing covert processes is an art form that is developed by understanding the many factors that can lead to them: organizational context, team history, cultural perspectives, and the dynamics of one-up/one-down relationships. One clue that something covert is going on is when you sense something is going on but you cannot figure out what it is. It is crucial that team members recognize their own covert behaviors and the reasons for them, and assess whether or not it is to the team's advantage that they reveal them. In multicultural teams, it may or may not be appropriate to discuss what is "under the water." Members who are from cultures that are diffuse may be more uncomfortable with such directness (see Chapter 2). Much will depend on the norms that are established within the team.

Power and Group Processes

Power has been the subject of numerous studies that cross disciplines, including sociology, psychology, anthropology, and organizational behavior. Analysis of power and control in organizations varies based on the theoretical approach and definition of power. A common working definition of power is that it involves a relative relationship in which an actor is able to influence another actor to act on his/her directions through position, numbers, or personal characteristics. Power differentials lead to unbalanced relationships, including dependency, which affect behavior and roles in teams (Sisaye and Siegel 1997). These differentials can include membership in one-up/one-down groups based on factors such as gender, race/ethnicity, social class, or age; relationships with other powerful people in the organization; and longevity or position in the organization.

Sisaye (2005) draws upon the work of Amitai Etzioni to analyze the use of power and members' responses in teams. Etzioni's research identified three aspects of power: normative, coercive, and utilitarian. *Normative power* is associated with symbolic rewards (e.g., prestige) and uses norms to incite positive responses from team members. Team leaders exercise normative power and practice normative decision making when making decisions by consensus. Team leaders can use *coercive power* by distributing rewards and punishment to ensure that team members comply with organizational goals. Rewards and punishment can be either material or symbolic. *Utilitarian power* refers to rational reasons why the team should follow a certain course.

Effective teams most often use normative power because exercising power coercively is not effective when decisions are supposed to be collaborative. Organizations are more effective when power and information are shared in collaborative teams (Conger 1989).

Size, organizational position, and one-up/one-down status influence the power of individual members. Within a team, groups that are larger, one-up, and have positional power are able to dominate discussions to have their opinions heard. In a predominately male team, one man may make a suggestion, another may endorse it, and all of a sudden, a decision has been made. Of course, they may have been discussing these ideas over lunch or in other places where they gather. When members of less powerful, one-down groups do give opinions, sometimes their opinions will be granted less weight, ignored, or challenged. They may form a subgroup, meeting outside the larger group to strategize methods to increase their influence (Kabanoff 1991). The two women on the team mentioned above may meet to strategize how they can be heard on the team. Methods of increasing influence such as appealing to members' sense of loyalty or moral values, will be discussed in Chapter 6.

Effective multicultural teams should strive for empowerment in order to enhance team collaboration in decision making and problem solving. As stated by Forrester (2000), empowerment implies that individuals and teams have the capacity to make decisions, not just make suggestions. In other words, empowerment means that a team has decision-making responsibility for a project. Further, empowered team members understand the relationship between the project and their organization's goals (Ford and Fottler 1995). Trust is a major component of empowerment, since leaders must have complete trust in teams to be task-oriented and to make decisions that uphold the organization's goals. Kirkman and Rosen (1999) found a positive correlation between team empowerment and outcomes such as productivity, job satisfaction and organizational commitment.

Components of Team Process

Principal components of team process—leadership, communication, conflict management, and decision making—will be outlined below and discussed more thoroughly in subsequent chapters.

Leadership

Empirical studies of differences in team processes across cultures have shown that perceptions of leadership affect team process. Perceptions of appropriate leader behavior vary significantly across cultures. Ayman and Chemers (1983) found that responsiveness to group norms explained leader behavior in Iran and Mexico, while group norms played a much smaller role for US team leaders. Similarly, Pillai and Meindl (1998) showed that charismatic (often referred to as visionary) leadership is common in collectivistic cultures. In this case, team members may have role perceptions that favor charismatic leadership. On the other hand, team members from individualistic cultures may base their roles on assigned tasks, and thereby prefer a task-oriented leader. For task-oriented leaders, a tension between behaviors that focus on individual power and the collaborative skills necessary for teamwork present a challenge.

There has been a global trend from authoritarianism to democracy, which has affected team leadership. Teams are more participatory, so that leadership is shared, and there are more self-managed teams (Burbidge 1994). Increased participation among team members requires strong leadership, which might seem paradoxical. As Rosabeth Moss Kanter (in Burbidge 1994, p. 3) notes, "It is almost a paradox. Participation requires better management than a machine-like bureaucracy. The leadership tasks may be shared or rotated, but they must be performed. And one of the leadership roles is to provide a structure for participative planning."

Team process benefits from a leader who can disseminate power, authority, and responsibility among team members rather than directing (Pfeffer and Veiga 1999). Delegating decision-making responsibility is essential for effective team process and accomplishment of tasks, but the leader needs to assess the developmental stage of the team since teams are more dependent on the leader in the forming stage. Also, team members from high-power distance or ascription- oriented cultures may lose respect for a leader who does not show sufficient direction. Leaders must have enough trust in their teams to empower them to access information, manage conflict, and make decisions (Forrester 2000).As mentioned in Chapter 1, in self-managed teams decision-making authority is turned over to the group. It has the responsibility of deciding which tasks should be carried out and how team goals will be achieved. Team members make decisions collaboratively, but often the team has an external leader who acts as a coach. Team autonomy allows members to learn from one another and make changes to team process as they see fit. It is important that the functions of leadership related to the task and the relationships of team members are clearly designated to various team members.

Communication

Multicultural teams have some advantages and potential traps in terms of team communication. They can have an advantage of increased communication, and differing perspectives, which helps creativity and generation of ideas. Milliken and Martins (1996) noted two studies in which diversity in organizational management teams correlated with more frequent communication within the team. Mutual knowledge in teams derives from such frequent and open communication. However, if team members do not share knowledge, individuals can resort to stereotypes that cause mistrust. Mutual knowledge is enhanced by setting up a decentralized communication network, or all-channel system (see Chapter 7), in which team members communicate with one another directly rather than through one team member.

Communication is essential for the development of a hybrid culture (Kopp 2005). This points to the need for meta-communication, defined as communication about the way the group communicates (Enayati 2001). By openly communicating needs, styles, and values, multicultural teams can develop a hybrid culture characterized by inclusive norms. Open communication involves stating one's needs as well as giving and receiving feedback about the impact of one's behavior on others.

Communication patterns are usually established such as who talks to whom, who supports whom, evenness of participation by team members, pacing and rhythm, pace, and circular or linear flow of ideas. It is important to watch for nonverbal clues, although the meaning may vary across cultures. For example, Japanese leave spaces between individual contributions, US Americans start as soon as the last person has spoken, and Brazilians tend to overlap on top of each other. What may be seen as polite in one culture would not seem so in another. It is important to watch for nonverbal clues such as eye contact, although the meaning may vary across cultures. Pacing is very important when there are language differences among team members. Different types of communication are needed to help the team function effectively on the task such as seeking opinions, clarifying the tasks, and creating harmony.

Virtual communication can have the advantage of slowing the discussion down and allowing greater participation, although nonverbal communication is lost. Some teams incorporate words such as *smile* or *frown* in parentheses to convey feelings.

In general, communication convergence is possible for multicultural teams, and national culture is not the most significant barrier to effective communication (Bargiela-Chiappini et al. 2003). Organizational culture and an individual's position or role has been shown to have a stronger influence on communication than national culture.

Conflict Management

Conflict can be overt or covert, and, as was mentioned earlier in the chapter, covert processes can be more destructive. Chapter 8 will discuss two types of conflict—*relationship conflict* and *task conflict*. Task conflict is more common and is related to issues such as differences in the content of important decisions that affect the work of the team, allocation of resources, and lack of role clarity. These can generally be resolved through discussion. In the forming stage, different points of view are often not addressed. Sometimes reasons for holding a point of view are related to deep-seated personal issues such as a threat to a team member's perceived status or competence, and real reasons for the difference remain covert.

Relationship conflict includes such deep-level issues as differences in values, perceived competence or status in the group, personality, and visible diversity. While the discussion of the difference may be around task issues, the covert process may be around relationship issues. In teams, visible surface-level diversity in areas around which there are societal one-up/one down status differences can increase relationship conflict (Pelled 1996). Studies have found that diversity in gender, race, ethnicity, and ability can aggravate relationship conflict (Jehn et al. 1999; Pelled et al. 1999; Iles 1995).

When there is common commitment to an overriding purpose for the team, which occurs in the forming stage, diversity is less apt to cause conflict (Jehn et al. 1999). When the team has developed norms related to decision making, coordination, communication, conflict management, and leadership, deep-level diversity issues are less of a problem (Mohammed and Angell 2004; Harrison et al. 2002). After sufficient trust and norms about openness have been developed, conflicts can be discussed openly and managed more effectively. Thus, there is both *preemptive* conflict management—preventing conflict by establishing a team climate of flexibility and compromise—and *reactive* conflict management—addressing conflicts after they occur (Marks et al. 2001).

Problem Solving and Decision Making

As teams approach problems, individual members can be defining the problem differently and a common definition of the problem is not clear. Once the problem is defined, alternative solutions need to be generated and their advantages and disadvantages discussed. The trap here is to not decide on a solution before a range of alternatives has been generated. Both who makes the decision and how it is made are important elements of this process. There is a range of methods for making the decision such as voting, consensus, and railroading that are discussed in Chapter 9. Sometimes teams continuously bring up problems, but no decision is made about the solution. Therefore, the status quo remains, and a decision is made by default. Other times, the perception of the decision that has been reached varies among team members.

Diverse perspectives are advantageous for decision-making processes. Team members with diverse perspectives can provide the team with alternative views on the team's task and strategies. Thus, diverse teams have great potential for enhanced performance and productive decision making (Enayati 2001). Diverse teams must be aware of the potential for social influence, even when problem solving and decision making are participatory. Participatory decision making, with all members involved in the decision-making process, reinforces individual commitment. Yet, power complicates this process. Decision making is not just rational information gathering; rather, decision making can reflect covert power disparities within the team (Enayati 2001). Social influence is another way of expressing power differentials between team members. Social influence privileges the ideas and input of more powerful team members. Research on decision-making processes has shown that formal procedures can decrease social influence (Enayati 2001). If some team members feel that their input or interests have been ignored in the decision-making process, conflict can arise. Team norms on decision making can help prevent conflict caused by social influence.

Formal and Informal Roles in Teams

Teams have both formal roles relates to jobs and responsibilities, and informal roles related to the team process.

Formal Roles

According to a study by Morrison (1994), cooperative team behavior depends on the way that team members define their team roles. Trust is a major factor in how team members view their roles and the roles of others. In a team where conditional trust is the norm, team members base their roles on expected team roles and behaviors. In teams characterized by unconditional trust, members are more likely to define their roles more broadly, which leads to behaviors that fall outside of assigned team roles. In other words, in teams that share unconditional trust, individuals will assume larger roles because they are willing to diverge from their assigned roles in order to contribute to team process and performance.

A corollary of research on unconditional trust is that in collectivist cultures, team members are likely to view teamwork as less temporal and more integrated with daily life. A study by Cox et al. (1991) demonstrated that collectivistic teams behave more cooperatively than individualistic teams. Further, collectivistic teams have fewer conflicts than individualistic teams, and employ cooperative rather than competitive strategies (Oetzel 1998). Members rotate roles and understand the jobs of others so that they can work more collaboratively, and so that they can step in if a member is absent for a period of time. One's work is done when the team is done. Job descriptions are more likely to be vague, with "leaky boundaries." By contrast, in individualistic cultures, team members are likely to see teamwork as isolated to a specific time and task (Gibson and Zellmer-Bruhn 2001). Individualistic cultures are likely to have formal and specific job descriptions. When jobs are defined in this manner, team members may be more concerned with their individual role at the expense of the team goal.

The following are role-related questions that teams need to address:

- How clear are individual jobs and responsibilities?
- How much agreement/commitment is there to individual jobs and responsibilities?
- Are jobs matched to skills of team members?
- Is the overlap of job responsibilities appropriate and clear?
- Is the workload and responsibility equitable?
- Are all the tasks that need to be done accounted for?
- Is the workload manageable?
- Are the rewards sufficient and appropriate?
- Are the rewards perceived to be equitable?

On multicultural teams, cultural identity may influence perceptions and stereotypes about the role members should have, as the following examples portray.

In one team in the U.S., a Euro-American administrative assistant asked an African American secretary to serve coffee in the morning to the staff. The other staff members were extremely uncomfortable with this arrangement and asked to have the responsibility rotated or dropped.

In Japan, it is common to have "office ladies" who are college-educated serving tea, although there is now some resistance to this type of role.

A nurse from the U.S. who was working in a rural community health clinic in Latin America rejected the expertise of the local staff. They could have helped her understand the belief system in the community regarding health practices and the availability of local substances for healing.

In an agricultural project in the Sudan, the Dinkas occupied unskilled and lower-level positions and the Equatorians filled the technical positions. The project was in the north, which is Dinka land. The Dinkas, who are quite traditional in their lifestyles and orientation, have historically preferred administrative, police, and political careers as opposed to technical professions. Traditionally, they live by cattle raising and herding. They consider themselves "born to rule." The Equatorians are more educated. This role differentiation contributed to strained relationships.

Informal Roles

In addition to formal job roles, informal roles and behaviors also influence team process. Kenneth D. Benne and Paul Sheats (1948) originally developed a classification of informal member roles (behaviors) based on an analysis of participation functions in the first National Training Laboratory in Group Development. Prior to this article, the assumption was that effective group process depended on the leader. Although it was initially developed for human development learning groups, this concept has applied to work groups, or teams.

Benne and Sheats divided behaviors into *functional roles*, those behaviors related to task and maintenance of the group which help it to accomplish its task, and *dysfunctional* or *individual roles*, those which are directed toward satisfaction of the participants' needs and which are not helpful to either the group task or the effective functioning of the group. Mudrack and Farrell (1995) have developed a similar list. The original roles are modified in the list below. Each member may, of course, enact more than one role in any given time period, and over the course of time, a wide range of roles.

Functional Roles Related to Task

These roles have as their purpose the facilitation and coordination of team efforts in the selection and definition of a common problem and its solution.

- Initiating—Proposing tasks, goals of action; defining team problems; suggesting a procedure or a new way of organizing the team for the task ahead
- Information or Opinion Seeking—Requesting facts or information about the team task
- Information or Opinion Giving—Providing facts, personal experiences, opinions or information about team concerns
- Consensus Testing—Checking with the team to see how much agreement has been reached
- Summarizing—Pulling together related ideas, restating suggestions, offering a decision or conclusion for the team to consider

- Clarifying—Interpreting ideas or suggestions, clarifying issues before the team; elaborating suggestions in terms of examples and trying to deduce how an idea or suggestion would work
- Evaluating—Questioning the practicality, logic, facts, or procedure of a suggestion or of some part of team discussion; questioning the direction the group is taking
- Recording—Recording team decisions or the product of the discussion

Functional Roles Related to Maintenance

These roles describe behaviors oriented to building team and interpersonal relations, morale, and motivation.

- Encouraging—Being friendly, warm, and respectful to others; showing regard for others; offering commendation and praise and in various ways indicating understanding and acceptance of other points of view
- Expressing Group Feelings—Sensing feelings within the team and sharing feelings with other members
- Harmonizing—Attempting to reconcile disagreement; reducing tension; getting people to explore differences
- Compromising—Offering a compromise that yields status when one's own idea or status is involved in a conflict; admitting error
- Gate Keeping—Attempting to keep communication channels open; facilitating and encouraging the participation of others; suggesting procedures that permit sharing remarks
- Standard Setting—Expressing standards for the team to achieve; applying standards in evaluating team functioning and production
- Observing—Recording various aspects of the team process and feeding such data back to the team

Dysfunctional Roles

These behaviors are attempts by members to satisfy their individual needs that are irrelevant or unhelpful to the team's task, and are either not oriented, or negatively-oriented, to team building and maintenance. These roles may be conscious or unconscious. Individuals may demonstrate these behaviors due to (1) their own long-standing needs for ego gratification, focus on self at the expense of the team, or insecurity; or (2) short-term physical or emotional problems they may be facing. When there is a high incidence of these behaviors occurring in a number of participants there may be one or more team issues related to the storming stage, morale issues, inappropriate leadership style, or an inappropriate or unachievable task. This indicates a need for team building and training of members, or for redefining the task.

- Showing Aggression—Deflating the status of others; expressing disapproval of opinions, acts, or feelings of others; attacking the team or the problem it is working on

- Blocking—Being negativistic and stubbornly resistant; disagreeing and opposing without or beyond reason; attempting to maintain or bring back an issue after the team has rejected or bypassed it
- Recognition-seeking—Working to call attention to oneself whether through boasting or reporting on personal achievements; showing envy toward another's contribution by trying to take credit for it
- Withdrawing—Psychologically leaving the team; showing no interest in connecting with the people or the task
- Dominating—Interrupting the contributions of others; asserting one's own opinion frequently and forcefully; giving directions authoritatively
- Distracting—Overuse of, or inappropriate, joking, horseplay, or other forms of inappropriate behavior, which make a display of the lack of involvement

Mudrack and Farrell (1995) named dysfunctional roles the stage hog, the clown, the cynic, and the blocker.

Which of the functional roles do you most often take? Which functional roles may have been missing in a team on which you were a member? Have you behaved in a way that was dysfunctional, and if so, what led you to do this?

Use of Informal Roles

The type of task of the group may influence the need for different roles. At the initial stage of problem solving, for example, initiating, and information or opinion giving and seeking are important, while in the stage of coming to a decision, roles of consensus testing, summarizing, and evaluating are more crucial.

Traditionally, many of the functional roles or behaviors identified above are seen as the responsibility of the leader. In low-power distance (ascription-oriented) cultures, it has been traditionally assumed that the designated group leader will run the meeting by keeping to the time schedule and assuming facilitation roles related to the task. Some leaders who have had training in group process will also assume maintenance roles, such as encouraging, harmonizing, offering process comments, and drawing out those who have not expressed their views. Often, however, these roles are shared, with other members assuming some of this leadership responsibility. If this happens, the leader is more able to be an equal participant. This concept of shared leadership is discussed more thoroughly in Chapter 6. This egalitarian approach to team leadership has been traditionally encouraged by organizational behavior literature (Benne and Sheats 1948), and more recently by the move to self-managed or empowered teams (Orsburn 1990; Wellins et al. 1991).

The American Friends Service Committee uses the Quaker business meeting style, in which the power to guide the course and outcome of the meeting is widely distributed. The formal role of the clerk, which rotates among members of a work group is to introduce the business at hand and facilitate the flow of discussion. This egalitarian approach to team leadership has been traditionally encouraged by organizational behavior literature (Benne and Sheats 1948), and more recently by the move to self-managed or empowered teams (Orsburn 1990; Wellins et al. 1991).

In high power distance (achievement-oriented) cultures the role of the leader is distinct from the participants. The leader is the one with the highest amount of formal authority. If there is no one with organizational authority, the leadership falls to someone with informal authority, based on factors in the hierarchical status such as age or gender. The leader moderates the discussion. In fact, leaders may seldom speak and appear to have little influence, but their influence is in controlling the agenda and in making the final decision after others have been heard.

Observing Team Process

For a team to function effectively, it is important for all team members to develop the skill of observing team processes such as covert behaviors, communication patterns, formal and informal roles, and decision- making. This is true for both self-managed and leader-led teams. In the latter, the leader does not have the entire responsibility for the effective functioning of the team if the team operates with democratic principles; members and the leader can jointly share this. The skill of process observation is the first step in intervening to improve effectiveness, either by providing missing functional roles, or by pointing out processes to heighten the group awareness and need for intervening or revisiting group norms.

The same behavior can be interpreted differently cross-culturally. Since members usually have the tendency to judge behavior by their own cultural standards, what might seem like opinion seeking or initiating by a young US participant may be seen as dominating by someone from a culture where younger people are expected to listen to older group members, or to allow more silence between interactions. A French participant, coming from a culture where disagreement is seen as a form of engaging with another, may seem aggressive to someone from a country where harmony and non-confrontational behavior is seen as important. Lack of eye contact, a sign of respect in some cultures, might be interpreted as withdrawing in other cultures. Therefore, when noting behavior in multicultural settings, it is very important to be able to describe the behavior rather than interpret the reasons for the behavior or pass a value judgment on it.

With increasing ability to identify behaviors of team members, individuals can intervene to improve team effectiveness. The following are some examples:

- *A team member can identify functional roles that are missing and consciously supply them. For example, if many team members are giving information and opinions, a team member could summarize, or check for consensus.*
- *A process observation may lead to an appropriate intervention. For example, if the group seems stuck or tired, a team member can simply express what she thinks the group is feeling and check it out with others. The intervention might be taking a break, or it could be identifying a covert protective disguise.*
- *With increasing ability to identify dysfunctional behaviors, any individual can assess his/her capability to be an effective team member, and can modify his/her behavior to be more effective.*

- *If one is in the cultural minority in a team as for example, a Canadian working in India, one can use the skill of process observation to learn about the normative behavior of the team in order to identify what behaviors are appropriate.*

It is a learned skill to be able to focus on both the process and content, although the more strongly a member feels about a content issue, the more difficult it is to simultaneously focus on process. The following suggestions may facilitate the development of process observation skills:

- A team can adopt a norm that anyone can make a process observation.
- A team can appoint a rotating process observer who will give feedback on his/her observations to the team. The process observer can use the assessment at the end of this chapter, Process Observation Guidelines. The process observer might interject at crucial points if the team is getting stuck on decision making, for example, or the team could agree to process observations midway through a longer meeting or at the end of a meeting. After making a process observation, it is important to check with the team for understanding.
- Although individual team members may have a proclivity for certain roles more than others, the individual and the team are more effective when many members are skilled in a variety of roles and can supply them as needed. Individual team members can be assigned specific functional roles that are missing.

Meetings

Many of us spend a lot of time in team meetings. Sometimes these are productive, but often people complain the meetings are not effective or productive. *Have you experienced meetings that were ineffective and unproductive? What leads to an effective meeting?*

Effective facilitation is very important. To facilitate means "to make easier" (The Merriam-Webster Dictionary, 1998). It is *fácil* in Spanish and *facile* in French. The facilitator may or may not be the team leader. Not all leaders or managers are effective facilitators (Weaver and Farrell 1997). Self-managed teams need facilitators, at least in the early stages of the team's development. The facilitator is responsible for setting up the meeting, conducting it, and seeing that follow-up work after the meeting is done.

The necessary work for setting up the meeting includes deciding on the outcomes, determining and distributing the agenda, making sure the right people are there for the topics to be discussed, and distributing relevant reading and pre-work that should be done before the meeting. The outcomes of the meeting can be to clarify issues, share knowledge, make decisions, or convey important information which cannot be left to memos. *Have you ever been in a meeting when it was not clear what the purpose of the discussion was, when the necessary information or people were not there, or when the information conveyed could have been more effectively given by a memo?*

The agenda may be set by the facilitator, or the facilitator may ask for agenda items from the team. The facilitator may want to ask others to facilitate a portion of the meeting about a topic on which they have been working, or, during a longer retreat meeting (1 or 2 days), in order to share the responsibility. Additionally, it is not usually possible to remain neutral and successfully facilitate a discussion around a topic about which you feel passionate; when this is the case, the facilitator should ask someone who does not have this personal stake to take over.

During the meeting the facilitator needs to clarify and get agreement on the agenda, and pay attention to process and content issues. The facilitator may want to ask for help from other team members with such tasks as recording, observing process, time keeping, or summarizing outcomes. One of the most frustrating aspects of meetings can be when the same topic gets rehashed in meeting after meeting, and no decision is made. I have found it helpful to ask what the purpose of the discussion is, or to ask for a summary of what was decided. *Have you experienced this frustration? What have you done about it*? Additionally, in groups which are at the forming or performing stages, all team members will be taking responsibility for supplying functional roles as needed. Particularly after longer meetings, it is important to have an oral evaluation of the meeting at the end. A quick round of statements by each person is helpful.

After the meeting, the facilitator needs to be sure minutes are distributed and someone has been assigned to act on decisions.

Virtual meetings have particular challenges in finding a time to meet when members are in drastically different time zones, and in the fact that members are not able to see nonverbal expressions. Both virtual and face-to-face meetings can take advantage of web technologies such as a wiki, which allows visitors to easily add, remove, and otherwise edit and change available content. This can be done with decisions and meeting notes.

The following is a checklist for facilitating a meeting:

- Before the Meeting
  - Identify the hoped-for outcomes
  - Determine who should facilitate specific topics
  - Identify who should be there
  - Determine the appropriate site, time, and setting
  - Distribute the agenda
  - Arrange for any necessary preparatory work, such as providing information on a problem to be solved
- During the Meeting
  - Conduct personal check-in, introductions
  - Clarify the purpose and expected outcome
  - Develop and/or clarify and agree on the agenda
  - Clarify and/or assign roles such as facilitator, process observer, note-taker, and interpreter
  - Define norms for how the work will be accomplished
  - Maintain a balance between content (what is discussed) and process (how it is discussed)
  - List and revise any decisions, including follow-up

  - Decide what to do with agenda items that were not discussed or were unresolved
  - Evaluate the meeting

- After the Meeting
  - Act on decisions made
  - Communicate the minutes

The factors that determine a meeting's effectiveness vary across cultures. Michael Olsson (1985) identifies some factors that vary across cultures as follows:

- Leader/participant roles (leader-audience; leader-participant; facilitator-participant; participant only)
- Sequence of participation (ordered/monitored/open)
- Topic control (fixed/flexible/open)
- Decision-making process (vote/vocal assessment/consensus)
- Pace (efficient/tolerant/patient)
- Space orientation (formal rows/layered circle/loose circle/unstructured)
- Punctuality (fixed/flexible/loose)
- Language choice (prestige/common/multilingual)
- Amenities (minimal/moderate/extensive)

Orientation toward time and space affect punctuality, the scheduling of an agenda, and where a meeting is held. In low-context cultures, it is expected that meetings start exactly or within five minutes of when they are scheduled, an agenda has been developed beforehand and is adhered to, and the meeting should end on time. Topics should be separated, and people should confine their comments to the topic at hand and not get off the subject. Furthermore, meetings should be as short as possible. In order to increase efficiency, it is best to hold a meeting in a closed-off room where distractions such as other people coming by or telephone calls will not interfere. The following are some examples of this:

> *In my initial experiences in a multicultural group, I found that the high-context African American and Latino members wanted to spend the first 30 minutes of the meeting socializing, while I wanted to get on with the task. When I relaxed about my need to start on time, I found the business was completed in the time allocated. The others were more ready to work once they had connected with each other.*
>
> *A Euro American woman who had spent several years in Brazil returned to the United States for several weeks for an operation. She arrived late to a work meeting with others she had worked closely with before going to Brazil. No one stopped the meeting to acknowledge her, and she was not able to successfully link up with the task, due to her need to connect with the people.*
>
> *Meetings in high-context cultures usually start after the agreed-upon time, which gives those who arrive earlier a chance to connect with others and settle in. Others may be late because they have been unwilling to cut short another interaction. Although there may be an agenda, the discussion may actually move*

among several items simultaneously. In fact, several meetings may be going on at once. The meeting will take place in an open area, or in a room with an open door, so that others who have business can get to those who are in the meeting.

The following describes meetings in Arab cultures, which are high-context:

> Arabs prefer consultation on a person-to-person basis; they hate committee and group meetings. Arabs make decisions in an informal and unstructured manner. Some of our professional business approaches seem to them rigid and impersonal. Their heritage is not one of enclosed offices but of open spaces, tents, and generous hospitality. As a result, you may find your meeting interrupted by the constant commotion of people coming and going, telephone calls, and servants offering beverages. If you insist on a more formal style, you may be at a disadvantage (Copeland and Griggs 1985, p. 124).

Another factor that varies across cultures is the purpose of a meeting relative to decision making. Low-context, time-oriented cultures view meetings as a time to exchange information and/or to hammer out decisions. A meeting is considered successful, usually, if some decisions have been made. High-context relationship-oriented cultures often view meetings as a time to further relationships in order to accomplish the task. A meeting may be used to announce a decision when the manager has explored people's views outside the meeting. The following excerpt describes *nemawashi*, a decision-making process in Japan:

> Nemawashi ("going around the roots") is a gardening term and is translated as the necessity of digging around the root system of a tree being transplanted. The gardener makes certain that he does not kill the tree by digging into the root system. In the same way decisions must be made in such a way that members' morale does not decrease and harmonious relations are not disturbed. The process of making a decision must contribute to the workers' morale as well as solving a problem.
>
> To the Japanese executive, a meeting achieves more than a decision or the exchange of information. A meeting allows the chairperson to evaluate the emotional temperatures of those involved. Voting or making the final decision is delayed until the feelings of all of those present are expressed. A meeting is held to "go around the roots" by making sure the interests of those involved and their feelings have been considered. Within the context of teams, this involves achieving agreement for a proposed project before members meet together (Alston 1985, p. 298).

A proposal sponsor will meet informally with others, hear their concerns, and modify the proposal. Concessions are made in private since public concessions are considered a sign of weakness and no one wants to lose face publicly. Whoever has made a concession or compromise can expect a concession from the other person at a later date. The Japanese keep careful accounts of their debts and there is a net balance of mutual debts and favors. To an outsider who is unfamiliar with this process, it may seem like an iceberg, with much below the water that cannot be seen or understood.

Relevant Competencies

- Observe and describe team process
- Recognize the possibility of covert process

- Recognize functional and dysfunctional roles on a team
- Contribute functional roles to the team as needed and appropriate
- Describe power dynamics in a team
- Plan and facilitate an effective multicultural meeting

Summary

In summary, group interactions always involve both content, the *what,* and process, the *how*. Team process is not often discussed, and teams can benefit from paying more overt attention to it. Some aspects of process, however, are covert and hard to discuss. Team members may be unconscious of or blind to them, making them hard to identify. Or they may be consciously self-protective or strategic; in this case it may or may not be appropriate to discuss them. It is also important to recognize one's own covert processes, and it is also important to understand the power dynamics of a team both internally and within the organization.

Four important components of team process are leadership, communication, conflict management, and decision making.

Roles can be both formal—related to job descriptions—or informal—related to behaviors of members. Informal functional roles include those related to task and those related to process. Dysfunctional roles may be either unconscious or attempts by individual members to satisfy their personal needs. A team member skilled in diagnosing functional roles may identify some that are missing and provide them for the team.

Meetings need to be carefully planned and facilitated, taking cultural differences into account.

Case Study: A Meeting of a US School Diversity Committee Whose Members Have Different Agendas

As you read the case study below, consider the following questions:

- *What could have been done before the meeting?*
- *What functional roles were or were not demonstrated by the facilitators?*
- *What was the outcome of the meeting?*
- *What do you think should have been done after the meeting?*

I am a U.S. Euro American female teacher in an independent female K-12 school. The population of the student body is 20% minorities with the largest group being first-generation Americans whose parents came from the Indian subcontinent and are both Hindus and Moslems. The school also has a sizable Jewish population. Other minority groups represented include Latinos, African Americans, and Asian Americans.

Last year a few minority members of the faculty approached the principal with their concern that the students in the school often displayed a lack of intercultural sensitivity. The principal formed a Committee on Diversity. The committee included three African Americans, including one who is a Baha'i who is married to a Czech, four Euro Americans including one who is of Jewish background and one who has an adopted Korean daughter, two Moslems, and a Hindu.

The first meeting was short, with two purposes—to clarify the purpose of the committee and to elect a chair. The principal asked the committee to make a list of recommendations of ways in which the school community could work to enhance appreciation of our diversity. Cynthia, one of the African Americans, and I, a Euro American, were chosen to be co-chairs. In preparation for the next meeting, Cynthia invited me to her home for dinner. After socializing during dinner, Cynthia and I sat down to plan our first meeting together. We began with a lengthy discussion of the term multicultural versus the term intercultural. Based on the articles I had seen in professional journals, I thought that multicultural referred to differences in race and ethnic background, gender, religion, sexual preference, and physical ability, but intercultural included international aspects. Cynthia was concerned that including all these dimensions would dilute the issues of race and ethnicity. We did not resolve this issue. We set the agenda for the meeting and included in it a discussion of the two terms. The intent was to begin to build awareness of the immensity of our topic. I left feeling stimulated but uncertain as to whether or not we had communicated effectively with each other.

The committee meeting was held a couple of weeks later, and Cynthia and I touched base by telephone to be sure we were clear about our plans. We agreed we would share facilitation in a fluid manner and that we would share the responsibility of taking notes. At the meeting, we presented the agenda: discussion of the terms multicultural and international, and recommendations. We passed the facilitation back and forth; when Cynthia was speaking, I felt that she and I were interpreting the direction of the meeting in two different ways. When I took the lead, I was concerned that she did not agree with what I was saying.

The discussion surrounding the terms was heated. Some members felt strongly that we were neglecting to include physically challenged students. Others discussed the need for the students to understand prejudice and exclusion, and differences in values and perspectives at a deeper level than some kind of "Mexican night." Others thought similarities were most important. The European American with an adopted Korean daughter said that her own extended family included three races and several nationalities, and that it was her constant struggle with her own children to teach tolerance and appreciation for the common bond of humanity. Several members agreed with her in passionate tones, and I thought that this was a difference of perspective that could immobilize the meeting and the work of the committee as a whole. I said something intended to validate both views, hoping to harmonize. Several others did not express their opinion and seemed disinterested in this topic; they thought we were spending too much time philosophizing and not getting anywhere.

We then moved on to brainstorming the kinds of activities that we might recommend. Time ran out, and we ended the meeting about 30 minutes later than we had planned. We had set the next meeting date, but both Cynthia and I felt that it was unclear what we should do next.

Through the months that followed, the tendencies that came to light in that first meeting returned repeatedly to stall meetings and raise tensions. Cynthia and I spent a great deal of time on the telephone with individuals who were withdrawing because they felt that their own agenda was not being addressed.

Assessment[1]

Process Observation

This is a suggested guideline for process observation. Your team may want to add additional questions. It is helpful to appoint a process observer at meetings sometimes and designate time occasionally to discuss what was observed. Additionally, the process observer could be responsible for intervening to supply necessary roles. As the team matures, all members will develop the skill of maintaining a balance between process and content. Track both individual behavior and patterns by relevant group (nationality, race, gender, age, position, etc.)

- Communication and Participation
- How even was participation?
- Was there any overlapping speech or cutting people off?
- How did people demonstrate they were listening to others?
- What was the pace and rhythm of communication?
- Were different points of view expressed?
- Were ideas and opinions acknowledged and expanded upon?
- What communication patterns were observable? Who talked to whom? Who followed whom?
- Was the flow of content and ideas circular or linear?
- Who had eye contact with whom?
- What other nonverbal behaviors were evident?

---

[1] Claire B. Halverson

Roles: Informal

- To what extent were task behaviors exhibited (initiating, information seeking and giving, opinion seeking and giving, clarifying and elaborating, summarizing, consensus testing and evaluating, coordinating)?
- To what extent were maintenance behaviors exhibited (managing conflict, encouraging, gate keeping, diagnosing and facilitating group functioning, active listening, acknowledging others)?
- To what extent were self-oriented behaviors exhibited (controlling, distracting, resisting leadership, forming alliances, over-depending on leadership, withdrawing)?
- How was leadership exhibited (directive or shared)?

Decision Making

- Was the issue or problem clear?
- How were alternatives proposed?
- What methods were used to make decisions (voting, railroading, consensus, default)?
- Were decisions clearly recognized and accepted by all?
- Were plans made to implement decisions?

Climate

- How would you describe the climate (humorous/serious, relaxed/tense, energetic/de-energized, cautious/tumultuous, etc.)?

References

Alston, J. (1985). *The American Samurai: Blending American and Japanese Managerial Practices*. Walter de Gruyter, New York.

Ayman, R. and Chemers, M.M. (1983). Relationship of supervisory behavior ratings to work group effectiveness and subordinate satisfaction among Iranian managers. *Journal of Applied Psychology*, *68*(2), 338–341.

Bargiela-Chiappini, F., Bülow-Møller, A., Nickerson, C., Poncini, G. and Zhu, Y. (2003). Five perspectives on intercultural business communication: Focus on research. *Business Communication Quarterly*, *66*(3), 73–96.

Benne, K.D. and Sheats, P. (1948). Functional roles of group members. *Journal of Social Issues*, *4*(2), 41–49.

Burbidge, J. (1994). A time of participation. *Journal for Quality and Participation*, 2–8.

Conger, J. (1989). Leadership: the art of empowering others. *Academy of Management Executive*, *3*(1), 17–24.

Copeland, L. and Griggs, L. (1985). *Going International*. New York: Random House.

Cox, T.H., Lobel, S.A. and McLeod, P.L. (1991). Effects of ethnic group cultural differences on cooperative and competitive behavior on a group task. *Academy of Management Journal, 34*(4), 827–847.

Enayati, J. (2001). The Research: effective communication and decision-making in diverse groups. In M. Hemmati (Ed.), *Multi-Stakeholder Processes for Governance and Sustainability—Beyond Deadlock and Conflict*. London, England: Earthscan.

Ford, R.C. and Fottler, M.D. (1995). Empowerment: a matter of degree. *Academy of Management Executive, 9*(3), 21–31.

Forrester, R. (2000). Empowerment: rejuvenating a potent idea. *Academy of Management Executive, 14*(3), 67–80.

Gibson, C.B. and Zellmer-Bruhn, M.E. (2001). Metaphors and meaning: an intercultural analysis of the concept of teamwork. *Administrative Science Quarterly, 46*(2), 274–303.

Harrison, D.A., Price, K.H., Gavin, J.H. and Florey, A.T. (2002). Time, teams, and task performance: changing effects of diversity on group functioning. *Academy of Management Journal, 45*, 1029–1045.

Iles, P. (1995). Learning to work with difference. *L Personnel review, 24*(6), 44–60.

Jehn, K., Northcraft, G. and Neale, M. (1999). Why differences make a difference: A field study of diversity, conflict, and performance in workgroups. *Administrative Science Quarterly, 44*(4), 741–763.

Kabanoff, B. (1991). Equity, equality, power, and conflict. *Academy of Management Review, 16*(2), 416–441.

Kirkman, B.L. and Rosen, B. (1999). Beyond self-management: Antecedents and consequences of team empowerment. *Academy of Management Journal, 42*(1), 58–74.

Kopp, R. (2005). Communication challenges between Americans and Japanese in the workplace. *Transcultural Management Review, 2* (Nov.), 70–77.

Marks, M., Mathieu, J. and Zaccaro, S. (2001). A temporally based framework and taxonomy of team processes. *The Academy of Management Review, 26*(3), 356–377.

Marshak, R. and Katz, J. (1997). Diagnosing covert processes in groups and organizations. *OD Practitioner, 29*(1), 33–42.

Milliken, F.J. and Martins, L.L. (1996). Searching for common threads: Understanding the multiple effects of diversity in organizational groups. *The Academy of Management Review, 21*(2), 402–434.

Mohammed, S. and Angell, L. (2004). Surface- and deep-level diversity in workgroups: Examining the moderating effects of team orientation and team process on relationship conflict. *Journal of Organizational Behavior, 25*, 1015–1039.

Morrison, E.W. (1994). Role definitions and organizational citizenship behavior: The importance of the employee's perspective. *Academy of Management Journal, 37*, 1543–1567.

Mudrack, P. and Farrell, G. (1995). An examination of functional role behavior and its consequences for individuals in group settings. *Small Group Research, 26*, 542–571.

Nadler, L.B, Nadler, M. and Broome, B.J. (1985). Culture and the Management of Conflict Situations. *International and Intercultural Communications Annual*, 87–113.

Oetzel, J.G. (1998). Culturally homogeneous and heterogeneous groups: Explaining communication processes through individualism-collectivism and self-construal. *International Journal of Intercultural Relations, 22*, 135–161.

Olsson, M. (1985). Meeting Styles for Intercultural Groups. *AFS Occasional Papers in Intercultural Learning*, 1–18.

Orsburn, J. (1990). Self-directed Work Teams: The New American Challenge. Homewood, IL: Business One Irwin.

Pelled, L. (1996). Demographic diversity, conflict, and work group outcomes: An intervening process theory. *Organization Science, 17*, 615–631.

Pelled, L.H., Eisenhardt, K.M. and Xin, K.R. (1999). Exploring the black box: An analysis of work group diversity, conflict, and performance. *Administrative Science Quarterly, 44*, 1–28.

Pfeffer, J. and Veiga, J.F. (1999). Putting people first for organizational success. *Academy of Management Executive*, *13*(2), 37–48.
Pillai, R. and Meindl, J.R. (1998). Context and charisma: A 'meso' level examination of the relationship of organic structure, collectivism, and crisis to charismatic leadership. *Journal of Management*, *24*, 643–671.
Sisaye, S. and Siegel, P.H. (1997). An analysis of the difference between organizational identification and professional commitment: A study of certified public accountants. *Leadership & Organization Development Journal*, *18*(3), 149–165.
Sisaye, S. (2005). New directions for managing work teams. *Leadership & Organization Development Journal*, *26*(1), 51–61.
Weaver, R. and Farrell, J. (1997). *Mangers as Facilitators*. San Francisco, CA: Berrett-Koehler.
Wellins, R.S., Byham, W. and Wilson, J. (1991). *Empowered Teams*. San Francisco, CA: Jossey-Bass.

Resources

Organizations
International Association of Facilitators: iaf-world.org
National Training Laboratories, Inc.: www.ntl.org

Books
Eitington, J. (2002). *The Winning Trainer*. Houston, TX: Gulf Publishing.
Gardenswartz, L. and Rowe, A. (1994). *Diverse Teams at Work*. Chicago, IL: Irwin.
Weaver, R. and Farrell, J. (1997). *Mangers as Facilitators*. San Francisco, CA: Berrett-Koehler.

Chapter 6
Effective Leadership for Multicultural Teams

Ken Williams

Leaders are not commanders and controllers, bosses and big shots. Instead they are servers and supporters, partners and providers.

–Jones et al. (1996)

Introduction

The literature on effective multicultural teams identifies leadership as an important factor in effectiveness. In some instances it has pointed out that there is a need for cohesion and a shared vision, while in others it has shown a need for a collaborative environment and expert coaching. This literature on the role of leadership does not agree on a coherent and systematic approach as to how multicultural teams can be effectively led. Although there is no one generic formula for the effective leadership of multicultural teams, there is a need to systematically approach leadership of multicultural teams in order to create a framework that takes into account the cultural dimensions as well as individual characteristics and behavior.

This chapter offers some insights on how multicultural teams can be effectively led that take account of their many features that present challenges for members and leadership alike. It focuses on a leadership approach that is not about controlling teams but about providing an atmosphere where members can flourish and be creative. This approach, referred to as shared leadership, aims at engaging all team members as full participants who are fully empowered in a manner that recognizes their worth and importance as equal members of the team. Shared leadership stresses interdependence and connectedness, where all members work in an influence relationship that is multidirectional between leaders and followers.

In order to build a platform for this shared leadership approach and to provide a context for how shared leadership might work in multicultural teams, the chapter first provides a definition of leadership that lays out the philosophical underpinnings for this approach. The chapter then discusses critical aspects of team leadership in general, and of multicultural teams in particular, that lay the foundation for the approach to be

C.B. Halverson and S.A. Tirmizi (eds.), *Effective Multicultural Teams: Theory and Practice,*

effective. Finally, special attention is given to the shared leadership approach, including a description of the conditions that are necessary before the approach can be successful and the steps that need to be followed in implementing it.

Learning Objectives

After reading this chapter you should be able to:

- Discuss how leadership can function as a multidirectional relationship with leadership roles being shared
- Distinguish coercive from noncoercive uses of power and influence tactics, and recognize the use of noncoercive influence tactics in teams
- Determine the different power styles that can be used in team situations
- Describe the appropriate uses of the leadership, management, and facilitation roles in the leadership of multicultural teams
- Identify effective leadership behavior for dealing with culture and gender in multicultural teams
- Recognize how elements of earlier leadership approaches might be useful in the leadership of multicultural teams
- Discuss the conditions that promote shared leadership in multicultural teams
- Describe a process for sharing leadership in multicultural teams

Defining Leadership

Many theorists in the field agree that the definitions of leadership are unclear and inconsistent, and that providing a unified and all-embracing definition is very challenging (Northouse 2004; Avery 2004). It is even more difficult when we think of defining leadership in the context of a multicultural team. Early definitions of leadership focused on notions of leadership as a single-handed phenomenon, with leaders having rare traits and being able to manage from the top in a manner that commanded and/or controlled others (Stogdill 1948, 1974). More recent definitions view leadership as a distributed phenomenon involving followers in an influence process (Antonakis et al. 2004; Lakey et al. 1995; Rost 1993). This chapter draws upon these more recent definitions as being most appropriate for multicultural teams.

Leadership as an Influence Process: Defining leadership as a process suggests that a leader affects and is affected by followers, and recognizes that leadership is not a linear unidirectional phenomenon but a series of interactive occurrences, making leadership multidirectional and available to everyone in the team (Northouse 2004; Rost 1993). The process can be seen as an influence relationship, which is concerned with how leaders affect followers and vice versa using noncoercive social influence tactics.

Leadership as Shared and Distributed: Definitions of leadership that focus on shared influence processes are especially important for leadership in teams. In Chapter 1, Tirmizi identifies interdependence and shared leadership roles as two of the elements that distinguish teams from groups. Leadership as an influence process emphasizes this interdependence and encourages sharing of leadership roles. Shared leadership, which is also referred to as participatory leadership, involves all members in decision making and leadership functions are distributed. Distributed leadership works through relationships, with team members assuming leadership in different circumstances depending on their expertise and with the focus on participation by all members (Bennett et al. 2003).

Leadership as Fostering Participation and Connectedness: Wheatley (2006) reminds us that all life depends on participation with its environment in the process of development, and that this applies to life within organizations and teams as well. As Wheatley points out, the participation process empowers individuals and recognizes the worth and importance of each individual within any given system. Nothing exists independent of its relationships, and encouraging full participation awakens the full potential of the interactions we create in working together. In terms of work teams, when team members believe they are full participants in a process, the work of the team can come alive as a personal reality, which can lead to commitment, and ownership of the work. For this to happen, it is critical that this interaction is real and that participation focuses on interconnectedness and the dynamic processes that value all team members as equals.

Leadership as a Multi-directional Influence Relationship: A definition of leadership that stresses a multidirectional influence relationship, providing a sharing of leadership functions, can create the type of team climate that produces effective multicultural teams. As noted by Tirmizi in Chapter 1 in his report of the study done by Thomas et al. (2000), allowing team members to be influential in charting the team's path is a significant element in moving teams towards success. This study indicated the importance of participation by team members in achieving team effectiveness.

In order to better understand how leadership can be shared in teams in a noncoercive manner, the following section examines power and influence and the different ways they can be used on teams.

Power and Influence in Multicultural Teams

Sources of Power

Within the context of teams, leaders are viewed as the ones exerting power, with power being defined as the capacity to influence beliefs, attitudes, or behaviors (Yukl 1998). *Personal* or *soft power* comes through personal characteristics and includes expert, referent, and information power. *Positional* or *harsh power* is based on formal position and includes legitimate, reward, or coercive power (see Table 6.1). *Authority* is power that is based on position, and includes legitimate or coercive power (Sennett 1993).

Leaders usually use personal and positional power in varying amounts, but overreliance on either can lead to a coercive atmosphere. *Coercion* involves the use of force to influence followers and often results in manipulation of penalties and rewards, resulting in the use of threats, punishment, and negative rewards (Levi 2001; Northouse 2004). Using coercion runs counter to the practice of shared leadership in teams, which works best with the use of soft sources of power rather than positional power. Decision making is best when members with the most relevant information on an issue dominate the conversation rather than members who rely on positional power or authority.

Creating a balance between the amounts of personal and positional power can be a challenge in a multicultural team where members have different orientations towards sources of power. In a study of 53 nations, it was found that leaders from some Asian, African, Latin American, and Caribbean countries relied more heavily on vertical or hierarchical sources of guidance for their leadership decisions than those from many Northern European countries (Smith 2003). This means that in multicultural teams there may be members who rely more on vertical or positional sources of power because of their cultural orientation.

It is desirable for leaders to have only moderate amounts of positional power. Although there can be occasions when positional power may be necessary and appropriate, too much dependence on it can restrict use of relationships as a means of influence and can result in exploitation and domination of followers. Personal power is less open to misuse since it erodes quickly if leaders act contrary to interests of followers, but it is also subject to abuse when a leader with charismatic appeal attempts to use this power for personal benefit. Studies of the uses of power at different levels of authority indicate that interactions between leaders and followers are most effective when there is a high degree of multidirectional or reciprocal influence, which may be the best way to restrict abuse of power (Bachman et al. 1966; Smith and Tannenbaum 1963).

Table 6.1 Types of power (Adapted from French and Raven 2004)

Personal or soft power
Sources:
Expert Power based on one's credibility or perceived expertise in an area
Referent Power based on another's liking and admiration
Information Power based on knowledge or information one has about a topic
Positional or Harsh Power
Sources:
Legitimate Power based on recognition and acceptance of a person's authority
Reward Power based on the ability to reward behavior that one wants to occur
Coercive Power based on the ability to threaten or punish undesirable behavior

Case Study: Sources of Power in a Multicultural Team

As you read the case study below, consider the following questions:

- *What are the sources of power being used by Kevin and Melanie?*
- *What mechanisms are being used to restrict the use of coercive power?*
- *Identify examples of reciprocal influences used in this case.*
- *What other recommendations would you give to this team to restrict abuse of power by Kevin?*

Kevin, an Indonesian male, was put in charge of a global team of a Danish male, a Columbian male, a Ugandan male, a Japanese male, and a Thai female (Melanie). The water resource management NGO for which they worked was recruited to help develop a sustainable water-safety management system for the Northern Indonesian region. The team's task was to work together to determine the best location to begin the project. Kevin told everyone to consult him before any action was taken because he understood the Indonesian people better than anyone else in the team, and he stated that he felt that the central Java island was where they should begin. He also announced that he had spent significant time with the chief regional manager, which gave him a clear understanding of what everyone needed to do for the success of the project. He assigned members to complete tasks according to their reported skills and gave them economic reports on Indonesia to study. Each person's progress would be reported to the regional manager and those making good progress were sure to join him on the next project. He stated that the criteria for joining him included demonstrating the ability to work in harmony with each other and completing all of their individual tasks. Kevin also asked members for feedback on his leadership, which he said could be given to his face or anonymously in writing.

Melanie immediately responded by identifying some of the errors in the regional resource management reports, which wrongly identified safe zone areas that had recently been declared as unstable tectonic regions. Kevin immediately recognized Melanie's knowledge of local geography and her obvious background experience in water resource management. Kevin pointed that Melanie was correct and he announced that he would be having some deeper discussions with Melanie before he made any final decisions. Melanie told Kevin that there were team members with much more knowledge about Indonesia than he had given them credit for and that he should he should let members discuss their strengths and areas of expertise, which she stated might be different from what was recorded on their resume. Kevin listened to Melanie carefully and acknowledged that he rushed things and that he should have given some time for members to discuss their areas of expertise and experiences in more depth, and he requested Melanie to lead the discussion on this.

At the end of the meeting, Kevin requested to have a private meeting with Melanie, where he told her that he felt as though she was challenging his authority and although she had some very good knowledge and experience, he would prefer if she would behave like an Asian woman and speak to him privately about her views. Melanie apologized to Kevin for any behavior that seemed offensive but reaffirmed the importance of letting team members have a say in the tasks that they wanted to work on since she felt that it could lead to greater success of the team. Melanie gained the admiration of the team (who perceived her as their informal leader) for the remainder of the project. Kevin reaffirmed what he said at the beginning about his expectations and the criteria for working on subsequent projects, and informed Melanie he would prefer that she write some of her thoughts and views on a piece of paper and pass it to him before she spoke openly about any issue that would challenge his credibility.

Influence Tactics

Central to this chapter is not only who exercises leadership within multicultural teams but also how this influence comes about. Power is about influencing other people, but it can be accomplished in a number of different ways. The manner in which power is enacted involves influencing behavior that may be based on positional or personal power, but team members can abuse either of these sources depending on the way they are used.

Influence tactics are means through which individuals attempt to influence others. These influence tactics could be grouped into direct, indirect, cooperative, competitive, emotionally based, and hierarchical tactics, as is shown in Table 6.2.

Table 6.2 Influence tactics (Adapted from Levi 2001; Yukl 2003)

Direct tactics	• Personal appeals: appeal to members' sense of loyalty or friendship • Gentle pressure tactics: use of advocacy and constant reminders
Indirect tactics	• Ingratiation: use of flattery or friendly behavior to get a person to think • favorably of you • Coalition tactics: seeking the aid and support of those with influential power to increase power of request
Cooperative tactics	• Rational persuasion: use of logical arguments and factual evidence to persuade team members • Consultation: seeking members' participation in decision making
Competitive tactics	• Harsh pressure tactics: use of demands, threats, or persistent reminders • Ingratiation: use of flattery or friendly behavior to get a person to think favorably of you
Emotionally based tactics	• Inspirational appeals: attempting to arouse enthusiasm by appealing to members' ideals • Personal appeals: appealing to members' sense of loyalty or friendship
Hierarchical tactics	• Exchange tactics: offering to exchange favors later for cooperation now • Legitimizing tactics: claiming that one has the authority to get obedience.

Direct tactics are explicit methods of influence, including the use of gentle pressure tactics and personal appeals, while *indirect tactics* use covert measures to manipulate team members.

Cooperative tactics involve rational arguments or consulting with team members, while *competitive tactics* influence members through pressure tactics. *Emotionally based tactics* rely on emotional appeals and include inspirational and personal appeals. *Hierarchical tactics* rely on positions of authority or resources associated with their positions, and include making offers in exchange for compliance by followers.

Team leaders often use pressure and legitimizing tactics on followers, while team members often use rational argument, personal appeals, and ingratiation to influence leaders (Levi 2001). However, research indicates that manipulative forms of influence are ineffective. In a study of influence mechanisms used by leaders in 12 countries, it was found that pressure tactics that involved using threats, demands, or persistent reminders to convince followers to complete work were the least effective methods for getting followers to complete work assignments (Kennedy et al. 2003). In this study, rational persuasion, consultation, and personal appeals were the most effective influence methods for leaders. These methods of influencing are noncoercive and can encourage participation among team members. Emotionally based tactics also have the potential to equalize and encourage participation among members, though there need to be mechanisms to ensure that leadership does not abuse their power. One such mechanism can be the use of multidirectional or reciprocal influence, where team members use noncoercive tactics to influence leaders and restrict their use of coercive influence tactics.

Differences in cultural orientations to power can affect team members' use of, and response to, influence tactics. Members from high power distance cultures may prefer leaders to use direct and hierarchical tactics, while members from low power distance cultures might prefer leaders to use indirect tactics (see Chapter 2). Individual characteristics based on personality and intelligences may also affect preferences for certain influence tactics. For example, members with logical/mathematical intelligences might tend to use rational persuasion, while members with intrapersonal intelligence might prefer to use inspirational tactics.

Power Styles in Teams

Team members express power through their behaviors, which can be categorized as passive, aggressive, or assertive, with emotional tones helping to define different power styles (see Table 6.3). The *passive* or *nonassertive power style* is polite, using pleasant emotional tones, with the aim of avoiding problems by not taking definite stands, and being unclear about positions. This style can send mixed messages, with receivers being uncertain about the beliefs and feelings of the passive communicator. This style is helpful in high conflict situations and is often used by members from a diffuse culture orientation (see Trompenaars's Value Framework in Chapter 2).

Table 6.3 Power styles (Levi 2001)

	Styles	Impact	Use
Non-assertive/passive	Polite and deferential	Resentment and confusion	Dangerous situations
Aggressive focused on winning	Forceful and withdrawn	Satisfaction and unequal status	Emergencies
Assertive confident problem solving	Clear and trust	Satisfaction equal status	Most situations

The *assertive power style* uses clear communication with little emotion attached and focuses on concern for others and self. This power style uses open communication, respect and relies on high trust in teammates to solve problems and conflicts. It is appropriate in situations where there is emphasis on equality (Lumsden and Lumsden 1997), but is not always successful, especially when there are team members from high context cultures as described by Griffin (see Chapter 7). Members from neutral cultures may perceive emotional expressions of members from affective cultures as aggressive or passive-aggressive (See Chapter 2).

The *aggressive power style* is forceful and critical, using negative emotions to appear powerful while being unwilling to listen to others. This power style may be appropriate in emergency situations where a forceful approach is needed, but is inappropriate for designated team leaders to use in most situations, especially in situations of unequal power. A combination of the passive and assertive styles may be more appropriate for use by leadership in team settings.

The use of these different power styles can present a challenge for the functioning of a team early in its development, as evidenced in the example below. The main task of leadership is to try to equalize power.

Case Study: Power Styles in a Multicultural Team in Graduate School

As you read the case study below, consider the following questions:

- *What are some examples of the power styles used, naming the persons using them?*
- *What power styles were effective?*
- *What were the influence tactics that were used by team members?*

Mary, Suki, Cheda, Ally and Josh are members of an international multicultural team recently formed in a graduate school class to create a team charter[1]

[1] Team Charter is a tool to gain clarity around the direction and purpose of the team. The purpose of the team charter is to serve as agreement between members around what the team s supposed to do and how they will move forward.

and get to know each other. Mary is an American female who has been working in the nonprofit field in various countries as a manager for many years. Suki is an Asian female, recently graduated, with one year of work experience as a Peace Corp volunteer. Cheda, also an Asian female, has worked in the corporate world for many years as a manager. Ally, a middle-aged African male, has worked as a project field officer for many years in different regions of the world. Josh, who is a much older western European male, grew up in several non-Western countries but now resides in Latin America and works as a farmer on a ranch. He has good relationships with Suki, Cheda, and Ally, having lived in all of their native countries and having spent time with them during the previous week of orientation.

Mary immediately identified what she thought should be the name of the group, stating with much enthusiasm and passion that she had spent much time in her job working on strategic plans and felt that the name of the group was a critical part in shaping its purpose. She provided information from several of her experiences and research, which supported her position. However, Josh verbally expressed his disagreement with Mary, stating that it was best to begin by getting to know each other better. He proceeded by stating all of the positive things he had observed about each team member, including Mary. His rationale was that this would give members a chance to know each other's strengths, and he also reassured Mary that her idea could then be pursued.

Cheda commended Mary for her knowledge and urged the team to listen to her because of her experiences, but also stated that the team should listen to Josh. Mary rebutted by stating how many years experience she had as a manager with organizations like the United Nations and Habitat for Humanity. Ally, after being very quiet, summed up what she perceived to be happening and said she felt they should approach the professor about the situation. She thought they needed to get one leader first so that they could have someone to follow on these issues. She asked Suki, who had not spoken, how she felt about the situation. Suki said that she did not have an opinion, and suggested that the team vote on the course of action.

Differentiating Leadership from Management and Facilitation

Leadership, management, and facilitation are often confused. They are different in function, though the roles may interchange. *Facilitation* is a process in which an individual either from within or outside the team helps a team improves how it works together (Weaver and Farrell 1999). The focus of facilitation is with helping team members do their own work, on the other hand, *leadership* focuses on setting direction for the team, and *management* focuses on directing and controlling the team. Leadership aims at producing constructive change and movement, while management seeks to help teams function more efficiently through coordination

Table 6.4 Comparing the roles of leader, manager, and facilitator (Weaver and Farrell 1999)

Leader	Manager	Facilitator
Takes long-term view	Takes short-term view	Helps people find a view and articulate it
Concentrates on what and why	Concentrates on how	Helps people concentrate and be clear in the here and now
Thinks in terms of innovation, development, and the future	Thinks in terms of administration, maintenance, and the present	Helps people think and communicate their thoughts
Sets the vision: the tone and direction	Sets the plan: the pace	Helps make meaning of tone and direction
Hopes others will respond and follow	Hopes others will complete their tasks	Hopes others will engage in the process
Appeals to hopes and dreams	Monitors boundaries; sets limits	Draws out meaning of hopes and dreams; pushes boundaries
Expects others to help realize a vision	Expects others to fulfill their mission or purpose	Helps others articulate a shared vision and common mission
Inspires innovation	Inspires stability, focuses on controlling and problem solving	Helps people respond to new and old things

and planning (Bennis and Nanus 1985; Kotter 1990). Leadership focuses on why and management on how (see Table 6.4).

Within a team, leadership may employ the use of any of these roles, with one person carrying out all of these functions, or leadership may use only one or two of these roles. Deciding which role to use depends on the situation, with the leader role being used if the main aim is to help members see the bigger picture and set direction. If the task involves setting deadlines, where team members share little responsibility for the work, then the manager role is best, while the facilitator's role is best if team members share full responsibility for the work. With the facilitator role, team members are more motivated to support the decisions made because they feel the decisions are theirs and not someone else's.

The stage of the team's development is critical, with teams at the earlier stages of development needing more direction from the leader role and more control from the manager role, while more advanced teams can function more effectively with the facilitator role. Below is an example of how this might play out in the early stages of a team's development.

Effective Team Leadership

Research on effective teams has identified characteristics of leadership related to building effective teams as including the leader's ability to inspire a shared and compelling vision in followers, provide enabling structures, provide a collaborative environment, and give expert coaching (Leithwood and Jantzi 2000; Barnett et al. 2001; Lafasto and Larson 2001). Leithwood and Jantzi found that effective leadership of teams includes the ability to motivate followers beyond their own self-interest, inspiring them to work for a sense of idealism, resulting in a shared and compelling vision. Barnett et al. (2001), on the other hand, found that behaviors that appealed to followers' self-interest contributed to team effectiveness. Lafasto and Larson (2001), in research conducted with a sample of 600 team members, found that teams were effective when leaders kept the team focused, helped create a clear structure where all group members understood their roles, and had a good communication system that allowed the easy flow of information.

Decision-Making Style

The particular style a leader uses in decision making also contributes to team effectiveness. Lewin et al. (1939) developed three leadership styles around how leaders use power in decision making. The first leadership style was *autocratic*, where leaders relied on positional power and were authoritarian. The second style was *participative*, where leaders involved followers in the decision-making process but maintained the final decision-making authority. The third style was *laissez-faire*, where the leader provided little or no direction and allowed followers freedom to determine goals, make decisions, and resolve problems on their own without any support. The autocratic style caused the highest level of discontent, causing a greater threat to team stability than either democratic or laissez-faire. The autocratic style also resulted in more exits from the team (36.7%, as compared to less than 10% for either democratic or laissez-faire styles, or a combination of democratic and laissez-faire styles; Van Vugt et al. 2004).

A fourth decision-making style that can be used and that might be more appropriate for leadership in multicultural teams is to give the decision-making responsibility to the team, with the designated leader facilitating decision making among team members. In Chapter 9, Gobbo describes decision-making steps in a synergistic model and provides insights on how decision making can proceed in a self-managed team. In this model, consensus building is described as being best for facilitating shared leadership.

Team Characteristics

To build an effective team, leaders also need to take into consideration the characteristics of the particular teams. Multicultural teams, with members from different cultural backgrounds and representing a variety of identities, present particular challenges for leadership. Leading multicultural teams requires a willingness to learn and the ability to be receptive to the different experiences brought to the team by various members.

Cultural Issues

Research has shown that followers resist leadership initiatives when the leadership approach clashes with their cultural values (Kirkman and Shapiro 2001). Members from high power distance cultures tend to accept leaders' authority more readily and may prefer authoritarian leadership, while members from low power distance cultures may prefer participatory styles (Connerley and Pedersen 2005). Participative approaches are considered to be desirable in much of North America and Western Europe but are not so desired in Asia and Latin America (Adler 2002; Hofstede 2005). In a global study it was found that participative leadership received the highest score in Germanic Europe and the lowest score in Middle Eastern countries. (Javidan et al. 2004). Leadership needs to critically assess the cultural make-up of teams before deciding on whether to use participative or authoritarian approaches or a combination of the two.

Leaders may display behaviors that are consistent with their own cultural orientation that can leave some members dissatisfied. One solution is for leaders to adopt approaches that appeal to members from both high and low power distance cultures at various times. For this to be successful, leaders would need to point out the benefits and challenges of having members from different cultural backgrounds on the team (see Chapter 2 for more discussion on this).

In the forming stage of team development, members from individualistic cultures tend to concentrate on tasks, while members from collectivist cultures stress interdependence and connectedness (see Chapter 4). Leadership needs to reconcile all of these divergent approaches without devaluing any member. The African concept of *Ubuntu*, which focuses on creating harmony among individuals, may provide lessons for leadership. In explaining the relevance of Ubuntu, Mbigi (1995a, b) developed the notion of the African tree. According to the African tree concept, there are three main branches that are important to leadership, leadership legitimacy, communal enterprise, and value sharing (Van der Colff 2003; Lessem and Nussbaum 1996).

Leadership legitimacy requires leadership to intentionally establish a personal connection with all team members and get to know their needs, being flexible and adaptable to them. *Communal enterprise* refers to the ability of the leader to help followers see the connection between their individual direction and the collective direction of the team. This can result in developing a vision that is inclusive of all needs. It is important that this vision be communicated in a manner to show that it grew out of the needs of the entire group. This requires leadership to become engaged in *value sharing*, where the critical values of the group are articulated verbally as well as lived out by the leadership.

The concept of *Ubuntu* can help develop harmony among members from different cultures as leadership gets to understand the needs and cultural backgrounds of members. According to Kirk and Bolden(2006), Ubuntu envisages individuals and community as a relational entity, with each giving value, purpose and identity to the other. Leadership needs to get all team members to see the connection between their individual directions and where the team needs to go as a whole. It is important for leadership to value the individual experiences brought by each member, whether they are from universalistic or particularistic, specific or diffuse cultures (see Chapter 2). The following example shows how difficult this can be in multicultural teams, but yet rewarding if leadership is able to effectively implement the concept of *Ubuntu*.

Case Study: Implementing Ubuntu in a Multicultural Team

As you read the case study below, consider the following questions:

- *What are the cultural dimensions that appear relevant to how the team functions together? Justify your response with specific reference to members' behaviors or statements.*
- *What issues other than culture seem to be relevant in this case?*
- *How effective was the facilitator's attempt to implement the concept of Ubuntu?*
- *What do you recommend as the next steps for the team in order to fully realize Ubuntu?*

In teaching the concept of Ubuntu in her graduate classes, Professor Gordo requested that members of her course on Team Effectiveness work in teams of five, and meet on five occasions after the first formal class session. In each of these sessions there was supposed to be a facilitator/leader, and a recorder, with these roles being rotated for each session, with everyone getting an opportunity to function in both roles. The aim of these sessions was for team members to get to know each other's style of leading meetings and any cultural backgrounds associated with their styles, and to discuss ways they would like to work together.

The following is an account of the interactions of one team comprising a West African female, a Central Asian female, an Eastern European male, a Midwestern American male, and a South American male. In the first meeting, the West African female was assigned to be facilitator. The facilitator arrived 15 minutes after scheduled time for the meeting, which was perceived by the European and the Asian as disrespectful. The facilitator greeted everyone with a hug and encouraged them to eat the food she had brought. The European and Asian commented on the late start and urged all to eat quickly so they could get to work. The facilitator smiled and asked people not to worry about the time, explaining that meetings in her culture involved ceremony. She introduced a song to the team, teaching the chorus to everyone and having them repeat it, although all team members did not do it enthusiastically.

After the team had eaten, the facilitator then explained the values that were important in her culture and invited members to describe how meetings in their cultures differed from how she conducted the meeting and to identify the most important values associated with these meetings. The European began by stating appreciation for the food, but indicated the importance of beginning meetings on time. The American expressed gratitude for the song, but stated that he was uncomfortable with the expressions of affection. The South American expressed comfort with affection, which he stated was part of his culture. The Asian female stated that in her culture, the facilitator would have been more assertive.

Gender Identity Issues

Social identities impact leadership of multicultural teams in a number of ways, with members from one-ups groups more likely to emerge as leaders (see Chapter 3). The effects of gender on leadership are seen all across the globe, with men in charge of the most important activities. This may be related to how women and men are perceived to lead. Some literature on gender and leadership promotes the view that men and women differ significantly in how they lead (Helgesen 1990). Earlier theories suggested that leadership was biologically determined, being innate for men and unattainable for women (Appelbaum et al. 2003). Another view is that women are fundamentally different from men in behavior, feelings, and thought, with women's way of leading claimed as superior (Gilligan 1982; Rosener 1990).

Table 6.5 shows that the stereotypical leadership qualities ascribed to women are more nurturing, while those ascribed to men are less so. Evidence for sex differences in leadership behavior is mixed. Earlier meta-analysis studies in laboratories found women manifested more interpersonally oriented and democratic styles of leadership while men demonstrated more task-oriented and autocratic styles (Van Engen and Willemsen 2001). Recent studies in actual organizations showed that women were more participative and less autocratic (Van Engen and Willemsen 2001). Assertiveness and abrasive behavior are associated with autocratic behavior and may be related to why men are dominant in teams, with women's participative styles seen as weaknesses. Members from more masculine-oriented cultures may prefer the strong autocratic style that is typical of men.

Table 6.5 Stereotypical gender leadership qualities

Female	Male
Transformational	Transactional
Participative	Autocratic
Relationship-oriented	Task-oriented
Use more referent and reward power	Use more coercive power
More team-oriented caring	More individualistic-oriented aggressive

When women exhibit autocratic behavior they are evaluated more negatively than men for the same behaviors. A meta-analysis of studies examining the evaluation of men and women leaders, found that women received lower evaluations than men for exhibiting autocratic behavior (Eagly and Carli 2004). Men are also more likely than women to give negative reactions to and deny women's leadership, and even competent women often receive less favorable evaluations than competent men (Eagly and Carli 2004). This can result in women's devaluing of their own leadership and in some instances may lead to their seeking to adopt what is perceived as male characteristics in order to lead teams.

Further research on the evaluation of men and women leaders has shown that as long as women leaders adopt a leadership style congruent with gender expectations, they were evaluated favorably (Klenke 2003). For example, when women's leadership was based on relationships, cooperation, sharing, and inclusion, they received positive evaluations (Eagly and Johnson 1990). On the other hand, when they adopted stereotypic masculine styles, such as being domineering and aggressive, they were perceived as ineffective leaders. This means that women will be more accepted if they adopt decision-making styles more congruent with socially accepted gender expectations.

Androgynous leadership, which integrates the effective skills that are associated with both masculine and feminine leadership, may be an effective approach to sharing leadership in multicultural teams. Effective leadership is not the restricted realm of either gender, and therefore men and women can learn from each other. One bright spot for leading multicultural teams is that gender appears to play a more important role in country-specific groups than in multicultural teams (House et al. 2004; Roffey 2000). This means that leaders might be able to utilize the different cultural perspectives on gender in the team to challenge stereotypes and create an inclusive atmosphere.

The next section looks at various leadership approaches that might be appropriate for guiding leadership in teams.

Approaches to Leadership

There have been various approaches to leadership through the years, and several of these theories can provide insights on effective leadership of multicultural teams.

Trait Theory

Traits are classified as stable patterns of behavior that are relatively immune to situational contingencies (Antonakis et al. 2004). Early research on leadership traits concentrated on physical characteristics but more recent research found that certain cognitive capacities, personality traits, problem-solving skills, and social

Table 6.6 Key leader attributes (Adapted from Zaccaro et al. 2004)

Cognitive capacities	Personality	Social capabilities	Problem-solving skills
General intelligence Creative thinking Metacognition	Extroversion Conscientiousness	Self-monitoring Social intelligence	Problem construction Solution generation

capabilities contribute more to effective team leadership (see Table 6.6). It was also found that high leader cognitive ability was positively associated with the accuracy of team decisions, but the effects were moderated by the degree of cognitive ability held by team members and the divergent thinking of team members (LePine et al. 1997).

Of the traits in the Big Five personality model presented in Chapter 3, it was found that extroversion had strongest relationship to leadership, followed by conscientiousness, with agreeableness having the weakest relationship (Judge et al. 2002). Ployhart et al. (2002), in a study of leadership growth and development, found that agreeableness was associated with increased displays of adaptability by leaders toward followers. However, analysis of leadership in working contexts has shown that it is not a static condition, but results from relationships between leaders and followers (Wheatley 2006).

In trait theory, there is an assumption that one leader possesses key characteristics that are necessary for leadership, with little thought given to the characteristics possessed by followers. Expecting one person to possess such a variety of characteristics is unrealistic, but it is possible that many of these characteristics may exist among team members. If a team allows sharing of leadership, it may be able to benefit from the multiple characteristics possessed by different team members, which can help to reduce some of the differences due to the different cultural orientations. For example, members with self-monitoring skills can help the team monitor social cues, which might help to reduce conflicts and misinterpretations that can occur as result of having members with different cultural orientations. Members with problem-solving skills can help the team generate a range of appropriate solutions to help solve difficulties encountered.

Transactional and Transformational Leadership

These two leadership approaches are discussed here together because of recent academic leadership research that suggests that they are two ends of a continuum (Yukl 1998). *Transactional leadership* motivates followers by appealing to their self-interest, using contingent rewards and management by exception. Contingent rewards influence followers with the use of strategic reinforcements such as praise and material rewards. Transactional leadership behaviors can be useful in the forming stage of team development, where expectations for team behaviors and success can be elicited and utilized in distributing rewards to gain compliance. For example, at the first meeting leaders can ask team members for expectations on how the team will work together and team rewards such as going to dinner can be given as incentives for accomplishments.

On the other end of the continuum is *transformational leadership*, where followers and leaders raise one another to higher levels of morality and motivation by appealing to ideals such as commitment, emotional engagement, or fulfillment of higher-order needs. Transformational leadership can use inspirational motivation, idealized influence, and individualized consideration to motivate team members. In a multicultural team a member can use inspirational motivation by communicating a compelling vision of what the team process or other outcomes could look like, incorporating symbols or music if appropriate. Idealized influence can be used to paint this picture by leaders modeling the behaviors desired. For example, if one of the visions of the team is to be inclusive, the leader needs to show that s/he is inclusive by being tolerant of the views and perspectives of all members. In individualized consideration, the leader acknowledges the individual needs, abilities, and aspirations of followers and uses these needs, strengths, and aspirations to help members become more integrated into the team.

Research has shown that both approaches are effective, although transactional behaviors showed relatively smaller effects on team outcomes when compared with transformational behaviors (House et al. 2004). The transactional dimension of contingent rewards is most positively related to team effectiveness and commitment of members (Davis and Bryant 2004). With transformational leadership, individualized consideration has the strongest effect on team satisfaction (House et al. 2004).

Servant Leadership

The servant leadership approach postulates that an individual emerges as a leader by first becoming a servant (Greenleaf 1977). Servant leaders focus on the needs of followers and help them to become more autonomous, shifting power to those being led. Servant leaders value all team members' involvement, and encourage respect, trust, and the utilization of individual strengths, with emphasis being placed on listening, empathy, and the unconditional acceptance of others. For example, if a team member begins to devalue another member because of gender status, the servant leader would seek to understand the cultural background of the member that is doing the devaluing as well as trying to understand the feelings of the member being devalued.

Servant leadership is an approach that can help to produce a climate that is needed for multicultural teams. At the heart of servant leadership is an ethic of caring, which is intended to protect followers and is an important ingredient in building trust and cooperative relationships which would help to provide the type of team climate described by Tirmizi in Chapter 1. Leadership of multicultural teams can use this approach throughout the stages of team development, which can result in the building of trusting relationships that can enhance team performance.

In a study of the impact of servant leadership on team effectiveness, Irving and Longbotham (2007) found that the servant leadership themes of providing accountability, providing support and resources, engaging in honest self-evaluation, fostering collaboration, communicating with clarity, and valuing and appreciating were strong predictors of team effectiveness. The focus of servant leadership on stewardship can help to provide accountability, and can help to foster ownership and responsibility, ensuring that leaders and followers are accountable for matters for which they are responsible.

Situational Approach

According to the situational leadership approach, effective leadership requires an individual to be able to adapt his or her leadership style to the demands of different situations (Hersey and Blanchard 1988). This approach emphasizes that leadership is made up of both directive and supportive dimensions, and each need to be applied appropriately in situations in order to be effective. Directive behaviors assist workers in task and goal accomplishment. Directive behaviors are more a one-way type of communication, with the leader focusing on clarifying and identifying what needs to be done, how it is to be done and who is responsible for doing it. Supportive behaviors, on the other hand, are two-way communication through which the leader shows social and emotional support and facilitates accomplishment of tasks.

The two dimensions of directive and supportive are further categorized into four styles: directing, coaching, supporting, and delegating. With this approach a leader must evaluate followers and assess how competent and committed they are to perform a given task, and then adopt the most appropriate of the four styles (see Fig. 6.1). The choice of style to be used is also affected by the workers' level of maturity, with the least matured teams receiving the most directive leadership behavior and the most matured workers given more control and responsibility over the work they do. In Fig. 6.1, the workers' maturity level proceeds from least matured in Style 1 to most matured in Style 4.

The leadership styles in this approach can be related to the stages of team development presented in Chapter 4. Leadership Style 1, *directing*, would be most appropriate for the forming stage, where leadership is needed to help the team clarify tasks and roles and set attainable goals. Style 2, *coaching*, would be used in the storming stage, where leadership is needed to help the team develop task-related and group-maintenance skills. Style 3, *supporting*, would be used in the norming stage, where team members are beginning to take on responsibilities previously carried out by the leader. Style 4, *delegating*, would be used in the performing stage, where there is less dependence on the leader. In the final stage of team development, adjourning, where a sense of loss and sadness can lead to stress and some regression to earlier stages of team development, the leader may need to increase both directive and supportive behavior and return to Style 3.

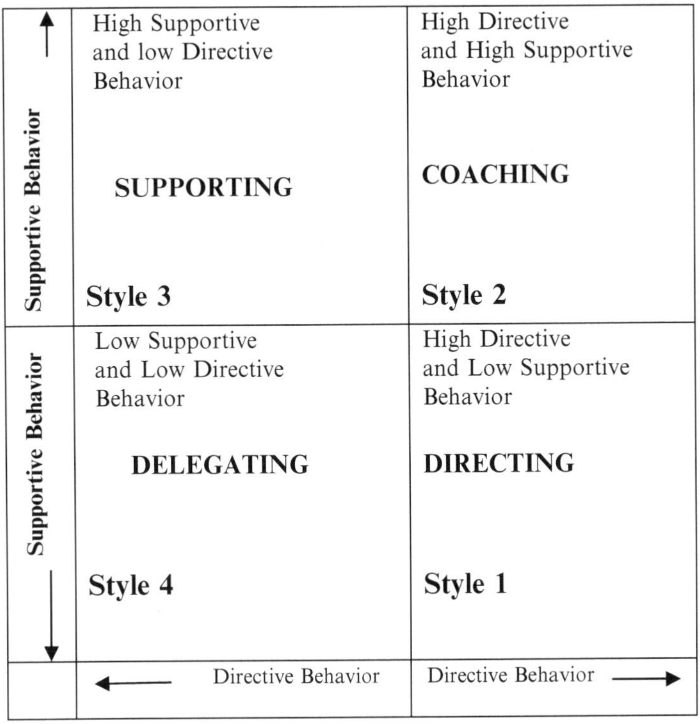

↑ Supportive Behavior	High Supportive and low Directive Behavior **SUPPORTING** **Style 3**	High Directive and High Supportive Behavior **COACHING** **Style 2**
Supportive Behavior ↓	Low Supportive and Low Directive Behavior **DELEGATING** **Style 4**	High Directive and Low Supportive Behavior **DIRECTING** **Style 1**
	← Directive Behavior	Directive Behavior →

Fig. 6.1 (Blanchard K., Zigarmi, P., and Zigarmi, D., 1985)

A small number of studies have been conducted to test situational leadership's use of maturity to divide workers into the four quadrants in the model and to see if the relationship between leader behavior and worker performance illustrated in the model held up. A few of these studies found that directive, structuring behavior was correlated more strongly with performance for low-maturity workers, but little support has been found for the model's overall prescriptions for leadership behavior in the four quadrants (Yukl 1998). A weakness of the theory is that it uses only one situational variable, when in reality there are many variables besides follower maturity that influence leadership behavior. However, the underlying idea is certainly generally useful, and its emphasis on the need for a supportive work environment is important for multicultural teams.

Shared Leadership

A critical factor addressed only to a limited extent in the approaches described above is helping to move team members from focusing on their own needs to concentrating on the good of the team and sharing leadership. In these approaches, leadership is in the hands of only a few individuals, which can lead to competition and fragmentation as members focus on their own self-interest, rely on their own cultural orientations to guide them, and compete for power. There is a need for an approach that provides a central role for followers within a multicultural context. When team members have a central role, they feel valued and are more apt to work well together and develop a sense of ownership.

Traditionally, approaches to leadership focused on individual leaders and concentrated on vertical or hierarchical approaches to organizing work tasks, where followers depend on a leader to direct activities and guide them in implementing decisions in which they were not involved (Pearce and Conger 2003). *Shared leadership* is the antithesis of this approach, focusing on leadership as a team-level phenomenon (Pearce and Conger 2003). Shared leadership has a number of predecessors that include-*empowerment and self-leadership* (Conger and Kanungo 1988; Manz and Sims 1989), *great groups* (Bennis and Biederman 1997), and *hot groups* - (LipmanBlumen and Leavitt 1999). Shared leadership as advocated in this chapter borrows from these concepts.

An ultimate aim of shared leadership is to get team members to share leadership functions, with no one person being designated as the leader and with decisions being made through consensus (Levi 2001). In order to get to this ultimate aim, teams may begin with a designated leader but then move towards a team structure where there is no designated leader but the leadership functions are shared, or they may decide to rotate leadership so that no one person retains the title of leader.

Shared leadership in this chapter emphasizes having a designated leader or leaders in the initial stages, but also draws on the concept of rotating leadership, which can be decided by the team at the outset. In the early stage of team development, the designated leader(s) might act as a coach and help team members to develop the necessary leadership skills. In this early stage of team development, leadership can be rotated, so that various team members get the opportunity to share some of the leadership functions. As team members develop their skill in team leadership, more responsibility can be turned over to them. Different multicultural teams might use different approaches, depending upon the situation, the characteristics of the members, and the tasks the team has been assigned, but the ultimate goal is for team members to share leadership, with all members feeling empowered, and the team being self-governed, with members having control over the team's work processes and major decisions.

Conditions Promoting Shared Leadership in a Multicultural Team

Certain conditions need to be present within a team for shared leadership to be implemented. These are illustrated in Fig. 6.2. Generally, it works better for teams not to embark upon shared leadership in the forming stages of development (see Chapter 4). It is best to wait until a later stage, when the necessary conditions are more apt to be in place.

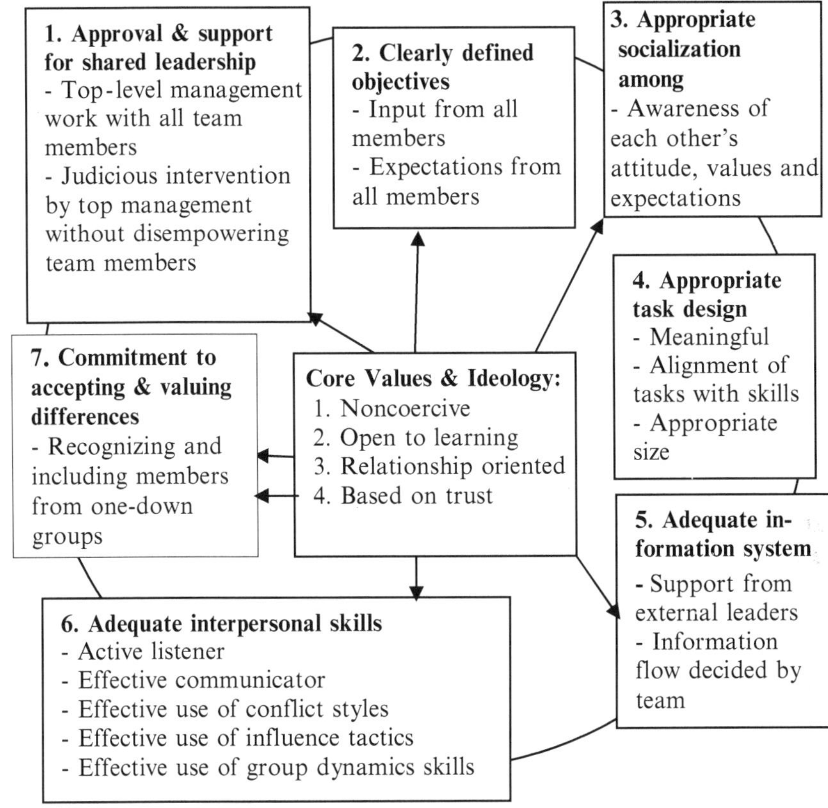

Fig. 6.2 Conditions promoting shared leadership (© Ken Williams)

Approval and Support from Top Management

A critical condition that needs to be in place for shared leadership to occur within a team is for top management to approve and support the practice of shared leadership in teams. Top-level management usually works with one or two members of a team, but for shared leadership to be successfully implemented, top-level leaders would need to be willing to work with all team members and this would impact the manner in which they relate to teams within the organization. The manner in which the team is structured would help to facilitate or limit the implementation of shared leadership and therefore it is important that top-level management endorse and support shared leadership. Top-level management's early team design decisions and expectations for team interaction and performance can contribute to the emergence of shared leadership. Although shared leadership as envisioned in this chapter would reduce dependence on top-level management, it is important that in the early stages of the team's development top-level management provide sparing, judicious intervention on an as-needed basis. This support could include providing varying resources for the team such as funding. The challenge for top-level leadership is to negotiate a gap-filling balance between abdication of leadership by team members on one hand; and disempowering seizure of control on the other.

Clearly Defined Objectives

The second condition promoting shared leadership is having clearly defined objectives for the team that are developed by the team. Initially, these objectives can be loosely developed by top-level management, after meeting with the team if appropriate, but as the team develops it should develop its own objectives (see Fig. 6.2). These objectives can include how team members would work together with regards to functional roles related to both tasks and maintenance behavior (see Chapter 5). Within the context of shared leadership, the team would need to be clear about how task and maintenance roles will be utilized, encouraging all members to function in roles according to their skills and preferences and not allowing one or two persons to dominate these roles. Shared objectives and priorities that are clearly defined and accepted, help to direct decisions about tasks to be done and also help with the coordination of efforts among team members. However, members from more particularist-oriented cultures may not be too comfortable with clearly defined objectives. This can also be exacerbated in the forming stage where team members do not know each other very well and lack of trust among members can derail the team. In order for the team to develop clearly defined objectives for themselves, sufficient time would need to have elapsed for team members to feel comfortable with expressing their feelings. The approach here would also depend on the maturity of team members.

Appropriate Socialization

The third condition is appropriate socialization, where team members become aware of each other's attitudes, values, and expectations. This awareness can help members build closer relationships, creating an atmosphere that leads to open communication. This condition doesn't usually come about until the later stages of team development (storming and performing), when members are more familiar with each other's strengths and challenges. As Halverson indicates in Chapter 4, leadership is usually challenged in the storming stage, and thus this may be an appropriate stage for members to begin to examine the possibility of shared leadership. However, it is recommended that leader and manager roles (see Table 6.4) be the main methods used in the forming stage, where hierarchical leadership is more easily accepted.

Appropriate Task Design

The fourth condition for sharing leadership is having an appropriate task design for the team. The task to be done should be meaningful, allowing members to have a vested interest in the work since it would have significance for stakeholders. Top-level management may design the task to be done, but once the team is in place, all members should have some input in making alterations to the task. Also, the work to be done should be such that needs the cooperation and interdependence of team members for its successful completion. This means that the task should be complex and require a variety of skills and knowledge, making shared leadership one of the most suitable and logical options for the team to pursue. The number of team members should also be appropriate to the tasks to be performed, with the optimum size being the smallest amount needed to do the task. Having too many members can be just as problematic as having too few.

Adequate Information Systems

The fifth condition is for there to be an adequate information system in place. It is important that all team members have access to the information that is necessary to help them regulate the team's activities and monitor its performance in relation to the organization's goals and mission. Top-level management should seek to provide equal access to information for all members and not seek to use one member as a conduit for passing information to the team unless the team requests that this be the case. In traditional teams, information is usually relayed through one person who is in a hierarchical position. Once leadership is shared, the team would have authority to make its own decisions about how information would flow (see Fig. 6.2). For example, the team could have a central location for information to be received rather than it being sent to one person repeatedly, and this information can be dispersed by various members as they take leadership, facilitation, or managerial roles.

Adequate Interpersonal Skills

Sharing leadership in multicultural teams involves coordinating activities and facilitating meetings, which requires members to possess adequate interpersonal skills. All members do not need to necessarily possess these skills initially but can be coached by a member who has them, who may or may not be the leader that is designated in the early stage of team development. These tasks require team members to be able to develop high levels of trust and cooperation with their teammates, which would require them to be able to listen actively and communicate effectively, use influence tactics appropriately, manage conflicts, and appropriately manage the various aspects of individual behavior, including their own.

As Halverson points out in Chapter 4, the performance stage of team development is when there is the highest degree of interdependence, and this is where shared leadership may be at its optimum.

However, before this level of shared leadership can be reached, team members would need to be able to receive and give feedback in a way that enhances cooperation, builds trust, and creates cohesion (see Chapter 7). Members would also need to be able to use the different influence tactics appropriately in facilitating and coordinating roles of leadership. In terms of managing conflict, members would need to become more adept at using collaboration and accommodation styles, and be able to recognize and counter other conflict styles (see Chapter 8).

Commitment to Valuing Differences

The seventh condition promoting shared leadership is the ability to value differences. Members from one-up groups tend to dominate leadership positions within teams in the forming and storming stages, and there is a tendency to challenge members from one-down groups if they become involved in leadership (see Chapter 3). Issues of differences in personality, identity, and culture may reach a zenith in the storming stage, and can severely affect how the team functions. In order for members to share leadership, there is a need for commitment to accept and value the differences among members, which would include recognizing and including women, ethnic/racial minorities, and members of other one-down groups, as equal partners in team processes. This may involve training on how to function effectively in a multicultural context.

Core Values of Shared Leadership

At the heart of shared leadership, as shown in Fig. 6.2, is an overarching mindset or ideology that relies on noncoercion, that is open to learning, that is relationship-oriented, and that is based on building trust. Establishing a noncoercive atmosphere is a very important element of shared leadership. This can come from developing a caring relationship among team members, which can result in members getting to know each other better. Team members need to discuss what the core values of the team are, which can include the four core values shown in Fig. 6.2. When team members are aware of the various conflict styles and influence tactics and can use them appropriately within a team context, this can help to create a relaxed atmosphere in which members develop trust with each other and become more willing to share their true feelings on issues. This kind of atmosphere, which engenders open and honest interaction, takes time to develop and may not be quite apparent in teams until the storming, norming, and performing stages of team development. This type of approach to team building can encourage members to be open to learning more about each other and to new ways to function within the team. With a relationship-oriented approach being at the heart of this method of shared leadership, members would be more inclined to develop trust of each other.

The core values should be the driving forces underlying the conditions that promote shared leadership, and the mindset behind all of the conditions. Top-level management must first possess this mindset as they put the teams in place, and need to help transmit the core values to team members. Their support for shared leadership must be rooted in these core values, which can help translate into the other conditions as they attempt to model these values in their interactions with team members. Team members need to have a commitment to these core values and efforts should be made by top-level management and by the team members in the initial stages to establish these core values as their overarching mindset.

Core Processes for Shared Leadership

The core processes for shared leadership will vary depending on the stage of team development. In the early stages of a team's development the core processes are focused on providing some structure around which leadership can function in the light of the multicultural nature of the team. These core processes include ensuring that the roles of facilitator, timekeeper, and scribe become a part of the meetings in the early stages of the team's development. This gives the team a regular structure by which to function, helps to resolve the issue of who is in charge, and reduces hierarchy, since more than one team member would have a critical role to play. At the same time, a process for rotating these roles needs to be developed. Systematic rotation of roles can help maintain equity and fairness, giving all members the opportunity to facilitate discussions and providing an inclusive atmosphere. Members can institute a method such as pulling straws of various lengths and members with the three shortest straws can serve the three roles in the first meeting, with the member holding the shortest straw being the facilitator, and the member with the second shortest straw serving as the timekeeper, while the member with next shortest serving as the scribe. Another suggestion is to institute a policy of rotating roles.

In addition, in recognition of the different cultural orientations that may be present in the team, different meeting formats can be utilized. For example, there may be members who are from particularistic-oriented cultures (see Chapter 2). These individuals would consider building relationships more important than getting tasks completed, and would prefer their meetings to be less structured, without formal roles. In this case, some meetings could be conducted without facilitators. Team members can utilize the tools of inquiry and advocacy, described in Chapter 7, to find out more about what teammates want and to state their own preferences.

In the later stages of team development the core processes could be less structured and team members could take more active roles in deciding how they want the team to function. During these later stages, learning will be directed through the relationships that have developed so tools such as inquiry and advocacy will not need to be relied upon, although they could still be utilized. The influence tactics used in these stages would mainly be noncoercive (see Table 6.2), indicating that the team is relying more on relationships and personal power to influence each other.

Steps for Developing Shared Leadership

Discuss Implications of Shared Leadership

Top-level management needs to discuss the implications of having a model of shared leadership in teams. Promoting shared leadership has implications for top-level management in terms of the resources that are needed to help it to be implemented successfully. Top-level management would need to recognize the time commitment and the need to shift the way in which they relate to the team. In the early stage of the team's development, the top-level management would need to meet with all team members rather than meeting with just one or a few team members (who may be the designated leaders), which is what is traditionally done. Once the team gets the opportunity to discuss their norms, they should have further meetings with top-level management in order to inform them about how the team will be operating and to let them know how they can provide assistance to members and to the team as a whole.

Establish a Process for Identifying Purpose and Goals

One of the first steps to be pursued is for the team to establish a process for identifying the purpose and goals of the team. When teams discuss their purposes and goals, the discussion usually centers around task-related issues. Since the heart of shared leadership is building lasting relationships, teams are encouraged to also include relationships as part of their purposes and goals. For example, teams can decide to have developing trusting relationships as one of the goals of the team along with specific task outcomes such as having an excellent team presentation. Including relationship-oriented purposes and goals can also help to stimulate discussion about the process for identifying these purposes and goals. For example, the team can include a relationship goal such as developing humor and identifying the purposes and goals of the team would be directed by the core processes identified above. Team members who score high on conscientiousness, low on neuroticism, high on agreeableness, and either high or low on extraversion in the Big Five personality model (see Chapter 3), can be encouraged to take active roles based on their personality traits, but this must be tempered with the inspirational motivation dimension of transformational leadership which could help to provide a vision for processes that will be pursued in the team.

Establish Norms for Multicultural Feedback and Communication

The third step is establishing channels for and methods of giving and receiving feedback that honor members from all cultural backgrounds, and establish communication norms for the team. As Griffin points out in Chapter 7, direct and indirect feedback are products of one's culture, and room must be provided for different forms of feedback to be given and received. Utilizing the tools of inquiry and advocacy can help teammates give and receive feedback interculturally. Griffin also identifies a number of overarching mindsets for enhancing competence as an intercultural communicator that can be utilized in establishing norms for team communication (see Chapter 7).

Identify the Skills and Work Experiences of Each Team Member

A fourth step is seeking to become familiar with the strengths and expertise of the various team members. Team members can accomplish this by sharing their skills and expertise at one of the early team meetings. It is critical for the team to know what skills members have that are well developed so that it can benefit from their expertise when sharing the functions associated with the leadership of the team. For example, there may be team members that are good at resolving disputes and conflict, while others may be better at motivating the team, and others may have strength in communicating a vision or using systems and procedures. It is critical for the team to know the skills that are possessed by members that are well developed so that the team can benefit from their expertise. The leadership assessment instrument at the end of this chapter provides an opportunity for members to examine their strengths and some of their areas of challenges.

Establish Norms for Team Culture

A fifth important step in the development of shared leadership is establishing general team norms for the kind of atmosphere that the team wants to function in. In this step the team collectively envisions the type of culture they want for their team. Allowing the core processes to influence the manner in which the vision is determined becomes very important since it can limit the influence of one member. Facilitators need to focus on building cohesion through consensus, ensuring that opposing views are discussed and clarified and that the team's norms are inclusive of all team members' input, with an emphasis on a noncoercive atmosphere.

Probably the most important norm a multicultural team can adopt is a *noncoercive atmosphere* that allows all team members to feel accepted, that is not based on "agreeableness," that allows members to be honest and trusting of each other and yet able to challenge each other's assumptions, can contribute to the kind of team culture that would promote shared leadership. A noncoercive atmosphere can encourage members to participate more readily in team activities and can promote greater connectedness and relationship-oriented interactions among members.

An important ingredient of a noncoercive atmosphere is the use of *influence tactics that are nonhierarchical* and cooperative (see Table 6.2). Challenges may arise when there are members from ascription-oriented cultures who might prefer to use hierarchical influence tactics, which might be perceived as coercive by members from achievement-oriented cultures. Establishing a norm where members agree to engage in *mutual learning* can help to reduce tensions and foster connectedness. Mutual learning occurs when team members develop a shared understanding of each other's background. For mutual learning to occur, team members need to be open to new perspectives, willing to learn, question assumptions, and understand concepts such as the ladder of inference, described in Chapter 7.

Another important norm teams need to establish is a *multicultural perspective on ethics*. Team members need to recognize that what may be perceived as right in one culture is not necessarily right in another culture. For example, a team member from an ascription-oriented culture may believe that it is wrong to challenge a leader, while a member from an achievement-oriented culture might have the opposite view. It is important to be able to value both perspectives. The team needs to draw on the experiences of members who have lived in different cultures and utilize some kind of inventory for storing ways of dealing with multicultural ethical dilemmas.

Provide Coaching for Members in Interpersonal Skills

A sixth step in developing shared leadership is to provide coaching for team members in using practices that promote shared leadership. In the initial stages of the team's development members may rely on approaches to leading teams that are more hierarchical, and this may especially be true of members from ascription-oriented cultures. In order to ensure that shared leadership practices become the heart of how the team functions, the team needs to identify members who are skilled in coaching who would provide feedback and insights on how members could more effectively use behaviors that promote shared leadership. These coaches should be skilled in intercultural communication (including giving and receiving feedback interculturally, and listening actively-described in Chapter 7-and be able to use various approaches to conflict, discussed in Chapter 8). It is important that the coaches not perceive themselves as the leaders of the team, and that as other members become more skilled in shared leadership, they also be given the chance to become coaches.

The coaching should take place predominantly in reflective meetings or in one-on-one situations which can be set up formally for evaluative purposes or can occur informally. In these meetings, members would have the opportunity to reflect on areas in which they think they need improvement and coaches would provide feedback on areas of shared leadership that are working well and areas where improvement is needed. Coaches would also receive feedback from team members.

An important element of this coaching would be empowering team members to participate more fully than they might have been accustomed to doing. The leadership approach that would be most appropriate would be a facilitative style (see Table 6.4). Team members who are facilitating need to place emphasis on listening, supporting, coaching, teaching, collaborating, and striving for consensus. This kind of approach is more likely to put the power into all team members' hands, with facilitators serving more as guides and catalysts, which helps with the power sharing. This can help motivate team members to support decisions made because they feel the decisions are theirs since they have significant input in discussions.

Establish a Process for Decision Making

In Chapter 9, Gobbo describes the various types of decision-making approaches available to self-managed teams which appears to be the type of decision-making most appropriate for the shared leadership emphasized in this chapter. In the shared leadership model, there might be a few individuals who might carry out most of the responsibility for leadership in the early stages of the team's development, and in this circumstance, it is best for the decision-making process to be more democratic. In this participatory model, all team members are consulted before any decision is made.

The consensus approach to problem solving and decision making might not be the most appropriate method for the team in the early stages of team development because not all members may be prepared to be fully involved in decision making, especially members who are from cultures that are ascription-oriented. However, as members begin to develop a team culture and as they become more familiar with the tasks the team is pursuing, the consensus approach to problem solving and decision making might become more appropriate.

Leadership of Virtual Teams

The concept of shared leadership as described in this chapter has significant application to virtual teams (VTs). Very few studies have examined how leadership roles are duplicated, substituted, eliminated, or shared on virtual teams, given that they are widely dispersed in time and geography (Balthazard et al. 2004). Research has suggested that leadership in VTs may be shared by team members, and may not be the domain of one assigned or emergent leader (Shamir and Ben-Ari 1999). A key challenge for leadership in VTs is to determine how leadership functions such as coaching, mentoring, team development, and envisioning can be accomplished in a shared leadership model.

Some scholars believe that physical distance makes it more challenging for leaders to engage in relational and task behaviors with team members (Napier and Ferris 1993; O'Hara-Devereaux and Johansen 1994). Other scholars contend that distance does not cripple team processes (Connaughton and Daly 2005; Kirkman and

Mathieu 2005). Not only is leadership in general more challenging for VTs, but when compared to face-to-face teams, VTs have showed lower levels of shared leadership (Balthazard et al. 2004). The separation in time and space can certainly present challenges to shared leadership, as VTs have fewer opportunities to recognize problems and are not able to anticipate them occurring the way they could if meeting face-to-face, which makes misunderstandings more likely to occur. In addition, most VTs use e-mail as their main method of communication, and it requires greater skill to use e-mails to foster trust or repair trust once it is broken. It can therefore become a significant challenge for leadership to foster cohesion and trust.

Leaders need to develop special skills for leading in cyberspace. First of all, they need to be aware of the time and space issues, which means becoming familiar with the time zones and national and religious holidays of team members and ensuring that all members take these factors into consideration when communicating. For example, teleconferences would need to be scheduled at times that do not disadvantage members from particular nations consistently. Leaders need to also lead the team as a whole and focus on building trust and cohesion early in the team's development. If possible, there should be a face-to-face meeting in the early portion of the team's forming stage, and if this is not possible, then the use of synchronous communication (which requires all parties involved in the communication to be present at the same time, and includes teleconference and telephone) should be encouraged. Whether meetings are face-to-face, using synchronous or asynchronous communication (asynchronous communication does not require all parties involved being present at the same time and includes use of e-mail), leadership needs to get team members to agree on expectations and clarify the roles for all team members, which can help with the development of a shared vision and the fostering of a new culture.

The underlying assumption of the shared leadership approach developed in this chapter is that the teams will be meeting face-to-face, but there are several aspects of the model that can be adapted and applied to leadership on VTs. Many of the conditions promoting shared leadership described in Fig. 6.2, although intended for face-to-face meetings, can also be adapted and applied to shared leadership in VTs. For example, conditions 1, 2, 4, 5, and 7 can be developed for VTs with little adaptation. However, conditions 3 and 6 require a good deal of adaptation. In order to develop appropriate socialization among team members in VTs, leadership needs to aim for more intentional integration of the core values and ideology and the conditions promoting shared leadership. There is a need for leadership to really work towards openness and providing an atmosphere where team members would feel comfortable presenting their viewpoints; the tendency not to speak readily in multicultural teams is exacerbated in VTs, where there is limited opportunity to learn about members' feelings through their body language.

Leadership needs to have a global mindset that recognizes how cultural differences can positively influence the team. Having first-hand experience of team members' culture might be helpful in helping to bridge the cultural differences. Leaders can encourage team members to augment text-only communication with charts and pictures which can help to provide deeper context, especially for those from diffuse-oriented cultures. Emoticons can be used to help provide clearer indicators of communicators' feelings and intentions, which can be useful for members from diffuse-oriented cultures. Leaders should also acknowledge seniority and titles of members, and celebrate their competencies and performance; this can be honoring for members both from achievement-oriented and ascription-oriented cultures.

Relevant Competencies

- Differentiate among the roles of leadership, management, and facilitation, and recognize when each is needed
- Collaborate with others to develop a vision
- Possess good interpersonal skills
- Understand the importance of, and be able to demonstrate, effective intercultural communication
- Listen actively
- Demonstrate trust in others
- Manage stress well
- Motivate and encourage others
- Demonstrate a clear perception of own strengths and weaknesses, and know how to utilize them
- Recognize the importance of empowering others, and know how to do it
- Value and respect varying perspectives

Summary

Leadership of multicultural teams presents a number of challenges, as identified in Chapter 2, with members having differing perspectives on power distance, uncertainty avoidance, individualism, and gender egalitarianism. A definition of leadership that perceives it as an influence relationship that is multidirectional, with followers and leaders both having significant influence in the relationship, and where purposes and goals are mutually pursued, provides an atmosphere wherein leadership of multicultural teams can be effective. In this definition, there is no one central leader; the key players are the entire group. The main sources of power are soft sources of power, using influence tactics that are predominantly cooperative, but may be both direct and indirect.

It should be noted, however, that providing an environment of shared leadership in a multicultural team presents a number of challenges that have not been completely resolved in this chapter. Shared leadership requires team members to be appreciative of low power distance and low uncertainty avoidance and to be more collectivist-oriented than individualistic. This is not easily attained in a multicultural group in which each member's culture is fully valued. There is a need for more research into this to ascertain the actual impact of using leadership approaches that are low on these cultural dimensions in multicultural teams.

Case Study: Safe and Productive Relocation of Refugees

As you read the case study below, consider the following questions:

- *What were the core processes used by the executive director to show that he was willing to share leadership?*
- *What leadership roles were utilized, and how successful were they?*
- *What influence tactics were utilized by the Asian director to influence team members to become fully involved?*
- *How could the executive director have shared leadership more effectively?*

Rescue Humanity (RH) is a human rights organization working in the Asian region to save the lives of people who are at risk for human rights abuses by their governments. It is also involved in providing vital information to policy makers in Washington D.C. on the state of human rights violations in several Asian countries. RH's headquarters is located in the United States, with a subsidiary office in Southern Asia. Recently, citizens have been complaining about the problems caused by immigrants being brought into their countries. Staff members from the Asian office have been complaining for years about the need for RH headquarters to give more autonomy to the Asian office so that they can respond to issues arising in Asia more quickly.

Rescue Humanity recently formulated a team to focus on addressing the issues related to immigrants whom they brought into these Asian countries, specifically looking at job opportunities, leadership issues, and the negative media attention RH was receiving.

The team that was formulated to look at the issues occurring in Asia consisted of the executive director, who is an American female (Tara); the Asian office manager, who is a Japanese male (Chi); the public relations officer, who is an Asian female; the organization's United States (male) lawyer; the female European human relations manager, and the chief program developer, who is a male refugee from the country with the worst human rights abuses, but recently became a legalized citizen after many years of petitioning the government. Tara was the only member of this newly formed team that was based in the United States; all of the other members were based in the Asian office.

Tara held a private meeting with Chi before meeting with all of the members of the team from the Asian office. The purpose of this meeting was to find out what might be the best way to conduct meetings with the members and how they should function as a team. During this meeting it was decided that Chi would take on the role of facilitator for the first meeting, while Tara would be the scribe. They felt that having the executive director performing the role of scribe would provide a symbolic gesture as to the manner in which she was intending to work with Chi and this new team. They also felt that it would give Tara the opportunity to understand and work with team members, since it would give her an opportunity to interact with team members but not dominate the meeting

In the first meeting, Chi asked team members to state their most important values and to describe how these values might impact the way that they work together. All team members except the American and the European, said that they wanted Chi as their spokesperson, stating that they wanted him to make final decisions, although they would like to be consulted about any decision. Chi stated that it was okay to have different views on how decisions were made, and encouraged anyone who had difficulty with the issue to speak openly about it or speak privately with him.

Tara requested that team members give her feedback about the way she interacted with them, emphasizing that she did not want to disrupt the way they did things. Chi informed team members that they were also welcomed to give feedback to anyone in the team, and that they could also do this through a third party rather than giving it to people directly. It was also requested that they state what they thought the goals and purpose of the team were and to identify ways in they would like to monitor their progress. Most of the goals that were stated by the members related to the way in which headquarters worked with the Asian office. Chi indicated that the other problems that arose, such as the escalating number of unemployed refugees brought into the border countries, were related to the limited authority and resources which the Asian office had, which resulted in their inability to respond appropriately to the developments within the Asian region. The American lawyer stated that the nature of the work in Asia was different than in America and the amount of networking needed to get the work done was much more complex than in the United States, and emphasized the need for more resources and expertise.

Chi asked the other team members who had not spoken if they had any special concerns that they would like to express, and he suggested that the team divide into pairs and talk about some of the issues and record them on sheets of paper and then present them to the team. During this time, the Asian team members were more candid about what they considered to be the issues related to employment and they also raised many issues related to internal relations within the Asian office. Some of the issues included the refusal of the non-Asian members of staff to contribute some of their salaries to help with providing jobs for the refugees; and the way they were talked to by some of the non-Asian staff.

Assessment Instrument[1]

The following list contains the key skills and qualities of an effective leader. Use the list to analyze your own skill level by giving yourself a rating for each skill/quality.

[1] Source: Elsevier Butterworth-Heineman (2005).

Next to each statement the ratings are marked one to four. These signify a sliding scale.

1 = totally underdeveloped

2 = significantly underdeveloped

3 = satisfactory

4 = fully developed

If you have no experience at all in any particular area, then leave the column blank. If you do not use these skills in your most recent job, you can draw on your experiences in other jobs and the activities you undertake outside work.

Once complete, ask a teammate to assess your skills by completing the chart in a different color, and then come together with that person to reach a consensus score of 1, 2, 3 or 4. Write this in as your overall score.

When you have agreed on an overall score with the same teammate, have a look at those items where you have a score of one or two and see if any patterns emerge: for example, are your scores more to do with communication, using systems and procedures, or managing difficult situations.

Discuss with the same teammate actions that you can take to improve the areas in which you are underdeveloped.

Differentiating among roles of leadership, management, and facilitation	1 2 3 4
Knowing when to use each of these roles	1 2 3 4
Working collaboratively with team members to develop a shared vision	1 2 3 4
Setting own goals and objectives	1 2 3 4
Working with team members to set their goals and objectives	1 2 3 4
Knowing what motivates different members of the team	1 2 3 4
Being flexible in dealing with different people	1 2 3 4
Managing time to set priorities and get tasks done	1 2 3 4
Providing feedback in multicultural setting effectively	1 2 3 4
Delegating tasks to others	1 2 3 4
Empowering others	1 2 3 4
Trusting others to complete a job properly	1 2 3 4
Expressing praise and giving constructive criticism	1 2 3 4
Sharing credit with team when things go well	1 2 3 4
Stimulating enthusiasm in colleagues and team members	1 2 3 4
Developing own skills and knowledge	1 2 3 4
Adapting to changes when necessary	1 2 3 4
Explaining difficult ideas to people	1 2 3 4
Putting own ideas forward assertively	1 2 3 4
Changing your mind in the light of new or better information	1 2 3 4
Using and interpreting body language effectively	1 2 3 4
Influencing the ideas and opinions of others	1 2 3 4
Facilitating meetings well	1 2 3 4
Respecting ways of doing things that are very different from yours	1 2 3 4
Providing the resources people need to do their jobs well	1 2 3 4
Helping individuals to plan their own development	1 2 3 4
Handling information in confidence and with tact	1 2 3 4

Listening actively to what others say	1 2 3 4
Asking open questions to obtain all of the information required	1 2 3 4
Solving arguments and disputes within the team	1 2 3 4
Sizing up a situation quickly to identify the source of the problem	1 2 3 4
Involving others in decision making	1 2 3 4
Negotiating with others to find the best way forward	1 2 3 4
Remaining calm and in control in a crisis	1 2 3 4
Communicating clearly to a group of people	1 2 3 4
Engendering enthusiasm and commitment in other people	1 2 3 4
Showing appreciation for other cultures	1 2 3 4
Managing stress well	1 2 3 4

References

Adler, N. (2002). *International Dimensions of Organizational behavior* (4th Ed.). Cincinnati, OH: South-WesternThomson Learning.

Antonakis, J., Cianciolo, A. and Sternberg, R. (2004). Leadership: Past, Present and Future. In J. Antonakis, A. Cianciolo and R. Sternberg (Eds.). *The Nature of Leadership*. Thousand Oaks, CA: Sage.

Appelbaum, S., Audet, L. and Miller, J. (2003). Gender and Leadership? Leadership and Gender? A Journey Through the Landscape of Theories. *Leadership and Organization Development Journal*, *24*(1), 43–51.

Avery, G. (2004). *Understanding Leadership: Paradigms andCases*. Thousand Oaks, CA: Sage.

Bachman, J., Smith, C. and Slesinger, J. (1966). Control, performance, and satisfaction: An analysis of structural and individual effects. In Yukl, G. (1998). *Leadership in Organizations* (4th Ed.). Saddle River, NJ: Prentice-Hall.

Balthazard, P., Waldman, D., Howell, J. and Atwater, L. (2004). Shared Leadership and Group Interaction Styles in Problem-Solving Virtual Teams. Proceedings of the 37th Hawaii International Conference on Systems Sciences.

Barnett, K., McCormick, J. and Conners, R. (2001). Transformational Leadership in Schools: Panacea, Placebo or Problem? *Journal of Educational Administration*, *38*(2), 24–46.

Bennett, N., Wise, C., Woods, P. and Harvey, J. (2003). Distributed Leadership. In Chrispeels, J. (2004). *Learning to Lead Together: The Promise and Challenge of Sharing Leadership*. Thousand Oaks, CA: Sage.

Bennis, W. and Biederman, P. (1997). *Organizing Genius: The SeCrest of Creative Collaboration*. London: Nicholas Brealey.

Bennis, W. and Nanus, B. (1985). *Leaders: The Strategies for Taking Charge*. New York: HarperCollins.

Conger, J., and Kanungo, R. (Eds). (1988). *Charismatic leadership: the elusive factor in organizational effectiveness*. San Francisco: Jossey-Bass.

Connaughton, S. and Daly, J. (2005). Leadership in the new millennium: Communication beyond temporal, spatial, and geographical boundaries. In Connaughton, S. and Shuffler, M. (2007). *Multinational and Multicultural Distributed Teams: A review and Future Agenda*. Small Group Research, *38*(3), June 2007, 387–412.

Connerley, M. and Pedersen, P. (2005). *Leadership in a diverse and multicultural environment: Developing awareness, know-ledge and skills*. Thousand Oaks, CA: Sage.

Davis, D. and Bryant, J. (2004). Influence at a Distance: Leadership in Global Virtual Teams. In Mobley, H. and Dorfman, P. (2003). *Advances in Global Leadership* (Vol. 3). Oxford: Elsevier Science.

Eagly, A. and Carli, L. (2004). Women and Men as Leaders. In J.Antonakis, A. Cianciolo and R. Sternberg (Eds.). *The Nature of Leadership*. Thousand Oaks, CA: Sage.

Eagly, A. and Johnson, B. (1990). Gender and Leadership Style: Ameta-analysis. *Psychological Bulletin, 108*, 233–256.

Elsevier Butterworth-Heineman. (2005). *Management Extra: Leading Teams*. Burlington, MA: Elsevier.

French, R. and Raven, B. (2004). The Bases of Social Power. In P. Northouse (Ed.). *Leadership: Theory and Practice* (3rd ed.). Thousand Oaks, CA: Sage.

Gilligan, C. (1982). *In a Different Voice: Psychological Theory and Women's Development*. Cambridge, MA: Harvard University Press.

Greenleaf, R. (1977). Servant Leadership: A Journey into Nature of Legitimate Power and Greatness. In Northouse, P. (2004). *Leadership: Theory and Practice* (3rd Ed.). Thousand Oaks, CA: Sage.

Helgesen, S. (1990). *The Female Advantage: Women's Way of Leadership*. New York: Doubleday.

Hersey, P. and Blanchard, K. (1988). *Management of Organizational Behavior: Utilizing Human Resources* (5th Ed.). Englewood Cliffs, NJ: Prentice-Hall.

Hofstede, G. (2005). Culture's Consequences: Comparing Values, Behaviors, Institutions and Organizations Across Nations. In M. Connerley and P. Pedersen (Eds.). *Leadership in a Diverse and Multicultural Environment: Developing Awareness, Knowledge and Skills* (2nd Ed.). Thousand Oaks, CA: Sage.

House, R., Hanges, P., Javidan, M., Dorfman, P. and Gupta, V. (2004). *Culture, Leadership and Organizations: The Globe Study of 62 Societies*. Thousand Oaks, CA: Sage.

Irving, J. and Longbotham, G. (2007). Team Effectiveness and Six Essential Servant Leadership Themes: A Regression Model Based on Organizational Leadership Assessment. *International Journal of Leadership Studies, 2*(2), Retrieved July 5th, 2007, from http://www.regent.edu/acad/global/publications/ijls/new/vol2iss2/IrvingLongbotham/Irving

Javidan, M., House, R. and Dorfman, P. (2004). A Non-technical Summary of Globe Findings. In R. House, P. Hanges, M. Javidan, P. Dorfman and V. Gupta (Eds.). *Culture, Leadership and Organizations: The Globe Study of 62 Societies*. Thousand Oaks, CA: Sage.

Jones, P., Palmer, J., Osterweil, C. and Whitehead, D. (1996). *Delivering Exceptional Performance*. New York: Pitman Publishing.

Judge, T., Bono, J., Ilies, R. and Gerhardt, M. (2002). Personality and Leadership: A Qualitative Quantitative Review. In Antonakis, J., Cianciolo, A. and Sternberg, R. (2004). *The Nature of Leadership*. Thousand Oaks, CA: Sage.

Kennedy, J., Fu, P. and Yukl, G. (2003). Influence Tactics Across Twelve Cultures. In H. Mobley and P. Dorfman (Eds.). *Advances in Global Leadership* (Vol. 3). Oxford: Elsevier Science.

Kirkman, J. and Mathieu, J. (2005). The dimensions and antecedents of team virtuality. In Connaughton, S. and Shuffler, M. (2007). *Multinational and Multicultural Distributed Teams: A review and Future Agenda*. Small Group Research, *38*(3), June 2007, 387–412.

Kirkman, B. and Shapiro, D. (2001). The Impact of Cultural Valueson Job Satisfaction and Organizational Commitment in Self-managing Work Teams: The Mediating Role of Employee Resistance. *Academy of Management Journal, 44*(3), 557–569.

Klenke, K. (2003). Gender Influences in Decision-making Processes in Top Management Teams. *Management Decision, 41*(10), 1024–1034.

Kotter, J. (1990). *A force for change: How leadership differs from management. New York*, New York: Free press

Lakey, B., Lakey, G., Napier, R. and Robinson, J. (1995). *Grassroots and Nonprofit Leadership: A guide for Organizations in Changing Times*. New Haven, CT: New Society Publishers.

LaFasto, F. and Larson, C. (2001). *When Teams Work Best: 6000 Team Members and Leaders Tell What it Takes to Succeed*. Thousand Oaks, CA: Sage.

Leithwood, K. and Jantzi, D. (2000). The Effects of Transformational Leadership on Organizational Conditions and Student En-gagement with School. *Journal of Educational Administration, 38*(2), 112–129.

LePine, J., Hollenbeck, J., Ilgen, D. and Hedlund, J. (1997). Effects of Individual Differences on the Performance of Hierarchical Decision-making Teams: Much More Than G. In Antonakis, J., Cianciolo, A. and Sternberg, R. (2004). *The Nature of Leadership*. Thousand Oaks, CA: Sage.

Lessem, R. and Nussbaum, B. (1996). Sawubona Africa: Embracing Four Worlds in South African Management. Johannesburg, South Africa: Zebra Press. In Van der Colff, L. (2003). *Leadership Lessons from the African Tree*. Management Decision 41/3, 257–261.

Levi, D. (2001). *Group Dynamics for Teams*. Thousand Oaks, CA: Sage.

Lewin, K., Lippit, R. and White, R. (1939). Patterns of Aggressive Behavior in Experimentally Created Social Climates. *Journal of Social Psychology*, *10*, 271–301.

Lipman-Blumen J., and Leavitt, H. (1999). *Hot groups: Seeding them, feeding them and using them to ignite your organization*. New York: Oxford university press

Lumsden, G. and Lumsden, D. (1997). Communicating in Teams and Teams. In Levi, D. (2001). *Group Dynamics for Teams*. Thousand Oaks, CA: Sage.

Manz, C. and Sims, H. (1989). Super Leadership: Leading Others to Lead Themselves. In Beyerlein, M., Johnson, D. and Beyerlein, S. (Eds.) (1993). *Advances in Interdisciplinary Studies of Work Teams: Team Leadership* (Vol. 3). Greenwich, CT: JAI.

Mbigi, L. (1995a). Towards a Rainbow Management Style, Enterprise, pp. 42–45. In Van der Colff, L. (2003). *Leadership Lessons from the African Tree*. Management Decision 41/3, 257–261.

Mbigi, L. (1995b). Ubuntu: The Spirit of African Transformation Management. Johannesburg, South Africa: Knowledge Resources. In Van der Colff, L. (2003). *Leadership Lessons from the African Tree*. Management Decision 41/3, 257–261.

Napier, B. and Ferris, G. (1993). Distance in Organizations. In Connaughton, S. and Shuffler, M. (2007). *Multinational and Multicultural Distributed Teams: A Review and Future Agenda*. Small Group Research, *38*(3), June 2007, 387–412.

Northouse, P. (2004). *Leadership: Theory and Practice* (3rd Ed.).Thousand Oaks, CA: Sage.

O'Hara-Devereaux, M. and Johansen, R. (1994). Global Work: Bridging distance, culture and time. In Mobley, H. and Dorfman, P. (2003). *Advances in Global Leadership* (Vol. 3). Oxford: Elsevier Science.

Pearce, C. and Conger, J. (2003). All Those Years Ago: The Historical Underpinnings of Shared Leadership. In C. Pearce and J. Conger (Eds.). *Shared Leadership: Reframing the Hows and Whys of Leadership*. Thousand Oaks, CA: Sage.

Ployhart, R., Holtz, B. and Bliese, P. (2002). Longitudinal Data Analysis: Applications of Random Coefficient Modeling of Leadership Research. In Antonakis, J., Cianciolo, A. and Sternberg, R. (2004). *The Nature of Leadership*. Thousand Oaks, CA: Sage.

Roffey, R. (2000). Strategic Leadership and Management in the Philippines: Dynamics of Gender and Culture. *Labour and Management in Development Journal*, *1*(10), 1–31.

Rosener, J. (1990). Ways Women Lead: The Command-and-control Leadership Style Associated with Men is not the Only Way to Succeed. *Harvard Business Review*, *68* (Nov/Dec), 119–125.

Rost, J. (1993). *Leadership for the Twenty-First Century*. Westport, CT: Praeger.

Senge, P. (1990). *The Fifth Discipline: The Art and Practice of the Learning Organization*. New York: Doubleday.

Sennett, R. (1993). *Authority*. New York: Norton.

Shamir, B. and Ben-Ari, E. (1999). Leadership in an Open Army: Civilian Connections, Interorganizational Frameworks, and Changes in Military Leadership. In Balthazard, P., Waldman, D., Howell, J. and Atwater, L. (2004). *Shared Leadership and Group Interaction Styles in Problem-Solving Virtual Teams*. Proceedings of the 37th Hawaii International Conference on Systems Sciences.

Smith, P. (2003). Leaders' Sources of Guidance and the Challenge of Working Across Cultures. In Mobley, H. and Dorfman, P. (2003). *Advances in Global Leadership* (Vol. 3). Oxford: Elsevier Science.

Smith, C. and Tannenbaum, A. (1963). Organizational Control Structure: A Comparative Analysis. In Yukl, G. (1998). *Leadership in Organizations* (4th Ed.). Saddle River, NJ: Prentice-Hall.

Stogdill, R. (1948). Personal factors associated with leadership: A survey of the literature. *Journal of psychology*, *25*, 35–71.

Thomas, D., Ravlin, E. and Barry, D. (2000). Creating Effective Multicultural Teams. *University of Auckland Business Review*, *2*(1), 11–24.

Van der Colff, L. (2003). Leadership Lessons from the African Tree. *Management Decision*, *41*(3), 257–261.

Van Engen, L. and Willemsen, T. (2001). Gender and Leadership Styles: A Review of the Past Decade. *Work and Organization Research Center* (paper 6). The Netherlands: Tilburg University.

Van Vugt, M., Jepson, S., Hart, C. and De Cremer, D. (2004). Autocratic Leadership in Social Dilemmas: A Threat to Group Stability. *Journal of Experimental Social Psychology*, *40*(1) 1–3.

Weaver, R. and Farrell, J. (1999). *Managers as Facilitators: A Practical Guide to Getting Work Done in a Changing Workplace*. San Francisco, CA: Berrett-Koehler.

Wheatley, M. (2006). Leadership and the New Science: Discovering Order in a Chaotic World. San Francisco, CA: Berret-Koehler.

Yukl, G. (1998). *Leadership in Organizations* (4th Ed.). Saddle River, NJ: Prentice-Hall.

Zaccaro, S., Kemp, C. and Bader, P. (2004). Leader Traits and Attributes. In J. Antonakis, A. Cianciolo and R. Sternberg (Eds.). *The Nature of Leadership*. Thousand Oaks, CA: Sage.

Resources and Web sites

http://www.shambhalainstitute.org/2004/2004_dialogue.html
http://www.nwlink.com/~donclark/leader/survstyl.html
http://hbswk.hbs.edu/item/4869.html
http://www.berkana.org/; http://www.ethicalleadership.org/
http://www.leadershiplearning.org/; http://wagner.nyu.edu/leadership

Chapter 7
Effective Intercultural Communication

Teresa Moore Griffin

Give every man thine ear, but few thy voice
–Shakespeare, Hamlet

Introduction

Today, effective intercultural communication is a required competency for every professional. Whether you are a global executive, a high potential professional, a member of a global or virtual team, the leader of a local team, a school teacher, lawyer, physician, programmer, plumber, or the owner of the corner bakery or dry cleaner, you are an intercultural communicator. A borderless world demands that you learn to communicate with people who come from many different backgrounds, some with cultural communication patterns that are not at all familiar to you. *Are you an effective intercultural communicator? Are you able to communicate with others, understand them, and be understood? Are you able to get your message across clearly and succinctly? Does your communication demonstrate awareness of, and respect for, the communication needs and preferences of the diverse others with whom you engage?*

Communication, which is culturally learned (Connerley and Pedersen 2005) and begins the moment you make contact with another, always occurs across differences. Sometimes the difference is based on interpersonal style. Sometimes it is based on professional expertise (lawyer, programmer, CEO, nurse, plumber, homemaker) or industry (financial, consumer, telecommunication, education, social services, pharmaceutical). At other times, the differences come from cultural background as described in Chapter 2, or dimensions of social identity (gender, religion, race/ethnicity, and so forth) as described in Chapter 3. Each dimension of diversity—individual, functional or cultural—can serve as a bridge to mutual understanding or as a barrier, increasing the potential for miscommunication.

Communicating across differences is a challenge that has magnified as we live and work with more and more people who come from different places intellectually, emotionally, and culturally. You must effectively respond to a range of differences

C.B. Halverson and S.A. Tirmizi (eds.), *Effective Multicultural Teams: Theory and Practice,*

if you want to achieve the goal of clear, respectful communication and expand your capacity for effectiveness and satisfaction. Competence as an intercultural communicator is vital to your ability to address challenges faced on multicultural teams (Matveev and Nelson 2004). Successful communication is an ongoing, dynamic, and active process which always results in mutual understanding. Understanding exists when there is shared meaning of a given behavior, gesture or symbol, or set of behaviors, gestures, or symbols.

While you are accustomed to attending to the content or subject matter of a communication, and even the mode of delivery, you are probably less accustomed to exercising intentional consideration of the cultural identities and orientations of the audience. Intentional consideration of this element, cultural identity, involves understanding your own culture and its influence on how you think and see the world, as well as the cultural norms of other group members (Matveev and Nelson 2004). Thinking about communication in this way may lead to important adjustments in behavior, adjustments designed to demonstrate respect for individual preferences and the cultural customs and expectations of others. Often the required adjustment goes beyond simply offering the current politically correct platitudes. It may require a redefinition of approach and process. Such a result can be achieved by challenging assumptions and developing a broader range of skills and processes for working with an ever-widening circle of people who further inform your perspective (Connerley and Pederson 2005).

The discussion in this chapter is intended to enhance your awareness of the competencies required for effective intercultural communication, on multicultural teams. With enhanced knowledge of intercultural communication, you can become a more effective listener, speaker, team member, and leader.

Learning Objectives

After reading this chapter, you should be able to:

- Describe the impact of culture on communication
- Communicate interculturally, whether speaking or listening, with confidence and increased comfort
- Understand the assumptions inherent in your own thought processes
- Identify ways to respectfully query others concerning the mental models they utilized in thinking and decision making
- Give and receive feedback

The Functions of Communication on Multicultural Teams

Tirmizi's Multicultural Team Effectiveness Model, described in Chapter 1, indicates that communication, one of the critical team processes, is influenced by societal and institutional factors; organizational factors; team dynamics; and team design.

The quality of a team's communication impacts, even defines, its climate and overall effectiveness. Where communication is effective, trust and commitment seem to be high. Members tend to perform better and express greater satisfaction with their role and participation.

Effective communication is at the heart of high-functioning teams, be they local, global, actual, virtual, cross-cultural, cross-functional, for profit, not for profit, government-sponsored, focused on community development, or corporate. Communication is the mechanism teams use to transfer knowledge, provide information, set direction, understand each other as individuals, ask questions, make decisions, take appropriate action, and simply relate to one another. When communication goes well, the transmission of information is complete: the sender delivers the message, and the receiver understands the message as the sender intended it. Effective communication can motivate you to act and achieve extraordinary results. Communication serves to support information sharing and decision making. It is a required tool for relationship and community building.

Because team members may come from different parts of the organization, including different geographic locations and divisions, a part of their charge is to bring a wide range of viewpoints and experiences to bear on problems and generate high quality solutions. Team members must have the capacity to communicate well when operating within the boundaries of the team and as they engage with a wider audience. Team communication goes well beyond what happens within the confines of the team. As they move back into their part of the organization, members must effectively communicate and sell the solution to local colleagues, on behalf of the team. The group's results and impact ripple out into the rest of the organization.

Multicultural teams face some particular challenges, above and beyond bridging from one set of personality preferences to another. Multicultural teams must bridge across cultures, with each culture having its own specific mental models and even language differences. This set of challenges adds layers of complexity to the work of effective communication in the intercultural context. A core process of teams (see Chapter 1) and a critical skill set for cross-cultural competence, effective communication is at the heart of individual and team effectiveness. *So, how does this process work? What are its component parts? What facilitates shared understanding, and what gets in the way?*

A Communication Model

Communication is a complex process, as shown by the traditional model of communication in Fig. 7.1. It involves a sender, a receiver, environmental factors, as well as personal and cultural filters. All of these elements affect both the sender and the receiver. Clarity of the message is driven by the words you choose to use and the accompanying nonverbal behaviors, including posture, tone of voice, eye contact, rhythm of breath, timing, and delivery of the message.

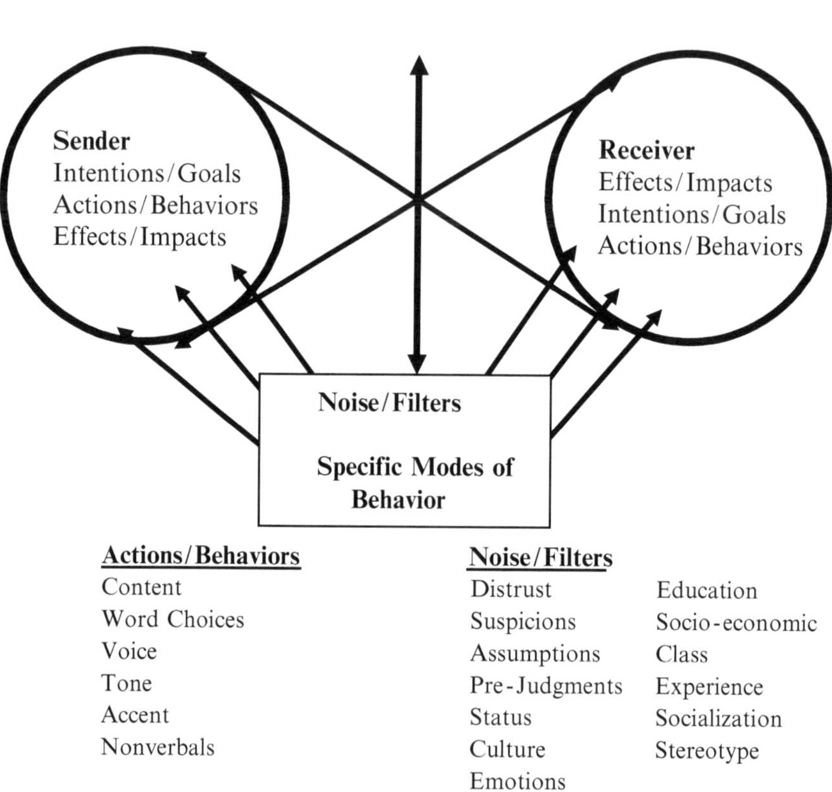

Fig. 7.1 A traditional communication model

As the sender formulates a message, her or his filters influence the content of the message and the way in which it is delivered. When the sender conveys the message, it encounters the receiver's filters. The receiver's filters are made up of personality preferences and values, in addition to being shaped by all dimensions of cultural diversity. The filters, also called noise, color and shape how the sender constructs the message and how the receiver interprets the message. This noise influences the content and meaning of the message. In a two-person interaction, when both people are from the same cultural background, the filters operating in their communication are primarily their individual personality preferences or style differences (see Chapter 3). For example, in the USA, for some people the word confrontation invokes images of a fight, a battle. For others, the word simply means that we are engaging in a dialogue about an issue that is difficult to discuss and a change in behavior is required. When you move across cultures, the layers and content of filters increase and become more complex. Interculturally, noise may involve a range of filters, such as mental models; prejudices and stereotypes; language and dialect differences; embellishment of information; level of animation; pacing and use of silence; directness of the message; formality of speech, as well as vocal tone and physical proximity. All of these filters create noise and potential interference, making communication even more challenging.

The specific meaning assigned to a particular behavior can vary within and across cultures. The same behavior can have an entirely different meaning in one culture than in another. For example, in the USA, when listening, shaking your head from side to side generally signals disagreement. Nodding your head in an up and down motion usually indicates agreement. In parts of India, head movement simply means that the person is engaged in listening. It is not the expression of an opinion, in favor of, nor in disagreement with the message. Without cross-cultural awareness of the meaning of specific nonverbal behavior, confusion and frustration abound.

The traditional communication model presented here is a mechanical description of an interactive, fluid, seamless, reflexive process. Much of what is depicted happens at rapid speed and, seemingly, involuntarily. The process begins with the sender, who has an important message to deliver. The message has as its goal the communication of a particular intention or idea. Looking out at the audience, be it one person or many people, the sender perceives them through a unique set of filters. The filters are specific to the sender's personal and cultural lens *and* to the individual or group that is the intended recipient of the message. If the individual or make-up of the group were different, the operative filters might also vary. The sender's filters include assumptions, history, fears, stereotypes, and the like about the individual or group with whom she is communicating. Her filters influence her word choices and all attendant behaviors, determining the pace of her speech, her tone of voice, the imagery she chooses to use, whether she sits or stands when delivering the message, the degree of formality of the communication, the way she holds her body, the depth and pace of her breathing, and so on.

Whatever the medium of communication—a face-to-face interaction, a telephone exchange, an email, or a videoconference—the sender's message lands in the world of the receiver, where it passes through filters. If the receiver is a group, the message passes through each group member's filters. The degree of understanding will vary depending upon the strength and intensity of the listener's filters. In groups, one person's filters will interact with those of another as people exchange their understanding of the meaning they have made of the sender's message. Naturally, everyone present will have their own interpretation of the message. In a team meeting of 25 participants, the sender is likely to experience several interpretations of the message. Some of the interpretations will be dramatically different from the sender's intention. Others will reflect subtle variations, some of which may be nearly imperceptible, until the receiver takes action. Then, the difference in interpretation becomes crystal clear. During a discussion, subtle differences seem meaningless. When acted upon, they become glaring. Investigating the subtleties is as important as delving into the more dramatic differences. In fact, the more dramatic the difference, the earlier the reality of the miscommunication tends to present itself, allowing for redirection. Subtleties often make themselves apparent much later in the process and so are more challenging to redirect before major disruption occurs. For example, if you ask team members to conduct two interviews to gather data on some relevant questions, the directions sound clear and straightforward. Yet, the potential for a subtle misunderstanding exists. Are you to conduct two interviews of two different people or two interviews of the same person at two different phases of the process? Another example might involve a Muslim colleague who says "Yes, if it is God's will." The non-Muslin colleague may hear this as a hopeful "Yes." Yet, the Muslim colleague may be respectfully expressing a lack of commitment which will not clearly present itself until the expected results are not delivered.

In Chapters 2 and 3 the authors discuss values, acknowledging that they differ from individual to individual and across cultures. *How do your values, individual and cultural, shape your communication? What are your individual and cultural filters? What has been their impact on your effectiveness when communicating across cultures?*

Both your style and your cultural differences can affect the way you hear others, and it can shape the way you construct and convey a message. Certainly the way a message is conveyed to a person who comes from a Collectivism orientation versus someone from an Individualism orientation (Hampden-Turner and Trompenaars 2000) would, by necessity, have to be different in order to achieve understanding and create alignment. For example, if the goal is to streamline a process, the message to the Collectivist would probably need to clearly describe how the change will affect all parties involved and demonstrate that the design and implementation plan serve the good of the whole team or system. The Individualist would most likely be motivated by hearing how the process will ease the burden in his functional area or lead to cost savings for the company, though it may have an adverse impact on some areas of the operation. To get buy-in to the goals of the project, the effective communicator must convey the goals in a way that addresses the needs and motivational levers of all team members, accounting for individual and cultural preferences.

Cultural stereotypes you hold about both individual and group differences, as addressed in Chapters 2 and 3, can lead to breakdowns in communication. For example, if a team member has a pattern of over-talking a point, other team members will often tune out as the individual speaks. The tuning out is felt by the individual, causing him to talk more because he wants to be heard, acknowledged, and understood. As the individual talks more, the team tunes him out even more. The cycle is vicious. How team members treat each other can facilitate communication and inclusion or lead to their disintegration. Considering this same behavior pattern, I have often noticed that over-talking by men is more easily tolerated than when the same behavior is exhibited by women. Women who over-talk are often talked over and therefore interrupted (Tannen 1990); (Tingley 199-, over-talk are usually allowed to finish speaking but perhaps no one resp. what they have said or their comments are simply acknowledged in a cursory fa. ion before someone transitions the team, redirecting focus. *What are some examples of communication barriers and breakdowns in the workplace? How do both individual and cultural differences lead to, or exacerbate, the presence and impact of communication barriers and breakdowns? In what ways have your preferences, individual and/or cultural, contributed to communication barriers or breakdowns on a team of which you have been a member?*

Formal and Informal Communication

Teams use various types of communication, to communicate both within the team and to other parts of the organization. At times, formal communication is called for, communication that follows the official chain of command or is part of the expected discussing and reporting that must be done to comply with the sanctioned organizational expectations or protocol. Formal communication, which usually involves announcements, written work plans, documentation of meeting output and new procedures, progress reports, presentations and recommendations, is engaged in most often in response to expectations of the organization's hierarchy and/or reporting structure.

In most organizations, the informal communication network is much more powerful than the formal process. It is where issues are negotiated and resolved. It is where agreements are reached and decisions are made. The informal communication network has the power to advance initiatives or derail them. All of the hurdles of the formal organization are surmounted by effectively navigating the informal communication system. Since all results are created through the efforts of people who decide to lend their support, teams that constructively use their influence through the informal channels create results faster. They satisfy the social needs of the organization, communicating alignment with business goals and respecting the political nuances of the system.

Communication Structures Used by Teams

There are several types of communication structures used by teams. As pictured in Fig. 7.2 (Fisher 1980), they include the chain, the wheel, and the all-channel networks. The *chain* reflects the traditional hierarchy, with communication flowing toward the formal chain of command, moving up and down the chain in a siloed fashion. In the *wheel* formation, communication flows in and out of the team through the leader. The leader is the center of the hub and transmits information to team members and other groups. The chain and wheel both require that information

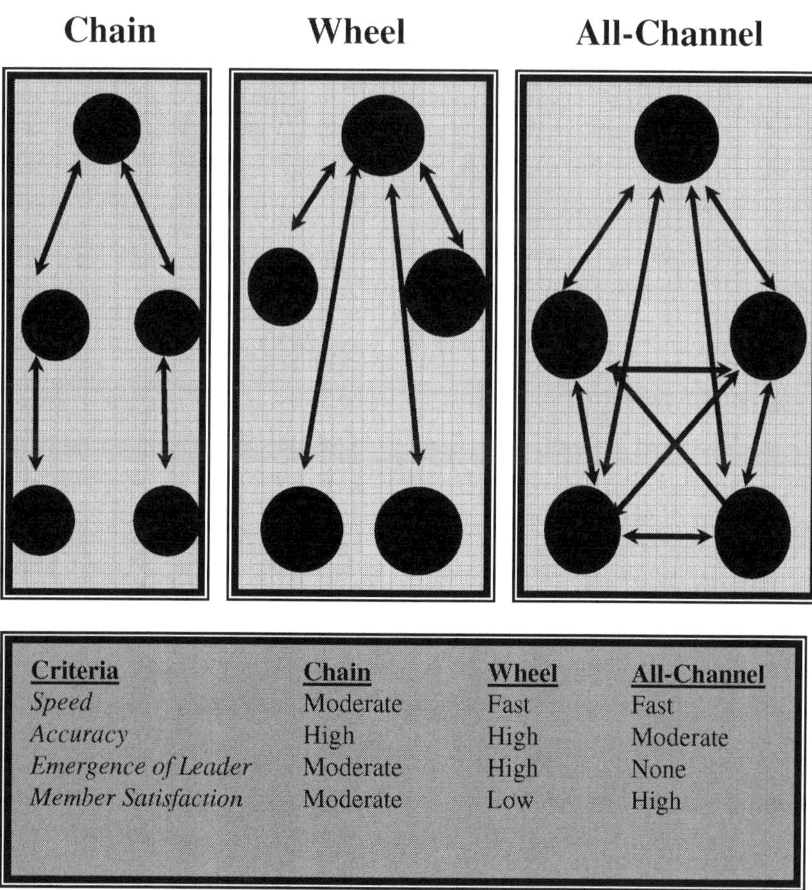

Criteria	Chain	Wheel	All-Channel
Speed	Moderate	Fast	Fast
Accuracy	High	High	Moderate
Emergence of Leader	Moderate	High	None
Member Satisfaction	Moderate	Low	High

Fig. 7.2 Communication structures and their effectiveness (Fisher 1980)

flow to a central point before it can be passed on to others. In these networks, communication requires more time. In the *all-channel* structure, communication flows freely among all members of the work team and out to the organization, as appropriate.

Teams benefit from making an explicit decision about the type of communication processes and structure they will use. The decision needs to be made with consideration for:

- The team's purpose and anticipated lifespan
- The structure of the team—hierarchical, flat, shared leadership, or self-managed
- The frequency of team meetings
- The individual communication and social needs of all team members
- Organizational expectations on communication from the team

The communication structure chosen should support the efficient and effective exchange of information, promoting understanding and facilitating right action.

Each structure has its inherent strengths and challenges. In terms of team member satisfaction, an important measure of team effectiveness, the all-channel network reports the highest degree of member involvement, energy, and motivation. It is also the one model in which leadership is more easily shared. Its power structure tends to remain flat. New teams may find the all-channel network to be most effective since all members are equally linked into the communication process. As teams develop, the preferred structure could change as member needs concerning issues of distance and centrality change (Fisher 1980).

Modes of Communication

High- and Low-Context Cultures

Culture plays a critical role in shaping team members' mental models (Adler 2001) and behavior. Accordingly, it stands to reason that the culture of each team member will have a significant effect on the way in which the team communicates. The skilled team member aims to understand the culture of his or her colleagues and their approach to relationships and tasks, as well as their approach to teamwork and decision making. Based on that understanding and knowledge, the wise team member makes adjustments in his or her communication style (Matveev and Nelson 2004).

As described in Chapter 2, anthropologist Edward Hall (1977) asserts that cultures exist on a continuum that reflects the degree, high to low, to which its members relate to context or the interrelated social and cultural conditions that surround and influence the mindset and behavior of an individual, organization, community, or society.

As documented by Halverson (1993), in low-context cultures such as Scandinavia and Germany, the message or communication depends on the words that are spoken, with little if any use of or emphasis on the meaning of the nonverbal elements of the communication. The verbal message tends to be direct and explicit. Things are spelled out in exact terms. The words are the message and, accordingly, are to be taken literally. Speed and efficiency in conveying the relevant facts and completing the interaction are of greatest importance, whether through an oral or written exchange.

High-context cultures use nonverbal communication as a powerful and vital part of the exchange. Significant meaning is conveyed through tone, gestures, facial expressions, posture, social status, history, the setting, even physical proximity and contact. While the verbal content of the message is implied, the power and importance of the conversation are related to the people, the situation, and the nonverbal elements. People speak, embellishing the point. Communication is seen and experienced as an art form and a way of engaging and connecting with others. Such exchanges lend themselves to oral communication and therefore, require time.

A meeting among women who, across cultures, tend to be high context in orientation will involve discussion of family and friends, an update on the people and current events in their lives, discussion of current challenges, and plans for the weekend or holiday. A request for similar information from the others present is a given. A similar kind of give-and-take relational dynamic would exist in a meeting or gathering among a group of Africans or Asians, whatever their gender. There is an interest in engaging and learning about the other. Face-to-face, or at least voice-to-voice, best enables this quality of interaction.

In her Cultural Context Chart, Halverson (1993) presents a discussion of interactions in high- and low-context cultures. Pay close attention to the information presented in Table 7.1. It provides useful insight into key dimensions of communication within high and low cultural contexts.

Not only is the style of communication different in high- and low-context cultures, the reasons for communicating are also different. Communication in high-context cultures appears to be more about the connection between people, the trust that evolves and the relationship that develops, *over time*. The first goal of the interaction is to know and connect with the other. In low-context cultures, the goal is to get the task done. Relationships begin and end and are seen as expedient, enabling a result. Then, *if* time permits, socializing and relating on a personal level can occur.

The High-Low Context model of cultures is useful in that it awakens awareness to the valid uniqueness and communication style of these cultural orientations. With this knowledge, constructive choices can be made about how and when to

Table 7.1 Cultural-context chart: Interaction (Halverson 1993)

High-context culture	Low-context culture
High use of nonverbal communication: Voice tone, facial expression, gesture, and eye expression carry significant parts of conversation	Low use of nonverbal communication: Message is carried more by words than by nonverbal means
Message implicit: Verbal message is implicit—the context is more important (situation, people, nonverbals)	Message explicit: Verbal message is explicit, and the context is less important
Indirect: The point is embellished and communication is circular	Direct: Things are spelled out exactly
Message is art form: Communication is seen as an art form, a way of engaging the person	Message is literal: Communication is seen as a way of exchanging information, ideas, and opinions
Disagreement is personalized: Sensitivity to conflict that another's nonverbal communication suggests. Conflict must be solved before work can progress or avoided because it is too personal	Disagreement depersonalized: Focus on rational solutions rather than personal ones, direct attention to others' bothersome behavior, and getting on with the task

communicate with others in ways that empower individuals and teams to become high functioning. When coming from a low-context culture, and working on a team with members who are from high-context environments, it is wise to be mindful of how meeting agendas are planned. In order to build an inclusive and comfortable communication environment for everyone, more time needs to be structured into the meeting design so that the relational connections can *begin*.

The success of the work and the health and vitality of the team is facilitated through team members' flexibility and acknowledgment of the different communication needs that exist on the team.

This pattern of difference in approach to communication—high/low context—will also affect the pace of the meeting, the way in which learning occurs, the preferred mode of communication, and all aspects of interactions. Low-context members of the team will do well to hear explicit instructions, spelled out clearly. Letters, memos, faxes, and e-mails are seen as perfectly appropriate. High-context team members' understanding will be enhanced if they hear instructions *and* have ample opportunity to discuss the information. Face-to-face interaction is preferred, allowing them to contextualize the interaction. On cross-cultural teams, meeting schedules need to include a variety of approaches and sufficient time to accommodate different needs and orientations. In many situations, providing oral and written instructions, coupled with time for demonstration, is of critical importance because it serves to reinforce understanding, particularly when language differences are present. Patience must be developed and exercised, as high- and low-context team members come together. *Are you a high- or low-context communicator? What is the impact of your orientation and communication style on teams? What can you do to modify your approach to communication, to support your colleagues whose orientations are different?*

Culture as Mirror Images

Charles M. Hampden-Turner and Fons Trompenaars (2000), in their book *Building Cross-cultural Competence*, present the idea that cultures share many of the same values and conceptions, though they have simply made different choices in how their values are sequenced (see Chapter 2).

Universalism emphasizes that which applies to a universe of people, while *Particularism* emphasizes the exceptions to the rule. Communication that spans this potential gap will need to address the universal rule, demonstrating fairness and sameness in application of the rule for all. The communication must also account for the particular exceptions and indicate the ways in which the rule is actually a guideline for establishing a more specific, unique agreement (Walker et al. 2003). In other words, communication will need to encompass both perspectives in order to address the needs and interests of all concerned. Effective communication will need to speak to that which is shared, the points of similarity and overlap, and that which is different and unique. With both orientations represented, it becomes apparent that all needs are considered. The experience of inclusion is more likely to result.

An *Individualist* orientation emphasizes the degree to which individual goals are valued over collective or group goals. Team members from Individualist cultures may have an intense focus on maximizing profits through the efforts of the team. They may push for the team to take risks and find creative, innovative approaches to business challenges. Their colleagues from Collectivist cultures may be more focused on the impact of the team's efforts on market share and customer satisfaction. They may suggest a business strategy that results in diminished profits in order to gain customer loyalty and capture market share. They might suggest this approach as a long-term strategy, enabling the company to capture an entire market. Japanese companies have often employed this approach. Team goals and agendas must account for what each orientation values and on what it places priority.

Specificity emphasizes precision, analysis, and getting to the point, while *Diffuseness* looks to the whole, the larger context. In communication, specificity orientation suggests that the starting point is with specifics (low context) and then the communication spins outward to include relationships. Diffuseness starts at the periphery (high context), relating broadly and then moves inward to encompass the specific aims. Communication styles that are specificity-oriented tend to be direct, forceful, and blunt, and may even be experienced as confrontational. Getting the message across is more important than the risk of offending the other. In the case of Diffuseness orientation, communication is more indirect. The sender of the message tends to drop hints, pointing in the direction of the core message and allowing the listener to interpret the message. The speaker tends to walk softly, hoping that the fullness of the message will be understood. Specificity can be likened to the orientation and practices of low-context cultures described previously. Diffuseness parallels the pattern of high-context cultures. In my experience, women, across cultures, tend to be more diffuse in their approach to communication. The style of men tends to parallel the cultural pattern of the nation with which they identify.

Trompenaars' (2000) model is a powerful tool for diverse teams. It suggests that diversity is an advantage since what a member of one cultural orientation misses seeing, the other sees in bold relief. The diverse team is able to see in multiple directions and communicate outward in ways that will capture the broadest numbers of constituents.

Each of these value perspectives is held by at least half of the world's population. On global teams, as well as local teams, differences in the order of values are bound to surface and impact the communication and work process. The response that is called for is to embrace the full spectrum of the continuum and explore issues using a holistic and inclusive approach. This mindset is essential as you work and communicate across individual differences and across cultures.

Virtual Teams and Communication

Today, many teams are virtual, brought together by technology. Technologies enable collaboration, information sharing, and decision making. While having reduced the constraints of time and distance, technology has left in place many of the old communication challenges. With most technology, context and nonverbal cues are dramatically reduced or distorted. Since nonverbal cues, tone of voice, and body language account for over 90% of the impact of communication (Mehrabian, 1981), much important information is lost. When we add the complexity of the use of technology to the inherent challenges of differences in first languages, idiomatic and colloquial expressions, as well as accents, the task of understanding each other becomes daunting. The absence of contextual information can lead to assuming a level of similarity between self and others that does not actually exist. Virtual teams have to find means, as they utilize global communication tools, to adjust their ways of communicating and understanding to fit the cultures involved (Adler 2001). *What techniques and approaches have you found to be most successful, across cultures, in making virtual meetings effective, particularly when there is not a shared first language? What can virtual teams do to mitigate the impact of diminished contextual information?*

Varner (2006) states that an individual's position in an organization has more of an effect on communication preferences and style than does the person's cultural background. Varner gives the example of computer programmers, who may prefer electronic communication with low levels of personal contact, regardless of their individual ethnicities. Electronic communication may be especially effective for diverse teams, depending on the task. Empirical studies have found that electronic communication produces greater heterogeneity in ideas and opinions (Enayati 2001). Both visible and deep-level diversity are somewhat neutralized by electronic communication. Nonverbal communication is essentially nonexistent, so team members can contribute without fearing a glance at the clock, a shrug, or a frown from another team member. E-mail is not appropriate for tasks requiring complex decision making. Therefore, the choice of a communication medium depends on team member preferences derived from organizational culture, as well as other cultural affiliations, and the complexity of the task. *Do you consider the neutralization of diversity on virtual teams to be a benefit or a detriment to the team's success?*

Nancy Adler (2001) suggests that intercultural communicators present messages through multiple channels, from visual aids to paraphrasing to summary statements. One team comprised predominantly of US and Swedish citizens applied Adler's recommendations. It began publishing a full agenda, complete with each speaker's key talking points, in advance of the meeting. The visual information, used as a point of reference during the meeting, proved to be helpful, providing clarity and focus. Pre-meeting notes, combined with the live teleconference or videoconference discussion and a post-meeting document that captured the key points of the discussion, emphasizing action items and decisions, supported a substantial improvement in the accuracy of the team's communications, its efficient use of time, and a higher level of involvement from all participants. A team that was floundering due to a lack of full participation and rampant misconceptions of purpose became high performing. Member satisfaction and productivity trended upward. *Have you ever been on a virtual team? What were or are your team's communication challenges? What are some strategies or processes your team utilized to improve communication and mutual understanding?*

.derations Concerning a Team's Communication Culture

: business of effective communication in an intercultural context requires thought and effort. The current, familiar way of operating and the rules that govern the reasons people communicate, as well as the way in which they communicate, will expand and change. New rules and patterns will be created. Those who are receptive to change will be the beneficiaries of learning and enhanced competence. Their effectiveness and value will increase.

Every team, intentionally and unintentionally, develops its own communication culture. When team members come from many places around the world or organization, the team's culture will be influenced by a multiplicity of experiences and preferences. High-functioning teams will establish an explicit culture, inclusive of a set of communication norms created by the group. The norms may be developed intentionally or may simply emerge as the group's life evolves. The more conscious the group can be of the norms it adopts and acts on, the more opportunities it has to choose which norms it will utilize in support of optimal communication and functioning. When a multicultural team develops operational norms that reflect the values and needs of its diverse membership, it is said to have developed a hybrid culture (Earley and Mosakowski 2000). The new team culture results from the overlapping cultures of its members. Hybrid cultures facilitate a strong sense of inclusion and foster mutual understanding.

When a team and team members are new to one another, it is reasonable for them to call upon what they understand about the culture of team members in order to make an educated guess about the most effective way to communicate with others (Adler 2001). As the team develops, it will evolve its own culture. Below are some specific considerations teams should explore. When properly implemented, these considerations help individuals and teams to become effective cross-cultural communicators.

Open-Mindedness

Open-mindedness helps to reduce the noise and filters in communication, increasing your ability and willingness to work well with others. Taking and holding a "position" gets in the way of seeing options and objectively considering their value. Open-mindedness holds the key to creativity (Von Oech 1998). It asks you to disengage from the "tried and true" and engage your ability to dream and imagine other realities, other ways of making things work. It invites you to push the boundaries, ask new questions, and allow creativity to flow without judgment or evaluation.

Open-mindedness facilitates listening, a critical communication skill, particularly in a cross-cultural context. In my experience, open-mindedness enables you to listen with your heart. In listening with the heart, you are better able to identify the place where you join with others, in spite of apparent differences. The contrast between people who are open-minded and those who are closed-minded is striking.

Open-mindedness helps to create a spirit of inclusion and excitement. Open-minded team members are more magnetic and influential than their counterparts. As communicators, they flex and flow to get things done. Others enjoy working with them and are stimulated by their energy and confidence. *Are you open-minded? What would it take for you to become an even more open-minded communicator? What would increase your level of open-mindedness, adding to your value and potential contribution? What can you do to encourage greater open-mindedness on the teams with which you work?*

Self-Awareness in the One Up/One Down Communication Dynamic

Many times, the challenges of the one-up/one-down dynamic in relationships (see Chapter 3) present themselves through a person's communication patterns. When you are one-up in terms of individual style or cultural group identity, you can easily slip into communicating with the one-down group member in a way that is condescending or puts the person in a subordinate position. You may speak over the one-down group member or correct what the person says or allow air time but not build on the comments or give them space and attention in the group's discussion process. In the one-up position, the individual whose culture is the prevailing one has the marked advantage of feeling relaxed, knowledgeable, in control, empowered, and powerful. The individual is advantaged through familiarity, privileged to make or know the rules for communicating and relating.

The one-down group member responds to the communication rules set by others. The territory is unfamiliar, presenting a psychological and practical disadvantage. Functioning may be diminished and constrained. Substantial energy is required to raise the experience of feeling one-down to the attention of others and deal with anticipated resistance in a way that does not damage the relationship. A cue for discerning when you are in the one-down position is when you have the thought that raising the issue of feeling one-down would be more work than it would be worth.

One-up group members can unconsciously behave in ways that shut down the voice and diminish the presence and contribution of one-down group members. The one-down group member feels marginalized, invisible, or too visible. The individual can begin to feel that it is too hard to push against the tide of the powerful ones who expect certain behavior. In reaction to the one-down group member's presence, the one-up group members may sometimes become patronizing. These are all barriers to authentic, effective communication.

In order to truly demonstrate that you value another, you must believe that all parties in an exchange are equally important and significant. I believe that all people, as human beings, have an equal right to be heard and understood. The proof of your values and beliefs is in your behavior, every day, moment to moment. The test is the degree to which your daily behavior offers tangible evidence to seeing, believing, and acting in ways that demonstrate that another's way of being is as correct as your own way of being.

When self-aware, you are conscious of your belief systems and behaviors (see Social Intelligence discussion in Chapter 3). Becoming conscious of the times when you are in the one-up position and the times when you are in the one-down position, holds many lessons concerning how to engage with others so that the power dynamics of one-up/one-down do not become the defining dimensions of your communication pattern and relationships.

Self-awareness requires deep knowledge of your behavioral tendencies, emotions, cultural conditioning, values and mindsets, idiosyncrasies, strengths and development needs (Adler 2001). Self-aware people are in tune with themselves *and* others. They are able to discern their motivation for acting in a given way and can listen to and learn from how others see them. The self-aware individual is usually a confident and competent person. *Are you self-aware? To what degree? What have been some situations in which you demonstrated self-awareness? What was the impact of your behavior? In what ways do you need to enhance your level of self-awareness?*

The Johari Window: A Tool for Enhancing Self-Awareness

Self-awareness can be enhanced. One simple model that teams and individuals can use to foster increased self-awareness is the Johari Window (Luft and Ingham 1955), Figure 7.3. It encourages you to be *Open*, to reveal information that is *Hidden* and not known to others, and to become aware of your *Blind Spot*. The Johari Window encourages an open exchange of information through self-disclosure and feedback. Receiving feedback is the primary tool available for diminishing the size and effect of your *Blind Spot*. The task of shrinking the size of your *Blind Spot*, learning what you do not know about yourself, is a worthy challenge. The more you are open to learning about yourself, the more likely you are to increase your capacity. The *Unknown* area shrinks accordingly. Learning requires personal courage, but is necessary as you work across cultures because there is so much that you do not know *and* are not aware that you do not know. The Johari Window supports you in increasing your level of Social Intelligence by providing you with insight into yourself.

The Johari Window, when used to enhance self-awareness, can stimulate interesting, useful dialogue, one-on-one or among members of a team. With the goal of expanding the size of the Open area, the primary techniques used are self-disclosure and feedback. Self-disclosure, telling others about yourself, places what is in the Hidden area out in the open. Feedback provides a constructive avenue for others to share their perceptions of you or the impact your behavior has had on them and/or the team. Feedback enables you to learn what may be in your Blind Spot.

	Known to Self	Not Known Self
Known to Others	**Open** *What you and others know about you...information that's out in the open*	**Blind Spot** *What others know or perceive about you that you do not know about yourself*
Not Known to Others	**Hidden** *What you know about yourself that others do not know*	**Unknown** *What you and others have not yet discovered about you*

Fig. 7.3 Johari window (Luft and Ingham 1955)

The depth and breadth of information about you that is out in the Open area may depend upon how long you have known the other or been a member of the team, the team's norms concerning self-disclosure, as well as your comfort, personally and culturally, in talking about yourself and making "public" information that may, to you, seem private or not relevant or appropriate to share in a work context. Certainly, you will decide what information you share and when you will expose any aspect of the Hidden area. You will also make mindful choices concerning from whom and when you will ask for feedback, opening up your ability to see into your Blind Spot(s). To one degree or another, you can make the Johari Window an active part of your strategy for enhanced self-awareness and positively impact your team's communication culture, enabling increased levels of openness through appropriate, respectful self-disclosure and feedback.

Here is an exercise you can use when you want to improve a relationship by sharing more information about yourself (Open and Hidden) and learning more about another or others, including how they see and experience you (Blind Spot).

You and another person, or you and your team members, can use the statements and questions in Fig. 7.4 to disclose the kinds of information suggested in the Open, Hidden, and Unknown panes of the window and request feedback on the kinds of questions noted in the Blind Spot. This exercise has the potential to open a window to increased self-awareness and enhanced competency. Keep in mind that what is comfortably revealed in one culture may be considered private and inappropriate for discussion in another. For example, women may be comfortable revealing emotional feelings about a topic, while men may be unable to identify specific feelings with the same ease, or may be less comfortable sharing such information.

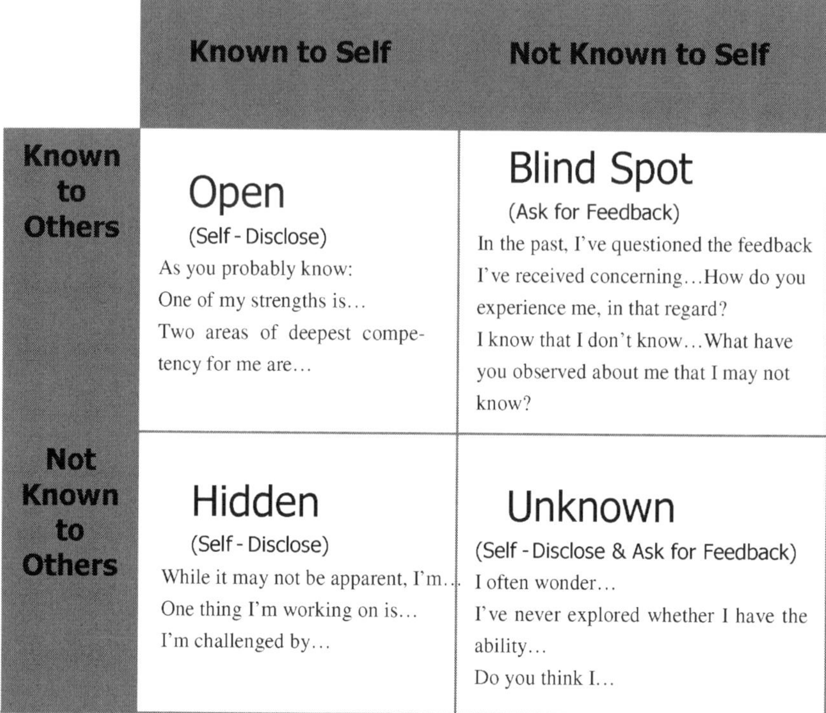

Fig. 7.4 Expanding the open pane through self-disclosure and feedback

As a woman of African descent, born and raised in the USA, I know that some African-Americans may be reluctant to openly share information with their white colleagues concerning the details of their lives. Backed by a history of one-down group membership, there can be lingering concern about how personal information may be used or misused, and the impact it may have on reputation and career opportunities.

Cultural tradition, as well as group and personal history, influence what and with whom you and others are comfortable sharing. *What kind of information are you willing to share in the workplace? How do your personal and cultural backgrounds influence your preference?*

Enhancing Competency as an Intercultural Communicator

Whether it is in your home, same-race community, same-religion, or same-gender gathering, or same-sexual orientation grouping, there are individual differences in communication style, needs, and expectations. In our multicultural world, differences are unavoidable and require a respectful, considered response if you want to be an effective, competent intercultural communicator. One model, which delineates several areas of required competence, is presented in the following section of this chapter.

The 3C Model

Competence as an intercultural communicator is a critical leverage point for all teamwork (Matveev and Nelson 2004). Matveev and Nelson provide additional perspective on this subject through discussion of their 3C Model. Here, in Table 7.2, Matveev highlights four dimensions of competence for the cross-cultural communicator. They include Interpersonal Skills, Team Effectiveness, Cultural Uncertainty, and Cultural Empathy.

Matveev's work, along with that of many others, suggests that communication, be it visual, verbal, written, sitting in silence, or contact across the ethers through the Internet or satellite links, is most effective when you are mindful. Mindful communication requires that you engage with the intention of being clearly understood and causing no harm to the relationship. Such goals suggest the need for awareness of what is likely to be most effective with a particular individual and/or what is culturally appropriate, given the context in which the communication occurs and

Table 7.2 The 3C model for cross-cultural communication competence (Matveev et al. 2001 in Matveev and Nelson 2004)

Interpersonal skills	Team effectiveness	Cultural uncertainty	Cultural empathy
Ability to acknowledge differences in communication and interaction styles	Ability to understand and define team goals, roles, and norms	Ability to deal with cultural uncertainty. Ability to display patience	Ability to see and understand the world from another's cultural perspective
Ability to deal with misunderstandings	Ability to give and receive constructive feedback	Tolerance of ambiguity and uncertainty due to cultural differences	Exhibiting a spirit of inquiry about other cultures, values, beliefs, and communication patterns
Comfort when communicating with foreign nationals	Ability to discuss and solve problems	Openness to cultural differences	Ability to appreciate dissimilar working styles
Awareness of your own cultural conditioning	Ability to deal with conflicts. Ability to display respect for other team members	Willingness to accept change and risk	Ability to accept different ways of doing things
Basic knowledge about the country, culture, and language of team members	Participatory leadership style. Ability to work cooperatively with others	Ability to exercise flexibility	Nonjudgmental stance toward the way things are done in other cultures

the cultural background of the listener(s). Awareness, achieved through mindfulness—intentionally devoting thought and mental attention to a matter—leads to enhanced effectiveness. A number of ways of thinking, and behaving facilitate improvement in communication skills, in all contexts.

The following section presents some helpful ways of thinking and behaving, when interacting cross-culturally. The author calls these important mindsets - mental attitudes or predispositions which establish an inclination or habitual response to a given situation. As you read this section, consider:

- What are some of the mindsets, or mental attitudes, which undergird your approach to cross-cultural communication?
- How do they impact your effectiveness?
- In what ways might you modify your mindsets for increased effectiveness?

Important Overarching Mindsets and Behaviors

A number of ways of thinking, mindsets, and behaving facilitate improvement in communication skills, in all contexts. When communicating within your cultural context, across cultures, one-on-one, or in teams, each of these mindsets will strengthen your competence as an intercultural communicator. Consistent utilization of the mindsets requires self-discipline. With self-discipline, more thought can be given to every interaction and a more conscious, mindful response developed. The assessment at the end of this chapter lists these mindsets and behaviors. Embed them into your daily behavior. Allow these mindsets and behaviors to support you in communicating effectively as you lead and influence others, as you relate to your family and friends, even as you reach across boundaries to interact with strangers. Because they facilitate the reduction of noise and minimize filters, these mindsets and behaviors enable sender and receiver to communicate with greater mutual understanding and respect. Many of the mindsets and behaviors suggested, all of which can be developed, resemble those of high-context cultures, inviting you to move closer to the mirror image of low context cultures, expanding competence and confidence as intercultural communicator. Thoughts and beliefs guide behavior choices. Accordingly, there are several mindsets that are useful for the intercultural communicator to adopt and use as a guide for expanding curiosity and strengthen the ability to reach through the boundaries of ones own culture to the culture of others.

First, the intercultural communicator must be committed to communicating effectively across cultures, facilitating an environment of mutual understanding and respect. Commitment is required to sustain your efforts through times of frustration and uncertainty.

Experience suggests the need for the intercultural communicator to exercise patience with self and others. Mistakes are often made. Forgiveness is required. Communicating across cultures takes a significant amount of energy and effort, as well as time. Speaking and comprehending the messages received is particularly energy draining whenever you are communicating in a language that is not your native tongue. This challenge is present even when you are fluent in that language.

When you are self-aware, and conscious of whom the other is personally and culturally, you can more consistently communicate with a quality of openness described in the Johari Window and acknowledge differences. Doing so can help to diminish the possibility of tension or conflict arising, born out of the differences. The simple act of acknowledging cultural differences may open the gateway to increased comfort and understanding. *When have you openly acknowledged cultural differences with another person? How did acknowledging the differences impact communication and understanding?*

A powerful and challenging practice is to clarify the core values that underlie any important communication or project, particularly when conflict may result. This practice enables you to focus on the deeper intentions, the core values, which are to be reflected in the message or project. The core values then become the touchstone for all actions and decisions, making it easier to be creative, solve problems, and reach consensus. One multinational team, charged with designing a new, organization-wide leadership model, reached an impasse as they struggled to define critical dimensions of leadership effectiveness. Release from deadlock occurred when team members clarified the core values they wanted leaders to exhibit. For example, aware of the impact of cultural differences on their understanding and ability to reach consensus, they acknowledged that leading with passion would look one way in Japan, and yet a different way in Egypt, Sweden, and Germany. They found a bridge to success once they made the core values their focus.

If you take a macro view, you see that people share the same core values, although the way they act them out may vary greatly. If you insist that everyone behaves in exactly the same way, you lose critical sparks of creative energy and become entangled in the web of the particulars. If you discipline yourself to connect with the core values you share with others, you can more readily find points of agreement and handle the particulars in ways that work best for each specific context.

Adler (2001) suggests that the effective intercultural communicator knows that there is much that is not known. To that end, it is important to be a learner, with deep curiosity. Actively ask the other about his or her customs and traditions. Let your natural curiosity stimulate learning. As often as you can, consult with colleagues who have had constructive experiences in various cultures. Ask them about the kinds of behaviors and communication practices they utilized which have been effective and have helped to foster mutual understanding. Always remember that, inevitably, something will get lost in the translation. It almost always does, even when you are communicating with those with whom you share a native language and culture. Remember, as the first of the overarching mindsets of the inventory states, commitment to effective intercultural communication is required.

Using International English

A simple and clear demonstration of the intention to make communication work well, cross-culturally, can be evidenced through the consistent use of International English, the language of most business exchanges. Here are some guidelines which will help you to use International English appropriately:

- When you are the speaker, clarify the message that you intend to communicate *before* you begin speaking. For people who tend to think out loud, extroverts, this could be a growing edge. Yet, the price of some internal discomfort is worth the reward of a clear, succinct message that the receiver understands.
- When conversing with those with whom you do not share a first language, speak more slowly, at the rate of fewer than 100 words per minute (Adler 2001).
- Speak in a straightforward manner, using everyday language. Eliminate slang, colloquial and culturally specific expressions, as well as imagery and metaphors. Imagery and metaphors may not translate well. Some people, as they translate from one language to another, translate word for word. Images and metaphors frequently defy literal interpretation.
- Use a simple, straightforward sentence structure. Each sentence should contain only one idea or concept.
- Use language that conveys sequence when organizing content or communicating procedures. Use phrasing like, "First... then...," or "Step one is...the second step is... next, you...lastly..." This is a practical approach for separating ideas and ordering longer descriptions.
- Direct questions, such as "Did you...?", are more effective than tag questions. A tag question is a question within a question. For example, "You did attend the meeting, did you not?" Tag questions add unnecessary complexity to the communication.
- Whole words, such as *cannot*, *would not*, *should not*, should be used instead of their contractions or reductions (*can't*, *gonna*).
- When writing, ask another person to read over your document, giving it their full attention. Solicit feedback on clarity of expression and completeness of content. Usually, someone from the host country, who has excellent skills in International English, will prove to be a valuable resource.
- Provide an extra measure of descriptive detail to insure that colleagues understand the nuances of points, offering examples to make the point and demonstrate the subtle aspects.
- Always summarize and clarify before transitioning from one point to the next or from segment to segment.
- Practice Inquiry and Advocacy, as described later in this chapter.

As an additional resource, readers may want to examine Adler's framing of "What do I do if they do not speak my language?" (2001). It contains a number of excellent ideas to consider.

Listening Actively

Listening is a valued communication skill. Some tips for listening actively include:

- Listen to understand. Adopt the other's perspective, suspending judgment and attachment to your own frame of reference.
- Allow the speaker to finish, permitting an uninterrupted sequence of thoughts.

- Model asking for clarification when confused or uncertain of the speaker's meaning. If you notice others looking or sounding confused, ask a clarifying question or make a clarifying statement to further understanding.
- Practice active listening, demonstrating engagement through nonverbal behavior. Summarize the speaker's message, accounting for the verbal and nonverbal components. The goal is to reflect full comprehension of the speaker's meaning, not simply the words that have been spoken (Adler 2001).
- Encourage active listening from others. On occasion, ask a question that allows listeners to demonstrate their understanding of the message communicated. Use a lead question like, "Would one of you summarize your understanding of the point we have been discussing? I want to be sure that we have a common understanding before moving on to the next subject."
- When witnessing a communication exchange, notice cues, verbal and nonverbal. If a lack of understanding seems evident, support the sender and receiver by acknowledging your perception of the potential misunderstanding. Ask a question of the speaker or listener or offer an interpretation of the message, stating an intention to support both in furthering clarity and understanding.
- Learn to listen deeply and discern the highest intention of the other. Look and listen beyond the words (Rogers and Farson 1979). Connect with the heart and spirit of the speaker.

Are you a good listener? What is your evidence? Under what circumstances is listening most challenging for you? What can you do to overcome this challenge? What can you do to listen even more deeply—to connect with the heart and spirit of the speaker?

Choosing Culturally Appropriate Nonverbal Behavior

Mehrabian (1971), in his study of nonverbal behavior, found that tone carries more meaning than words. Specifically, his findings indicate that when communicating in the same language, only seven percent (7%) of the message is conveyed through the spoken word. Thirty-eight percent (38%) of meaning is suggested through vocal tone and fifty-five percent (55%) is implied through other aspects of body language. With over ninety percent (90%) of a spoken message being defined by tone and body language, the nonverbal components are undeniably of critical importance.

Individuals differ in the size and sweep of hand gestures; in the frequency and intensity of their smile; in the vocal range they are comfortable utilizing; in their eye contact; and the amount of physical distance they prefer. The differences in nonverbal expression can be even more evident across cultures, particularly as you compare and contrast nonverbal expression across high- and low-context cultures. What is considered an appropriate gesture in one culture may be inappropriate, offensive, or viewed as unusual behavior in another.

For example, in my experience, touching beyond a handshake is thought to be inappropriate and an aggressive invasion of boundaries in Japan, China, and Korea.

Yet in Arabic countries, kissing on the cheek is expected. In the USA, across genders, handshakes, even hugs, can be exchanged among business associates. Consistently, I have noticed that Arab men sit closer to one another than do men from the West.

Perhaps the single nonverbal expression that seems to have universal meaning is a smile. Smiling is the same in every language, or is it? *What has your experience been with the universal message in a smile? Where and when might a smile mask emotions? Which gender is more likely to hide surprise or fear? Which gender is more likely to mask feelings of anger or disappointment? What have you determined to be the best strategy for nonverbal communication across cultures?*

Using the Ladder of Inference and Practicing Inquiry and Advocacy

So often when you communicate with another, mutual understanding is assumed. Action is taken based on assumptions. The Ladder of Inference (Ross in Senge 1994) reveals how you make inferences based on limited data and act based on those inferences. The mental pathway for this innate, reflexive process is shown in Fig. 7.5.

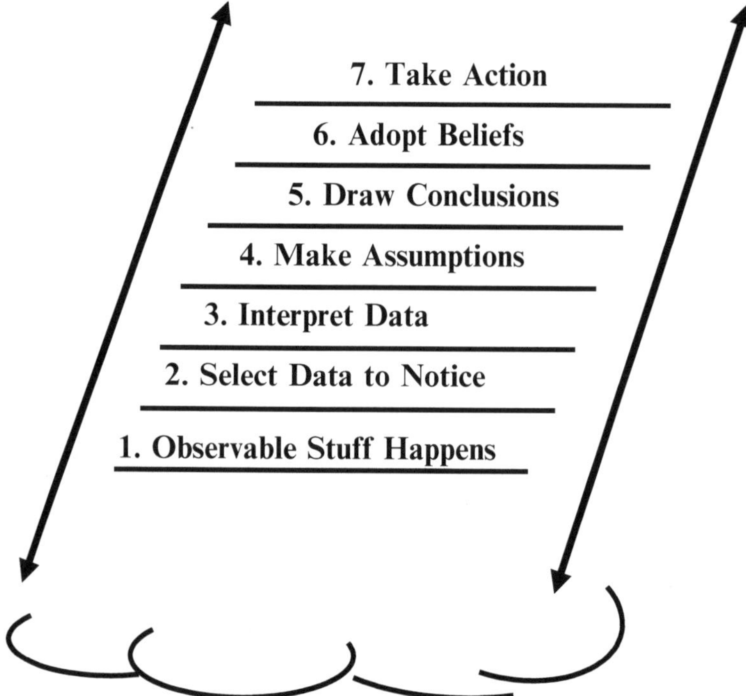

Fig. 7.5 The ladder of inference—a mental pathway (Ross in Senge 1994)

Inference is central to survival, saving you from data overload and the necessity of analyzing a myriad of inputs. Inference allows you to make decisions quickly, using limited data and a rapid sorting process. Inference can also create difficulties when you neglect to acknowledge the data with which you are working, the assumptions you have made, the conclusions you have drawn or the action you have taken. When you neglect acknowledging and testing generalizations, you limit communication to the selling of your ideas and pushing for what you want. The opportunity to discover deeper levels of truth about your own thinking, as well as the perspectives of others, is lost. Communication is short-circuited. The Ladder of Inference is a constructive tool enabling you to understand the process through which you gather data and reach conclusions. It lays out the journey along your mental pathway, from data input and selection to taking action.

Assumptions need to be revealed and probed before taking action. The skills of Advocacy and Inquiry, developed by Ross and Roberts (in Senge 1994), help to slow down the communication process, allowing assumptions to be uncovered and tested through dialogue. These skills are outlined in Table 7.3.

When you are at the point of making assumptions, drawing conclusions, adding to your beliefs about the other or taking action (Steps 4 through 7 on the Ladder), you can take the initiative to stop and share your logic with those present. The process, called *Advocacy,* invites you to communicate openly and fully. In doing so, you make your thought process transparent and implicitly invite others to do so as well. Thereby, you move your thoughts and feelings from the Hidden domain of the Johari Window into the Open area. Through conversation, you disclose your thinking. Then you can use *Inquiry*, asking others what they think, inviting dialogue, sharing your point of view, and asking about the thinking of others.

Table 7.3 contains examples of statements which can be used to reveal your thought processes and test the reality or accuracy of your assumptions. This technique models the power of self-disclosure as a communication tool, facilitating openness, self-awareness, and shared clarity. The figure also contains examples of questions you can pose to draw out and more deeply understand the thinking of

Table 7.3 Inquiry and advocacy: valuable ways of seeking information (Ross and Roberts 1994)

The ladder of inference Advocacy	Inquiry
Reveal your thought process. Invite dialogue.	Respectfully probe the thinking and reasoning of others.
My assumptions are…	What do you mean when you say…
The data I am working with…	What leads you to say…
Since…, I am concluding…	What data are you using to support your conclusions?
How do you see the situation?	How are you using the word…
What is your reaction to what I said?	Please walk me through your reasoning.
In which ways do you see it differently?	Help me understand your thinking.
If…then…	Make a process comment, e.g., "You've been quiet, what's going on?"

others. It is important to understand what the others are thinking. Finding appropriate ways to explore and gain insight into the thought processes of others is essential. The process of Inquiry can provide a direct avenue into their reasoning. Respectful probing can help to surface useful information, avoiding the pitfalls of acting based on assumptions. For example, you may have data that suggest that a team member is making assertions based on an interpretation of an individual's behavior or on specific biases related to personal philosophy or cultural conditioning. Asking questions, inquiring, gives the speaker an opportunity to hear his or her own logic and reasoning, in addition to allowing others to have a window into his or her thinking. When questioned, stepping through your logic can provide a glimpse into your own thought process, with its strengths and/or limitations. You can begin to see both logical and unfounded assumptions, or disciplined and undisciplined reasoning.

Inquiry is a powerful tool when used constructively. Misused, Inquiry can be experienced as a way of wielding power over others, shaming and embarrassing or controlling others through co-optive means. Used respectfully, however, it helps to expand openness by allowing information to flow from the Hidden dimension of the Johari Window into the Open area. Inquiry can also be a window into Blind Spots, shedding light on beliefs and thought processes that were unconscious.

Teams can use the Ladder of Inference, powered by Inquiry and Advocacy, to share and test assumptions and uncover buried truths, as team members reveal their logic and thought processes and inquire about the logic and thought processes of others.

Using Feedback—A Powerful Communication Tool

Feedback aids in increasing self-awareness and can result in enhanced competence and confidence. In a world of differences—individual, group, and cultural—feedback can help to bridge gaps. Feedback is a means to seeing yourself through the eyes of others, gaining clearer perspective on the impact of your behavior from their vantage point.

Feedback occurs directly when you are told, straight-out, that what you said or did was not clear or outright offensive or breeched a cultural norm. Sometimes, feedback is more indirect. You learn that the listener(s) did not understand the message. More often than not, you learn about your ineffectiveness when there is an unexpected response to what you said or did. Or, what occurs is different from what was desired or what you thought was agreed upon. Often, the cues indicating a lack of understanding are expressed and yet go unattended.

Feedback completes the communication loop and closes the communication gap, when one exists. It helps you to know when you have been heard and understood and when you have missed the mark. In its highest form, properly framed, feedback supports growth and development. Feedback, be it appreciative or developmental, is a generous gift that can influence you to continue an effective behavior or change an undesirable behavior. *Appreciative feedback* provides information on any aspect of another's behavior which you value, find to be effective, and would like them to continue doing. *Developmental feedback* is offered in instances where a change in behavior is warranted to enhance effectiveness. The skill of giving and receiving both kinds of feedback—appreciative and developmental—are needed to improve your effectiveness as a communicator.

People from remarkably similar cultural backgrounds encounter filters and noise as they reach out to provide feedback to one another. In such instances, the filters can be the quality of the relationship between the giver and the receiver, the mood of the giver or receiver, or the organizational level or power relationship between the parties. Vocal tone, word choices, and nonverbal behavior impact the quality of the message and how it is received. Certainly, the forum in which the feedback is delivered, including its timeliness, is of critical importance and influences the listener's receptivity. Moreover, if the listener has requested the feedback, the reception of the information may be dramatically different from those cases in which the feedback is unsolicited. For most people, unsolicited feedback can engender defensiveness. This can be especially so when the feedback is developmental.

The cultural background of the person giving the feedback operates as a filter, influencing what is said and how it is said. Adding layers of complexity, the cultural background of the receiver operates as a filter as well, affecting how what has been said is heard, experienced, and subsequently acted upon. In high-context cultures, which tend to be very relational, it is considered disrespectful to challenge an authority figure. In low-context cultures, however, challenging authority is seen as a right, even a responsibility. In such cultures, the social structure tends to have, at its philosophical foundation, an egalitarian principle.

Frequently I find my German clients outwardly deferential to perceived authority. Even when asked for, feedback tends to be provided in an indirect fashion. I have to listen very carefully, both to what is said and what is not said and then blend that information with what has been noticed when the topic was previously discussed. My British clients, while polite, are more direct in providing critical feedback. The New York based clients, on the other hand, tend to address the critical, developmental feedback first. In fact, it is often challenging for them to acknowledge what has worked well. Cultural differences account for these group-level variations. Despite these distinctions, in most cultures, receiving constructive feedback is a rare and precious gift. Individual and team effectiveness, as well as relationship building (Matveev and Nelson 2004), require you to be able to give and receive feedback constructively.

How to Give Feedback Constructively

Here are some basic guidelines to utilize when giving feedback (Porter 1982):

- You must begin by insuring that your intent is to be helpful. If you are angry or have a bias against the other person, find a graceful way to refrain from giving feedback.

- If the recipient has not made a direct request for feedback, ask permission to give feedback.
- Describe the person's behavior and its impact specifically.
- Whether the feedback is appreciative or developmental, offer only one or two points.
- Focus only on behavior that can be changed. If a person is physically challenged and walks with a limp, it is unconstructive to provide feedback about the limp. Or, if a person takes time to carefully phrase his thoughts because English is not his first language, it is not helpful to ask him to speak faster, without pausing.
- Provide feedback close to the occurrence of the behavior about which you are speaking.
- Frame the message in a way that is nonjudgmental. Describing behavior will facilitate such an outcome. For example, instead of saying, "You are lazy about your work," which is judgmental, you could say, "I have noticed that over the last 2 weeks, you have missed the deadline on two of your major tasks and you seem to be significantly behind schedule on the third. The missed deadlines are impacting the team's ability to complete the project on schedule."
- Use language, vocal tone, and nonverbal behavior that are respectful and support clear communication. Make sure the nonverbal behavior is congruent with the content of the message. When expressing disappointment in a behavior and outcome, smiling is not appropriate. On the other hand, when expressing appreciation about behavior that has led to positive outcomes, smile and offer encouraging nonverbal cues.

How to Receive Feedback

Ask directly for the remarkable gift of feedback (Porter 1982). Select people who will be honest, providing a clear picture, from their perspective, of your behavior and its impact. Then:

- Ask behavior-specific questions to elicit behavior-specific feedback.
- Be open-minded, and breathe. Relaxed breathing will improve your ability to hear and understand the information provided.
- Listen carefully to fully comprehend the speaker's message. Whether you agree with the speaker is of no relevance. Listen and learn.
- As needed, ask questions to clarify the speaker's comments. You must make certain that questions are truly questions, intended to deepen or broaden your understanding of the message. If your questions contain a point of view, or are designed to defend your behavior, be silent and breathe.
- Respond to the speaker's comments with a nondefensive "Thank you for the feedback."
- Apart from the feedback discussion, examine the information received. If any of it is new, investigate its validity with others who will provide an honest

perspective. Be mindful of how the request for information is phrased. Ask a behavior-specific question, such as, "I would appreciate your perspective concerning the way I…What have you noticed?"

- Determine any appropriate action warranted by the feedback. In the case of appreciative feedback, will you continue the behavior? If the feedback is developmental, what adjustments will you make, if any? You always have the choice of acting on feedback or, with gratitude toward the giver, letting it go.
- When feedback is initiated by another, you may decide to listen or choose not to listen to what the other has to say.

How to Ask for Coaching on Giving and Receiving Feedback Interculturally

Ask a knowledgeable source, someone who is competent at communicating in the specific cultural context of concern, about the most appropriate way to engage in giving and receiving feedback. For example, when asking for feedback in Asia, I was encouraged to provide a series of questions framed in future-oriented terms. Questions were suggested such as, "If we were to discuss this topic again, how might we approach it to insure an even more effective outcome?" Framing the question in this way acknowledges that the feedback will aide in preparing for future discussions. With this quality of distance from potential insult or challenge to authority, the door to feedback was opened.

When you work interculturally, mistakes can occur as a result of cultural blindness. When such mistakes happen, the best you can do is learn from them. Giving feedback on a business issue or a cultural faux pas is often difficult to do. This is particularly so when the recipient of the feedback is not well known to you or there is a notable difference between job levels or the person seems to be especially sensitive to feedback. Additionally, you can feel arrogant or inappropriate saying what of another's culture-specific behavior needs to be corrected. The clearest way to decide when to provide feedback in this area is when the person's behavior could result in physical danger, breaks the law, is in violation of company policy, or measurably negates the individual's or the team's effectiveness.

For example, at times it is appropriate to provide feedback on behavior patterns that affect how others view the individual in question. It may be necessary to give an employee or colleague feedback on body odor if the problem is causing colleagues to avoid being in his or her presence. In such cases, the person may lose out on some aspects of team camaraderie, during which information is shared and team spirit is enhanced.

Hence, providing feedback is an important responsibility. As is always the case with feedback, the recipient can choose to act on the feedback or not. It is fair and appropriate for the person to have the information and equally as fair and appropriate for the individual to determine their response to the feedback. Constructive feedback is a contribution to the individual. Always, you must remember that the recipient of information has freedom of choice about how to respond.

How to Give and Receive Team Feedback

Teams can engage in giving and receiving feedback as a group. The process can be accomplished utilizing the guidelines cited above for giving and receiving feedback. For each team member, in turn, the feedback can be focused on a specific, finite question or set of questions. Also, team members can each design their own behavior-specific questions, to ask the group. These kinds of activities, when managed constructively, enhance openness and trust, deepening relationships and potentially increasing team effectiveness. Feedback addresses and shrinks the Blind Spot described in the Johari Window. For individuals and teams, surveys can also be an effective means of collecting feedback. Be they custom designed or purchased off the shelf, they can provide a wealth of information about effectiveness and opportunities for improved functioning. Links to several organizations that design and market such tools are provided at the end of this chapter.

Relevant Competencies

Enhancing Competence as an Intercultural Communicator: An Inventory of Mindsets and Behaviors

Using the inventory, place an "S" in the boxes which represent your strengths and a "D" in the boxes which offer you the greatest opportunity for development. Ask for feedback on both areas from your colleagues.

Practicing overarching mindsets	☐ Be committed to communicating effectively ☐ Demonstrate patience with yourself and others ☐ Openly acknowledge cultural differences which may impact understanding ☐ Explicitly clarify core values and use as touchstone ☐ Be a learner with curiosity
Speaking using international English	☐ Clarify your message before speaking ☐ Speak slowly ☐ Use common, everyday words ☐ Share one idea per sentence ☐ Use words that convey sequence to separate and order your ideas ☐ Ask direct questions ☐ Use whole words ☐ Solicit feedback on the clarity of documents before distribution ☐ Offer specific examples to clarify subtleties ☐ Summarize before transitioning or closing

(continued)

(continued)

	☐ Practice Inquiry and Advocacy
Listening and witnessing	☐ Actively listen to understand ☐ Allow the speaker to finish the thought ☐ Facilitate clarity by practicing Inquiry ☐ Discern highest intention of the speaker
Inquiring and advocating	☐ Reveal and investigate mental models utilizing skills of Inquiry and Advocacy ☐ Inquiry—ask one question of speaker to uncover and reveal logic and reason ☐ Advocacy—openly and fully disclose your thought processes and feelings
Giving and receiving feedback	*Giving feedback* ☐ Test your intent ☐ Ask permission to speak ☐ Describe behavior and its impact ☐ Offer only one or two points ☐ Focus on changeable behavior ☐ Make it timely ☐ Choose nonjudgmental language ☐ Use supportive, respectful nonverbal behavior *Receiving feedback* ☐ Ask specific questions ☐ Listen with openness and a desire to understand the message ☐ Ask only clarifying questions ☐ Respond without defending your behavior ☐ Offer appreciation for the information ☐ Consider the information and any warranted action *Ask for coaching on giving and receiving feedback cross-culturally*
Choosing nonverbal behavior	☐ Choose behavior to support the message ☐ Use visual aids ☐ Engage in culturally appropriate nonverbal behavior

Summary

Communication is the primary vehicle for influencing others, getting things done, breaking down barriers, getting to know strangers, and deepening your knowledge of those who are familiar to you. Communication, the tool used to share your reality and explore the reality of others, is successful when the sender's message is received and understood as intended. To achieve that end, individuals and teams must master the ability to convey a message, facilitate buy-in to ideas and initiatives, and bridge individual and cultural differences within the team and across the organization. Through the consistent application of flexibility in approach, open-mindedness, self-awareness, and the willingness to honor the communication needs of different cultural groups, based on their values and the priority they place on them, teams can develop effective intercultural communication.

While respectful acknowledgment of differences is a challenge when communicating face-to-face, it becomes even more difficult when working virtually, lacking many communication cues. In such instances, multiple communication tools and techniques prove helpful, ranging from the use of written agendas, to the distribution of talking points, to the use of summary statements. Whether communicating virtually or actually, techniques such as International English, the Ladder of Inference, Inquiry and Advocacy, Active Listening, and Giving and Receiving Feedback are of critical importance as teams seek ways to communicate effectively.

As the world becomes more diverse and boundaries shrink, communication becomes more dynamic and challenging. Yet, it is the only way that human beings have of exchanging information. By necessity, communication must be mastered if you are to diminish confusion, anger, resentment, and derailment of initiatives. Successful communication facilitates collaboration, inclusion, innovative solutions, and the establishment of strong relationships. Successful communication enables you to make your best contribution to the team and the organization.

Communicating with clarity conserves your most precious resources. With effective communication, a spirit of collaboration, productivity, harmony, and peace exists. Life on teams becomes easier and more fulfilling.

More happens in communication than the mere exchange of words. Understanding on the intellectual and emotional levels can and should occur. All progress, be it in teamwork or any level of relationship, is made through communication—what you hear and see, what you feel and sense, and ultimately, what you understand. While the measurable aspects of communication are its visible dimensions, I believe the most powerful aspects are invisible. The power and clarity of any communication is contained in the dynamic energy or feeling tone of a given exchange. Frequently, the energy of an exchange stays with you much longer than the words that were spoken. The energy or intention of the exchange has the most lasting effect because it relays the deeper message. Yet, this aspect of communication defies definition or measurement.

As the physical world and its boundaries continue to shrink, organizations are relying on teams more and more. Some teams will work face-to-face and some will be virtual. Creative and effective ways of spanning the gaps created by differences—individual and cultural—will need to be discovered. Consistently, you will have to rely on learning how to know what others want, need, and are intending to convey. A more effective system for knowing will be needed.

When working on a team, explicitly define the communication norms and traditions by which the team will operate. Make sure that they represent the needs and preferences of all and will serve the team well, as it establishes open communication and builds trusting relationships, enabling it to accomplish its task. Publicly acknowledge differences and their potential to generate creativity, as well as miscommunication. Solicit the help of all concerned to join in making the communication process work. Practice Inquiry and Advocacy. As a communication practice, document meeting highlights, action items, and key decisions. Distribute the notes as a support, with the suggestion that the recipients respond to the document, including raising questions for clarification.

I believe that, at the transpersonal level, everything is already known and understood. You *can* see into the hearts and minds of colleagues and neighbors. Knowing at this level requires a still mind, relinquishment of the ego, and investment in knowing with more than what the conscious mind is aware of. You will need to allow the witness within to be the knower, the part that is connected to everyone else and to the Universal Mind.

A challenge is to bring this high quality, a more-accurate-than-words kind of knowing and communicating, into conscious awareness. Communication and understanding will improve when life is lived in responsible relationship to *the whole* and to individual needs, neither subordinate to the other. *What do you think?*

Assessment Instruments

ITAP International www.itapintl.com

With offices in the Americas, Africa, Asia, Asia Pacific, the Middle East, and Europe, ITAP International delivers a range of business solutions and services, all designed to "Build Human Capability—Globally." ITAP has the expertise to develop and implement customized assessments or administer a proprietary survey called "Culture in the Workplace." The results of this instrument, licensed by Dr. Geert Hofstede, provide practical, behavior-focused suggestions on ways to modify your behavior and approach to communication so that you are more likely to be understood and experienced as relevant and appropriate.

Training Management Corporation—TMC www.tmcorp.com

TMC provides learning and consulting solutions based on the book *Doing Business Internationally*. Their "Cultural Orientations Indicator" is a web-based, self-reporting instrument that assesses individual preference along ten cultural dimensions. The profile you receive will enable you to compare your individual results with you team's aggregate data, as well as with national norms from various countries of your choice. The survey is available in a number of languages, for ease of administration.

Case Study: He Threatened Me!

As you read the case study below, consider the following questions:

- *What might be some of the cross-cultural communication dynamics that played a part in this situation?*
- *Given the potential cultural differences, what kinds of nonverbal behavior might have contributed to the researcher's interpretation of the executive's message?*
- *What cues do you look for as an indication of a miscommunication?*

A large international firm was facing a major issue with their largest product. The regulator community and customer advocacy groups were challenging the integrity of the data the company supplied to the industry's regulatory body. As the investigation grew in size and scope, many people who were involved in the testing were interviewed. During one such interview, an outside researcher said that she had been threatened by a company executive. The executive accused of making the threatening comments was a man, native to Japan. The outside researcher, a woman who was born and raised in Madras, said that this was the first time since her arrival in the United States three years prior, that she felt fearful in a work setting. She said she felt certain that her personal safety was at risk, given the treatment she received from the Japanese executive. The executive pointed out that he was simply doing his job, motivating the researcher to keep focused on producing a satisfactory and timely outcome for the business they both served, as well as the consumers who would benefit from the product.

Case Study: What Did She Say?

As you read the case study below, consider the following questions:

- *When you are speaking with an international audience, what must you be aware of and take into account?*
- *In what ways does the behavioral example you set—what you say, how you say it and the context in which it is said—impact how comfortable or uncomfortable others feel?*
- *What would you have done to diminish the negative impact the following presentation had on the rest of the meeting?*

An international financial firm convened its Human Resources leadership team, key executives from around the world, on the coast of Spain for a retreat and strategic planning meeting. One segment of the meeting featured a skilled and highly successful speaker from the United States, who talked about change—organizational and personal change. Being less accustomed to working internationally, during her presentation she used a number of personal examples from the private parts of her life; the parts of her life that involved relationships and situations outside of the workplace. Her culturally mixed audience had mixed reactions to her comments. Many members of the audience were offended by what they viewed as inappropriate and unprofessional remarks. The speaker had crossed a boundary, bringing the very private into a public, professional context. Some of the meeting participants felt pressured, wondering if they too were expected to share at an equally personal level. They wondered if they would be judged negatively by their leadership, those who sponsored the speaker, if they too did not use examples from their private lives. The presentation had a negative effect for the remainder of the meeting.

Case Study: Changing the Cook Stove: A US Peace Corps Volunteer in Senegal

As you read the case study below, consider the following questions:

- *Was feedback solicited and provided?*
- *Was this a culturally sensitive approach to feedback or an approach that reflected the Peace Corps worker's preferences?*
- *What are some alternative approaches which may have been more efficient and successful?*

As a U.S. American male Peace Corps volunteer in Senegal, West Africa, I acted as a regional coordinator for an appropriate technology project. The purpose of the project was to spread knowledge and use of homemade, fuel-efficient cook stoves, in order to reduce the pressures on rapidly dwindling forest resources partly caused by the use of firewood. In my role as coordinator of the effort in the northern part of the country, I was responsible for setting up one-week trainings in interested villages, preparing the participants, and loosely supervising the trainings themselves. I worked with a team of three trainers, Tapha, Thiarra, and Pape (all Senegalese men), who lived in the villages during the trainings. As supervisor, I would drop in for a day or two at a time to make sure everything was working as planned.

The stove was made from a mixture of clay and sand, a technology imported from Guatemala. Since this was a nontraditional material, it seemed unlikely to gain easy acceptance. It was also extraordinarily labor-intensive to produce and use, requiring extensive pounding of dry clay in preparation and much barehanded beating to get a solid, packed mass during construction.

During the latter part of my time in Senegal, I helped introduce a new stove model into the program. The new model, developed in Burkina Faso, looked quite similar in design but took advantage of more traditional building materials. A combination of clay, manure, straw, and a little water was mixed and left to sit for a week. This was similar to the process used in building adobe houses in the region. This "fermented' mixture was then used to form a stove right around and above the three rocks used in the traditional three-rock fire.

I felt strongly that the new stove was more appropriate than the old. It involved introducing only a new form, not a new material, and might therefore be more easily accepted. It took a third of the time to make, and involved modeling the materials instead of packing and pounding. The adobe mixture also allowed for a stove with thinner walls, involving less material and absorbing less of the heat from a cooking fire. Finally, it used the built-in rocks to form a stand for the cooking pot (the old stove had no stand), and the door to the firebox was reinforced with scrap metal from tin cans. It was therefore less likely to cave in. There seemed enough distinct advantages to warrant trying it out, and I was excited at the prospect of contributing to a useful innovation.

I first trained the trainers in the new technology, since I was the only person in the organization who had learned how to use it. This put me in the position of acting as both the technical authority and supervisor of the training team. We then began a pilot effort to use the new model in training people in villages, to see how it would work in practice. For the first few days, I stayed with the team and participated in the training. When it seemed as though things were well under way, I returned to my previous pattern of occasional visits.

The team of trainers proved quite successful in adapting to the new materials. However, problems arose in two areas: wall thickness and building technique. I saw quickly that all three trainers had a great predilection for making the stove walls as thick as ever (twice what they should have been). This used more materials to build a less efficient (more heat-absorbent) stove. They also seemed stuck in their habits of pounding and beating the new, more elastic materials, instead of modeling and shaping them. Rather than making it solid, the beating simply made the new stove lose its shape. It worried me to see my pet project losing some of its ease and efficiency unnecessarily.

I tried a number of tactics to change these habits. At first, I simply explained why thin walls and modeling made a better stove and made it easier. I announced that this was how this stove should be made. This tactic had very little apparent success; fat walls and pounding continued, much to my chagrin.

Rather than forcing the issue, I chose a gentler approach. I made it a point to visit more frequently than usual and at each visit I praised the work they were doing. I also threw in a little pitch for thin walls and modeling. I particularly praised thinner-walled stoves; I urged and encouraged the trainers to change their old ways. I held back from making a big fuss about it, but I brought it up gently whenever the occasion arose, and often with individual trainers instead of the whole group. I was mildly frustrated by the situation, but my appreciation of the team's generally excellent work helped me to relax and have patience.

As a result, the stove walls eventually thinned down (though not quite as much as I might have liked), and the trainers gradually accepted the smooth handling that the mixture demanded. In the other areas of the new stove model, the team had been extremely adaptable and resourceful, picking up the new system quickly and adding a few very useful innovations of their own. Overall, I felt very satisfied with what we had achieved, and pleased that changes had happened cooperatively instead of through an exercise of authority.

References

Adler, Nancy J. (2001). *International Dimensions of Organizational Behavior* (4th ed.). Cincinnati, OH: South-Western College Publishing.

Best Books and Articles on Organizational Communication: http://www.questia.com/Index

Clark Wilson. Provides organizational core competency assessments and surveys. http://www.cwginc.com

Connerley, M. and Pedersen, P. (2005). *Leadership in a Diverse and Multicultural Environment*. Thousand Oaks, CA: Sage.

Earley, P.C. and Mosakowski, E.M. (2000). Creating Hybrid Team Cultures: An Empirical Test of Transnational Team Functioning. *Academy of Management Journal, 43*(1), 26–49.

Enayati, J. (2001). The Research: Effective Communication and Decision-making in Diverse Groups. In M. Hemmati (Ed.), *Multi-Stakeholder Processes for Governance and Sustainability—Beyond Deadlock and Conflict*. London, England: Earthscan.

Fisher, B.A. (1980). *Small Group Decision-Making* (2nd ed.). New York: McGraw-Hill.

Hall, E.T. (1977). *Beyond Culture*. New York: Anchor Press/Doubleday.

Halverson, Claire B. (1993). Cultural Context Inventory: The Effects of Culture on Behavior and Work Style. In W. Pfeiffer (Ed.), *The Annual(1993)Developing Human Resources*. San Diego, CA: Pfeiffer.

Hampden-Turner, C.M. and Trompenaars, F. (2000). *Building Cross-Cultural Competence: How to Create Wealth from Conflicting Value*. New Haven, CT: Yale University Press.

Luft, J. and Ingham, H. (1955). *The Johari Window, A Graphic Model of Interpersonal Awareness*. Los Angeles, CA: UCLA.

Matveev, A. and Nelson, P. (2004). Cross Cultural Communication Competence and Multicultural team Performance. *International Journal of Cross Cultural Management, 4*(2), 253–270.

Mehrabian, A. (1971). *Silent Messages*. Belmont, CA: Wadsworth Publishing Company.

Porter, L. (1982). Giving and Receiving Feedback: It Will Never be Easy, But it can be Better. In L. Porter and B. Mohr (Eds.), *Reading Book for Human Relations Training*. Alexandria, VA: National Training Laboratories Institute.

Rogers, C. and Farson, R. (1979). *Active Listening*. In D. Kolb, I. Rubin and J. MacIntyre (Eds.), *Organizational Psychology* (3rd ed.). New Jersey: Prentice-Hall.

Ross, R. (1994). Ladder of Inference. In P. Senge (Ed.), *The Fifth Discipline Fieldbook* (pp. 242–252). New York: Doubleday.

Ross, R. and Roberts, C. (1994). Balance Inquiry and Advocacy. In P. Senge (Ed.), *The Fifth Discipline Fieldbook* (pp. 253–259). New York: Doubleday.

Tannen, D. (1990). *You Just Don't Understand*. New York: Ballantine Books.

Tingley, J. (1994). *Gender Flex, Men and Women Speaking Each Other's Language at Work*. New York: AMACOM Books.

Varner, I.I. (2006). The theoretical foundation for intercultural business communication: A conceptual model. *Journal of Business Communication, 37*(1), 39–58.

Von Oech, R. (1998). *A Whack on the Side of the Head* (Revised ed.). New York: Warner Business Books.

Walker, D., Walker, T. and Schmnitz, J. (2003). *Doing Business Internationally*. New York: McGraw-Hill.

Resources

Communicating Across Cultures by Elaine Winters. Elaine Winters is a Cross-cultural educator and Instructional Designer. She is the co-author (with Rob Sellin) of: *Cultural Issues in Business Communication*. http://www.bena.com/ewinters/xculture.html

Diversity Inc. An on-line magazine that provides news, resources, and commentary on the role of diversity in strengthening the corporate bottom line. http://www.diversityinc.com

Denison Consulting. Bringing organizational culture and leadership to the bottom line is the focus of this global leader's research-based model. Denison will also support you in custom designing assessment and feedback tools. http://www.denisonculture.com

Emergence of Communication Networks— www.tec.spcomm.uiuc.ed

Tom Finn, Consultant, Coach and Author of *Are You Clueless? Crack the Cultural Code...and Profit*. Tom Finn coaches leaders on cultural competency and handling business pressures. (703) 709–7947. tfinnman@aol.com

MeridianEaton Global. GlobeSmart, Meridian's leading edge, web-based tool provides detailed knowledge on how to conduct business with people from around the world. http://www.meridianeaton.com

Pachter and Associates Barbara Pachter, President. Pachter and Associates, a worldwide business communications training company, teaches global communications for effectiveness in a global context. Contact: Joyce Hoff, Office Manager, PO Box 3680, Cherry Hill, NJ 08034 (856) 751–6141. Pachter@ix.netcom.com http://www.pachter.com

Sietar Europe. SIETAR offers an array of cross-cultural assessment instruments. http://www.sietar-europa.org

Chapter 8
Conflict

John Ungerleider

Peace is not the absence of conflict but the presence of creative alternatives for responding to conflict—alternatives to passive or aggressive responses, alternatives to violence.

–Dorothy Thompson

Introduction

The goal of this chapter is to (1) provide insight into the sources and dynamics of conflict in multicultural teams and (2) review some fundamental competencies in self-awareness and communication that can facilitate engagement with conflict in groups. The chapter integrates thematic perspectives from the fields of Conflict Resolution/Transformation, Intercultural Communication, and Organizational Behavior.

Learning Objectives

After reading this chapter you should be able to:

- Analyze the causes of conflict in multicultural teams
- See the constructive as well as destructive potential of conflict
- Assess diverse personal styles and cultural norms for addressing conflict
- Begin to identify your own personal and cultural style of dealing with conflict
- Recognize how conflicts are integral to natural stages of group development
- Distinguish between task and relationship conflict
- Assess some social-psychological dynamics of identity-based conflicts
- Define terminology and concepts in the field of Conflict Transformation
- Introduce basic principles of negotiation, mediation, intervention, and peacebuilding
- Identify communication skills for dialogue about a conflict

C.B. Halverson and S.A. Tirmizi (eds.), *Effective Multicultural Teams: Theory and Practice*,

Defining Conflict

Conflict is a natural part of social existence and destined to be a reality for human beings working together. In the field of Conflict Resolution, *conflicts* have been defined as deep-rooted differences that are hard to resolve, versus simpler and easier to settle *disputes* (Burton 1986; Burgess and Spangler 2003). On a multicultural team, negotiable disputes are more prevalent that non-negotiable conflicts, but are often based on fundamentally different needs, interests, perceptions, or cultural norms. For the purpose of this chapter, the general term "conflict" will be used. *Conflict on teams* is defined here to mean a struggle, or state of disharmony or antagonism, or hostile behaviors, resulting from contradictory interests, needs, or beliefs, or mutually exclusive desires.

The roots of conflict in work teams can be understood and approached from different professional and academic perspectives, e.g., by framing conflict analysis through the varying lenses of the following field fields:

- Organizational behavior sees conflict in work teams coming from negative emotions, fear, and competitiveness arising from perception of differences or scarce resources.
- Intercultural communication sees conflict as coming from misunderstandings due to culturally differing perspectives.
- Conflict resolution sees conflicts as growing from unmet human needs and competing interests.
- Conflict transformation looks holistically at systems of conflict: historical roots and structural causes as well as inter-group dynamics.

Conflicts arise when needs and desires are stifled, or when someone feels threatened. Conflicts on work teams can come from confusion about roles, poorly run meetings, private agendas, and conflicting personalities (Levi 2001). Conflicts may arise in self-directed teams from the ambiguity of non-hierarchical decision-making processes, or if managers feel their authority is threatened by participatory group decisions (Appelbaum et al. 1999). Conflicts may be driven more by "top-down" issues like a scarcity of organizational resources or authoritarian management, or "bottom-up" concerns between individuals who clash for a variety of interpersonal reasons.

Orientation Toward Conflict: Constructive or Destructive

Conflict can feel dangerous and its potential benefits may not be recognized. Conflicts undermine team goals when disagreements block effective communication and collaboration. Yet conflict is a dynamic force for change. Without the creative tension that is often expressed through conflict, groups may remain stagnant. Without the catalyst of conflict, repressed needs and desires may remain ignored and unmet. Hidden, passively angry, controlled, or indirect conflict may be as dangerous to a team's survival as open, aggressive, uncontrolled, or direct conflict. Without an inclusive conflict resolution process, affective disenchantment can result in withdrawal from group participation (Amason et al. 1995), or a team will become stuck in conformist groupthink (see Chapter 9).

If conflict is probable, and it is unhealthy to eliminate expression of conflict in a group, how can a team prepare to optimize the way conflicts are managed? Productive struggle, rather than destructive attacks, builds team capacity for understanding differences and finding creative solutions. Awareness of conflict dynamics, cultural differences, and simple communication skills increases the chance of constructively transforming a conflict situation. Multicultural teams in particular require creative and culturally diverse approaches to addressing conflict (Appelbaum et al. 1998). When teams engage with conflicts directly, deepened communication and honest self-examination can lead to creative, positive energy. Negotiating and integrating the varying perspectives and interests of group members are part of what give a team creative dynamism.

Task Versus Relationship Conflicts

Conflicts on teams can be understood as *task* (resource distribution, procedures, facts, etc.) versus *relationship* or *emotional* (e.g., feelings, preferences, values, style) conflicts. Some organizational behavior theory sees relationship conflicts as rare, but more likely to have negative impact on teams, whereas task conflicts are more common but can be constructive or destructive, depending on how they are managed (Jehn 1997; De Dreu and Weingart 2002). In this view, constructive conflicts operate more at the *cognitive* than *affective* level of team interaction. If conflict can be clearly understood for its components and dynamics, it can move forward as a functional conflict. This should not be misconstrued to mean that emotions should be ignored in a conflict.

A dysfunctional relationship conflict is emotionally hard on people, as opposed to analytically hard on the problem—the opposite of one core precept of *principled negotiation*: to be hard on the problem, not on the people (Fisher and Ury 1983). Well-managed cognitive-style conflict encourages communication of options, innovation, and consensus, rather than dominance by individuals (Appelbaum et al. 1999). Often conflicts on teams are not personal, and many of the conflicts that appear on teams are not significant enough to disrupt the functioning of the team; they may be addressed by remembering the common purpose and general agreement of the team (Kline 1999).

For task conflict to remain constructive, members should stay focused on substantive issues, while respecting and seeking to better understand differences. Communication channels stay open, members are accepted, and diverse member skills and views are used to make decisions and resolve differences of opinion. A destructive conflict gets personalized—negative feelings and private agendas detract from team goals. Frustration increases, while trust, individual input into decisions, and commitment are lost.

Constructive conflict patterns can be encouraged—and destructive conflicts discouraged—by managers through group facilitation (Esquivel and Kleiner 1996). For example, an academic manager in a graduate school held private meetings with faculty members who were generating disagreements on academic committees, but also made public comments praising effective collaboration leading to successful achievements by the committee. On a self-managed team, interpersonal feedback sessions can help clarify which communication and behavior patterns are beneficial and which harmful to the mood and productivity of the team.

What look like task conflicts on the surface, may have hidden relationship components that can sabotage rational, cognitive approaches to conflict resolution. Like the 88% of an iceberg that is hidden under water, buried issues, attitudes, histories, wounds, and emotions can dangerously impact a negotiation if they are not revealed as an explicit dynamic of the conflict. Relationship conflicts require affective as well as cognitive strategies for intervention and healing.

Sometimes asking how someone is feeling about a problem, or offering an apology is worth more than any amount of explanation or problem solving. Sometimes an apology is required for reconciliation to begin. This is also true in international diplomacy, such as when the Chinese demanded a formal apology for an American spy plane entering its airspace in 2001 before they were willing to return the plane to the United States, or when Korea and China demand that Japan apologize for war crimes committed in World War II for the sake of normalizing contemporary international relations.

Conflict in Stages of Group Development

Conflict in teams is more predictable in certain stages of group development. Two prominent theories name the stages of group development as *forming*, *storming*, *norming*, and *performing* (Tuckman 1965—see Chapter 4), or *inclusion*, *control*, and *openness* (Schutz 1973—see Chapter 4).

During the formation of a group, members are typically optimistic and on their best behavior, so conflicts are rare. During this orientation phase of a team, attention to relationship building can pay off when conflicts eventually emerge. *Trust-building* and *team-building activities* pursued early in a group's existence can create stronger and more open relationships between members. Establishing effective communication channels and habits can prevent conflict, and will facilitate more effective responses to conflict when it does occur. In the MBI (mapping, bridging, integrating) model for bridging differences on cultural teams (Maznevski and DiStefano 2000), building early understanding of and communicating about differences are important for managing those differences and resolving conflicts. Dissonant cultural norms in the early phases of a group can cause dissatisfaction and impede progress to productivity, as this example shows:

A Liberian woman working on an otherwise American team of women was unfamiliar with their jokes about U.S. television shows. This led her to thinking that

Americans are shallow and insensitive, and she refused to participate actively in setting group norms and decision-making processes, becoming argumentative in ways that seemed unreasonable to her teammates. The group required long meetings to finish simple assignments.

Conflict is most likely to emerge in the middle stages of a group's development. During the *storming* stage, team members experience dissatisfaction as they readjust ideal hopes for their team experience to the realities of the actual group. There is a natural struggle with how much to merge one's individuality with group needs and norms. As members have already developed a sense of *inclusion* in the team, they feel enough ownership for the team to begin struggling for *control* over team direction and decisions. If feelings and conflicts are not effectively addressed, the team may remain stuck in a stage of dissatisfaction, with either overt or covert struggle for control. At this stage, effective and well-timed communication is critical in ensuring that a conflict does not escalate out of control. If conflicts are addressed effectively and their underlying causes are adequately resolved, teams will move to the next stage, where increased cohesion and agreement about group norms lead to feelings and expressions of *openness* and high *performing* productivity.

Personal Styles of Addressing Conflict

Individual styles of addressing conflict are based on differences in personality (see Chapter 3), the influences of family, and cultural norms. Individuals from any culture may be ready or reticent to take initiative and confront a conflict directly. Still, without stereotyping cultures, we can be aware that different communities and nationalities have evolved differing acceptable norms for engaging in healthy conflict. When a conflict arises, some cultures exhibit more direct and overt argument, while others favor more indirect communication, even via a third party. There are cultural realities that allow us to more easily imagine people from Mediterranean cultures in a public argument than people from East Asian countries, whether over a minor or major issue. The fact that we don't see an argument on the street in Japan or Thailand does not mean there is no conflict, and, similarly, if we witness an energetic argument among Italians or Israelis, it doesn't mean that a serious conflict exists. Influenced by television and radio talk shows, the United States has developed into an increasingly argumentative culture (Tannen 1998). Traditional cultures may involve an extended family or social network in reaching out to address a conflict—for example, when parents, grandparents, and in-laws offer advice to a struggling young couple in Cyprus or Nigeria.

In multicultural work teams influenced by the presence of diverse cultural perceptions, practices, and personalities, differing styles of dealing with conflict will impact group dynamics. A widely used system for categorizing conflict styles is Thomas' (1976) matrix of *avoiding, accommodating, competing, compromising, or collaborating*—drawn from an individual's relative behavioral predisposition in a conflict situation, measured along the contrasting dimensions of assertiveness or

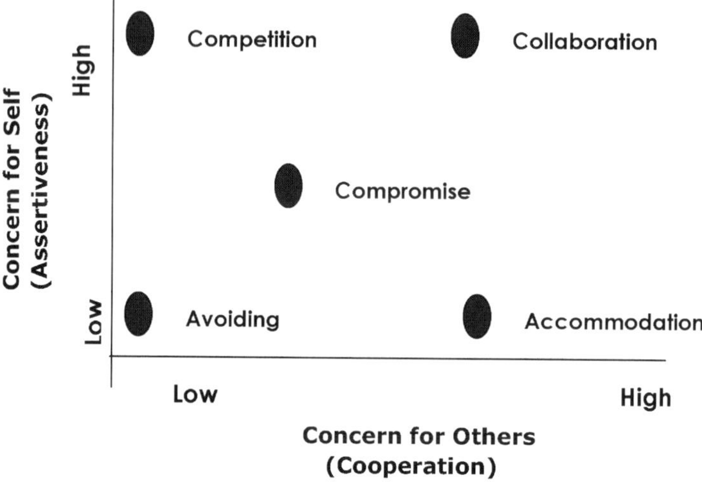

Fig. 8.1 Conflict management styles (Thomas 1976)

cooperativeness. These five styles of addressing conflict can be thought of in terms of needs (see Fig. 8.1). There are pros and cons to each conflict style.

If I am only concerned with my own needs (vertical axis on the chart), I will be likely to *compete* or coerce. *Competition* may resolve a conflict quickly, but may sacrifice friendships. When I am only concerned with seeing that another's needs are met (horizontal axis on the chart) in order to preserve a relationship, I completely *accommodate* the other. If this is not an important issue, this can be satisfactory, but if it is important or happens repeatedly, I can build up resentment. *Accommodation* may preserve friendships on the surface, but lead to brewing resentments. If I *avoid* a conflict, I don't take care of my needs or anyone else's. I can use sarcastic comments or subtly hostile behaviors such as ignoring someone, or simply remove myself from the conflict. *Avoidance* may be wise for averting danger in the short run, but cannot resolve the problem. With a clever *compromise*, I can partially meet of my needs as well as the needs of others. *Compromise* may meet some needs of each party, but not all. If we *collaborate* as equal partners in trying to communicate effectively, we take on the challenge of trying to meet everyone's needs. I take responsibility for my needs and feelings, giving clear feedback about what I feel in response to another's actions (see Chapter 7), and I listen to understand the actions of others. *Collaboration* may devise a wise solution, but may require a lot of time and effort to achieve.

Individuals approach different conflict situations with varying styles. For example, in a more formal conflict at work I may be more coercive, while I may be more accommodating with friends. It can be useful for individuals to assess their own preferences and styles in addressing conflict to see what pros and cons arise when applying their particular style:

Rahim (1983) developed a parallel system for conflict resolution style preference based on relative concern for self or others creating a similar system based on combinations of high or low concern: The various styles in this system are named:

avoiding, obliging, dominating, compromising, or integrating. Differing styles of addressing conflict may reduce or increase stress levels: Integrating has been shown to reduces stress by lowering task and relationship conflict; avoiding and dominating styles can increase stress by raising task and relationship conflict; obliging can reduce the experience of conflict-induced stress, but also increase stress due to the inability to assert one's interests (Friedman et al. 2000).

Avoiding means withdrawing and not engaging with an uncomfortable situation; accommodating/obliging leads to focus on similarities rather than differences and giving away ones own interests in pursuit of maintaining a harmonious relationship; competing/dominating means seeking to win and control the outcome of a dispute even if it means forcing one's will and interests on others; compromising involves giving up something of one's own interests in order to achieve a mutually acceptable, if imperfect, solution to a conflict; collaborating/integrating implies open sharing of information about opposing vs. shared interests in order to reach truly satisfactory, and possibly creative, solution for all parties.

Exercise: Analyzing Your Style of Dealing with Conflict

It is possible to assess one's own conflict-handling style via self-reflection, getting feedback from friends or colleagues, or more formally by using the Thomas-Kilmann Conflict Mode Instrument, available on the Internet.

Self-reflective questions include:

What works and what is difficult for me in resolving interpersonal conflicts? How does my culture or background influence the way I deal with conflict? How does my cultural style help or hinder me in dealing with conflict? Are there exclusive symbols and rituals of in-group identity that bring pride or fear while predisposing me to hostility towards those outside my group? (Morrow and Wilson 1996) Where have these habits come from? How does my cultural socialization dispose me to act in future conflicts?

Much of this behavioral diversity in conflict is due to personality (see Chapter 3), but personality is not deterministic. The theory of *psychosynthesis* (Assagioli 1971) proposes that we can overidentify with parts of the self, or *sub-personalities*, blinding us to the freedom we have to incorporate a wide range of possible behaviors in response to dynamic social situations. Understanding how our own psychological patterns function can help us act more objectively in conflict situations. Other aspects of behavioral variation in conflict are due to culture.

Cultural Styles of Dealing with Conflict

Culture can be viewed as a unique combination of values, behavioral norms, and symbols, or alternately, perceptions, practices, and products (Moran 2001). Myriad factors make members of two distinct cultures either compatible or likely to clash on a work team. To prevent conflict, cultural differences in approaching problems, communicating, gender roles, or time management may need to be explicitly acknowledged and group norms altered in order to meet the needs of group members with different national, ethnic, religious, gender, or cultural identities. Differing perceptions and assumptions shape how individuals approach a given conflict. In a multicultural team or an intercultural conflict, perceptions of a conflict situation may be dramatically different when seen through the lens of diverging *cultural frameworks* (see Chapter 2). This point is illustrated in the following example.

Professor Stephen Worchel describes a time he planted bananas in his yard in Hawaii and they spread into his neighbors' yards. In the multicultural milieu of Hawaiian society, his neighbors were Japanese, Portuguese, Chinese, and Hawaiian. Each of them responded differently: the Japanese neighbor was affronted by this encroachment as an example of American insensitivity and arrogance; the Portuguese neighbor became competitive and tried to grow larger bananas; the Chinese neighbor chopped down the banana plants that had entered his own yard late at night without even discussing the issue; and the Hawaiian neighbor laughed off the issue and blamed the land itself for the problem (Worchel 2005). Even though there were individualistic, and perhaps even culturally atypical in the Japanese case, approaches to this minor agriculture dispute among his various neighbors, it brought into clear view the ways cultural diversity can impact responses to conflict.

To act differently from one's own cultural norms can feel uncomfortable to the point of feeling that one's sense of identity is threatened. In more collectivist societies, open conflict has traditionally been seen as dangerous to social cohesion (Triandis 1995). Still, recent organizational behavior research shows that openly addressing conflict, even in collectivist societies, can be constructive, improving problem-solving and developing (rather than threatening) interdependence. Paradoxically, avoiding open conflict may lead to more competitive interaction and less interdependence (Tjosvold et al. 2003).

Individuals with *high- or low-context* cultural styles may need to be approached differently in a conflict situation (Ting-Toomey 2003). For example, a lower context individual should consider being less direct and urgent in trying to resolve a conflict than they are accustomed to being when approaching a higher context individual; when dealing with a conflict involving a lower context person, a higher context individual may have better success by trying to be more direct and forthcoming than would feel appropriate within his or her home culture.

Conflict Through the Lens of Culture

Imagine a circle of people standing around a complex sculpture. Without moving, each person can only see a particular view of this sculpture. They may miss key portions of the structure that are hidden on the sides of the sculpture that are out of their line of view. This is similar to individuals with differing needs or from different cultures trying to understand a common conflict. Subjective perspectives are influenced by personal or political histories and norms of cultural understanding. Diverse cultural norms within one group create complex interactions—as in a mandala, sculpture, or puzzle—that influence emotional expression, power, and persuasion within intragroup conflicts. Not only understanding but also legitimating another's perspective on a conflict creates connections across difference. This allows the team members to speak more freely, and to build collective understanding of how each has contributed to the conflict in question (Kolb and Williams 2003).

Differing cultural norms lead to divergent perspectives: relative cultural frames, such as varied approaches to power distance relationships between managers and employees, individualism versus collectivism, temporality and the management of time, and even the dynamics of interpersonal space or habits of eye contact (see Chapter 2), should be considered when beginning to address a conflict with someone from another cultural background. For example individuals from a society where there is high power distance or strong collective loyalties, may find it difficult as subordinates to directly address a conflict with a superior. High uncertainty avoidance tendencies in members on a self-directed team may cause unacceptable levels of tension and reactive conflict (Hofstede 1980). This status-based obstacle to early resolution of a problem could lead to escalation of the conflict and even to open rebellion. Regarding time and personal space issues, simple discomfort with divergent norms can bring conflict-producing tensions. Team members at different points on a continuum of universalist versus particularist values may disagree more severely than seems warranted over a discrepancy in following a rule or procedures. The following example highlights this point.

A young female Scandinavian diplomat working in West Africa confronted the mayor over the telephone about a development spending issue. He hung up on her: she was overstepping her bounds as a young woman, whom he saw as having too much power coming with her control over development funds. She wanted to talk with him the next time they met to tell him that hanging up on her was not acceptable and that he could tell her directly if he was angry with her. Before she could do this, her ambassador recounted the incident to the mayor's older cousin, who approached the mayor. In West Africa, when an older cousin points out a blunder, admonishing the mayor's behavior in this case, the younger cousin must apologize. The next time the diplomat saw the mayor, he apologized and even gave her champagne for her birthday. Since he had admitted that he was wrong, she could no longer directly address his behavior and talk through their differences. Rather, she was conciliatory in order to help him save face: she acknowledged that he probably hadn't really meant what he did. The roots or dynamics of the conflict were never truly resolved or transformed, though the conflict was defused, albeit in a manner that was not satisfying to the diplomat.

Differing linguistic norms and discursive styles can also lead to misunderstandings between team members. Intercultural communication theory reminds us that what is said may not be what is heard, particularly where there are cultural filters at work between the speaker and the listener (Fantini 1991). The actual meaning of specific words, even the word "peace" itself, may have different definitions to people on two ends of a verbal exchange (Cohen 1998). William Safire (2005), in his *New York Times* column "On Language", has noted that there is no term for compromise in Arabic, though *taarradhin*, a conflict resolved without humiliation, comes closest to a Western notion of a win-win solution.

New York Times columnist Thomas Friedman (2005) recounts this story about intercultural linguistic misunderstanding:

> Last September, Deputy Secretary of State Robert Zoellick gave a speech to the National Committee on United States-China relations in which he repeatedly urged China to become a responsible "stakeholder" in the international system. It turns out there is no word in Chinese for "stakeholder," and the initial Chinese reaction was puzzlement and reaching for a dictionary. Did Zoellick mean "steak holder"? After all, he was speaking at a dinner. Maybe this was some Texas slang for telling China it had to buy more U.S. beef? Well, eventually the Chinese got a correct interpretation (p. 12).

A comparable anecdote is of the Ghanaian bureaucrat who was invited to a "brown bag" lunch in Copenhagen. The intention for such a meeting is that everyone brings their own lunch, whether in a brown bag or not, but in Ghana "brown bag" signifies a bribe! The confusion and cross-cultural misunderstanding of the Ghanaian about the nature of this meeting was somewhat comic in this case, and easily cleared up, but it could have created more serious ethical judgments with longer-term implications for international collaboration. Common-sense human social behaviors, such as *self-restraint*, *humor*, or *separation*, are effectively employed in traditional as well as modern societies to diffuse tensions and de-escalate conflict (Bonta 1996).

Conflict can grow from misinterpreted nonverbal cues or tone of voice. In a multicultural context, the chances for miscommunications increase. A simple misunderstanding can lead to an incorrect interpretation of intention, which can initiate the Ladder of Inference (see Chapter 7) and set into motion a retaliatory cycle. A wrong assumption can draw an unexpectedly hostile reaction, leading to hidden animosity or open argument, setting off a cycle of reactive negative exchanges. Kelman describes how conflicts escalate—not only from reciprocal misunderstandings, but from perceived threats, pride, defensiveness, and inflexibility—into an *interactive self-escalatory process* (Kelman 1998). The following is an example of miscommunication escalating to conflict.

> *A Sudanese man and an American woman were working together on an academic team. The American woman had a habit of making mildly sarcastic comments and on one occasion jokingly suggested that the group did not want to hear from the Sudanese man, intending actually to mean the opposite by teasingly encouraging him to speak. He took this very personally and publicly said he felt this was a disrespectful racist comment and refused to speak to her again. She tried to speak with him in private and apologized profusely, but he refused to talk with her or accept her apology. At a later point, and after other members of the team had tried to engage him to speak with the woman, he decided that it was no longer an issue and said so publicly. The incident was never directly*

discussed, and the woman felt the issue was never actually resolved; she never felt safe enough to speak openly with her colleague again.

Such issues of direct versus indirect communication in team members operating from *specific* versus *diverse* cultural frames must be managed in a manner that allows colleagues to retain their dignity during the management of a conflict. Even on virtual teams, misunderstandings require responses with adequate interpersonal and intercultural sensitivity to keep them from escalating into damaging conflict. On virtual teams there are novel linguistic opportunities for miscommunication, since only written words are shared without any socially moderating nonverbal cues, such as tone of voice or a smile. The following is an example of virtual team miscommunication.

A Danish development aid administrator sent an e-mail about decision on a project issue to all relevant parties. One member of the team from Ivory Coast sent an aggressive response—cc'ed to everyone on the e-mail list and others not directly involved in the issue—that she had not received any e-mail message leading up to this decision. In fact, she had been away from the office for some time and had not received the earlier e-mail communication that went out. This public and aggressive style of dealing with conflict was one that had been faced before by this administrator in Ivory Coast. She sensed that her Ivorian colleagues want to make sure they are heard and that other people know about a conflict. Rather than being confrontational in response and sending a public e-mail message that pointed out the team member's mistake to everyone, the administrator won respect by sending her only a private e-mail response with a copy of the earlier communication. The team member appreciated that her mistake had been underplayed and not made public, and this greatly improved the relationship between the administrator and the team member in the long run.

Improving *interpretability* (i.e., speech that facilitates understanding) and checking that intended meanings are clearly understood, are key to keeping conflict constructive (Ayoko et al. 2001). Recent research suggests that the existence of social *advice networks,* and team leaders who are capable of initiating structure for their team, moderate the impact of values diversity as a cause of team conflict (Klein et al. 2004). What awareness of my own identity, my patterns of behavior, and my ways of perceiving or communicating might be needed to prevent as well as resolve conflicts? Transparency about differing styles is a simple step toward coordinating and harmonizing group norms for addressing conflict. Cultural styles of conflict and strengths in conflict resolution can be elicited via storytelling—telling stories within a multicultural group that shed light on ways that we have dealt with conflict in the past.

Exercise: Group Storytelling to Analyze Conflict Styles

Have the members of a group or class sit in a circle. Each person tells one sentence of a story that the group creates. For example, the first person says "Once upon a time there was a conflict..." The next person continues and then the next person until everyone in a circle has spoken and the group has developed a story about a conflict and how it was addressed in their particular cultural style, specifically mentioning who are the parties and stakeholders that get involved in the conflict dynamics and develop strategies for resolution.

I have used this activity with groups in conflict from various countries who share similar cultural styles of dealing with conflict. This activity helps them understand their cultural commonalities in ways that allow them to proceed to mutually address a specific conflict in the group or between their ethnic or national communities.

Identity Issues

In a multicultural team, functioning in ways that are culturally unfamiliar can feel threatening to one's identity. Unrecognized identity needs can simmer into open conflicts.

Identity-based conflicts are more complex and deeply personal than disputes over tangible issues such as resources (Rothman 1997; Maalouf 2002). Social identity differences need not disappear in order to eliminate conflict; rather, successful conflict management strategies work with those identities and capitalize on recognition of real diversity (Haslam 2001). Catholic and Protestant teenagers from Northern Ireland who participated in peace-building dialogue reported that they felt a stronger sense of their own identity even as they came to appreciate differences and similarities in relation to members of the other community (Ungerleider 2003).

Fundamental psychoanalytic theory defines a variety of psychological defense mechanisms that work to protect the safety of the ego when it feels threatened (Freud 1946). One of these defense mechanisms is *projection*, in which I project my own faults onto others in order to see myself in a better light and preserve my self-esteem. Though these thoughts may begin unconsciously, they can lead to blaming; sometimes one member is isolated and made into a *scapegoat* for problems in the group.

Scapegoating is often employed to reinforce membership within a community. Positive conceptions of belonging to an in-group are contrasted to negative stereotypes and enemy images of an out-group (Ashmore et al. 2002). Reinforcement by the in-group will protect members from seeing their behavior as intolerant. Ethnic or national groups maintain traditional scapegoats. When members of a multicultural or multi-ethnic work team come from identity groups with a history of identity-based conflict—such as Greeks and Turks or Japanese and Koreans—even mild criticisms or pointed jokes could escalate tensions. If there is a power imbalance in an intergroup relationship, an actual or perceived *one up/one down* relationship (see Chapter 3) may develop. A team leader will want to address this potentially divisive dynamic in a proactive manner by building trust and communication capacity.

Gender socialization cannot be ignored as an identity factor that impacts team communication and conflict dynamics. Gender stereotypes can lead to false assumptions, or even bias against team members. Different styles and goals of communication have been identified for men and women—for example, men tend to communicate in order to seek status while women talk to achieve intimacy (Tannen 1991; Wood 2000). In keeping with socialized norms concerning gender roles, men may act more overtly aggressive in a conflict, while women tend to withdraw.

The pressure to conform to dominant social norms and mores can lead to fear that I will be rejected if I'm not "normal." This internalized fear of my own difference, translated to guilt, shame, or anxiety, is projected onto others who diverge from group norms. This projection of socially unacceptable qualities translates into *enemy images*, then to fears of victimization and reactive attacks (Keen 1986). In interpersonal conflicts, just as in intergroup conflict, this dynamic can emerge as *mirror images* between two enemies—the innocent self (victim) versus the aggressive other (perpetrator) (Kelman 1998). This is easier to see in intergroup relations. Tensions between Muslim immigrants and European natives have erupted into riots, as in Oldham, England in 2003, and Paris, France in 2005 each group saw the other as both culturally different and threatening to its security.

The issue of security is central to both personal and political conflict behaviors. Where there is perceived insecurity, either personally or politically, irrational reactions and defensive attitudes escalate potential differences into aggressive behaviors in a pattern of *self-fulfilling prophecy*: "a false definition of the situation evoking a new behavior which makes the originally false conception come true" (Merton 1957, p. 423). Arguably, Israelis and Palestinians, by seeing each other as a threat, have implemented aggressive and violent practices towards each other, which have in turn proved the reality of each their respective fears. Rather than seeking to build security through power and force—or *collective security* (i.e., ganging up with allies to intimidate potential opponents)—conflict transformation principles suggest seeking to build *cooperative security* (Forsberg 1992), where people work together to eliminate injustice and create healthy social systems that prevent conflict.

Preventing Escalation

For preventing violence and healing historic wounds, Staub (1989) emphasizes shifting a culture of antagonism to one of positive reciprocity. Developing pro-social attitudes and behaviors, such as showing interest in others, sharing openly about one's own perspective, and appropriately timing remarks, are helpful in laying the groundwork for trust and team harmony. Relationship-building leads to mutual confidence.

Within a multicultural team the emergence of some kind of unifying *transcendent identity* (Kelman 2002) among team members can override the divisive potential of identity-based differences. Consolidating mutual linguistic and behavioral customs within a group reduces potential misunderstanding and build common team identity. A team leader can build trust and common identity through team-building activities, establishing *super-ordinate goals* (common objectives), and keeping communication honest and open.

Approaches to Conflict Resolution

The growing field of *conflict resolution* offers a toolbox of perspectives and interventions relevant to a wide variety of conflict situations, ranging from *negotiation* strategies and third-party *mediation* to using systematic *conflict transformation* interventions and *peacebuilding* to shift relationships sustaining intractable, deep-rooted conflicts.

Logical analysis based on sound theory, plus intuitive insight, sensitivity, and awareness of conflict dynamics, are all needed to devise interventions that will de-escalate a growing conflict. Ideally, the timing, contextual framing, and level of directness of an intervention will be sensitive to the needs and identities of the parties in conflict. A third-party consultant or mediator may be required if internal efforts to intervene are ineffective.

Negotiation

Conflict resolution theory and practice focuses on developing appropriate approaches for negotiating a conflict. Similar to cultural styles of dealing with conflict, *negotiating styles* are described as being (1) *soft*: concerned with preserving the relationship between the negotiating parties; or (2) *hard*: focused on winning the negotiation. In their landmark book about negotiation, *Getting to Yes*, Fisher and Ury (1983) developed the notion of *principled negotiation,* in which negotiators focus on alternative approaches that are neither soft nor hard: trying to understand mutual needs and seek joint solutions; working together to uncover underlying (and potentially common) interests, rather than digging into competing positions; proceeding independent of whether or not trust has been established; and being hard on the problem rather than the people in negotiation. In cooperative, interest-based *integrative bargaining* (Pruitt 1981), parties collaborate to find *win-win agreements* that meet the needs of both parties. In game theory, a win-lose result is called *zero sum*: that is, where a win equals +1 and a loss equals −1, the sum of the equation is zero: +1 −1 = 0. A win-win solution could result in a positive sum: 1 +1 = 2.

Allowing for informal *pre-negotiation* (Cohen 1991) or *circum-negotiation* sessions (Saunders 1999), meetings to build trust and communication norms before a negotiation session, can establish effective and potentially face-saving ground rules to insure a more successful formal process. Participants might agree to the setting and procedures to be used for the formal negotiation, what are possible areas for potential agreement, and whether there are some topics that just shouldn't be raised. To build confidence and momentum in a negotiation it may be necessary to address less controversial issues first. What is important is to clarify mutual understanding of the essential conflict, and verify the main issues and interests for each party.

Cultural styles impact negotiations by adding *cross-cultural "noise"*—i.e., the verbal and nonverbal messages that cannot be clearly understood across cultures, and lead to linguistic or symbolic misinterpretation (Fisher 1980; Cohen 1991; Avruch 1998). Assumptions about national negotiating characteristics, even if once useful, have become diluted by rapid international globalization. Like in the cartoon in which an Englishman bows while a Japanese businessman reaches out for a handshake, international negotiators are fast learning to adapt to the complexities and uncertainties of intercultural negotiation. Principles for intercultural negotiations that apply to communication in multicultural teams include:

1. Be flexible, get to know the other culture, employ approaches that will facilitate communication, avoid what may be irritating.
2. Be careful not to get stuck in stereotypical assessments and assignment of traits.
3. Be aware of language barriers, check understanding from time to time, go slow, ask questions.
4. Be careful about attributing meaning to nonverbal behavior; nonverbal communication is significant and may even contradict verbal input.
5. Be aware that mistrust can breakdown communication and communication is essential (Casse 1985).

Mediation

In the professional field of *mediation*, or *alternative dispute resolution* (*ADR*), a neutral third party facilitates an agreement between parties in conflict. Mediators also look beyond the ultimate goal of a reaching agreement to consider the importance of relationships and cultural differences in the mediation process. An emerging focus on *transformative or humanistic mediation* brings awareness to the importance of transforming and developing relationships between parties in conflict. Transformative mediators believe that building relationship can be even more important than penning a formal agreement, which may end a dispute in the short term but not resolve the underlying causes of the conflict (Baruch Bush and Folger 1994).

In a multicultural team, there may be a need for a neutral third-party to mediate a dispute between team members with culturally diverging norms for dealing with conflict. An interculturally sensitive mediator will *interpret*, *buffer*, and *coordinate* dissonant linguistic or nonverbal messages and negotiating styles to protect the *face* (self-respect and honor) of adversaries and keep communication flowing (Cohen 1998). A mediator working across cultures should elicit relevant cultural behaviors, norms, and wisdom that can be useful in transforming a conflict (Lederach 1995). In traditional societies, a social leader or elder will be engaged as a mediator. An example is Burma, where *respected insiders* are called on as a neutral third party who will use informal methods for mediating a serious conflict (Leone and Giannini 2005).

Conflict Transformation and Peacebuilding

Conflict transformation stresses the need to deal not only with the *problem*, but also with the *people* involved, the *process* of addressing the problem, and the sources or *politics* underlying the presenting problem. Conflict transformation recognizes that systems of conflict, and the wounded relationships that sustain them, must be deeply transformed if there is to be sustainable peace (Diamond and McDonald 1996; Green 2002; Lederach 2003). Conflict transformation moves from situational analysis to strategic intervention, assessing the sources and dynamics of a conflict, then trying to transform the structures and relationships that sustain a conflict system, working at both personal and political levels.

Conflict transformation seeks to build "positive" as well as "negative" peace (Galtung 1969), where there is not only an absence of overt violence (the calm of an oppressive Pax Romana), but healthy social systems and relationships between people. Conflict transformation seeks to promote nonviolent approaches to conflict, to transform conflictual relationships, and to build peace culture. Successful conflict transformation practice requires creative problem solving, lateral thinking, coping with complexity, addressing multiple tasks, and dealing with confusing emotions in challenging situations. Systematic conflict analysis and strategic intervention must incorporate diverse cultural values and even opposing views of reality.

The goals of conflict transformation, which are oriented toward intercommunal and international violence, are also relevant to intragroup conflict. Just as in conflict transformation, dialogues or *problem-solving workshops* between representatives of groups in conflict, *mutual reassurance* and *confidence building* must be developed to reopen the bridges of effective communication between conflicting parties (Kelman 1998). Within multicultural teams, just as in multiethnic societies, there must be informal and formal mechanisms established for minority representation and consultation, power sharing, and participation, along with tangible as well as perceived recognition (Boulding 1992).

During his tenure as UN Secretary General, Boutros Boutros Ghali defined the roles of peacekeeping, peacemaking, and peacebuilding in *An Agenda for Peace* (1983). Roles outlined for international peace missions apply to building peace on work teams as well: *Peacekeepers* (to police behaviors or intercede and keep feuding members apart), *peacemakers* (negotiators or mediators), or *peacebuilders* (team and trust builders, systems reformers) may need to emerge in order to heal the dynamics in a team. Conceiving of myself as a potential peacemaker or peacebuilder can change my ability to respond to conflict. Peacebuilders need to look deeply to see what may be hidden under the surface of a contentious negotiation or conflict. *What might I do as a peacemaker or peacebuilder when a conflict begins to escalate?*

As peacebuilders, we can imagine what well-placed interventions will have a ripple effect throughout our societies, organizations, or teams. The challenge is to create a harmonious, team culture that values diverse styles and contributions, rather than a culture of conformity, or conflict, or even emotional violence—a culture of peace. It is useful to imagine a yogurt or sourdough starter, a small but poten that changes the quality of all that is around it. A spoonful of yogurt turns gallons milk into yogurt. In many ancient languages around the Mediterranean there is the expression, "slowly slowly" (*siga siga*—Greek; *yavash yavash*—Turkish; *leyat leyat*—Hebrew; *shway, shway*—Arabic). This expression can be seen as an approach to life, as well as a sensible approach to transforming seemingly intractable conflicts.

Traditional and tribal societies have developed their own conflict resolution mechanisms for *reconciliation* and *restorative justice*. For example, the Polynesian *Ho'o ponopono* approach to reconciliation is a holistic system that incorporates restitution to victims and forgiveness of perpetrators (Galtung 2001). The *Gada'a* system of training young men about their social responsibilities among the Omara in Ethiopia includes mechanisms for conflict resolution (Solomon 2005). Rwanda brought back its traditional *gacaca* tribunal system to deal with a huge backlog of cases and overcrowded prisons after the 1994 genocide (Lambourne 2001). The peaceful, aboriginal Semai people in Malaysia use the *becharaa'* process of informal discussions and formal speeches to exhaustively assess communal consensus for a just solution based on Semai traditional values—values which, as in other peaceful traditional societies, emphasize *peacefulness* through a world view emphasizing nonviolence as a fundamental component of humanity (Bonta 1996).

Collaborative Conflict Transformation on Teams: Communication Skills for Dialogue

While there are a growing number of theories and methods of conflict resolution coming from professionals in the field, there are still few experts better than each of us in understanding our own unique cultural and personal context in relation to the kind of conflicts we experience in our daily life and in our socio-political environment. Any work team can collaboratively analyze its specific multicultural dynamics and can deepen cross-cultural dialogue to develop more effective responses to conflict.

In order for conflict dynamics to shift, group processes, communication styles, and relationships may need to be addressed through an honest dialogue in which perceptions are openly shared and actively heard. With diverse communication, negotiating, and conflict styles, with differing cultures, perspectives, identities, and needs, how can a multicultural team have an effective dialogue? Will team discussion about conflict have the dynamics of (1) a positional debate, (2) a problem-solving task force, or (3) a dialogue designed to create understanding of differences, relationships, and trust?

When team members are empowered to express themselves honestly and are recognized for their perceptions and feelings, a deeper level of dialogue and communication is possible. In order to have honest dialogue with the goal of

…ding of diverse perspectives, norms for dialogue must be agreed …sh an atmosphere of respect and open communication. For example, …reements not to interrupt or to use words that are recognized as divisive …event predictable conflicts from arising. Fundamental skills of speaking and …ening must a sharpened and deepened for effective conflict dialogue. *Authentic expression* (Kelman 1998) combined with *active listening* ideally leads to a sense of *deep dialogue* (Diamond 1996).

Authentic Expression

Authentic expression means openly and honestly sharing my perspective about a situation. One technique for speaking authentically is taking ownership for my opinions, or speaking from "*I*" statements, rather than using the general, dominant, and impersonal "*we*." Directly expressing my feelings is an approach for giving honest interpersonal feedback (See Chapter 7). This is particularly important in a conflict situation. In a multicultural setting, directly expressing my point of view on a controversial topic may stretch the limits of what is culturally appropriate, particularly in a mixed-gender setting. When cultural complexity makes the appropriate level of honest expression confusing, it seems to be a fairly universal human phenomenon that *conciliatory language* will achieve more harmonious results that hostile words.

Active Listening

Active listening consists of such techniques as providing supportive nonverbal cues, asking clarifying questions, and summarizing or offering reflective statements to show understanding (see Chapter 7). The goal of active listening is confirming what has been heard, and that hearing has actually taken place, establishing a foundation for genuine communication. Often we don't communicate, we compete. We don't really listen but rather prepare our next rebuttal point for debate. Really listening shows respect and openness, that I will sincerely consider the views and needs of others. Listening can actively defuse aggressiveness by:

- Exhibiting receptivity to new ideas and openness to statements that I may not agree with
- Giving value to the speaker
- Displaying a willingness to hear—neutrality and a lack of hostility (Turk 1997)

In trying to understand the dynamics of a conflict, it is important to listen to the context as well as content of what is being said, including the observation of nonverbal and symbolic messages. When working interculturally, it may be more complicated to assess what is effective active listening and what makes someone feel heard. For example, a common nonverbal feature of active listening is keeping eye contact. This may be inappropriate, particularly between genders, in specific cultures.

Through practicing *authentic expression* and *active listening*, team members will feel a sense of *recognition* and *empowerment*—(1) recognition of who I am and the value of what I have to contribute, and (2) empowerment to honestly express my perspectives, needs, and feelings.

It is important to ascertain effective verbal and nonverbal cues within a specific culture in order to be accurately understood and to ensure that others feel heard. As a member of any group, we can experimentally determine whether speaking authentically and actively listening has improved communication.

Check-in/Check-out

A common technique in dialogue about conflict is to use a *check-in* at the beginning of a group or a *check-out* at the end. In both of these activities, group members each take a turn sharing something about how they are doing or feeling about events. In a check-in activity, each team member may say how they are, or share a recent event or something personally significant that has happened since the group last met. During a check-out activity, participants each express how they personally felt about the group meeting. A check-out is an explicit opportunity to find out whether a session felt productive, whether communication was effective, and whether group members felt that their perspectives and positions were heard and considered by those with conflicting perspectives or positions.

In a check-out, we can ask ourselves and let the team know: Did I feel heard? We can find out from other team members: Did you feel heard? It is important to recognize how we feel when we are heard (valued) versus when we are ignored (worthless). The resentment and anger that can be planted by group members who are not feeling listened to—even about unrelated issues—can translate quickly into open conflict. Unresolved feelings and resentments can be a source of disgruntlement and resistance to group productivity, which can devolve unexpectedly into conflict.

Nonverbal Communication Activities

While dialogue is an important tool for conflict transformation, there may be times when talking is ineffective or inappropriate in multicultural teams. Common words may not exist that can adequately communicate emotions or cultural conventions. At those times, nonverbal aesthetic or artistic alternatives—even silence—may provide a more appropriate format for dealing with emotional conflict (Van Gligow et al. 2004). Formal or informal inclusive rituals that welcome members of all traditions can also be practically employed for peacebuilding (Schirch 2004).

Communicating Using Exercise: T'ai Ch'i Chuan

Employing activities that increase sensitivity and awareness of interpersonal dynamics can facilitate the ability to perceive escalation of conflict versus enhanced communication. An example is a push hands exercise from the Chinese exercise practice in the martial arts tradition T'ai Ch'i Chuan. Two partners stand facing each other with legs in a balanced position (feet shoulder width, one foot in front of the other) and gently touch the backs of their wrists together. Partners experiment with pushing each other's wrist, slowly moving together in a circular motion, experimenting with varieties of force and sensitivity, trying to stick together and yield enough to each other's force to keep active communication open. It is quickly apparent how your partner reacts when you are overly aggressive, or how the relationship is lost when you are too passive. Employing force against force leads to stalemate and impasse. By contrast, give and take leads to flexibility, working together, and fine-tuning the dynamics of interpersonal communication into a sense of blending and harmony (Crum 1987). The give and take of negotiation can be experienced tangibly in such a game; the sensation of interacting rather than fighting may be then translated via metaphor to verbal communication or conflict situations. Physical 'listening' characteristics, such as following and attending, can be translated to more general relational skills such as paying attention or caring. Both empowerment and recognition are heightened as the rhythm of communication develops.

Deepening Dialogue: Building Empathy and Reconciliation

Interactive conflict resolution approaches using dialogue are beneficial in promoting empathy (Fisher 1997) and reconciliation when there are conflicts on multicultural teams. *Joint narrative storytelling* about a conflict's impact on individuals promotes compassion and healing (Hadjipavlou-Trigeorgis 1998). Using *reflexive dialogue* (Rothman 1997), group members build a sense of a shared responsibility through introspective interaction in which participants speak about their needs and interests, rather than blaming and arguing, or even problem-solving; this creates a forum for mutual empowerment and recognition.

A relevant concept from the field of international diplomacy is *GRIT* (*gradual reduction in tension*), in which each party makes graduated and reciprocated initiatives to reduce tension and build confidence and trust (Osgood 1962). At youth peace-building camps, dialogue proceeds from the relatively low-risk sharing of similarities and differences, through higher risk discussions of stereotypes and differing perspectives on history, to more deeply personal sharing of family stories (Ungerleider 2001). To achieve *forgiveness* between parties that have wounded each other can be one of the deepest goals, yet the act of forgiveness itself has a power to transform and heal a conflict that should not be underestimated (Henderson 1999).

Relevant Competencies

- Capacity to analyze the causes of conflict
- Ability to recognize the creative potential of conflict and engage with conflict constructively
- Ability to respond sensitively and appropriately to diverse cultural styles of addressing conflict
- Awareness of one's own predominant conflict style and the flexibility to use different styles as appropriate
- Skills for working through conflict in normative stages of group development
- Ability to distinguish between task and relationship conflict and respond appropriately
- Willingness and ability to apply conflict interventions: negotiation, mediation, conflict transformation, and peacebuilding
- Willingness to collaborate to transform conflict dynamics on teams
- Communication skills for open dialogue

Summary

In summary, members of multicultural work teams need to develop an orientation toward conflict to bring out its constructive potential and avoid its destructive ramifications. Team members will have diverse personal and cultural styles of engaging in and seeking to resolve conflict. Conflict is more likely to appear in the middle stages of group development, when members are adjusting their expectations to the reality of a group's dynamics and wrestling for their share of control. Team members would be wise to develop coherent communication norms and trusting relationships that will serve them when conflicts do arise. The social-psychological dynamics of identity play a critical hidden role in interpersonal and intercultural relationships in teams, just as they do in intergroup or international relations. Work teams facing more serious conflicts may choose to integrate various approaches for conflict resolution, from negotiation to third party mediation, to more systematic conflict transformation and peacebuilding. Multicultural work teams can work collaboratively to become aware of and transform the dynamics of intragroup conflict by applying communication skills for dialogue that will surface the issues in a conflict and transform the relationships and structures that sustain conflict.

Case Studies

As you read the case studies below, consider the following questions:

- *What tools from this chapter can be used to assess the conflict dynamics at work in this multicultural team?*
- *What are the characteristics, tendencies, differences and potential conflicts between members of different gender, age, and professional experience level?*
- *What are the styles of dealing with conflict for each group member? What parts of these styles are personal versus culturally influenced?*
- *How can the underlying interests and needs of various group members be surfaced? How do these hidden factors and feelings influence member behaviors and team interactions when conflict emerges?*
- *How should the conflict be addressed appropriately, from a culturally as well as interpersonally sensitive manner?*

Selecting a Peace-Building Project Site

The members of an internationally mixed work team for an International Non-Governmental Organization (INGO) based in Washington DC are having challenges managing a conflict over a decision about which country should be the base for their next training of youth peace-building trainers. Leading contenders are Sri Lanka, Nepal, Nigeria, and Burundi.

Paul is from northern, rural Ghana. He is in his late thirties, old enough to be considered an elder in his tribe. He has worked for twelve years on development projects in West Africa. Alicia is from San Francisco. She is just back from a year doing humanitarian work in Sudan. Naoko is from Japan and this is her first job. David is from New York and just got his Master's degree in Conflict Transformation, which included an internship in Sri Lanka. Bernhard is from Germany and is spending a year in DC on leave from his job with a government agency that does development and aid projects in South and Central Asia.

Paul is the oldest member of the group and often calms tense situations by telling stories. Alicia considers herself a feminist and really wants to push herself professionally in the context of this team. Bernhard tends to be very direct in his communication style and work-oriented in the team, keeping the group on task and starting meetings on time. David considers himself easy going with a good sense of humor. Naoko tends to be very quiet in the group, but will sometimes make a comment at the end of a meeting about how she doesn't feel supported by the group. Other members of the group feel like they are bending over backwards to include her.

Paul has recently missed a few meetings. Alicia and Bernhard want to give him feedback about his participation, but he has mentioned that in his culture it is inappropriate in particular for a younger woman to give direct feedback to an older man, who should approach him indirectly through an appropriate third party. They are feeling frustrated by delays in making the decision to move forward with the next project and what they see as the lack of focus and contribution from the other team members.

David and Bernhard really want the next project to be in South Asia – Sri Lanka or Nepal—while Alicia and Paul want the project to be in Africa – Nigeria or Burundi. A decision must be made within a week in order to respond on time to a USAID Request for Proposal (RFP). Meetings have become more tense, there is arguing, particularly between Alicia and Bernhard, while Naoko is becoming more withdrawn, David is saying less and Paul has been increasingly absent. The situation comes to a head when Paul arrives an hour late for a meeting without having told anyone and Alicia raises her voice at him. Naoko gets upset and walks out.

The Middleperson: A US American in Thailand

As a U.S. American female supervisor in Thailand, I found that basically all examination of group dynamics in Thailand must be done indirectly, on an individual level. In order to find out how the group is doing, you have to add up the sum total of each individual perception. For example, if there is some kind of a problem or conflict within the group, it will never come out in the open during any kind of group meeting. What will probably happen is that one or two people will either come to you in person, or they will let someone else who isn't directly involved know. This person will then talk to you. It often takes a great deal of detective work to find out exactly what the issue is, but if you talk casually with enough group members, you will probably end up with a fairly accurate picture of the problem, and no one will lose face in the process.

Once you know what the issues are, you have the option of taking it back to the group and discussing it together, or of taking it up in an indirect way by discussing alternative solutions with individual group members. What needs to be kept in mind is that every conversation you have with an individual is a conversation with the group, as all discussions go directly back to the rest of the group. As long as you can deal with this manner of handling conflict, you will have access to information on how the group is doing, and a channel of communication and problem-solving strategies. Discussing conflict areas directly as a group is not generally accepted in Thailand as a way to solve problems, because group members will not usually disagree with each other in public. However, once trust is built up with individuals, you can get more accurate information about their feelings, as well as those of the rest of the group. Therefore, in Thailand, the individual is the group, and issues are dealt with more outside of the group than within it. All of this has taken some getting used to, but it is extremely interesting to watch it work. Things generally function smoothly if you can plug into the Thai system of information gathering.

Another interesting, but frustrating, dynamic is the functioning of the supervisor-coordinator work group. The new coordinator, Alice, was a U.S. American and had never lived in another culture before. Since she was unused to adapting her very direct style of communication, our dealings as a group were less than productive. I became the spokesperson for the group of supervisors. The two Thai supervisors felt strongly about certain issues and wanted Alice to know their feelings. They were, however, very hesitant to talk to her themselves at first because of the Thai code of indirectness.

Because I am a fairly direct person, I was less hesitant to discuss concerns, especially things that were really affecting all three of us in a very negative way. Unfortunately, I lost credibility with Alice, because, although I assured her that I was speaking for the group, she didn't trust my assessment of the Thai perspective. She wanted to hear directly from them, not understanding why they were not coming to her directly. The end result was that Alice looked upon me as a troublemaker who was trying to come between her and the Thai supervisors. I still am not sure how I could have handled this better. What started out as observations and suggestions which Alice had requested, ended up being perceived as threats to her leadership. This resulted in an unhealthy sort of competition between us. Having never experienced this in any previous work situation, I probably did not react well to it. It seemed like anything I did to try to help the situation was taken as a confrontation and a test of her authority. In the long run, I withdrew and stopped taking the role of the middleperson, and the two supervisors became more direct about the important issues.

Assessment Instruments

Team Assessment: Styles, Emotions, Needs, Sensitivity

The following four-step 'SENSe' collective assessment exercise is a participatory self-reflective exploration to be undertaken by a multicultural team or task group. The goal is to reveal the many hidden dimensions of personal style, cultural socialization, emotions, and needs that impact conflict dynamics in groups. Once these underlying influences are made transparent by the process of bringing them to the

surface, the team can creatively address how to address its conflict
and more effective manner.

Styles: Have all members of the group reflect about conflicts th
involved in during the past few years either privately, by journal writi
ing personal stories with a partner. Applying some of the catego
chapter as well as creatively describing personal behaviors, each person should characterize his or her own style of dealing with conflict and try to assess which parts of their tendencies are personal versus culturally influenced. Each team member can list 3–5 characteristics of their personal and/or cultural conflict style, and communicate those that feel safe to be shared with the team.

Emotions: Everyone on the team anonymously writes a list of possible private emotions or other hidden factors potentially within group members that might influence their behavior in a conflict. Each team member should write some of their own needs and feelings as well as what they imagine belong to others in the group without distinguishing between their own and others.

Needs: The team brainstorms how underlying interests or needs might impact member behaviors and team interactions, either in a current conflict, or a conflict that might surface.

Sensitivity: Based on the information gathered from generating these three previous lists, the team discusses potential ways to take effective action and appropriately address a intra-group conflict in a culturally and interpersonally sensitive manner: Try to make SENSe of it all.

Tools for Assessing Individual Conflict Styles in Groups

There are two notable instruments for measuring individual styles of dealing with conflict, based on (1) personal preferences (Thomas-Kilmann Conflict Mode Instrument), and (2) culturally learned behaviors that influence approaches to conflict (Hammer Intercultural Conflict Style Inventory).

Personal Conflict Styles

The *Thomas-Kilmann Conflict Mode Instrument* (TKI) is "designed to assess an individual's behavior in conflict situations" (Thomas and Kilmann 2001). The TKI can be taken, or a copy purchased, online. The TKI creates a score that reflects one's repertoire of conflict-handling skills along the dimensions of assertiveness and cooperativeness, one's primary preference among the five conflict styles of *avoiding*, *accommodating*, *coercing*, *compromising*, *or collaborating*, and suggests when to most effectively apply each style. The Rahim Organizational Conflict Inventory (ROCII) can also be used to measure preferred conflict styles using similar categories: *avoiding*, *obliging*, *dominating*, *compromising*, *and integrating* (Rahim 1983).

Cultural Conflict Styles

The Hammer Intercultural Conflict Style Inventory (ICS) Inventory assesses "culturally-learned approaches for managing disputes" (Hammer 2005) along dimensions of direct versus indirect and emotionally expressive versus restrained approaches to conflict. Combinations of these culturally-influenced preferences for conflict engagement result in four distinct styles for cross-cultural conflict resolution: discussion, engagement, accommodation, and dynamic styles.

References

Amason, A., Thompson, K., Hochwarter, W. and Harrison, A. (1995). Conflict: An important dimension in successful management teams. *Organizational Dynamics*, *24*(1), 20–34.

Appelbaum, C., Shapiro, B.T. and Elbaz D. (1998). The management of multicultural group conflict. *Team Performance Management*, *4*(5), 211–234.

Appelbaum, S.H., Abdallah, C. and Shapiro, B.T. (1999). The self-directed team: A conflict resolution analysis. *Team Performance Management*, *5*(2), 60–77.

Ashmore, R., Jussim, L. and Wilder, D. (2002). *Social identity, intergroup conflict, and conflict reduction*. Oxford: Oxford University Press.

Assagioli, R. (1971). *Psychosynthesis*. London: Penguin.

Avruch, K. (1998). *Culture and Conflict Resolution*. Washington D.C.: United States Institute for Peace.

Ayoko, O., Hartel, C. and Callan, V. (2001). Disentangling the complexity of productive and destructive conflict in culturally heterogeneous workgroups: A communication accommodation theory approach. In D.H. Nagao (Ed.). *Academy of management best paper proceedings*, CM: A1–A6.

Baruch Bush, R.A. and Folger, J.P. (1994). *The promise of mediation*. San Francisco, CA: Jossey-Bass.

Bonta, B. (1996). Conflict resolution among peaceful societies: The culture of peacefulness. *Journal of Peace Research*, *33*(4) 403–420.

Boulding, E. (1992). Ethnicity and new constitutive orders. In J. Brecher, J.B. Childs and J. Cutler (Eds.), *Global visions*. Boston, MA: South End.

Boutros Ghali, B. (1983). *An agenda for peace*. New York: United Nations.

Burgess, H. and Spangler, B. (2003). Conflicts and disputes. In G. Burgess and H. Burgess (Eds.), *Beyond intractability*. Boulder, CO: Conflict Research Consortium, University of Colorado.

Burton, J. (1986). On the need for conflict prevention. *Institute for conflict resolution and analysis occasional paper #1*. Fairfax: George Mason University.

Casse, P. (1985). *Managing intercultural negotiations*. Washington, DC: SIETAR.

Cohen, R. (1991). *Negotiating across cultures*. Washington, DC: United States Institute for Peace.

Cohen, R. (1998). Cultural aspects of international mediation. In J. Bercovitch (Ed.), *Resolving international conflicts* (pp. 107–125). Boulder, CO: Lynne Rienner.

Crum, T. (1987). *The magic of conflict*. New York: Touchstone.

De Drue, C. & Weingart, L. (2002). Task versus relationship conflict: a meta analysis. *Academy of Management Proceedings*.

Diamond, L. and McDonald, J. (1996). *Multi-track diplomacy: A systems approach to peace*. West Hartford, CT: Kumarian.

Esquivel, M. and Kleiner, B. (1996). The importance of conflict in work team effectiveness. *Empowerment in Organizations*, *4*(4), 10–15.

Fantini, A. (1991). Becoming better global citizens: The promise of intercultural competence. *Adult Learning*, *2*(5), 15–19.

Fisher, G. (1980). *International negotiation: A cross-cultural perspective*. Yarmouth, ME: Intercultural Press.

Fisher, R. (1997). *Interactive conflict resolution*. New York: Syracuse University Press.

Fisher, R. and Ury, W. (1983). *Getting to yes: Negotiating agreement without giving in*. New York: Penguin Books.

Forsberg, R. (1992). Why cooperative security? Why now? *Peace and Democracy News*, Winter, 9–13.

Freud, A. (1946). *The Ego and the mechanisms of defence*. New York: International Universities Press.

Friedman, R., Tidd, S., Currall, S. and Tsai, J. (2000). What goes around comes around: The impact of personal conflict style on work conflict and stress. *The International Journal of Conflict Management*, *11*(1), 32–55.

Friedman, T. (2005). The axis of order? *New York Times*, January 13, A23.

Galtung, J. (2001). After violence: Reconstruction, reconciliation and resolution. In M. Abu-Nimer (Ed.), *Reconciliation justice and coexistence* (pp. 3–21). New York: Lexington.

Galtung, J. (1969). Violence, peace, and peace research. *Journal of Peace Research*, *3*, 167–191.

Green, P. (2002). CONTACT: Training a new Generation of peacebuilders. *Peace and Change*, *27*, 97–105.

Hadjipavlou-Trigeorgis, M. (1998). Different relationships to the land: Personal narratives, political implications and political possibilities in conflict resolution. In V. Calotychos (Ed.), *Cyprus and its people* (pp. 251–273). Boulder, CO: Westview.

Hammer, M.R. (2005). The intercultural conflict style inventory: A conceptual framework and measure of intercultural conflict approaches. *International Journal of Intercultural Research*, *29*, 675–695.

Haslam, S.A. (2001) *Psychology in organizations: The social identity approach*. London: Sage.

Henderson, M. (1999) *Forgiveness: Breaking the chain of hate*. London: BookPartners.

Hofstede, G. (1980) Motivation, leadership, and organizations: Do American theories apply abroad? *Organizational Dynamics*, *9*(1), 42–63.

Jehn, K. (1997). Qualitative analysis of conflict types and dimensions in organizational groups. *Administrative Science Quarterly*, *42*(3), 538–566.

Keen, S. (1986). *Faces of the enemy: Reflections of the hostile imagination*. San Francisco, CA: Harper & Row.

Kelman, H. (1998). Social-psychological dimensions of international conflict. In W. Zartman and J. L. Rasmussen (Eds.), *Peacemaking in international conflict: Methods & techniques* (pp. 191–233). Washington, DC: United States Institute for Peace.

Kelman, H. (2002). The role of national identity in conflict resolution. In R. Ashmore, L. Jussim and D. Wilder (Eds.), *Social identity, intergroup conflict, and conflict reduction* (pp. 187–211). Oxford: Oxford University Press.

Klein, K., Saltz, J., Lim, B.C., Knight, A.P. and Ziegert, J. (2004). When team members' values differ: The moderating effects of team leadership and network structure. In K.M. Weaver (Ed.) *Academy of management proceedings*. St. Louis: Academy of Management.

Kline, T. (1999). *Remaking Teams*. San Francisco, CA: Jossey-Bass.

Kolb, D. and Williams, J. (2003). *Everyday negotiation: Navigating for hidden agendas in bargaining*. San Francisco, CA: Jossey-Bass.

Lambourne, W. (2001). Justice and reconciliation: Postconflict peacebuilding in Cambodia and Rwanda. In M. Abu-Nimer (Ed.), *Reconciliation justice and coexistence* (pp. 3–21). New York: Lexington.

Lederach, J.P. (1995). *Preparing for peace: Conflict transformation across cultures*. New York: Syracuse University Press.

Lederach, J.P. (2003). *The little book of conflict transformation*. Intercourse, PA: Good Books.

Levi, D. (2001). *Group dynamics for teams*. Thousand Oaks, CA: Sage.

Leone, F. and Giannini, T. (2005). Traditions of conflict resolution in Burma: Respected insiders, resource-based conflict, and authoritarian rule. Washington, DC: Earth Rights International.

Maalouf, A. (2002). *In the name of identity: Violence and the need to belong*. New York: Arcade Publishers.

Maznevski, M.L. and DiStefano, J.J. (2000). Global leaders are team players: Developing global leaders through membership on global teams. *Human Resource Management, 39*(2/3), 195–208.

Merton, R.K. (1957). *Social theory and social structure*. Glencoe, IL: Free Press.

Moran, P.R. (2001). *Teaching culture: Perspectives in practice*. Boston, MA: Heinle & Heinle.

Morrow, D. and Wilson, D. (1996). *Ways out of conflict: Resources for community relations work*. Belfast: Ulster University Press.

Osgood, C.E. (1962). *An alternative to war or surrender*. Urbana, IL: University of Illinois Press.

Pruitt, D. (1981). *Negotiation behavior*. New York: Academic.

Rahim, M.A. (1983). A measure of styles of handling interpersonal conflict. *Academy of Management Journal, 26*, 368–376.

Rothman, J. (1997). *Resolving identity-based conflict in nations, organizations, and communities*. San Francisco, CA: Jossey-Bass.

Safire, W. (2005) Mishegoss. *New York Times magazine*, April 17, 2004.

Saunders, H. (1999). *A public peace process: Sustained dialogue to transform racial and ethnic conflicts*. New York: St. Martin's Press.

Schirch, L. (2004). *Ritual and symbol in peacebuilding*. Bloomfield, CT: Kumarian.

Schutz, W. (1973). *Elements of encounter*. Big Sur, CA: Joy Press.

Solomon, B. (2005). *Ways of knowing among the Oromo*. Capstone Paper. Brattleboro, Vermont: School for International Training.

Staub, E. (1989). *The roots of evil: The origins of genocide and other group violence*. Cambridge: Cambridge University Press.

Tannen, D. (1991). *You just don't understand; women and men in conversation*. New York: Ballantine Books.

Tannen, D. (1998). *The argument culture*. New York: Random House.

Ting-Toomey, S. (2003). Managing intercultural conflicts effectively. In L. Samovar and R. Porter (Eds.) *Intercultural communication* (10th ed., pp. 373–384). Belmont, CA: Wadsworth.

Thomas, K.W. (1976). Conflict and conflict management. In M.D. Dunette (Ed.), *Handbook of industrial and organizational psychology* (pp. 889–935). Chicago, IL: Rand McNally Publishers.

Thomas, K.W. and Kilmann R.H. (2001). *Thomas-Kilmann conflict mode instrument: Profile and interpretive report*. Mountain View, CA: Consulting Psychologists Press.

Tjosvold, D., Hui, C., Ding, D. and Hu, J. (2003). Conflict values and team relationships: Conflict's contribution to team effectiveness and citizenship in China. *Journal of Organizational Behavior, 24*(1), 69–88.

Triandis, H. (1995). *Individualism and collectivism*. Boulder, CO: Westview.

Turk, A.M. (1997) *Mediation training manual*. Unpublished.

Ungerleider, J. (2001). Bicommunal youth camps and peacebuilding in Cyprus. *Peace Review, 13*, 583–589.

Ungerleider, J. (2003). Entrusting young leaders to improve their world. *The New Body Politic, 1*(1).

Von Glinow, M.A., Shapiro, D. & Brett, J. (2004). Can we talk and should we?: Managing emotional conflict in multicultural teams. *Academy of management review, 29, 4*, 578.

Wood, J. (2000). Gender communication and culture. In L. Samovar and R. Porter (Ed.), *Intercultural communication* (9th ed., pp.170–179). Belmont, CA: Wadsworth.

Worchel, S. (2005). Culture's role in conflict and conflict management: Some suggestions, many questions. *International Journal of Intercultural Relations, 29*, 739–757.

Chapter 9
Problem Solving and Decision Making

Linda Drake Gobbo

If you can dream it, you can do it.

–Walt Disney

Introduction

Problem solving and decision making in multicultural work teams are the last of the skill areas to be covered in this book. This topic will be discussed from the cultural, individual, and organizational levels of multicultural team development, building on the frameworks that have been presented in previous chapters. Many theorists consider problem solving and decision making as synonymous—all decisions are made in response to a problem or opportunity. Simply stated, if *problem solving* is the process used to find a solution to the problem, challenge, or opportunity. However, how one solves problems can be quite varied. An individual can use analytical tools based on logic, deduction, or induction, or intuition based on an understanding of principles, or creative thinking. Problem-solving abilities and approaches may vary considerably, actually using different paradigms or frameworks. In this chapter one approach, with the steps and methods to do problem solving in work teams, will be presented.

Decision making involves making choices, determining an outcome, or making up one's mind about something. It also occurs by progressing through a prescribed set of steps. Although there are many different techniques from which to choose in each of the steps, the decision-making steps themselves are the same. Many decisions are routine or operational, and once initially made can be repeated in the same way until the conditions under which it was first made change. There is really no *problem* to be solved. For example, when a team needs to organize materials for a training, some of the decisions to be made can include where the materials will be assembled, who will do the editing, what information should be delivered in the session, how the materials will be produced, when the research for the documents will be done, and who will be the contact person for the training. If the division of the work is acceptable to all of the team and the end results are positive, the team may

C.B. Halverson and S.A. Tirmizi (eds.), *Effective Multicultural Teams: Theory and Practice*,

decide to use the same approach for all future training presentations. There are two items worth noting here: (1) several decisions have been made in order for the team to complete its work together; and (2) there was no problem needing to be solved. Is it possible that a problem may have developed somewhere in the process of the team's completing its task? Certainly it is possible, but it is not a requirement! In the work cycle of a team there are many routine or operational decisions made daily. If a problem does arise the team will need to revisit the decision-making process and determine what, if anything, might need to be completed in a different way.

There are also decisions made that are more tactical, or strategic, and require more creativity or time spent in the preliminary phases of the process. This happens because the outcome of the decision is less well understood by the team, or there may indeed be a problem, challenge, or opportunity that requires more attention. The actual decision is only a part of the whole process. Problem solving has a broader scope than decision making, and strategic decision making uses many of the same steps used in problem solving. For example, the same team above may find the workload among team members is uneven and the timeline for completing the work too short for all team members to complete what they had decided to do. In order to resolve this problem for future tasks the team may need to look more strategically at how each understood the task assigned, and what their expectations of the members were for the task and their role in it. In resolving a problem there can be one or many decisions made, and strategic decisions will require more work than routine decisions. So what does this mean? *All problem solving involves some decision making; decision making does not always involve problem solving.*

There are six steps to the problem-solving model described and demonstrated in this chapter. Several of those steps within the model are used for decision-making, and are covered as well. *How* a team makes the decision, and *who* on the team makes it are important elements and will also be discussed. As prior chapters have noted, membership of multicultural teams varies greatly. The procedures each member follows, the different value orientations guiding their behavior (Smith et al. 2002), the nature of the tasks they must complete, and the communication tools they employ (face-to-face and/or technology-based) all impact how they approach problem solving and decision making. When done effectively, problem solving, which includes decision making, moves through all the steps described here equally, engaging the knowledge and skills of all team members.

This chapter will first present theoretical frameworks for problem solving, then define the steps that comprise problem solving and decision making within them. This will be followed by a discussion of the cultural variations, and impact of individual styles and societal assumptions on decision-making. Shared mental models and consensus are offered as methods to equalize participation in team decision making, and an overview of other methods provided. The last section will look at ways to coordinate the stages of team development with the variety of problem-solving and decision-making techniques in order to maximize a team's effectiveness.

Learning Objectives

After reading this chapter you should be able to:

- Compare traditional problem solving and appreciative inquiry
- Describe a synergistic model for problem solving, including decision making, that can be used in multicultural groups
- Identify factors that influence decision making in a team
- Discuss how cultural considerations impact the individual's view of problem solving and what they value in decision making
- Describe ways in which individual personality and social identity impact our problem-solving and decision-making processes
- Define shared mental models and consensus, their value in problem solving and decision making, and their misuse in groupthink
- Name and describe various techniques for problem solving and decision-making and relate their use to different stages of team development

Approaches to Problem Solving

A Synergistic Approach to Problem Solving

There is wide cultural variation in the definition of problem solving as a team or management process. When we look at problem solving as a method for organizational change and development, there are two approaches that are useful for a team to be familiar with, and to be comfortable in using. As a team process these approaches provide different ways to conduct problem solving. The origins of each are quite different, and can mean very different mindsets on the part of team members to the entire topic of problem solving, and whether problem solving can, or should, even be done.

The first, *traditional problem solving*, has been valued through the years for its ability to find the "true," objective answer. The traditional problem-solving approach uses as its theoretical framework classic scientific inquiry, which is based on the belief that there is one objective reality, and that reality is discernable. It involves understanding the current situation, whether a problem or opportunity, identifying problems and/or gaps, brainstorming solutions, selecting and testing a solution, and analyzing the results. The traditional problem-solving approach concentrates on the opportunity or issue that needs the attention of members in the organizational system. Accurate description of the task at hand, and expansive treatment of the possible actions to be taken will lead to the best decision and implementation plan. It concentrates on *fixing* the problem.

Beliefs that resonate with traditional problem solving and classic scientific inquiry:

- There is a model or method for objectively viewing the world
- It is possible to do complex planning because the world is predictable
- Things can be best understood if they are broken down into parts

In recent years an approach to organizational change and problem solving called *appreciative inquiry* (AI) has gained in popularity. Originally used in action research, its roots are in non-Western cultures, and in the new sciences framework, which is based on the belief that there is no one objective reality, and that "reality" can be created by what one focuses on. Initial research attests to its usefulness as an alternative to the more widely known traditional problem-solving approach to change and management. Appreciative inquiry relies more on the emerging new sciences framework (Watkins and Mohr 2001). The basic assumption of the appreciative inquiry approach is that changes happen through the process of identifying what all individuals value or appreciate in an organization, and think contributes to the success of the organization and accomplishment of its mission. Information is collected from members within the whole system on best practices in the organization; results are shared and then framed with an emphasis on the perceived strengths of the organization. Appreciative inquiry looks at what is being done well now, and how that can be built upon for the future.

Beliefs that resonate with appreciative inquiry and the new sciences approach:

- The world is complex and subjective
- Planning is part of a continual on-going re-evaluation process
- All things are interconnected and should be considered as part of a whole

Table 9.1 highlights some of the broad differences between traditional problem solving and appreciative inquiry:

Table 9.1 Traditional problem solving vs. appreciative inquiry (Adapted from Cooperrider et al. 2005)

Problem solving	Appreciative inquiry
Identification of the problem or opportunity to be addressed	Identification of a need or opportunity to be addressed
Gathering information and analysis of the causes for the problem or opportunity	Appreciation of the best of what exists currently, and a desire to foster more of this in the environment
Identification of solutions	Envisioning what might be possible in the future
Analysis of possible solutions	Discussing what should be
Action planning for resolution	Innovating towards improvement

As you read the case study below, consider what information they will need to gather using the traditional problem solving method and what information they will need to gather using the appreciative inquiry method.

Case Study: Faculty Exchange Program

A higher education institution is about to design a faculty exchange program with institutions in two other countries. An alumna from the agricultural sciences department made the initial contact, but faculty from other departments and the administrators of all the institutions are very excited about the possibilities. An inter-institutional work team has been in face-to-face (f2f) meetings for two weeks now, sharing information about the academic programs and administrative systems that should be carried forward to the joint design. They are given a start date 18 months from now, but will not meet again as a whole team in a face-to-face (f2f) setting before the start of the program.

At today's meeting they begin on an agenda that includes:

- *Developing a survey to be distributed to faculty and administrators that will capture what each sees are the possibilities for collaboration across institutions*
- *Determining a method for collating this information as a basis for building a vision for the future joint program*
- *Setting a timetable to gather this information so it can be analyzed and discussed with the administrators from each institution*
- *Deciding how they will communicate with each other—how often, in what formats*
- *Determining the process they will use to make decisions as a work team for the coming months*

Proponents of the traditional problem-solving approach believe this can be one of the team processes where people are most focused in their work. There is emphasis on the issue at hand and creative alternatives are identified. Success in the traditional problem-solving method depends on all the steps in the problem-solving process being completed accurately. Appreciative inquiry posits that the traditional problem-solving approach is limiting, and can potentially lead to inaccurate results because the focus is on finding the best solution.

Proponents of the appreciative inquiry framework believe that in every organization, group, or individual there are some strengths that can contribute to their success. In a time when change must happen rapidly it is easier to move to the future if the most treasured parts of the past are retained. Traditional problem solving advocates are concerned that the emphasis on future may not resolve the issue currently in front of the team or organization, leaving the potential for the problem to grow.

Clearly these two approaches, while grounded in the idea of scientific inquiry, have taken very different paths and each will lead teams to a different orientation to problem solving and the decision making within it. Traditional problem solving looks at and resolves the issue. In the appreciative inquiry approach there is no mention of a *problem* that needs solving; but more an opportunity to be in touch with those aspects of the organization that are of value, and should be built upon as the organization improves. Neither framework captures the whole picture—traditional problem solving may not lead to positive transformation, while appreciative inquiry may leave real and immediate needs unattended.

Some authors have termed the comparison of the two approaches *deficit-based change* (traditional problem solving) to *asset-based change* (appreciative inquiry) (Whitney and Trosten-Bloom 2003). One thing is certain—a diverse work team will need to understand both orientations in order to be successful. Using the following exercise, try each approach and see how the varying emphasis of each framework might change the focus of the topic at hand.

Case Study: Recognizing Different Orientations to Problem Solving and Resolution—Community Nonprofit Housing Program

As you read the case study below, consider the following questions:

- *If you were to approach this problem using the traditional problem-solving approach, how would you suggest the team define the issue?*
- *How would you approach solving the problem?*
- *If using an appreciative inquiry approach, how would suggest the team define the issue?*
- *How would you approach solving the problem?*

A nonprofit community-based organization that provides subsidized housing for low-income community residents has a wonderful reputation in the community for offering housing referrals and placement services, while also providing emotional support and childcare for parents who are at work. A core team of five people, all with relatively equal levels of responsibility, manages the organization. Each person manages a different aspect of the organization. The gap between clients' earnings at minimum wage employment and the costs of shelter and food has placed increased demand for affordable housing in the community.

When the core team meets to set their goals for the next year in preparation of their annual budgeting exercise, they need to determine how their agency might respond to this gap in the coming year.

Most useful for multicultural work teams is an approach that captures the best attributes of both, such as the synergistic approach below.

One of the desired outcomes of a culturally synergistic organization is for the management processes to reflect the cultural and individual diversity of its work teams. Culturally synergistic organizations create new work processes that transcend the distinct cultures of their members (Adler 2002). They recognize the similarities and differences of the individuals and their cultural approaches to the processes of work teams. No matter what type of team, or teams, are formed, problem solving, and the decision making within it, are processes they must perform.

Creating a culturally synergistic problem solving model that recognizes the problem solving orientations of each of its members and allows the cultural and individual diversity of the team members to be used beneficially for the team requires that the contributions of all be heard, valued, and considered. Borrowing some of the practices and perspectives from the appreciative inquiry approach and incorporating them into the traditional problem-solving framework may be useful.

Adler proposed a model for developing a culturally synergistic approach to problem solving (Adler 2002). She was interested in the fact that cultural orientations towards time and acceptance of an existing situation as unchangeable, rather than a problem to be addressed, would drastically change how a team would manage the problem-solving and decision-making process. This example is one of many possibilities where the fundamental way in which an individual sees the world would impact the approach to problem solving.

Building upon this idea, the choice of approach—traditional problem solving or appreciative inquiry—would also significantly alter how a team viewed a problem. This is before even taking into account individual decision-making styles or societal assumptions.

As Chapter 5 suggests, before a team begins to work on the task(s) assigned to them, the procedures and norms to be used should be discussed and agreed upon. In order to set the stage for effective team problem solving and decision-making, I have adapted the Adler model to incorporate the principles of both appreciative inquiry and traditional problem solving. This framework will encourage team members to share preferred approach to problem solving.

- *Describe the situation.* Each team member should describe the situation they have been asked to resolve from their own cultural and individual perspective. *What are the attributes of the situation/problem, and which of those are valuable to retain?* Allowing all members to voice their views will contribute to developing an understanding of the members and their relationship to the situation and each other;
- *Culturally interpret the situation.* Each member should identify the cultural and societal assumptions that explain their perspective regarding problem solving and decision making as much as possible. *Which assumptions might explain the perspective and behavior of others? Where are there similarities and differences across the members?* In this way, members can present not only their cultural perspectives, but also their own as individuals or as a subculture within the larger cultural frame of reference. This also allows for asking questions to better understand.
- *Share and discuss the impact.* Each member should discuss with the team how they can make collective use of the information received before beginning to

work on the situation/problem at hand. *What can be learned from the various cultures and individual styles represented that will enhance team effectiveness in problem solving? How can we combine these approaches into our problem-solving strategies?*

Discussing the perspective and value each individual brings to the team will promote more creative options without losing sight of the problem at hand. This has been illustrated here using the Community Nonprofit Housing Program.

Case Study: Creating a Synergistic Approach to Problem Solving Revisited—Community Nonprofit Housing Program

A nonprofit community-based organization that provides subsidized housing for low-income community residents has a wonderful reputation in the community for offering these housing referrals and placement services, while also providing emotional support and childcare for parents who are at work. A core team of five people, all with relatively equal levels of responsibility, manages the organization. Each person manages a different aspect of the organization. The gap between clients' earnings at minimum wage employment and the costs of shelter and food has placed increased demand for affordable housing in the community.

As the core team meets to set their goals for the next year in preparation of their annual budgeting exercise they need to determine how their agency might respond to this gap in the coming year. Before the meeting begins the facilitator suggests they go around to each staff member and ask:

- *What do you think are the most important aspects of this issue the team needs to address?*
- *What would a positive outcome look like to you?*
- *How did you make this choice?*

Once all have answered these questions they are invited to ask for clarification or more information about the contributions of each of the members. Each is then asked how they think the team should proceed to determine a goal-setting approach for the year. The questions are repeated as often as needed to move the staff to a consensus on an approach to setting their goals for the year.

By asking these questions the team continually moves towards using synergistic problem-solving techniques that are acceptable to the cultural norms and individual behaviors of all team members while creating an environment in which they can choose to participate in a manner that is most appropriate for each of them. This synergistic approach will guide all the steps used in the actual problem-solving-process as described here.

A Synergistic Model for Problem Solving and Decision Making

In addition to determining the frame of reference to be used in problem solving, the team must have a method or multiple methods for solving the problems and making the actual decisions. There are several basic, useful models for actual problem solving and decision making available. Some of the models most appropriate to multicultural teams are noted here, and a synergistic model that combines elements of each is then presented.

Adler (2002) believes there are five steps in the decision-making process and that there are cultural variations, which she demonstrates, in each. She does make reference to problem solving specifically. The steps she describes are: problem recognition, information search, construction of alternatives, choice, and implementation.

Other problem-solving models (Kayser 1994; Halverson 2004) are similar in identification of the steps, but break them down more completely and add a step for evaluation of the decision. Some of these use the visual representation of a wheel, where a team can move freely from one *spoke* to another as it realizes the need to be more comprehensive in its thinking at one step or another. For example, if a team makes the realization at the Choice phase that it does not really believe as a team that any of the alternatives are viable, it can return to the Information Search phase and generate more ideas.

Harrington-Macklin (1994) begins the process with the gathering of ideas, step two of the other models mentioned, and does not include evaluation, but she does include an additional step for analysis. The value of her model is in the wide variety of tools she suggests as useful in each step, allowing for many visual and verbal possibilities for each step in the process.

Combining the major ideas from these models, I offer below a model for understanding and working with problem solving and decision making in multicultural teams. It builds on the synergistic approach already discussed. This is followed by Table 9.2, which compares the traditional problem solving and appreciative inquiry approaches, cultural and individual variations, implications of these variations on the problem-solving and decision-making process, and tools and techniques that might assist the team during each phase of the synergistic model. The cultural and identity considerations, and descriptions of how to use some of the tools and techniques, will be discussed more fully later in the chapter. Each team must choose what is best for it at the particular point in its team development.

Problem-Solving Steps in a Synergistic Model

1. *Developing problem awareness.* A situation or problem is identified that the team believes they should address. The parameters of the situation and what exactly needs attention is yet to become clear.

2. *Gathering information.* Additional data on the problem is collected from a variety of sources. This can be factual and/or perceptual. As the team completes this step, a clear definition of the problem should emerge. A statement of the goal or result desired will determine the scope of the problem and what the team feels can be accomplished by its resolution.
3. *Identifying alternatives.* It is important to generate as many alternatives and have as much team participation as possible. This supports the broad worldview of team members and the creative options they can generate.
4. *Selecting a solution.* The choice of the solution itself is only one aspect of this step. While the goal is to make a decision to address the problem, there are additional factors to consider in this step. The team should also agree on *who* makes the decision, and *what method* will be used to make it.
5. *Implementing the solution.* The implementation plan must consider who will be affected by the solution, and if it is supported by the whole team. There should be agreement on the scope of the work and who will complete it.
6. *Evaluating the outcomes.* The solution should solve the identified problem. The team should agree when the evaluation should be conducted, using what criteria, and who will do it.

Decision-Making Steps in a Synergistic Model

In the introduction it was stated that there are occasions where the steps in decision making are made repetitively with no problem solving required. Decision making in these cases includes steps two (gathering information), three (identifying alternatives), and four (selecting a solution)—predominantly steps three and four. If the procedure is successful, the team can repeat this decision-making approach in future similar situations.

Who Makes the Decision on Self-managed Teams

As noted in Chapter 1, there are several categories of teams. For each of these teams the method employed for decision making is related to the purpose of the team. For instance, a task force may be formed with the expressed purpose of making a decision, or series of decisions, on a specific topic. In self-managed teams most decision-making responsibility is given to the team, which then works independently. In these well-defined instances the decision-making authority has been given to the team. How that team handles this responsibility among themselves is not always dictated.

Decision making on teams can be approached in a number of ways, varying in the degree of participation team members are allowed. Self-managed teams often have an internal leader to facilitate self-management of the team. In teams that are leader-led, the decision making can be *collaborative* or *participatory,* where the leader shares all pertinent information with the team and all team members participate fully in the decision; *consultative,* where the leader makes the decision on his or her own after consulting the team; or *autocratic*, where the leader makes the decision without input of the rest of the team.

Some self-managed teams have joint facilitation or shared leadership (see chapter 4). In these cases, decision making is more challenging. It is advisable for the team to discuss in advance how decision making will be handled. Will decision making always be collaborative? There might be certain types of decisions where other decision-making approaches would be more appropriate or where perhaps the decision-making authority should lie with one individual rather than being shared. Criteria for deciding how the decision should be made are: amount of time available, importance and impact of the decision, and who has the expertise.

Methods for Making Decisions

Once the approach has been decided upon, the team needs to decide how it will make the actual decision. The most common ways in which decisions get made on teams are listed below. *Which have you observed? How would you assess the outcomes of each?*

- *Consensus*. Consensus is a process that not only seeks the agreement of team members, but also seeks to resolve any objections of the minority to achieve the most agreeable decision. With consensus, each member should be able to state "I believe you understand my point of view; I believe that I understand your point of view; I may not prefer the decision that is being made, but I will support it because it has been made in an open and fair manner."
- *Voting*. This is simply a tally of opinions for or against available choices. It can be unanimous and all must agree, or by majority (more than half).
- *Railroading*. A suggestion that was made in the team is acted on without discussion or a formal decision being made.
- *Default*. No decision is made, so the status quo remains.

Developing Consensus

Having shared leadership roles on a team and a decentralized communication network (see Chapter 7) will assist in all members developing a common understanding of team processes. As stated in Chapter 5, collaborative decision making reinforces normative change in the team and the commitment of the individuals on it. Using the consensus method can support development of a collaborative process and ownership of decisions made by the team. One useful set of guidelines for the consensus method was written by Hare (1982; Enayati 2001). They include:

- Participants are urged to seek a solution that incorporates all viewpoints.
- Participants must argue on a logical basis, giving their own opinion while seeking out difference.
- Participants are asked to address the group as a whole, while showing concern for each point of view, rather than confronting and criticizing individuals.
- A group coordinator is useful to help formulate consensus.
- It is essential not to press for agreement, but to hold more meetings if necessary and to share responsibility in the group for the implementation of the consensus.

Table 9.2 Work team problem solving and decision making: steps and tools

Traditional problem solving and decision making:	Appreciative inquiry	Cultural, societal, and individual variations	Implications of different perspectives	Synergistic model: tools/techniques to use in each step
1. Problem recognition There is a problem identified which should be resolved	1. Team reframes the central issue of their inquiry in a positive light	Some situations should be accepted as they are and no intervention is required The full understanding of the problem may be different among team members and can impact comfort level in discussing it in team	Level of change or improvement desired may be defined differently; will impact future steps in the model	1. Developing problem awareness Complete open dialogue on description of the situation and agreement on what the team wants to change or improve
2. Information search This can include relevant facts (soft and hard data)	2. Team gathers information on what works well and what could be	Who should be gathering ideas and possibilities Leaving outcome to chance may mean a need for less information, and might limit possible solutions Orientation to moving quickly may limit search	Allows for a wider range of information to be collected Who, what, where, and when answered not only with hard data but information on perceptions and feelings of those involved	2. Gathering information Written and Internet search, surveying members on perceptions regarding the decision and what information should be considered
3. Identification of alternatives Select as many as possibles	3. New, future-oriented alternatives are identified	There can be past-, present-, and future-oriented alternatives How alternatives are identified can mean quick action, or systematic collection	A limitation of alternatives identified is possible if the worldview of the situation by team members differs radically	3. Identifying alternatives A variety of techniques to generate alternatives and increase participation. Some of these include: brainstorming, round robin, delphi method, mind mapping, role playing, simulations

4. Choice of solution or course of action	4. There is more confidence to journey into the future when they carry forward the best parts of the past	Individual or team decision making methods can vary Decisions are made at a different pace or speed Individual styles can mean let others choose; agonize over options; need systems/reasons for making choices	Certain members of work teams may be reluctant to engage in a group process, or comment on a course of action they do not feel is in their area of responsibility	4. Selecting the most appropriate solution Must decide if team wants a collaborative or majority-voting outcome, and whether discussion on alternatives happens inside or outside of formal meeting setting. Possible techniques: nominal group, voting, consensus, force field analysis
5. Implementation	5. All assist in constructing the new scenario	Implementation can involve the whole team or responsibilities can be delegated depending on expertise, or role The time needed for implementation should be considered The necessity for a detailed plan should be considered	A different commitment of time for implementation can mean less time in the process to monitor or make adjustments to the decision, or the level of buy-in from those who must do the work associated with the decision	5. Implementing the solution Discuss and agree on scope, time estimates for completing work, and who (individual, team, other) will responsible, for each step
6. Evaluation May generate a new set of decisions to be made, determine criteria for review, who will conduct, when, how quickly solved	6. Continual improvement through repetition of the process	The time period for evaluation, determination if change has occurred; if it's positive There may be a need to be systematic or to be right	Different assumptions may affect team's perception of success	6. Evaluating the outcomes Discuss methods and possible outcomes before beginning the evaluation

Cultural Considerations in Decision Making

Different cultural values and assumptions about decision-making can impact how a work team views their responsibilities to each other and within the organization. The understanding of which decisions are within the purview of the team, and their approach to making them will vary across cultures. Chapter 2 presented an integrated cultural framework for working in multicultural teams. Such dimensions as time orientation, achievement-ascription, individualism-collectivism, gender egalitarianism, and intellectual autonomy all impact how problems are solved, decisions are made and who makes them. The dynamics of each team will be different and some aspects of this framework will play more of a role than others. This happens because each team member brings her/his own unique cultural and individual imprint to the team.

A cross-cultural analysis of participatory decision-making processes was conducted that provides some current examples of the impact of culture on work teams. Using Hofstede's dimensions of individualism/collectivism, and low/high power distance (achievement-ascription in the integrated framework in Chapter 2), the study looked at participatory decision-making (PDM), and examples of where they are found (Sagie and Aycan 2003). The authors contend culture plays a role in the meaning managers and subordinates give to participatory decision making at the national, organizational, and work team levels; and approaches vary by country, culture, subcultures within a region, and within organizations. This study was conducted on teams whose decisions were of an operational nature, and not at the strategic level. They analyzed how the cultural dimensions of individualism and power distance affect human *cognitive processes* (sharing knowledge and expertise of all participants), and *motivational processes* (identification with the team or organization) in different settings around the world. The cognitive processes help improve the quality of the decisions, while motivational processes increase acceptance of and commitment to the jointly made decisions.

Some of the ways in which they found participatory decision making being used that most impact work groups or teams are noted here:

- *Face-to-face participatory decision making (PDM).* In individualistic cultures this is direct leader-member interaction, usually more cognitive-based. It tends to focus more on the task than on the relationships between superiors and subordinates, or team members. This is more common in English-speaking countries that share the US American individualism/collectivism and power distance patterns (Hofstede 1980).
- *Collective PDM.* This combines low or medium individualistic orientation with low or medium power distance. Another way to say this is an orientation to working in groups rather than individuals and a sharing of power between management and the workers. It can be seen in pockets of the USA (trade unions), and countries in Western Europe such as Germany, Sweden, and Norway (Hofstede 1991). It is considered to be more motivational than cognitive, and more egalitarian than face-to-face PDM.
- *Paternalistic PDM.* This category combines low individualism and high power distance, and is frequently observed in countries such as Korea, India, Turkey, and Mexico. In these situations the management does not really transfer power, and the

employees do not really seek it. The role of the superior is to provide guidance, nurturance, and care to the subordinates. On the employee side, the leader/representative has the role of consulting with the subordinates and communicating the final decision with them. The main mediating process is motivational (i.e., employee acceptance of and commitment to the decisions) rather than cognitive (improvement of joint decisions). Although the Japanese system has low individualism and high power distance the Japanese managers do delegate authority to team members, making it different than paternalistic PDM. The practices of *nemawashi* (prior consultation) and *ringi* ("bottom-up" approval before management sign-off), described below, demonstrate this variation on paternalistic PDM.

- *Nemawashi*, translated as "tend to the roots", is an important aspect of consensus building, problem solving and decision making in Japanese organizations. It suggests that once the roots are stable the tree will grow, and ideas will flourish on a solid foundation. If they do not, then there are some difficulties with the roots of that idea. *Nemawashi* is "a tactic implemented by the Japanese to bring about consensus through various pre-meeting consultations, where a strong foundation is being built so that the result will create a general agreement amongst those involved in the decision" (Tomlinson 1999).
- *Ringi*, or bottom-up decision making, is the practice wherein a proposal is commented upon before the meeting, so that people can have the opportunity to think about the proposal and add ideas. It is used in conjunction with nemawashi, while the preliminary meetings of the nemawashi process are not in session. The proposal is reviewed at each stage, and improvements and adjustments added on, so when it reaches the ultimate decision makers every team and person involved has had the opportunity to comment, and share concerns and support with others.

Self-Managed Teams PDM

Many multicultural teams are self-managed and employ participatory approaches. These teams are autonomous or semi-autonomous, and blend low power distance and high individualistic needs. In the interest of achieving more independence in their work, more interesting work, and more responsibilities, the team members contain their personal ambitions for the sake of the team and the benefits they will get as a work team. This form of PDM is currently flourishing in many, mostly Western countries—Australia, Canada, Sweden, the UK, and the USA (Salem and Banner 1992 in Sagie and Akcan 2003).

All of these PDM styles demonstrate the balance of the *cognitive* and *motivational* aspects of the team's work. Even in situations where the cognitive aspects dominate, the cultural context will influence what each team member brings to and expects from the work team in terms of participation in decision making. As discussed in Chapter 4, the team should consider cultural differences when establishing norms.

It is useful here to return to the difference between work groups and work teams as outlined in Chapter 1. In groups there is an identified leader, individual accountability, and the group's purpose is the same as the larger organizational mission. In a team there are *shared* leadership roles. Within work teams the individual members may be practicing different forms of participatory decision making, and this will influence their participation in the process. There will be cultural variations in how team members view who has the authority *within* the team to make a decision *for* the team. Whether these variations are based on cultural background or experience in social identity groups is not as important to remember as is the fact that they exist. Using the synergistic approach described above will help to bring these variations in assumptions to the entire team's attention.

Individual and Social Identity Considerations in Decision Making

Individual personality characteristics and preferences also impact the functioning of a work team in decision making. A quick review of Chapter 3, including the Five Factor/Big 5 personality models, the Myers-Briggs Type Indicator, and Howard Gardner's Multiple Intelligences, will demonstrate how an individual's personal preferences surface quickly in a work team environment. As previously stated, the factor of openness/intellect is linked to problem solving and decision making.

In each work team there are infinite combinations of approaches to the decision-making possibilities that arise. It is useful to look at how these will present themselves in decision making in actual work team situations. Psychological blocks based on personal characteristics can make it difficult for individual members of a team to allow the openness needed for a creative problem-solving approach, which contains making decisions, to evolve within the team. Examples of this might be a preference for predictability, or orderly approach to the problem; a need to decide each issue as it arises without allowing it to remain open for additional thought, rather than considering several different options at once; or a difficulty tolerating ambiguity. Environmental blocks related to the actual work environment, such as distractions in the workplace, or the method in which success and/or failure are dealt with in the workplace and on the team, can also be factors in developing effective decision-making procedures for a team. Individuals have different preferences or needs in their workspace, and if not apparent can hinder the team's ability to problem solve or make routine decisions (Gardenswartz and Rowe 2003).

Gardenswartz and Rowe (2003) have also identified seven style preferences for how individuals approach decision making. Though these ideas have not been fully tested for their validity and reliability, they provide a starting point for team discussion on what individuals consider to be their dominant style when making decisions. These include: (1) leaving outcomes to chance, (2) agonizing over decisions and options, (3) procrastinating, (4) being paralyzed by having to make a decision, (5) plunging quickly into making decisions, (6) methodically weighing alternatives, and (7) leaving the decision making to others so you don't need to accept responsibility for it. The authors are quick to point out that all individuals use all styles, but usually have a preferred style. They suggest team members discuss the styles represented on the team and how that may influence the team's work. The Myers Briggs Type Indicator is also often used to help team members identify their individual characteristics and preferences, and may also be a useful tool in that discussion.

Devising a truly synergistic approach to decision making involves using a broader definition of diversity, not solely the cultural considerations discussed previously. As Table 3.1 in Chapter 3 suggests, identifying who is in one-up/one-down social identity groups may help us to keep our unconscious assumptions from interfering with team processes. When specifically discussing decision making, this dimension may influence who team members think can make decisions on the team, and how members see themselves in relationship to others in the team. This will impact their contributions or willingness to take risks on the team. In Chapter 5, research (Enayati 2001) was presented on how social influence can privilege the ideas and suggestions of more powerful members of a team. Having formal procedures to equalize participation and share all information relevant to the problem at hand can decrease this factor.

Working with the individual and social identity factors that impact the team dynamics can put quite a burden on a team while it is in the midst of completing its tasks. But the ability to do so guarantees it will have the widest range of options available to it for the tasks that require creative problem solving and decision making. The case below illustrates these points.

Case Study: Individual and Social Identity Considerations—Community Nonprofit Housing Program

As you read the case exercise below, consider the following questions:

- *What factors might be at work here?*
- *Using the cultural, societal, and individual frameworks studied, what assumptions should be discussed in the team?*
- *How might the team move forward?*

The core work team of the community nonprofit organization decided to design a training program to be submitted as part of a grant proposal. The timeline for completion of the proposal was short. Although they had worked together previously, they had never completed a team task such as this before. In previous projects, each had had their own teams and would complete the work prior to coming together in this iteration. In an activity to introduce themselves more fully to each other before beginning the task at hand, the members described their own backgrounds as follows:

- *Esteban, a homosexual male in his early 30s, from Miami, with a Cuban mother and Venezuelan father*

- *Jeanine, a 27-year-old female who grew up in Detroit; her mother was from the Philippines and father from Puerto Rico*
- *Anna, 24 years old from Ukraine, has been in the U.S. for one year; English is not her first language but she is fluent and works in it quite well*
- *Joanie is in her early 40s, a mother of two, and grew up on a dairy farm in New England*
- *Bill, a Euro-American male in his 50s, from California*

In the beginning of their time together on this proposal the decision-making process was somewhat undefined. It appeared they would reach consensus with a collective nod. Shortly into the time together, they realized this was too ambiguous for most of the team, and each person had a different understanding of prior decisions that had been made. They next moved to a "thumbs-up/thumbs down" vote. Although this worked for a while, the team realized that members tended to give a thumbs-up even if they didn't really always agree. They were better off than before, but there was still room for improvement.

Additional Factors That Impact the Decision-Making Process

There are several factors in addition to cultural and individual preferences that influence the decision(s) to be made by a work team (Maier in Kayser 1994), These are the quality of the decision, acceptance of the decision, time pressure, and influence of the organization.

Quality of the decision refers to the technical quality required of a decision. When a decision is viewed in a totally objective fashion, there is clearly one option that fits best with a particular decision. *Acceptance of the decision* refers to the commitment to, and emotional support for, the decision that is required by those who must execute it. These two factors are measured against each other in the decision-making process.

There are four possibilities, called the quality/acceptance grid, which can be produced when measuring these two factors:

1. *Neither quality nor acceptance is important*. The alternatives are equally good so quality is not an issue, and the final choice makes little difference to those who have to execute it.
2. *Quality is important but acceptance is not*. The decision doesn't require a commitment from all to execute it, and/or certain technical expertise is required to make the decision.
3. *Acceptance is important and quality is not*. The differences in choices is not significant, but buy-in from the team is, such as taking on additional tasks or committing the team to additional work.
4. *Quality and acceptance are both important*. The decision requires high quality and commitment from the team. These decisions must draw upon the team's

expertise to make them, and at the end must have the full commitment of the team to the decision.

When *time pressure* is involved, most teams will move to a decision-making method that is less time-consuming than consensus. For example, when faced with many decisions or a quick deadline, a team may decide to forego obtaining full consensus on a decision and determine a stance of not actively working against a decision, or voting by majority to carry a decision forward. The time pressure is related to total understanding of the decision at hand. Not all decisions require total understanding of all the options by all those on the team. Because all may not be needed to help execute the decision, engaging the entire team in the decision-making process may not be the best use of their time.

The *organization influences* teams. Work teams operate within an organization that has structures and systems that dictate how it conducts its business. Parameters set by the organization because of resources, congruence with the mission, or strategic direction can influence the decisions made by its work teams. Knowing what these parameters are will allow the team to be more efficient in their work, and may dictate which decisions require the most time and thought be spent on them.

Because most teams are faced with multiple decisions at any given point in time, the importance of these factors will be constantly changing with each decision faced by the team.

Creating Shared Mental Models

The idea of having an agreed-upon approach for problem solving and decision making in a work team is not new. Research dating back 20 years supports the importance of developing cognitive models, more recently termed mental modeling, to enhance decision making (Jeffery et al. 2005). A *mental model* is a mechanism by which an individual can put order or structure to reality. It provides a system for understanding purpose or meaning to something. This can be extremely useful in the actual decision making, providing a structure or example of how the team will approach making a decision.

A shared mental model is one that is held by a team as a way to inform their work together. The model, or knowledge structure (Jeffery et al. 2005), is used by the whole team, and becomes a guide for obtaining goal congruence and task completion. There are three elements that are part of a shared mental model:

- *Knowledge*: how the team organizes and structures task-relevant information
- *Attitude*: the individual interpretation of the team environment and activities
- *Behavior*: shared expectations team members have of each other

For example, if the members of a team all began on a project they would have discussions about how each member envisioned the task in front of them. They will discuss what the finished product should look like, how they might approach completing it, how much time each step might take to complete, even what work environment or tools they might need for the task. The team might also consider the skill set of each member as it relates to the project at hand, what decisions could be made by individual members of the team and what needed to be a group decision. What would emerge is a shared mental model of the project and the team and its processes. If the team took on new projects, or new membership, all the prior conversations would need to be transferred or revisited.

Team processes are more effective, and performance is higher, among teams that share goal congruence, and high quality mental models. If done well, shared mental modeling can be very synergistic—allowing team members to share new information, process ideas, overlap knowledge, and communicate effectively. With shared mental modeling, all team members need not be skilled in every aspect of the work of the team, and they have a common language from which to integrate new information and make efficient use of individual contributions.

The literature also supports the idea that shared mental models can evolve over time and become more efficient and developed. As a work team gains experience, they are able to refine the model they use, expand on their communication within the team, and be responsive to new information as the external organizational environment changes. With a shared mental model, it becomes easier to orient new team members, and internalize as a team the contributions of existing or departing members.

Groupthink

The only cautionary note about the use of shared mental models is the need to protect against the development of a phenomenon termed *groupthink*, introduced in Chapter 5, in the discussion about conformity versus consensus. Groupthink is a concept that was identified by Irving Janis (1972) and refers to faulty decision making in a team. The concept of groupthink is that once a group, or team, becomes highly functioning, its members can become reticent to voice a dissenting opinion. Usually there is an outside pressure being exerted on the group that causes groupthink to occur. Examples of outside pressures are: the time in which to make a decision is limited, the decision is a particularly important one, other organizational stresses enter that do not allow the team to use their established processes, or the established communication and decision-making processes are in need of adjustment but the team, or individuals within it, do not trust that the team can make these adjustments successfully.

Some of the symptoms of groupthink are:

- Having illusions of invulnerability and believing the team is invincible in its actions and decisions
- Being dismissive of critical thinking and ignoring alternatives that have adverse solutions

- Exerting direct pressure on a team member who disagrees with the direction the group is taking
- Stereotyping the opposition negatively
- Mindguarding by making little or no effort to gather opinions or advice from outside the team that might change its course of action

Methods for counteracting groupthink include:

- Inviting outsiders or content experts to team meetings.
- Asking all team members to be critical evaluators of the work the team's doing. This can be done in each session or at the point of critical decision making. Sometimes dividing into smaller groups or dyads will allow more critical thinking about an idea to emerge.
- Encouraging open discussion on factors influencing critical decisions in the team. Silence doesn't always mean consent. Open discussion can be encouraged by setting aside time in meetings for discussion, or asking the person who brought the information on the decision to step out of the discussion until all other members have been able to share their perspectives with the team.
- Protecting the team from making premature decisions by double-checking time frames and postponing decisions if more time is needed.

Table 9.3 McFadzean's levels of team development (McFadzean 2002)

Attention steps	Problem-solving and decision-making responsibilities
Level 1: The task	Concerned with getting the task done, the task is simple or routine, or it is a period of crisis and the job must be completed quickly. At this level the team must have a focused goal in mind, as sticking to the task at hand is most important.
Level 2: Meeting process	There is a compromise between time and the depth of analysis or discussion that can occur on agenda items, making congruence in the process used as important as congruence in the goal of the team's tasks.
Level 3: Team structure	There is an understanding of the characteristics of the particular team members and the roles and responsibilities that fit each, what the knowledge and skill areas are within the team, and what information must come from outside the team to solve the problem at hand.
Level 4: Team dynamics	The team members strive for equal participation, conflict is understood as being beneficial to the team when handled constructively, and the team is able to examine and manage its behavior in order to enhance creativity and effectiveness.
Level 5: Team trust	Members are truly committed to the growth and success of each individual member of the team. If this commitment is not shared by all members of the team, there will be hesitance to communicate ideas, or to participate in problem-solving activities that require that level of shared trust or belief that all contributions of knowledge and ideas will be considered equally or without undue criticism.

Developing Problem-Solving and Decision-Making Techniques in Teams

How does one develop creative problem solving and decision making teams? In Chapter 4, there were several different models of team development presented. I would like to add to these models by looking specifically at team development and its relationship to problem solving and decision making. McFadzean suggests that the most appropriate creative problem-solving techniques used by any team are directly linked to the level of team development and facilitation present. Using techniques that do not fit the team's current level of development will compromise the creativity of current solutions, and could jeopardize the future productivity of the team. This correlates to the stages discussed in Chapter 4, which suggest that certain processes can be done better at different stages in the team's development.

McFadzean calls these levels *attention steps*, and believes team development to be a sequential process (see Table 9.3). As teams develop and move up the levels, they devote attention to different aspects of their development. I suggest this sequential process is somewhat different than the Tuckman or Gersick models, which focus more broadly on the stage of group development in relationship to the tasks as a whole, not just problem solving and decision making performed by the team. It is important to keep in mind that teams have different tasks assigned to them, and that not all tasks require the same level of team development in order to be performed well.

McFadzean believes that techniques will produce the most creative and useful ideas if they are selected for use based on the level of trust on the team, its level of development, and facilitator skills used. She divides problem-solving techniques into three categories: *paradigm preserving, paradigm stretching*, and *paradigm breaking*. What follows are her definitions of these categories and when they might be used. I have then selected representative techniques for each category and described how they can be used.

Paradigm-Preserving Techniques

Paradigm-preserving techniques do not redefine the boundaries of the problem; rather, they explore the best approach to be taken with the existing problem. They use free association but use less imagination. For this reason they can be more comfortable for team members to use. *These techniques can be used by all levels of teams, 1 through 5.*

Brainstorming

In this method, any alternative is considered, no criticism is allowed on any alternative until all team members have presented alternatives they perceive as valuable. No contribution can be edited, but can be added upon by any team member. The object is to generate a quantity of ideas, and narrow down the list later using filtering. This method tries to encourage wild, exaggerated, and humorous ideas. Filters, or criteria for selection, are then used to help narrow down the list. Possibilities for filters are cost, time, availability, fit with the philosophy of the team or organization, resistance/acceptance of the idea, and/or practicality. Apply all filters to each idea to edit out or in some of the ideas. A variation of this is the *round robin* or freewheeling method of generating ideas in which one person at a time gives out an idea, and the rounds continue until all ideas are out for discussion. Anyone can pass on any turn and all ideas are listed as they are offered. The strength of this approach is that it can help determine possible causes of issues, and generate solutions. It is a good method when the team wants inclusiveness, for planning implementation steps, and for non-routine decisions that require more creativity.

Consensus Card Method

This *consensus card method* is used to help move teams to consensus more quickly, and to get a commitment from all to a decision that has been made. It uses a visual aid to indicate positions of team members in relation to any decision being made. The issue is first defined and presented, the ideas are discussed fully by the team, questions are asked by any member, preliminary judgments made by individuals, and when the facilitator believes all conversation is done, then members are asked to display the color card that represents how they feel about the topic. Once the decision is reached, it is recorded.

Variations

Fist-to-Five—State what is believed to be what the team has decided upon and ask for a fist-to-five finger demonstration. 5 fingers up = I support this and will take a leadership role, 4 = I support this, 3 = I am neutral, 2 = I am not comfortable with this and need to talk, and 1 = I am against this, and fist up = I am against it and will block it. Any fists, 1s, or 2s means a consensus has not been reached and the question should then be asked what will people need to change their position.

Red-Yellow-Green Cards—Used in two ways: one for discussion and the other for decisions. For the discussion, the group member who wishes to speak, holds up a card. A *green card* means "I have something to say" or "I have a question." When several group members hold up a green card, they are noted and placed in a queue of people waiting to speak. Each person speaks in turn. A *yellow card* means "I can clarify" or "I need clarification (on what was just said)." The *red card* is for process. A red card might say: "Are we getting off track, here?" or "What is our objective in doing this?" It gives all members an equal chance to be facilitator. When it is time to make a decision, a green card means "I agree with the decision and will support it." A yellow card signifies "I can live with the decision and commit to supporting it." The red card is disagreement with the decision at hand, "I don't agree, but am willing to work to find a better way, taking into account what has been said by all group members." A red card does not block progress; the person who displays it will work with others on the issue and bring it back to a subsequent meeting. The team must have all yellows and greens for the decision to have been made by consensus. The strength of this method is that it will get many opinions voiced in a face-to-face environment by allowing discussion and disagreement or support on complex issues. This method also allows for identification of new options through the discussion and participants know right away about potential disagreements or roadblocks to the issue at hand.

Nominal Group Process

The *nominal group process* allows more time for individual thought, and ensures that all of the team's opinions will be included. In the initial team discussion or prior to the use of this technique the team must define the problem to be solved, then in silence generate and record ideas, state them to the team, clarify if needed, then tally responses. This method is appropriate for sensitive issues that might have contrary opinions and many details that may paralyze the discussion. It ensures equal participation by all team members. Nominal group process is also good in situations where the cause of the problem has been identified and agreed upon, but determining the course of action is problematic.

Multi-voting

Team members vote for as many ideas as they like, and the ideas with the most votes are circled. The ideas with the least votes are clustered where possible, then each person votes again but for half the number of ideas left. This process is repeated until there are three to five ideas left in total. This becomes the list of possibilities from which to work.

Force Field Analysis

Force Field Analysis is a useful technique for looking at all the forces for and against a decision. It is a method of weighing pros and cons. By conducting the analysis one can plan to strengthen the forces supporting a decision, and reduce the impact of opposition to it. Describe the plan or proposal in writing on a chart for all to see. List all forces for change in one column, and all forces against change in another column. Assign a score to each force, from 1 (weak) to 5 (strong). Once the analysis is completed, you can decide whether your project is viable. When the decision to carry out a project has already been made, Force Field Analysis can help you to work out how to improve its success rate. Here you have two choices: (1) reduce the strength of the forces opposing the project, or (2) increase the forces pushing a project. By assigning a "weight" to each force there is a more thorough consideration of how powerful each is in reality; discussion and assigning value will allow the team to test their own assumptions of each force.

Mind Mapping

Mind Mapping provides a structure that encourages creative problem solving, and then holds information in a format that is easy to remember and quick to review. Mind Maps abandon the list format of conventional note taking in favor of a two-dimensional structure. They are more compact than conventional notes, often taking up only one side of a sheet of paper. To make notes on a subject using a Mind Map, write the title of the subject in the center of the page, and draw a circle around it. For the major subject subheadings, draw lines out from this circle. Label these lines with the subheadings. If there is another level of information belonging to the subheadings above, draw these and link them to the subheading lines. Finally, for individual facts or ideas, draw lines out from the appropriate heading line and label them. As you come across new information, link it in to the map appropriately. Maps can use simple phrases, colors, and symbols for ideas, making language differences less problematic and allowing different concepts to be linked together easily.

Delphi Technique

This technique refers to the solicitation in writing of ideas and anonymous comments from team members, summarization of the comments, and dissemination back to the team for further comment. The team should reach consensus in a predetermined number of rounds, usually three to four. This technique generates input from all team members without bias and requires that all team members support the decision. It works well when the team is not all in the same location. The technique can also remove some of the impact of dominant members of the team, or mitigate pressure to commit to certain ideas.

Paradigm-Stretching Techniques

Paradigm-stretching techniques are designed to develop new ideas or ways to look at the problem. Examples of these methods are connecting two unrelated aspects of the problem at hand, or looking outside of the problem to stimulate new ideas, connections, and humor. The teams with the widest variety of skills and diverse composition will produce some of the most creative solutions. Because they require a significant level of trust within the team, *these techniques will be most successful with teams at levels 3, 4, and 5 of development.*

Paired-Choice Matrix

Working from a list of alternatives that the team has generated, pair together those that are most opposite from each other and generate decisions that will make use of both alternatives. This will provide the team with more alternatives, but the team will have either more unique decisions, or will be able to determine some alternatives to be eliminated. Make sure all alternatives are considered, tally responses, and keep those that are most likely to succeed. Repeat the process until there is only one choice left.

Variation: Pair together those alternatives that are most similar to each other. The first method allows for more creative decisions that challenge assumptions of the team about what "fits" together, the variation is more methodical. Both allow a complex problem to be broken down into smaller discussion points and eliminate options by limiting how many items it is considered with at one point in time.

Six Thinking Hats Technique

Six Thinking Hats is a technique used to look at decisions from a number of important perspectives. This forces team members to move outside habitual thinking patterns, and helps to get a more rounded view of a problem. This tool was created by Edward de Bono in his book *Six Thinking Hats*. If you look at a problem with the Six Thinking Hats technique, then you will solve it using all approaches. Six Thinking Hats can be used in meetings or individually. Each thinking hat represents a different style of thinking. Team members don one of the "hats" and look at the problem from the perspective of that color hat. In meetings it has the benefit of blocking the confrontations that happen when people with different thinking styles discuss the same problem. It is a good technique for looking at the effects of a decision from a number of different points of view. It allows necessary emotion and skepticism to be brought into what would otherwise be purely rational decisions.

- *White hat*: This thinking hat focuses on the data available. Look at the information and see what can be learned from it. Look for gaps in knowledge, analyze past trends, and try to extrapolate from historical data.
- *Red hat*: Look at problems using intuition, gut reaction, and emotion. Also try to think how other people will react emotionally. Try to understand the responses of people who do not fully know your reasoning.
- *Black hat*: Look at all the bad points of the decision. Look at it cautiously and defensively. Try to see why it might not work. This highlights the weak points in a plan. It allows them to be eliminated, altered, or to prepare contingency plans to counter them.
- *Yellow hat*: The yellow hat helps to think positively. It is the optimistic viewpoint that helps to see all the benefits of the decision.
- *Green hat*: This hat stands for creativity. This develops creative solutions to a problem. It is a freewheeling way of thinking, in which there is little criticism of ideas.

- *Blue hat*: The Blue Hat stands for process control. This is the hat worn by people chairing meetings. When running into difficulties because ideas are running dry, they may direct activity into different "hat" thinking.

Paradigm-Breaking Techniques

Paradigm-breaking techniques can produce the most creative ideas. These methods use unrelated stimuli and forced association in methods such as wishful thinking, drawing, and role playing to communicate different ideas about the problem at hand. Because these methods can be considered "alternative" forms of expression, they should be used with teams that have developed a high level of trust in each other, and the work they do together. *These techniques can be used with teams at level 5 of development.*

Role Playing

Role playing is acting, as a character that you either create or pick from a spectrum of pre-created characters. You set your mind into this character, and play it out by improvising the characters' moves. The action of role playing goes beyond games and plays, and can be used to "play out" different decisions. Role playing is often used in training and/or teaching situations. Team members are required to assume the role of the appropriate individual where they are tested upon their ability to react appropriately to a hypothetical situation.

The Right Answer

In the *Right Answer* activity, each team member looks at the problem and generates what he/she believes is the right answer. These are shared, and the team adopts one right answer, or combines aspects of several.

The power of McFadzean's is twofold: (1) it links appropriate techniques and tools to levels of team development; and (2) it offers a number of techniques to choose among within each category. The relationship between team, facilitation of the process, and creativity techniques used must be considered in order to get the best results. In self-managed teams the responsibilities of the facilitator are assigned to a team member or shared by the team as a whole. As a team develops and moves to the next level in the hierarchy of team development, they have a wider range of problem-solving techniques available to them.

As stated before the problem-solving and decision-making techniques mentioned here can be used with other models of team development. The key is to use techniques that (1) are the most creative, (2) cause the least apprehension in the members, and (3) use various modes of communication and expression so all team members can contribute.

The following case study illustrates these techniques as well.

Case Study: Choosing Tools and Techniques—Community Nonprofit Housing Program

As you read the case study below, consider the following questions:

- *What level of team development was the team in?*
- *What problem-solving and decision-making techniques might be available to yield the best results for the decisions at hand, and increasing the overall effectiveness of the team?*

Let us return to the team faced with the increased demand for affordable housing. They were using a "thumbs up/thumbs down" method of making decisions with some limited success.

In the words of one team member:

"There were many different factors impacting our problem-solving and decision-making process. We did not communicate the same way, and did not respect the perceived stubbornness to each other's ideas. Added to that, many on the team were extremely sensitive to feedback. People on the team simply could not come together very easily to complete the task in front of us when we had to make decisions as our own work team. This was due mostly to a lack of comfort, openness, and willingness to communicate. Personality differences, cultural differences, and radically different work styles further augmented these difficulties."

"All of our meetings generated amazing ideas, but a lack of a decision-making process, coupled with a desire to incorporate every idea, was a hindrance. When we finally stepped back from the task to look at where we were stuck, it was clear choosing one solution and generating the implementation to follow through on that choice was our own 'problem' to solve.

"With that understanding we began using fist-to-five to reach consensus, the technique we all valued most. This allowed us to make the actual decisions and move on to getting the proposal finished. If we still had choices that were difficult to make, we would use fist-to-five consensus in conjunction with nominal group process. This would allow us to remove alternatives that we really weren't attached to. When forced to remove the alternatives that were the least likely to succeed, we could focus in on one or two choices we really liked and talk each through more fully. We agreed to use a written timetable with action steps to be taken at each marker for the implementation. This approach also gave us the opportunity to be more creative and willing to take more risks with new ideas in the earlier stages of problem solving. All of our team now had a way to share their own knowledge and expertise, in an environment that was more comfortable in which to work."

And the proposal was finished.

Virtual Teams

Many times new organizational structures include virtual teams, where certain team members must interact through technology, or in a limited face-to-face environment. In these situations, there must be a clear understanding of the alternatives for problem-solving and decision-making methods. Can all members participate equally in all activities? If the answer to this question is "no," then other methods must be selected. Virtual teams also must discuss the affect of the quality/acceptance grid and time pressure on the methods by which they make their decisions and solve problems faced by the team. Inability to change and develop new communication patterns as membership and expertise change will adversely affect the work of the team. When these changes occur, the team must repeat some of the steps they have taken in their team development and check to make sure they are still inclusive and that they integrate the expertise of the new membership.

Case Study: Virtual and Blended Teams—Faculty Exchange Program

As you read the case example below, consider the following question:

- *Given what you discussed about the team and the task in front of them when you were introduced to them earlier in the chapter, what else might you suggest they consider?*

The earlier case of the faculty exchange work team provides a good example of a mixed format face-to-face (f2f) and virtual team. Once they return to their home institutions, each will need to report back to their supervisors, and continue to build the exchange program.

- *How often will they meet and how?*
- *Must their electronic meetings be synchronous, or is asynchronous satisfactory?*
- *Are conference phone calls or video conferencing necessary, and if so, how often?*
- *Are there certain decisions they must all participate in, or can tasks be delegated to individuals within the team?*
- *Are the techniques that had been agreed upon in the f2f planning session still the best to use in a virtual meeting?*

The work team found that a monthly telephone conference call that all attended was a must. They found all agendas and notes needed to be distributed at least two days in advance so they can think about materials and ask questions in advance of the meeting. Problem-solving sessions that required questions and discussion were the best topics for conference calls.

Follow-up actions and decisions and implementation-related issues could all be handled by electronic meetings. Work to be done was separated into clusters, and smaller teams took on cluster topics and reported back virtually to the group.

The team was able to continue meetings, but needed to review the norms that had been established while in the f2f environment. Meeting processes and procedures were reviewed to make sure that all were able to participate. Two members felt their contributions were more creative because they needed to write more specifically about their ideas.

Having problem-solving and decision-making procedures that work seamlessly in mixed formats will be increasingly important in the years to come. The realization that cultural, societal, and individual factors will continue to influence how work teams function is important as these factors may not be “visible” in the same way in electronic formats.

Relevant Competencies

- Be able to recognize different approaches to problem solving as a team process and make use of traditional problem solving and appreciative inquiry in an integrated way
- Know the six steps of problem solving and decision making, what occurs in each step, and the appropriate tools and techniques to use to be successful at each step
- Be aware of internal and external factors that influence the team’s ability at problem solving and decision making in their work
- Understand how the culture, social identity and individual factors of members impact a particular team and its method of problem solving and decision-making
- Select and use the most effective problem-solving and decision-making techniques for the work team at its stage of team development

Summary

In this chapter there is a distinction made between problem solving and decision making. It is quite possible for decision making to be a routine procedure, without becoming a problem to be solved. However, problem solving always involves one or more decisions being made. Problem solving and decision making are necessary team processes that must be mastered by work teams. This happens by developing a synergistic approach to problem solving, which includes aspects of the traditional problem-solving and appreciative inquiry approaches. By combining these approaches, work teams will be able to involve all team members and better understand their worldview. Discussions among team members to better understand the perspectives of each of the members, before beginning to problem solve or make decisions, are recommended.

Although there are several models of problem solving and decision making, a six-step model is adopted and described in this chapter. Team members need to learn the steps in a synergistic problem solving model, and use some of the tools and techniques suggested in each. These steps are: (1) developing problem awareness, (2) gathering information, (3) identifying alternatives, (4) selecting a solution, (5) implementing the solution, and (6) evaluating the outcome. Decision making uses steps two, three, and four regularly. The team must be understand who will make decisions on the team and what method will be used for making them.

Teams need to understand the factors that impact the decision-making process. External factors are the quality/acceptance grid, time pressure, and organizational culture. Internal factors are cultural, societal, and individual considerations.

Developing shared mental models and using a wide variety of appropriate tools and techniques will assist work teams in creative problem solving and effective decision making processes.

Case Study: Selecting a New Teacher for a Community School in Latin America

As you read the case study below, consider the following questions:

- *Can you identify which steps in problem solving and decision making were followed fully and which were not?*
- *Can you articulate what tools and techniques might be used by the school committee to resolve the initial hiring problem and make the decision?*
- *How would you have advised them to approach this hiring problem, given what you have read in this chapter?*

I am a U.S. male and a Quaker who was a member of the school committee of a private school in a small, rural community in Costa Rica. The community was founded by Quakers who left the U.S. to find a simpler lifestyle in the 1950s, and now consists of Quakers and non-Quakers from the U.S., in addition to the indigenous Costa Ricans. The school was run by a committee overseen by the Quakers. The school committee consisted of three U.S. Quaker expatriates including myself, the chair, and the head teacher; two women of the original Quaker families, Mary and Jania, who were born in Costa Rica and married to Costa Ricans; and two Costa Ricans who were Catholic. The two Costa Ricans spoke English marginally. Meetings were held in English. The U.S. expatriates had the highest education, and pursued their own agendas much more than the Costa Ricans.

As we were looking for candidates for teaching grades 1 to 3, I had recommended Sara, who taught that level, was fluent in Spanish, and who was lesbian. I knew she had been turned down by another private school in the area because, as she had been told, "We live in a Catholic country, and all of the parents would pull their children out of the school if they knew we'd hired a homosexual." I knew it would not be easy to gain approval of Sara, but no other good candidates turned up.

At the meeting to decide which teachers to hire for the next school year, we all arrived with much trepidation, ready for a long, difficult meeting, for we had to reach consensus. During the preceding weeks there was much discussion throughout the entire community, and the tension level was high. The chair began the round table discussion offering that Sara should be evaluated only on her educational merits, and that her personal life was none of our business. The head teacher and Jania echoed her views. Both of the Costa Ricans said that they had heard the views of homosexuality in the U.S., but that's not the way it was here. They could not accept hiring a homosexual teacher, in part because of the Bible's view of homosexuality, and they would expect most of the parents would pull their children out of the school. Mary later added that she, too, had heard the view that homosexuals should be treated the same as "normal" people, but deep inside she did not believe this to be true, and she could not accept her children being in the presence of a homosexual teacher.

I mentioned that I had spoken with Sara on the phone and that she described how both she and her partner had been in the Peace Corps in Central America, and later adopted their children and lived in South America. People in all of those places got to know and love them, and when they later found out about their living arrangement, they accepted it. I said that in the U.S. it took a long time, but people have accepted that is a natural occurrence such as being left-handed, and that research also supported this view. I said that I believed that, if given the chance, the community would eventually learn to accept Sara and homosexuality by actually getting to meet and live with her rather than reacting to what they have been told about homosexuality.

The meeting went on for four hours, when we broke without any hope of reaching consensus. There were many tears, accusations of immorality on both sides, and nobody had budged from their original positions. A few days later I received a note from Mary charging me with being arrogant and condescending. How dare I come from the U.S. and tell these "simple country folk" what is right and what is wrong, that the U.S. is the latest in moral advancement, and that if Costa Ricans just followed my advice they would also learn what is right. I wrote back and told her that I did not intend to be arrogant or condescending. I told her that I felt that everybody had different opinions, and that I respected hers. I admitted that I do believe that it is okay to believe that another person's beliefs are wrong not just different, based on one's own belief system. However, I told her I could not tell her that she was wrong; that I must accept that she believes what she believes, and that she may believe what I believe is wrong.

I got no response.

Problem-Solving and Decision-Making Assessment

Efficient problem solving and decision making in a work team is dependent upon shared communication between team members and an understanding of the individual styles and preferences of team members. This assessment is designed to elicit information about these preferences. Complete these questions individually and then discuss the answers with the team. Complete the exercise by identifying how the team's responses will support and challenge the ongoing work of the team.

Look at the preferences listed below and check which represents your strongest preference when working with a team:

Work Environment	Very important	Neutral	Not at all important
Workplace considerations			
An organized, shared, consistent meeting space where I am physically comfortable			
A quiet private space with little or no distractions			
A shared team space with lots of creative distractions happening around us			
Regular breaks and interruptions so ideas can settle			
The opportunity to revisit decisions the team has made			
Organizational considerations			
The organization supports the work of the team by making time and resources available for us to work on projects			
The team works in a fast-paced environment, with outside pressures to keep the motivation and production levels high			
The organization allows the team to make some mistakes, we do not have to always have the right answer			
The organization gives ambiguous or loose parameters for projects to the team			

Team Problem Solving

When problem solving as a member of a team, I am most comfortable with my contributions to solutions to problems when (check all that apply):

_____We are very orderly in working through the problem in front of us
_____I am interested in the problem at hand, and highly motivated to achieve

_____We do not take forever to get it done
_____The problem is ambiguous and takes a lot of investigation, design, and discussion to sort through
_____No idea team members contribute is too crazy
_____We work on a lot of ideas at once

When problem solving as a member of a team, I am most satisfied with my contributions in the following steps:

Problem solving step	Where I am most satisfied with my contribution	Techniques I like to use most often when at this step
Problem recognition		
Information search		
Identifying alternatives		
Choosing solutions		
Implementing solutions		
Evaluating outcomes		

Individual Decision Making

When you think about your preference in making decisions, meaning what you do most often, please check the answer that best represents you:

Individual preference	In daily decisions	In professional decisions	I make my best individual decisions
Let the decision get made on its own, don't interfere with it			
Make lists, consider all the possible outcomes/options, and choose one			
Make lists and consider options, but vacillate when you have to choose			
Wait until the last possible opportunity to make the decision			
Make the decision quickly and move on to the next thing			
Let other people make the decision			

Team Decision Making

Think about your own work preferences first and make and mark YES for those items that are preferences you have as an individual; NO for those that are not. Then go through the list again and mark YES/NO if these hold true in team situations (check all that apply):

_____ Let someone else make the decision, I'd rather work with the concept or project after the decision's been made

_____Have input, but I do not need to make the final decision
_____ I want to be part of all major decisions, but let other team members work out details
_____ I want to work collaboratively on all decisions

References

Adler, N.J. (2002). *International Dimensions of Organizational Behavior* (4th ed.). Cincinnati, OH: South-Western.

Cooperrider, D.L., Whitney, D. and Stavros, J.M. (2005). *Appreciative Inquiry: The First in a Series of AI Workbooks for Leaders of Change*. Brunswick, OH: Crown Custom Publishing.

Enayati, J. (2001). The research: Effective communication and decision-making in diverse groups. In Hemmati, M. (Ed.), *Multi-Stakeholder Processes for Governance and Sustainability-Beyond Deadlock and Conflict*. London, England: Earthscan.

Gardenswartz, L. and Rowe, A. (2003). In L. Gardenswartz and A. Rowe (Eds.), *Diverse Teams at Work: Capitalizing on the Power of Diversity* (1st ed.). Alexandria, VA: Society for Human Resource Management.

Halverson, C.B. (2004). *Effective Multicultural Teams* (5th ed.). Brattleboro, VT: School for International Training.

Harrington-Macklin, D. (1994). *The Team Building Tool Kit: Tips, Tactics, and Rules for Effective Workplace Teams*. New York: American Management Association.

Hofstede, G. (1980). *Culture's Consequences: International Differences in Work-related Values*. Thousand Oaks, CA: Sage.

Janis, I. (1982). *Groupthink: Psychological Studies of Policy Decisions and Fiascos* (2nd ed.). Boston, MA: Houghton Mifflin.

Jeffery, A.B., Maes, J.D. and Bratton-Jeffery, M.F. (2005). Improving team decision-making performance with collaborative modeling. [Electronic version]. *Team Performance Management, 11*(1/2), 40–50. Retrieved December 20, 2005, from the Emerald In sight database.

Kayser, T.A. (1994). *Building Team Power: How to Unleash the Collaborative Genius of Work Teams*. New York: Irwin.

Kelly, K.P. (1994). *Team Decision Making Techniques*. Irvine, CA: Richard Chang Associates.

Kline, T. (1999). In M. Holt, D. Ullius and P. Berkman (Eds.), *Remaking Teams: The Revolutionary Research-based Guide That Puts Theory into Practice*. San Francisco, CA: Jossey-Bass/Pfeiffer.

Magruder Watkins, J. and Mohr, B.J. (2001). *Appreciative Inquiry, Change at the Speed of Imagination*. San Francisco, CA: Jossey-Bass/Pfieffer.

Mathieu, J., Heffner,T., Goodwin, G., Cannon-Bowers, J. and Salas, E. (2005). Scaling the quality of teammates' mental models: equifinality and normative comparisons. *Journal of Organizational Behavior, 26*, 37–56.

McFadzean, E. (2002). Developing and supporting creative problem-solving teams: Part 1—a conceptual model. [Electronic version]. *Management Decision, 40*(5), 463–475. Retrieved December 20, 2005, from the Emerald Insight database.

McFadzean, E. (2002). Developing and supporting creative problem solving teams: Part 2-facilitator competencies. [Electronic version]. *Management Decision, 40*(6), 537–551. Retrieved December 20, 2005, from the Emerald Insight database.

McKenna, R.J. and Martin-Smith, B. (2005). Decision making as a simplification process: New conceptual perspectives. [Electronic version]. *Management Decision, 43*(6), 821–836. Retrieved December 20, 2005, from the Emerald Insight database.

Sagie, A. and Akcan, Z. (2003). A cross-cultural analysis of participative decision-making in organizations. *Human Relations, 56*(4), 453–473.

Selart, M. (2005). Understanding the role of locus of control in consultative decision-making: A case study. [Electronic version]. *Management Decision, 43*(3), 397–412. Retrieved December 20, 2005, from the Emerald Insight database.

Simon, T., Pelled, L.H. and Smith, K.A. (1999). Making use of difference: diversity, debate, and decision comprehensiveness in top management teams. *Academy of Management Journal, 42*(6), 662–673.

Smith, P.B., Peterson, M.F. and Schwartz, S.H. (2002). Cultural values, sources of guidance, and their relevance to managerial behavior. [Electronic version]. *Journal of Cross-Cultural Psychology, 33*(2), 188–208.

Tomlinson, S. (1999). Comparison of consensus Japanese style and Quaker style. [Electronic version]. Retrieved July 1, 2006, from http://www.earlham.edu/~consense/scott2.shtml

Watkins, J.M. and Mohr, B.J. (2001). *Appreciative Inquiry: Change at the Speed of Imagination*. San Francisco, CA: Jossey-Bass/Pfeiffer.

Whitney, D. and Trosten-Bloom, A. (2003). T*he Power of Appreciative Inquiry: A Practical Guide to Positive Change*. San Francisco, CA: Berrett-Koehler.

Chapter 10
Multicultural Teams—Some Considerations for Present and Future

S. Aqeel Tirmizi

I am enough of an artist to draw freely upon my imagination...
–Albert Einstein

The previous chapters provided a comprehension discussion of theory and practice of multicultural teams. Our aim was to provide a bridge between emerging theory and practice-based knowledge in intellectually challenging and practically engaging and useful ways. It is not necessary to attempt a meta-summary of our previous discussions. However, it is important and useful to offer some overall questions and considerations as the readers proceed with their thinking and practice of multicultural teams.

Levels of Analysis

In this book we looked at multicultural behavioral dynamics at the team level. However, a multicultural team's effectiveness may be impacted by variables or dynamics at higher levels, as noted in the Multicultural Team Effectiveness Model in Chapter 1. Therefore it is extremely important that as managers, leaders, and members of teams we effectively diagnose and intervene at the appropriate organizational level. Consider the following example. A new monitoring and reporting system is introduced for project management in an international organization. After the first year of using this system the organization is receiving complaints that the data and information reported by some of the teams is incomplete and inaccurate in some cases. It is possible that these teams are not effective in performing one of their important tasks. However, it is also possible that some of these teams did not receive adequate training and guidance. Another possibility is that the information available is insufficient. Only careful attention to levels of analysis would reveal the level at which the problem may be occurring and identification of appropriate solutions.

C.B. Halverson and S.A. Tirmizi (eds.), *Effective Multicultural Teams: Theory and Practice,*

Organizational Commitment

A number of chapters in the book make a case for the importance, need, and advantages of multicultural teams. The notion of teamwork and its usefulness for contemporary organizations is fully embraced today. We have all heard the question "Are you a team player?" as part of an interviewing process. While the commitment to supporting multicultural teams is often there in organizational settings, this commitment is incomplete in many cases as it is not supported through organizational systems and structure. I would like to highlight some of these systems as examples. While many organizations may encourage teamwork, they continue to evaluate and reward people based on individual performance and achievement. If we look at organizational performance management and compensation systems, with very few exceptions, these systems are geared towards individuals and not teams and teamwork. Effectiveness and sustainability of multicultural teams depend on introducing and maintaining organizational systems that support these teams. Similarly, creation and maintenance of organizational culture that promotes and reinforces teamwork is extremely important in encouraging and maintaining effective multicultural teams.

Difficult Choices and Decisions

Throughout the book we have employed and explained ideas and approaches that are inclusive and devoted to developing and capitalizing the best of human potential, with special attention to multicultural settings. However, there may be some situations where individual members do not perform and should be held accountable and in other cases more difficult decisions may be necessary when desired and expected performance goals are not met. Sometimes these difficult decisions have to be made and we should be prepared to make them fairly and effectively. Brett, J., Behfar, K. and Kem, M. et al. (2006) offer four broad approaches to manage such and other major challenges faced in multicultural teams. These are adaptation, structural interventions, managerial interventions, and exit. Adaptation refers to consciously addressing and working with cultural differences; structural interventions refer to adjusting the team design such as adding team members; managerial interventions which include mechanisms such as developing and following team norms; and exit strategies include removing and replacing team members when other interventions do not work.

Learning to Working Effectively in Multicultural Teams

We feel that that this book contains a comprehensive set of knowledge and skills related to working in multicultural teams effectively. These provide a good blend of intellectually stimulating conceptual frameworks and highly applied tools and instruments to understand and manage the complexities of working in multicultural teams. Developing individual effectiveness in multicultural team settings occurs not only through acquiring the relevant knowledge but in practicing and testing it. In the opening pages of this book we argued that we see multicultural teamwork as a discipline. Developing the mastery to understand and work effectively in this discipline requires continuous personal investment over a period of time. Central to developing this mastery is openness to learning, taking some risks, and on-going commitment to personal and professional development.

The Future

We see the future of multicultural teams characterized by exciting challenges and possibilities. Throughout the book we noted the trends and challenges around working virtually across cultures. In the future we anticipate that virtual multicultural teams will continue to increase. This presents a dilemma. This trend is bringing individuals closer when working in teams across cultures in terms of speed and efficiency of communication. However, these new work arrangements present challenges in terms of lack of personal connections and psychological distance among team members.

It is increasing the distance between individuals as more and more people are in contact with each other with increasing frequency, with little or no face-to-face contact. At the same time, working virtually is decreasing the distance because our technology infrastructure allows communicating across cultures with speed and efficiency unprecedented even in the last 10 years. As this trend further unfolds, it will continue to bring opportunities and challenges for virtual multicultural teams.

The 2004 Human Development Report, titled "Cultural Liberty in Today's Diverse World", advocates for identifying just and robust ways of working with multicultural societies around the world. The report draws special attention to the large immigration populations in Western Europe and the USA and the importance of integrating these populations into these societies. The increasing globalization of businesses, international development, and closer cooperation in the humanitarian sectors will continue to make our organizational environment more multicultural. The implications of these trends are clear—we need professionals who are competent to work in multicultural teams and organizations across a variety of sectors.

References

Brett, J., Behfar, K. and Kern, M. (2006). Managing Multicultural Teams. Harvard Business Review *84*(11), 84–91.

Human Development Report (2004): Cultural Liberty in Today's Diverse World. New York: United Nations Development Program.

Author Index

Subject Index

Seborrheic keratosis